D1035453

Bending the Law

BENDING THE LAW

The Story of
the Dalkon Shield
Bankruptcy

Richard B. Sobol

 The University of Chicago Press
Chicago and London

RICHARD B. SOBOL, a Washington, D.C., attorney, has specialized in
class action litigation asserting the civil rights of minorities and women.

The University of Chicago Press, Chicago 60637
The University of Chicago Press, Ltd., London
© 1991 by Richard B. Sobol
All rights reserved. Published 1991
Printed in the United States of America

00 99 98 97 96 95 94 93 92   5 4 3 2

ISBN: 0-226-76752-3 (cloth)   0-226-76753-1 (pbk.)

Library of Congress Cataloging-in-Publication Data

Sobol, Richard B.
    Bending the law : the story of the Dalkon Shield bankruptcy /
Richard B. Sobol.
        p.   cm.
    Includes bibliographical references and index.
    1. A.H. Robins Company—Trials, litigation, etc.   2. Bankruptcy—
United States.   3. Products liability—Intrauterine contraceptives—
United States.   4. Dalkon Shield (Intrauterine contraceptive)
I. Title.
KF228.A3S6   1991
346.7303'8—dc20
[347.30638]   91-14129
CIP

♾The paper used in this publication meets the minimum requirements
of the American National Standard for Information Sciences—Perma-
nence of Paper for Printed Library Materials, ANSI Z39.48-1984.

To Zachary
in loving memory

Contents

Preface

When I began work on this book in the spring of 1987, I had practiced law, specializing in civil litigation, for twenty-five years. During that time, I frequently lamented the insufficiency of news reports of cases in which I was involved or of which I had direct knowledge. Despite widespread interest in the legal process in our society and widespread appreciation of the profound social, political, and economic implications that judicial decisions can have on our lives, popular coverage of consequential litigation tends, with some notable exceptions, to skim the surface and to miss the significance of what has transpired.

This book represents my effort, as a lawyer, to describe an important legal proceeding in terms that are accessible to lay readers and yet allow real understanding of what went on. The book tells the story of the reorganization of the A. H. Robins Company, a proceeding precipitated by Robins's overwhelming liability to women who suffered injuries as a result of their use of the Dalkon Shield intrauterine birth control device. The case was played out in the arcane and specialized field of federal bankruptcy law, yet the underlying contest—the fight between the company's shareholders and the injured women for the available dollars—is quite elemental.

By means of the reorganization proceeding, Robins's managers and shareholders were able to eliminate all individual and corporate liability for injuries related to the Dalkon Shield. In exchange, the American Home Products Corporation, which acquired the A. H. Robins Company as part of the resolution of the bankruptcy case, paid $2.3 billion to a trust that is responsible, to the extent its funding permits, for settling or defending, and paying the claims of the injured women. Because Robins was able to obtain this limit on its liability, its shareholders received American Home Products stock worth four times the prebankruptcy price of their Robins stock. In fact, for the year 1987 while the company was in bankruptcy, Robins's stock had the highest rate of appreciation of any security on the New York Stock Exchange.

The Robins bankruptcy is important to the hundreds of·thousands of women whose rights it determined, and for the precedent it provides for

ix

other situations in which manufacturers of dangerous products seek refuge in bankruptcy. The case also provides a vivid picture of the functioning of the judicial process and of provincial and idiosyncratic factors affecting the resolution of issues of broad significance.

The A. H. Robins Company was founded in Richmond, Virginia, over one hundred years ago. In the last half-century, under the leadership of E. Claiborne Robins, Sr., grandson of the founder and until the recent acquisition the chairman of Robins's board of directors, the company grew into a Fortune 400 corporation, marketing internationally such well-known consumer products as Chapstick and Robitussin. Despite this growth, the A. H. Robins Company remained headquartered in Richmond and was a major economic force in the city, providing employment to thousands and, as a company and through the Robins family, providing major philanthropic support to local charities and institutions, most notably the University of Richmond. At the University, several buildings and programs, including the athletic center and the business school, are named after members of the Robins family.

Before the bankruptcy, Robins was forced to defend litigation related to the Dalkon Shield in hundreds of federal and state courts throughout the United States. Robins was opposed by highly skilled litigators who, over the company's determined and, it has been suggested, improper resistance, succeeded in proving that Robins had marketed the Dalkon Shield without investigating its safety and that, after they had learned of the propensity of the device to cause life-threatening pelvic infections, company officials had withheld and even destroyed this information while the Dalkon Shield was still being sold and used.

Robins's managers had come to believe that the company was suffering an unfair disadvantage defending itself not only in hundreds of places at once but in hostile surroundings. Robins had suffered particularly stunning defeats in the courts of Kansas, Colorado, and Minnesota, where juries had imposed millions of dollars of punitive damage judgments against it. In the year before Robins filed for bankruptcy, the company had made several unsuccessful efforts to consolidate Dalkon Shield litigation in the federal court in Richmond before United States District Judge Robert R. Merhige, Jr. These efforts had been successfully opposed by a coalition of lawyers representing injured women. Robins finally achieved the consolidation of Dalkon Shield litigation in Richmond before Judge Merhige by filing for bankruptcy.

Judge Merhige is a product of the University of Richmond Law School and is an enthusiastic booster of both the city and the university. He is also a neighbor of E. Claiborne Robins, Sr., who is a celebrated figure in Richmond. Three weeks before the bankruptcy filing, Merhige met in his home with Robins, Sr., and E. Claiborne Robins, Jr., the president of the A. H. Robins Company, to discuss the company's plans with respect to bankruptcy. Merhige has established a reputation as an innovative and unorthodox judge more interested in and more adept at results than at theory. Much of the story of the Robins bankruptcy is the tale of this feisty and determined judge, acting with the unquestioning support of three judges of the United States court of appeals in Richmond, making the decisions that were necessary, often without support from or in contradiction of existing law, to transfer liability for Dalkon Shield injuries from the A. H. Robins Company and its officers, directors, attorneys, and insurer to a trust with limited funding, and to allow Robins's shareholders to be paid the value of the company in excess of the fund before it could be determined whether the individual entitlements of the women injured by the Dalkon Shield exceeded the amount of the fund or, indeed, the total value of the company.

My attention was called to the Robins bankruptcy by an unusual coincidence. On August 21, 1985, the day the proceeding began, I was retained to file suit against Robins by a friend in Washington, D.C., who had recently undergone a hysterectomy as a result of a pelvic infection attributable to her use of the Dalkon Shield. I had no previous involvement in litigation related to the Dalkon Shield. The next morning, I saw newspaper reports of the bankruptcy filing. The Bankruptcy Code prohibits anyone from filing suit against an entity that has filed a petition in bankruptcy.

Concerned over this development, I traveled to Richmond to read the available documents in the office of the clerk of court and I began to follow the proceeding. On behalf of my client, I filed a claim against Robins in the bankruptcy case. Later, when I decided to write about the case and before any action had been taken on the claim, I asked my client to retain different counsel and she did so. I have no financial interest in her claim or any other matter related to the Robins bankruptcy.

The major sources on which this book is based are public documents (motions, memoranda, affidavits, exhibits, reports, transcripts, opinions) filed in the record of the bankruptcy proceeding and my observation of hearings before Judge Merhige and before the United States Court of Appeals for the Fourth Circuit. In addition, I was fortunate to be granted interviews by Judge Merhige and by many of the other important figures in the case including Frederic Bremseth, Penn Ayers Butler, Michael Ciresi, Murray Drabkin, Peter B. Edelman, Mark C.

Ellenberg, Louis L. Hoynes, Jr., Stanley K. Joynes III, Kenneth R. Feinberg, Joseph S. Friedberg, Ralph R. Mabey, Robert E. Manchester, Alesia Ranney-Marinelli, Joseph F. McDowell III, Francis E. McGovern, Alan B. Morrison, Ralph D. Pittle, Michael A. Pretl, Judith J. Rentschler, James C. Roberts, Michael M. Sheppard, S. David Shiller, James F. Szaller, Georgene M. Vairo, and Timothy Wyant. I spoke with most of these people on more than one occasion. Everyone I approached was willing to be interviewed, with the single exception of counsel for Aetna Casualty & Surety Company, John G. Harkins, Jr. I thank each of the people who spoke with me for their time, their courtesy, and their frankness in discussing the case with me.

I encouraged that frankness in two respects. I did not tape-record interviews, and, when asked, I agreed not to attribute statements without returning and asking for specific permission. In the end, I cited to interviews only infrequently, as my account usually reflects an amalgam of information.

Consistent with my purpose of writing a book accessible to nonlawyers, I have tried to avoid legal terminology. When it was unavoidable, I stopped to define the word or phrase, and entered it in the index. I have relegated legal citations and technical legal discussions to the endnotes. (The notes do not include citations to hearing transcripts where the source is clear from the context, and a note would contain only a transcript citation. These citations are collected in a separate table that appears after the endnotes.)

The preparation of this book consumed most of my time for three years, far longer than I had anticipated. My main source of help and advice was my wife, Anne Buxton Sobol, an attorney of rare insight, who discussed the subject with me on what must be one thousand occasions, providing perspective, criticism, and ideas. It was possible for me to write this book only because of Anne's support, encouragement, and patience. My daughter, Joanna Sobol, read the manuscript in both an intermediate and a late stage and offered astute suggestions. I also received help and encouragement from Michael B. Trister, James G. Abourezk, and Winn Newman, my former law partners, and from Henri Norris, Ralph J. Temple, Marcus Raskin, George Cooper, Lynne Bernabei, and Karen Judd. I am particularly grateful to Douglas G. Baird, Harry A. Bigelow Professor of Law, the University of Chicago Law School, who provided invaluable suggestions on and corrections to my manuscript. Finally, I thank the University of Chicago Press, and particularly John Tryneski for his confidence in the project and Jennie Lightner for her careful work on the manuscript.

1   The Dalkon Shield

Efforts to prevent pregnancy by placing a foreign object in a woman's uterus date back many centuries. Devices made of glass, ivory, wood, wool, silkworm gut, silver, gold, copper, zinc, and pewter in a variety of sizes and shapes have all been used for this purpose. The reason for the contraceptive effect of an intrauterine device (IUD), which does not create a barrier to the entry of sperm into the uterus, has never been established. One theory is that in reaction to the device the body produces white cells that destroy the sperm or the fertilized egg. Another is that the IUD somehow interferes with the ability of the fertilized egg to attach itself or to remain attached to the wall of the uterus.[1]

Infection and injury have always been associated with IUDs, and they were not widely used until the late 1960s. Then, growing dissatisfaction with the adverse effects of birth control pills, together with mounting concern over the "population explosion," caused renewed interest in the development of a safe IUD. The possibility was enhanced by two scientific advances. One was the development of antibiotics that provided a method of treating uterine infections that did occur. The other was the invention of malleable, inert plastic, which could be compressed during insertion and then regain its intended shape, and which would not break down or chemically interact with bodily fluids.

The Dalkon Shield intrauterine device was designed in 1968 by Hugh Davis, a gynecologist on the faculty of the Johns Hopkins Medical School, and by Irwin Lerner, an electrical engineer and part-time inventor. In 1964 Johns Hopkins had opened a family planning clinic under Davis's supervision, and, through this clinic, Davis was able to test various newly developed IUDs, mostly on poor, black women from Baltimore. A major design problem with most of these IUDs was the frequency with which they were expelled as a result of the body's natural efforts to rid itself of a foreign object.

The Dalkon Shield was specifically designed to control the problem of expulsion. It is a piece of flexible plastic, about three-quarters of an inch across, shaped like a shield to approximate the shape of the uterine cavity. The device has four or five prongs jutting out of each side at a

1

downward angle. Because of their direction, the prongs resisted the expulsion of the device. As it turned out, however, the prongs often made insertion or removal painful and difficult, and they were responsible for the tendency of the device to embed itself in the uterine wall or to perforate the uterus.

A more serious design problem of the Dalkon Shield related to its string. One end of the string was tied to the bottom of the plastic shield and the other end was tied in a knot. When the device was in the uterus, the string passed through the cervix into the vagina. Its purpose was to allow the woman to check that the device was in place and to assist in its removal.

"Tailstrings" designed to serve these purposes are found on all IUDs, but on IUDs other than the Dalkon Shield the tailstring is made of a single plastic filament—a "monofilament"—in order to avoid the absorption of moisture, and with it bacteria. The entry of bacteria from the vagina into the uterus is a major cause of dangerous and potentially life-threatening uterine infections, known as pelvic inflammatory disease, or PID. Frequently, a hysterectomy must be performed to overcome PID, and even when a hysterectomy is not necessary, infertility often results.

Davis and Lerner did not use a monofilament string on their new Dalkon Shield. The monofilament strings they tested either were too weak and would break during removal because of the resistance offered by the prongs, or were too stiff and would cause discomfort to the man during intercourse. Instead, Davis and Lerner used a multifilament string, named Supramid, which was composed of hundreds of tiny nylon strands encased in a nylon sheath. Supramid was made by a company in West Germany and used primarily in the repair of horse tendons. Davis and Lerner hoped that the sheath would prevent vaginal fluid from entering the spaces between the strands and moving up into the uterus, a phenomenon called "wicking."

For two reasons the sheath did not do its job. First, inexplicably, Davis and Lerner failed to seal its ends. Fluid from the vagina could enter the open end at the bottom of the sheath and wick up past the knots to the open end at the top inside the uterus. Indeed, the nylon sheath made the problem of wicking worse because it shielded the bacteria inside the sheath from the antibacterial action of the mass of viscous fluid in the cervix known as the cervical plug. Second, the sheath developed holes either in the initial tying process or as a result of decomposition after the IUD was in place. These holes allowed the bacteria to escape into the uterus without even reaching the top of the string.

In the fall of 1968, Davis and Lerner formed the Dalkon Corporation (owned 55 percent by Lerner, 35 percent by Davis, and 10 percent by

Lerner's lawyer) and assigned to it all rights to the Dalkon Shield. The two men arranged for the manufacture of several hundred Dalkon Shields at a plastics factory in Brooklyn, and for twelve months, between September 1968 and September 1969, Davis inserted the device in 640 women, most of whom were patients at the family planning clinic at Johns Hopkins.

In October 1969, Davis submitted a study entitled "The Shield Intrauterine Device: A Superior Modern Contraceptive" to the *American Journal of Obstetrics and Gynecology*. The study, published in the February 1, 1970, edition of that journal, reported that there had been only five pregnancies among Davis's 640 subjects in a twelve-month period.[2] Davis reported an annual pregnancy rate of 1.1 percent, well below the rates of almost 3 percent that had been reported for other commercial IUDs and about the same as pregnancy rates for oral contraceptives. Davis made no mention of any adverse effects more serious than ten expulsions and nine removals for unspecified medical reasons. Davis concluded his study with the assertion that "the superior performance of the shield intrauterine device makes this technic a first choice method of conception control."

Davis's study was misleading in several important respects. First, the number of women in the study was far too small to yield results that would be predictive. The accepted standard for studies of the effectiveness of a contraceptive is a minimum of 1,000 patients with an average use of twelve months. Only 8 women among Davis's 640 patients had had the Dalkon Shield inserted during the first month of the study, and the average length of use for all the women was less than six months.

Second, Davis neglected to mention that he had advised patients to use contraceptive foam during the first two or three months after the insertion of the Dalkon Shield. Months of nonconception were being credited to the Dalkon Shield when another method of contraception was also in use; the average length of experience with the Dalkon Shield alone was substantially below six months.

Third, Davis compiled his statistics within three days after the end of the twelve-month period. He did not wait the time necessary to discover that additional women in the study had become pregnant during the twelve months. After he had submitted his study but before it was published, Davis learned of enough additional pregnancies during the study period to increase the annual pregnancy rate to over 5 percent. He nevertheless allowed his 1.1 percent figure to be published.

Finally, Davis did not reveal either his role in the development of the Dalkon Shield or his financial interest in the product.

In January 1970, just before the publication of his study, Davis gave widely publicized testimony before a subcommittee of the United States Senate, in which he condemned the birth control pill as "giving rise to health hazards on a scale previously unknown to medicine" and touted "modern intrauterine devices that provide a 99 percent protection against pregnancy and can be successfully worn by 94 percent of all women."[3] In response to questioning from counsel to the committee, Davis denied that he had any "particular commercial interest in any of the intrauterine devices."[4]

Under the terms of the Federal Food, Drug and Cosmetic Act, no drug can be sold in the United States without the approval of the Food and Drug Administration. The FDA will approve a drug only after review of a New Drug Application reporting on scientifically sound clinical tests of 1,500 users over two years, with results showing efficacy and safety. But in 1970 IUDs were classified as "devices" rather than "drugs," and the requirements of premarketing approval did not apply.[5] As a result, the Dalkon Corporation was able simply to begin selling the Dalkon Shield without obtaining any governmental or medical approval. With the publication of Davis's study in February 1970, the Dalkon Corporation began commercial distribution of the Dalkon Shield.

Although some sales were made on the strength of Davis's study, Davis and Lerner soon concluded that they would be unable to realize the full commercial potential of the Dalkon Shield unless it was marketed by a large company with an established distribution system. Efforts to sell rights to the Dalkon Shield to a major pharmaceutical company were undertaken, and in May 1970 the product came to the attention of the A. H. Robins Company.

The A. H. Robins Company, Incorporated, traces its history to 1866, when Albert Hartley Robins, an ex-Confederate soldier, opened an apothecary in Richmond, Virginia. Thirty years later his son Claiborne organized the A. H. Robins Company as a separate business to engage in packaging and selling to doctors a remedy for stomach disorders— Robins Cascara Compound—developed by Albert in his shop. Claiborne died at an early age, and the company, run by his widow, remained a small business, primarily engaged in the distribution of this single product, until 1933, when their son, E. Claiborne Robins, received a degree in pharmacy from the Medical College of Virginia in Richmond. Young Claiborne set out to expand the business by acquiring and developing drugs and other products that could be marketed on a wide scale.

Over the next fifty years, E. Claiborne Robins built the A. H. Robins

Company into one of the 400 largest corporations in the United States. Still primarily engaged in the manufacture and distribution of pharmaceuticals, it had subsidiaries and distribution systems throughout the world. Its best-known over-the-counter products were the Robitussin line of cough medicines, Dimetapp cold remedies, and Chapstick lip balm.

The A. H. Robins Company became publicly owned in 1963 and its stock was listed on the New York Stock Exchange, but it remained a family-controlled business, with a distinctly local cast. The Robins family continued to own almost half of the outstanding shares and to manage the company. In 1975, Claiborne Robins relinquished the position of chief executive officer but remained as chairman of the board. E. Claiborne Robins, Jr., became president and chief executive officer in 1978. The company remained headquartered in Richmond, and all its directors were drawn from the Richmond community. The A. H. Robins Company was one of Richmond's largest employers, and the Robins family was among the city's most generous philanthropists.

Before its acquisition of the Dalkon Shield, the A. H. Robins Company had had no experience with contraceptive devices. It first received information relating to the Dalkon Shield, including Davis's published study, through a member of its sales force on May 21, 1970. On June 12, 1970, rushing to beat a competing bid from the Upjohn Corporation, Robins purchased rights to the Dalkon Shield from the Dalkon Corporation for $750,000 plus 10 percent of net sales. During that twenty-two-day period, Robins gathered information concerning the Dalkon Shield during meetings with Davis at Johns Hopkins in Baltimore and with Lerner at the Dalkon Corporation offices in Stamford, Connecticut. In the process, company officials learned that Davis, the author of the only study of the Dalkon Shield, was the co-inventor and co-owner of the product; that Davis's own data showed a minimum pregnancy rate of 5.3 percent, not the 1.1 percent that his study claimed; and that no information was available relating to the safety of the Dalkon Shield when it remained inside a woman's uterus for an extended period.

Company officials also learned that the Dalkon Shield being sold by the Dalkon Corporation was different from the device used in Davis's study. After the study, Davis and Lerner had added copper and copper sulfate to the mixture from which the device was molded. They did this partly to increase the visibility of the IUD under x-rays but also because there were suggestions in the work of others that the release of copper in the uterus might provide an additional contraceptive effect. In addition, Davis and Lerner had developed and were marketing a smaller Dalkon

Shield, which they called a "nullip" version, intended for women who had never borne a child. Up to that point, the general medical consensus was that IUDs were not suitable for women who had not had a full-term pregnancy. An IUD that could be used by these women had the potential of opening up a vast new market. These variations on the original device had not been tested, even by Davis.

Although none of these factors deterred Robins from purchasing the Dalkon Shield, the purchase agreement provided that, should Robins ever be required "to prove safety or efficacy of the product," it could deduct the cost of doing so from the royalty payments to the Dalkon Corporation.

Robins promoted its new product intensively. The company supplied its sales force with reprints of Dr. Davis's study showing a 1.1 percent pregnancy rate. Advertisements in medical journals proclaimed the Dalkon Shield to be "safe and effective," "trouble free," and "truly superior" and emphasized the availability of the untested nullip version. The Dalkon Corporation had recommended on the label accompanying the Dalkon Shield that a painkiller be administered before insertion and that contraceptive foam be used for the first three months after insertion. To boost sales, Robins eliminated these cautions.

Robins's medical advisory board advised the company to market its IUD only to gynecologists, warning that

general practitioners . . . who do not routinely do pelvic examinations [are] . . . almost certain to have problems. Enough problems arise when competent physicians perform insertions. Under no circumstances should the Dalkon Shield be "pushed" on a physician who is just casually familiar with pelvic anatomy.

The company ignored this advice and heavily promoted the Dalkon Shield to general practitioners.

Robins went further and promoted the Dalkon Shield directly to women who might use it. The product could only be sold to doctors, but Robins proceeded on the theory that doctors would supply the IUD requested by their patients. According to one company memorandum, "Mr. Robins has assigned top priority to special promotions of the Dalkon Shield in other than medical and trade magazines." The company employed a public relations firm with the mandate to "mount an all-out campaign to publicize the product" in print media and on radio and television programs directed to women. As a result, stories favorable to the Dalkon Shield—often exaggerating Davis's findings beyond his own false claims—appeared throughout the country.

All of these efforts paid off. In 1971, 1972, and 1973 more Dalkon Shields were sold than all other brands of IUDs combined. By the end of 1973 more than 3 million had been sold. By this time Robins was using its success in selling the product as a basis for its promotion.

Remember, the DALKON SHIELD wouldn't be NUMBER ONE in sales if it wasn't NUMBER ONE in effectiveness.

All the while, Robins ignored repeated danger signs. Within days of the purchase, Robins's management received a warning of the potential problems with the multifilament string from Irwin Lerner, co-inventor of the Dalkon Shield. A June 29, 1970, "orientation report" from a Robins official to thirty-nine top executives stated: "The string or 'tail' situation needs a careful review since the present 'tail' is reported (by Mr. Lerner) to have a 'wicking' tendency." No review was conducted.

In the spring of 1971 Wayne Crowder, the quality control supervisor at the Chapstick plant—the Robins facility assigned to manufacture the Dalkon Shield—questioned how the sheath could serve its intended purpose of keeping the tailstring dry and avoiding the transmission of bacteria when the sheath was open at both ends. Crowder conducted a simple experiment. He tied knots in several pieces of the string material and placed an end of each piece, but not the knot itself, in water. Several days later Crowder found moisture had crept past the knot to the other end of the string. Crowder reported this finding to his supervisor, Julian Ross, and suggested heat-sealing the ends of the string. Ross reacted angrily and advised Crowder that the design of the string was not Crowder's responsibility. When Crowder replied that his conscience required him to say something, Ross told him that his conscience didn't pay his salary.

Nevertheless, the following month Crowder described his wicking experiment and his idea for heat-sealing the sheath to the president of Chapstick, Daniel French. French discussed the matter with a staff physician in Robins's medical department who, in turn, reported to Robins's medical director that French had advised that "the open ends [of the tail-string] will wick water. It seems to him if this is so then the ends will wick body fluids containing bacteria." The possibility of changing the tailstring was considered in response to Crowder's experiment but was rejected because Robins did not want to slow down production in the face of the great demand for the product that the company's marketing efforts had created.

In April 1972 Robins learned of the additional problem of the sheath developing holes after its insertion. An expert in plastics advised that there is "a definite problem with [the sheath] because historically it has been shown that nylon does deteriorate *in situ* over a period of time." Again, the possibility of replacing the tailstring was considered and rejected.

To the contrary, in its promotional efforts Robins aggravated the danger caused by the deterioration of the sheath. The Dalkon Corporation had included on its labels a recommendation that the Dalkon Shield be replaced every two years, a recommendation that placed some control on the problem of deterioration and wicking. Later studies would show that prolonged use of the Dalkon Shield sharply increased the rate of pelvic infections. When Robins began its promotion of the Dalkon Shield, it continued the two-year-replacement recommendation. But its salesmen began to report that this recommendation was creating resistance among physicians because other IUDs carried no similar recommendation. In July 1972, just after it was warned about the deterioration of the sheath, Robins adopted language encouraging use of the Dalkon Shield "for five years or longer."

During the years that Robins marketed the Dalkon Shield, the company was constantly engaged in stemming the tide of adverse information—information reporting high pregnancy rates with the Dalkon Shield and information indicating the hazards of the product. Ironically, the two problems intersected, because the first reports of serious injuries associated with the Dalkon Shield concerned women who had become pregnant with the device in place and had suffered septic abortions. A septic abortion is a spontaneous termination of a pregnancy resulting from an infection of the reproductive system.

An early indication of this problem was a June 1972 letter from Thad J. Earl, a physician practicing in Defiance, Ohio. Originally Earl was enthusiastic about the Dalkon Shield. In early 1970 he had purchased an interest in the Dalkon Corporation, and when the Dalkon Shield was sold, he had been retained by Robins as a consultant. In his letter, which was sent to more than a dozen Robins executives, Earl reported that six of his patients had become pregnant with the Dalkon Shield in place. He had removed the device from one, and the woman carried to full term. He had not removed the device from the other five, and each had suffered a septic abortion between the third and the fifth month of her pregnancy. "I therefore feel it is hazardous to leave the device in . . . I am advising physicians that the device should be removed as soon as a diagnosis of pregnancy is made." What was happening was that the tailstring—laden with bacteria—was being drawn into the expanding uterus and causing infection.

Earl's conclusion that the Dalkon Shield should be removed from pregnant women was, as Robins's Dalkon Shield project manager noted in an internal memorandum, "completely in reverse of what we have been recommending since it was felt that the pregnancy would have a better chance of continuing to term if the Dalkon Shield were left in place." No action or investigation was undertaken in response to Earl's advice. To the contrary, several months later, in October 1972, Robins put out a promotional brochure intended for patients that encouraged *not* removing the Dalkon Shield in case of pregnancy: "When pregnancy does occur, the bag of water pushes the IUD to one side and the developing baby is not really touching the device at all."

During 1972 and 1973 Robins received a stream of other reports of spontaneous septic abortions, as well as reports of uterine infections among nonpregnant women using the Dalkon Shield. In several instances women had almost died as a result of virulent infections. Robins deflected these as isolated or insufficiently documented incidents and did nothing to address the problem.

The matter took on a critical dimension in May 1973, when Robins received reports of the deaths of two young women who had become pregnant while wearing the Dalkon Shield. A twenty-four-year-old woman in Texas fitted with a Dalkon Shield entered the hospital with flu symptoms on one day, aborted her twenty-week-old fetus the next day, and died the third day. The same thing then happened to a thirty-one-year-old woman in Arizona. Robins's only reaction to these reports came five months and several hundred thousand Dalkon Shield sales later, when, in October 1973, the company printed new labels that acknowledged the risk of "severe sepsis with fatal outcome, most often associated with spontaneous abortion following pregnancy with the Dalkon Shield *in situ*."

In the spring of 1974 Robins learned that Donald Christian, head of obstetrics and gynecology at the University of Arizona Medical Center in Tucson, had prepared an article about the Dalkon Shield, entitled "Maternal Death Associated with an Intrauterine Device," that was scheduled to be published in the June 1974 issue of the *American Journal of Obstetrics and Gynecology*. In May 1974 Robins sent a letter to 120,000 physicians urging the removal of the Dalkon Shield from any woman who became pregnant with the device in place, essentially adopting the advice Dr. Earl had suggested two years earlier.

Within weeks Robins was forced by the momentum of negative developments to withdraw the Dalkon Shield from the domestic market. On May 28, 1974, the Planned Parenthood Federation instructed its 183 clinics around the country to stop using the Dalkon Shield. Other public health facilities quickly followed suit. Shortly thereafter, Dr. Christian's article was published and generated devastating publicity. Christian reported on five cases of women who had died from infection after becoming pregnant with the Dalkon Shield in place, and he described the alarming speed with which pelvic infections can turn fatal.

The greatest concern is the rather insidious yet rapid manner in which these patients become ill . . . The first symptoms, which were disarmingly innocuous in and of themselves, occurred within thirty-one and seventy-two hours of death . . . The margin of safety that time ordinarily provides is not present.[6]

In June 1974 the Food and Drug Administration's Medical Devices Panel held hearings on the issue of septic abortions and IUDs. Robins's medical director, Fred Clark, appeared and argued that the risks presented by the Dalkon Shield were no different from those of other IUDs. In his testimony Clark did not reveal what was then still unknown to the FDA and to the medical community—that the Dalkon Shield had, not a monofilament string, but a multifilament string disguised inside a nylon sheath. Nonetheless, on June 26, 1974, the commissioner of the FDA, Alexander Schmidt, requested that Robins suspend sales of the Dalkon Shield while the safety issues were given further study. Two days later Robins announced a "voluntary" suspension of domestic sales of the Dalkon Shield. An accompanying Robins press release stated that "neither A. H. Robins nor the FDA has any reason at this time to believe that women now using the Dalkon Shield successfully should have the device removed."

Robins continued to sell the Dalkon Shield in at least forty foreign countries for another ten months. Foreign sales had climbed in 1973 and 1974, even as domestic sales were declining. Robins continued to advertise the product in foreign markets, using the same claims it had used when it introduced the Dalkon Shield in 1971 ("highly sophisticated," "almost no comparison with older generation [IUDs]," the 1.1 percent pregnancy rate), with no reference to the problems that had led to the withdrawal of the product in the United States.

In July 1974 the Center for Disease Control in Atlanta issued a report that singled out the Dalkon Shield as being associated with septic abortions. At FDA hearings in August 1974 Dr. Howard Tatum, a leading researcher in contraception, revealed publicly for the first time that the Dalkon Shield had a multifilament tailstring. Tatum had performed the same "wicking experiment" that Wayne Crowder (and presumably Irwin Lerner) had performed more than three years earlier, with the same result. He had repeated the experiment using a solution containing the type of bacteria found in the vagina and found that after forty hours the bacteria had reached the base of the upper knot in the string, a point well inside the uterus. Tatum went further and microscopically analyzed thirty-six strings from used Dalkon Shields and found that thirty-one of them were infectious. Comparable tests on monofilament strings showed no transfer of bacteria.

In February 1975 a summary of Tatum's experiments with the Dalkon Shield tailstring was published in the *Journal of the American Medical Association*.[7] In April 1975, with 15 fatal and 245 nonfatal septic abortions now reported, Robins announced the cessation of foreign sales.

Robins's decision to discontinue sales of the Dalkon Shield did nothing to reduce the threat of injury to the women who were still using the device. Some 3.6 million Dalkon Shields had been implanted in women all over the world, and many, if not most, of these devices were still in place. Robins had the choice of acknowledging that the Dalkon Shield was unsafe and recalling the product, thereby limiting the number of future injuries and the number of future claims, or not recalling the Dalkon Shield and continuing to proclaim its safety in defense of the claims for injuries that had already occurred. Robins chose the latter course. When it announced the final cessation of sales, the company blamed negative publicity and stated that it "remains firm in the belief that the Dalkon Shield, when properly used, is a safe and effective IUD." Robins never deviated from that position.

By 1975 several hundred suits had been filed against Robins claiming damages for a long list of injuries associated with use of the Dalkon Shield: death related to septic abortion, nonfatal septic abortion, pelvic inflammatory disease with or without a hysterectomy or other infertility, perforation of the uterus or embedment of the device requiring surgical removal, ectopic (extrauterine or tubal) pregnancies with resulting abortions, and birth defects.

Initially, Robins's strategy in the defense of these lawsuits was to point the finger at the physicians who had inserted the Dalkon Shield. Robins claimed that it supplied the product to physicians, not directly to women, and that any problems were the result of incorrect use by the physicians. Perforation injuries, according to Robins, were the result of improper insertions. Infections were the result of physicians' failure to determine the presence of preexisting infections. In furtherance of this strategy, Robins would bring the plaintiff's physician into the case as an additional defendant if the injured women had not already done so. In the words of Roger Tuttle, the attorney who administered this early strategy for Robins:

In retrospect this was poor tactical judgment because it drove Robins' natural ally, the prescribing physician, to cooperate with the plaintiff and oppose Robins. The net result was that invariably the physician denied receiving the promotional literature and instructions and blamed Robins for leading him astray in treating his patient.[8]

The first Dalkon Shield trial began in December 1974 in Wichita, Kansas. The plaintiff, Connie Deemer, had become pregnant with a Dalkon Shield in place. Although she successfully carried her baby to term, the IUD perforated her uterus and lodged itself in her abdominal cavity. During her pregnancy she lived in fear that the Dalkon Shield would damage her baby, and later she was forced to undergo surgery to have the device removed. Mrs. Deemer was represented by Wichita attorney Bradley Post, then a forty-five-year-old specialist in products liability and medical malpractice. Post later became one of Robins's principal nemeses in its efforts to contain its Dalkon Shield liability.

Post sued both Mrs. Deemer's doctor and A. H. Robins, but because he was aware of several other cases in which a Dalkon Shield had perforated the uterus, he thought that there was good reason to believe that the product itself and not the doctor was responsible. Robins's position was that the doctor had erred in using the Dalkon Shield because of the particular tilt of Mrs. Deemer's uterus.

In the course of pretrial discovery, Post secured from Robins's files a copy of a memorandum sent by Fred Clark, the company's medical director, to top company officials on June 9, 1970, before Robins had bought the Dalkon Shield. Clark had examined Hugh Davis's patient records and had reported pregnancies at a rate of more than 5 percent, not 1.1 percent as Davis claimed. Robins's intentional misrepresentation of the pregnancy rate by a factor of five directly related to Connie Deemer's unwanted pregnancy.

Another valuable piece of evidence also concerned Hugh Davis. Prior to the *Deemer* trial, Davis had successfully concealed his financial interest in the Dalkon Shield. In pretrial testimony in the *Deemer* case, Davis again denied any financial interest, adding piously that Irwin Lerner had offered him stock in the Dalkon Corporation but that he had refused it to avoid any conflict of interest with his role in evaluating the Dalkon Shield. After this testimony Roger Tuttle, Robins's attorney, learned the truth of the matter and confronted Davis with it. When

Davis testified at the *Deemer* trial, he reversed himself and admitted his financial interest in the Dalkon Shield.

Robins presented nine expert witnesses in the *Deemer* trial, but Post skillfully argued that the Clark memorandum and Davis's belated confession of a conflict of interest discredited Robins's truthfulness and showed its lack of care in testing the Dalkon Shield. The jury returned a verdict against Robins for $10,000 in compensatory damages and $75,000 in punitive damages. It found Mrs. Deemer's doctor not liable.

Although the amount of money awarded was not great, the precedent was alarming both to Robins and to its insurer, the Aetna Casualty & Surety Company. In response to the *Deemer* verdict, Aetna insisted that responsibility for the direction and coordination of all Dalkon Shield litigation be taken away from Roger Tuttle and transferred to McGuire, Woods & Battle, a large Richmond law firm that was close to Robins and had also done work for Aetna.

McGuire, Woods & Battle restructured Robins's basic defense. Instead of blaming the doctor, Robins defended the product and contested causation, arguing that the plaintiff could not prove that her injury was caused by the Dalkon Shield and not by some other factor. McGuire, Woods assembled a panel of medical experts to testify that the Dalkon Shield was not defective or materially different from other IUDs, and that infections were attributable to the presence of an undetected infection at the time of insertion or to exposure to infection from other sources while the IUD was in place.

Ostensibly to support this defense, attorneys for Robins would interrogate plaintiffs about their sexual and hygienic habits. Robins took the position that multiple sex partners, with the accompanying increased risk of contracting sexually transmitted diseases, were a more likely cause of uterine infections than was the Dalkon Shield. Attorneys for the company would ask the plaintiff to identify her sex partners so that these men could be subpoenaed and asked about their medical histories. Women were also asked to describe their sexual practices and the details of their personal hygiene, on the theory that these might relate to the risk of pelvic infection. The courts divided on whether to require answers to these questions, but the mere fact that questions suggesting uncleanliness, promiscuity, or sexual aberration were asked dissuaded many women from pressing forward with their claims (or from making claims at all) and induced others to accept cheap settlements offered by Robins.

Meanwhile, plaintiffs' attorneys were pressuring Robins for information. The Federal Judicial Panel on Multidistrict Litigation administers a procedure for consolidated pretrial proceedings in one federal district court when numerous cases involving common factual issues are pending in several federal district courts. Its purpose is to save time and expense by avoiding repetitive discovery (fact-finding) proceedings, such as the deposition (pretrial testimony) of the same witness on the same subject numerous times, or the adjudication of objections to the production of the same document by several different judges.[9] In 1975 the Multidistrict Litigation Panel consolidated all the hundred or so Dalkon Shield injury claims then pending in the federal courts for pretrial proceedings before Judge Frank Theis in the United States District Court in Wichita, Kansas.

Counsel for the plaintiffs in the consolidated cases elected Bradley Post lead counsel. From 1976 to 1980, under Post's leadership, depositions were conducted of Robins officials and employees and of the principals in the Dalkon Corporation, and thousands of documents were produced. The proceedings were reopened in August 1981 and again in September 1982, when Post learned of additional relevant documents that Robins had not produced. The results of this effort were available to all Dalkon Shield plaintiffs.

At least until 1979, McGuire, Woods & Battle's strategy was successful. The plaintiff lost in each of the handful of cases that were tried in the four and a half years after the *Deemer* trial. McGuire, Woods threw enormous resources in terms of lawyers, doctors, and other experts into each of the trials and pressed every possible demand for information, every possible objection, and every possible defense. The plaintiffs were typically represented by attorneys from small firms, working on a contingent fee and without substantial resources to devote to a major battle with a huge corporation. By 1979 some three thousand cases had been filed and the vast majority of these had been settled at a relatively affordable average cost of $11,000.[10]

A major break in this situation occurred in the summer of 1979 when a jury in Colorado awarded $600,000 in compensatory damages and $6.2 million in punitive damages, the largest judgment ever imposed against a pharmaceutical company, to a woman named Carrie Palmer. Mrs. Palmer became pregnant while wearing a Dalkon Shield in August 1973 and suffered a near-fatal septic abortion. Her attorney, Douglas Bragg of Denver, relied heavily on Robins's failure to act on Thad J. Earl's June 1972 letter, which had warned of the risk of septic abortions and urged the removal of the Dalkon Shield from pregnant women.

In March 1980 Diane Hilliard, a woman who had experienced an extrauterine pregnancy while wearing a Dalkon Shield and who, as a result, underwent nine operations over five years before all her reproductive organs were finally removed, was awarded a $600,000 judgment against Robins by a California jury. The same month, the company paid $1.3 million to settle a case involving a child born with brain damage as a result of an infection linked to his mother's use of the Dalkon Shield. In 1980 almost a thousand new Dalkon Shield injury cases were filed, far more than the number resolved in that year. Many of the new cases were based on injuries that had occurred after the cessation of Dalkon Shield sales.

Until this point, to protect its legal position, Robins had done nothing to encourage doctors to remove Dalkon Shields still in use. In February 1977 Bradley Post had asked Robins to write to doctors and recommend the immediate removal of all Dalkon Shields, but the company had refused. Later that year Post appeared before a panel of the Food and Drug Administration in Washington to ask that agency to recommend the removal of all Dalkon Shields. The FDA panel, unconvinced by the scientific evidence, declined to take any action on Post's request.

In September 1980, following the *Palmer* and *Hilliard* verdicts, Robins finally decided to act. The company sent a "Dear Doctor" letter to two hundred thousand physicians recommending removal of the Dalkon Shield.[11] As the basis of the recommendation, the letter referred generally to reports that women who use an IUD for more than three years are exposed to an increased risk of an infection. "Since any present users of the Dalkon Shield are in the long-term use category, we now recommend removal of this IUD from any of your patients who continue to use it, even though they may not be experiencing any pelvic symptoms at this time." The letter was designed to reduce the number of women who continued to use the Dalkon Shield without acknowledging any defect in the device; the advice in the letter was equally applicable to any IUD that had been in place more than three years.

Although Robins's string of successes in court had been broken by the *Deemer* and *Hilliard* verdicts, in the years 1980, 1981, and 1982, McGuire, Woods & Battle continued to defend the increasing volume of Dalkon Shield litigation on the grounds it had staked out. The results in the thirty or so cases that went to trial in these years were evenly divided. Robins was frequently able to prevail in the argument that the plaintiff had failed to establish that her pelvic infection had been caused by the Dalkon Shield rather than some other risk factor. In these years, there was only one award of punitive damages, that in the amount of $500,000.

During this period the vast majority of the cases were resolved by out-of-court settlement, although by 1982 the average settlement had increased to $40,000. Robins's insurance policies with Aetna covered most of the costs associated with the Dalkon Shield claims, and a substantial amount of insurance coverage still remained. Robins's uninsured Dalkon Shield costs for the years 1980 through 1982 totaled $15 million; the company's net profits after taxes for those years (after deducting its Dalkon Shield expenses) were over $118 million. The situation was disturbing but not threatening to the company's well-being.

In 1983, events were set in motion in Minnesota that shattered Robins's strategy of "toughing it out" case by case.[12] A disproportionate number of Dalkon Shield cases were pending in Minnesota as a result of out-of-state advertising by lawyers in Minneapolis. A small firm in Minneapolis was charged with improper advertising and was forced to relinquish more than two hundred cases involving Dalkon Shield injury claims. The cases were transferred to the Minneapolis law firm of Robins, Zelle, Larson & Kaplan.[13] Robins, Zelle is a firm with almost two hundred lawyers, substantial resources, and a widely varied practice—quite unlike any firm A. H. Robins had yet faced in Dalkon Shield litigation. The firm assigned Dale Larson and Michael Ciresi, attorneys experienced in representing plaintiffs in industrial disasters and products liability cases, to work full time on the Dalkon Shield litigation.

The federal court in Minneapolis had assigned all the Dalkon Shield cases pending in that district to a single judge, Donald Alsop. In the first of the cases to be tried before Judge Alsop, Larson and Ciresi represented Brenda Strempke. Four years earlier, while wearing a Dalkon Shield, Mrs. Strempke had contracted a rampant pelvic infection. Emergency surgery was performed, one of Mrs. Strempke's fallopian tubes was removed, and she was left sterile.

To bolster their claim for punitive damages, Larson and Ciresi asked to take depositions from several top Robins officials. Bradley Post had already deposed these officials in the multidistrict litigation, but he had focused on the defects in the Dalkon Shield rather than on the witnesses' early knowledge of those defects and of the dangers they posed, which is what Larson and Ciresi wanted to explore. Nonetheless, consistent with what was then the general practice in courts throughout the United States, Judge Alsop would not allow any witness who had been deposed in the multidistrict proceeding to be deposed again.

The *Strempke* trial began in March 1983 and lasted nearly four months. Robins's attorneys objected to virtually every document Larson and Ciresi sought to introduce. Robins raised questions about Mrs. Strempke's health, her personal hygiene, and her sex partners. The jury heard contradictory testimony from a total of eighteen expert witnesses for the two sides. What may have been decisive was that during the trial, in time for the information to be made available to the jury, the Center for Disease Control in Atlanta issued a major study reporting that the pelvic infection rate for Dalkon Shield users was five to ten times higher than the rate for users of other intrauterine devices and recommending that all Dalkon Shields be removed.

The jury found that the Dalkon Shield was defective in design, that it was inadequately tested, and that Robins had "willfully" failed to warn of the known risks. It awarded Brenda Strempke $1.75 million in damages, including $1.5 million in punitive damages. Before the year was out, Larson and Ciresi tried another Dalkon Shield case, and they won again, this time recovering $550,000.

In response to the length of the *Strempke* trial, Judge Alsop requested that the other judges of the federal district court in Minnesota share the burden of the large number of Dalkon Shield cases, and, on December 9, 1983, the hundreds of Dalkon Shield cases pending in that court were redistributed among all of the sitting judges. Twenty-three cases, including eight in which the plaintiff was represented by Larson and Ciresi, were assigned to Judge Miles Lord.

Miles Lord, a former attorney general of Minnesota and a former United States Attorney for Minnesota, is known for his vigorous, some would say excessive, opposition to corporate misconduct. In 1976 the United States court of appeals removed Lord from a case in which the Reserve Mining Company, one of Minnesota's largest employers, was charged with polluting Lake Superior. The court of appeals stated that "Judge Lord seems to have shed the robe of the judge and assumed the mantle of the advocate."[14] In 1981, in a widely publicized speech to the Minnesota Council of Churches, Lord condemned the lenient treatment of corporate wrongdoing—what he referred to as "crime in the skyscrapers"—in American courts.

After examining the record of the *Strempke* trial, Lord concluded that it was senseless to separately litigate common factual issues concerning the design, testing, and safety of the Dalkon Shield or the conduct of company officials. Lord announced his intention to consolidate all twenty-three cases for a joint trial on common issues. This joint trial would be followed by separate hearings on the individual issues relating to injury and damages.

This unusual procedure was inconsistent with both prongs of Robins's defense strategy: making trial as unpleasant and expensive as possible for the plaintiff and her lawyer, and placing the primary focus of the trial on the plaintiff rather than on the Dalkon Shield or the conduct of company officials. Robins's defense that the plaintiff's injury was attributable to her own sexual behavior or personal hygiene would be unavailing before a jury considering the claims of twenty-three women whose only common characteristic was their use of the Dalkon Shield at the time of their injuries. The company objected vociferously, but unsuccessfully, to the planned consolidation.

Lord also announced that he would allow Larson and Ciresi to reopen discovery both to secure additional documents and to depose top company officials, including E. Claiborne Robins, Sr., concerning their knowledge of the company's handling of the Dalkon Shield. A. H. Robins filed half a dozen motions to reverse or modify this decision, but Lord could not be moved. For example, when the company claimed that the elder Robins had a heart condition that prevented him from testifying, Lord ordered that Mr. Robins's medical records be produced and be analyzed by an independent physician. After this had been done, Lord ruled that the deposition would be taken at the company offices and would be interrupted every hour and a half so that Mr. Robins could rest. But he would not back down on the basic point that Mr. Robins must testify.

The depositions began in Richmond in January 1984. The answers of Claiborne Robins, Sr., were evasive; he claimed that he had no recollection of any decisions relating to the Dalkon Shield. In response, Lord ordered that the minutes of the company's board of directors' meetings be produced to refresh the witness's memory. The company produced only segments of the minutes, claiming that the rest were subject to the attorney-client privilege. Lord ordered that the full minutes be brought to his court for his review. The minutes convinced Lord that Robins, Sr., was intimately involved in all significant company decisions. The next day, Judge Lord took the extraordinary step of flying to Richmond and presiding personally over Robins's deposition, ordering him to make responsive answers to the questions as they were put to him. Robins, Sr., testified for eight days.

On February 8, 1984, Lord issued an order requiring A. H. Robins to produce ten categories of documents that Robins had failed to disclose in the multidistrict proceeding. The most sensitive of these concerned studies or tests of the Dalkon Shield tailstring that McGuire, Woods & Battle had commissioned. Most of these studies—dubbed by plaintiffs' lawyers the "secret studies"—had never been used by Robins in litigation, giving rise to the inference that they confirmed, rather than rebutted, the hazards of the tailstring. If that were so, these company-sponsored studies would be invaluable to the plaintiffs. Robins contended that the studies were privileged and not subject to disclosure because they had been commissioned by its attorneys for use in litigation. Lord overruled these objections. Apparently unwilling to trust Robins to make complete responses to his order, Lord took the unusual step of appointing two Minneapolis attorneys as "special masters" to go to Richmond and physically supervise the production of the documents.

Robins responded by asking the United States court of appeals to overturn Judge Lord's discovery order. The company also filed a motion asking Lord to remove himself from the cases because of an "unprecedented degree of hostility and bias towards Robins." The court of appeals rejected Robins's appeal on February 23, 1984, and gave the company fifteen days to comply with Lord's order. That same day Lord refused the request to remove himself from the case.

Over the course of the preceding weeks, Robins had moved methodically to settle the cases assigned to Judge Lord. Under the circumstances, the demands of the plaintiffs' attorneys were high, but Robins met them. By February 23, when the court of appeals ruled, only two of the cases pending before Judge Lord—two in which Larson and Ciresi represented the plaintiffs—remained unsettled. Robins decided to settle these at any cost rather than to comply with the discovery order and go to trial before Judge Lord.

Larson and Ciresi had two hundred other cases to consider, and they were reluctant to settle the cases in Judge Lord's court just as they were about to receive long-sought documents they believed would be highly incriminating. Judge Lord's special masters were at Robins's headquarters in Richmond, and the review and copying of the documents to meet the court of appeals deadline were under way. But Robins offered to settle the remaining two cases in Judge Lord's court, plus five other cases in which the plaintiffs were represented by Larson and Ciresi, for $4.6 million—more money than the plaintiffs had demanded in their complaints. In addition, Robins agreed to pay the judgments in the two cases that Larson and Ciresi had tried and won (Robins had forestalled these payments by taking appeals). The offer was too good to refuse.

Larson and Ciresi extracted additional concessions. A settlement of the last cases pending before Judge Lord would moot his discovery order before any documents were produced. Robins agreed to the entry of an order by another federal judge, Robert Renner, before whom other Dalkon Shield cases were pending, prohibiting the destruction of any document covered by Judge Lord's order. Larson and Ciresi would be able to seek production of these documents in Judge Renner's court. Robins also agreed to the personal appearance of E. Claiborne Robins,

Jr., and two other top Robins executives in Judge Lord's court when the settlement was presented. Larson had demanded their presence to preclude arguments made by Robins in other cases that settlements entered into by counsel had not been authorized by management and that management had no information as to what had transpired in the Dalkon Shield litigation.

The Robins letter to doctors in 1980 had not satisfied critics, who demanded a full-scale recall of the Dalkon Shield. They contended that the letter understated the urgent need for removal by failing to explain how the multifilament tailstring on the Dalkon Shield can cause pelvic infections. Critics also contended that the dangers posed by long-term use of the Dalkon Shield were so great that it was necessary to go beyond a letter to doctors and communicate directly with women who were still using the device. In April 1983 Robert Manchester, a Burlington, Vermont, attorney associated with Bradley Post in the multidistrict proceeding, submitted a "Citizen's Petition" to the Food and Drug Administration, in which he asked the agency to initiate a recall of the Dalkon Shield and to require Robins to pay the costs associated with removal of the device. Robins opposed the petition, and on February 29, 1984, when the settlement of his last two Dalkon Shield cases came before Judge Lord, the FDA had done nothing about the matter.[15]

Company president E. Claiborne Robins, Jr., general counsel William Forrest, and research director Carl Lunsford were in court when the settlement agreement was presented to Judge Lord. Before he approved the settlement, Lord castigated these men for defending rather than recalling the Dalkon Shield.

Under your direction, your company has in fact continued to allow women, tens of thousands of them, to wear this device—a deadly depth charge in their wombs ready to explode at any time . . . The only conceivable reasons you have not recalled this product are that it would hurt your balance sheet and alert women who have already been harmed that you may be liable for their injuries . . .

If this were a case in equity, I would order your company to make an effort to locate each and every woman who still wears this device and recall your product. But this court does not have the power to do so. I must therefore resort to moral persuasion and a personal appeal to each of you . . . Please, in the name of humanity, lift your eyes above the bottom line . . . Please, gentlemen, give consideration to tracing down the victims and sparing them the agony that will surely be theirs.

The response to this statement was not repentance but outrage. Robins lodged an appeal and retained former United States attorney general Griffin Bell to file judicial misconduct proceedings against the judge. Judge Lord retained former attorney general Ramsey Clark to defend him, and after a public hearing the misconduct proceedings were dismissed. But in the appeal, the court of appeals ordered Lord's statement stricken from the record on the ground that he had denied the due process rights of the Robins officials by rendering judgment when no trial had occurred and when they had had no opportunity to defend their conduct.[16]

Nonetheless, Robins's situation rapidly deteriorated. Judge Lord's statement, together with the size of the settlements of the cases in his court, received wide publicity and provided substantial impetus both to Dalkon Shield victims and to their lawyers to pursue their claims vigorously. In addition, in the Dalkon Shield cases in his court, Judge Renner adopted Judge Lord's February 8 discovery order verbatim. By July 1984, Renner, like Lord, concluded that it was necessary to appoint special masters to supervise Robins's production of the documents. Larson and Ciresi soon began to receive the documents identified in Judge Lord's order.

On July 30, 1984, there was another remarkable development when Roger Tuttle, the attorney who had been in charge of Dalkon Shield litigation for Robins until 1975, appeared in Minneapolis for a deposition scheduled by Michael Ciresi. Tuttle was now a professor of law at Oral Roberts University and a born-again Christian. The preceding year he had published an article critical of Robins's handling of the Dalkon Shield litigation.[17] Robins had filed suit against Tuttle in Oklahoma, seeking to prevent his testimony in Minnesota, but to no avail.

During the deposition, Tuttle suddenly revealed that in 1974 he had destroyed incriminating documents relating to the Dalkon Shield on the orders of William Forrest, Robins's general counsel. According to Tuttle's testimony, Forrest had been furious because of the disclosure in the *Deemer* case of documents contradicting Hugh Davis's claimed pregnancy rate. To prevent anything similar from happening in the future, Forrest had ordered Tuttle to destroy all documents that could be harmful to the company in future Dalkon Shield litigation. Tuttle described how the files of senior Robins officials had been systematically searched, with particular focus on documents that would demonstrate top company executives' knowledge of the dangers of the Dalkon Shield, and how hundreds of documents had been removed from these files and burned in an incinerator.

Tuttle testified that as a salve to his conscience he had secreted away and retained the originals of the most damaging documents, and in front of startled observers he began to pull these from a large envelope he had brought to the deposition. Copies of many of these documents had previously come to light, but one damning document had never before been revealed. It was a memorandum to top Robins management from Roy Smith, the company's director of product planning, dated June 10, 1970, reporting that Davis and Lerner had added copper sulfate to the Dalkon Shield in the hope that the released copper would enhance the IUD's contraceptive effect. Tuttle testified that Robins had concealed this information because it would have caused the FDA to classify the Dalkon Shield as a drug and to require that Robins prove its safety and efficacy before the product was put on the market. Tuttle's testimony created another round of national publicity adverse to Robins.

The pressure continued. Within days of Tuttle's testimony, Larson and Ciresi initiated proceedings seeking monetary penalties against A. H. Robins for destruction of documents. They took depositions from the company officials who were implicated by Tuttle, all of whom denied any knowledge of or involvement in the destruction of documents. Also in the summer of 1984, CBS's "60 Minutes" aired a segment critical of the Dalkon Shield and of Robins's failure to recall it. In September 1984 there were reports of three additional deaths related to the Dalkon Shield, these from pelvic infections without pregnancy.

Later that month A. H. Robins settled the remaining 198 cases in which Larson and Ciresi represented women injured by the Dalkon Shield for an average of $192,000, a total of $38 million. The settlement ended Larson's and Ciresi's participation in Dalkon Shield litigation, but the agreement provided that the evidence they obtained would be available to other attorneys. In fact, the Robins, Zelle law firm prepared and widely distributed a 160-page catalog listing and describing the materials generated in the Dalkon Shield litigation all over the country—deposition and trial testimony of hundreds of witnesses, company documents, videotaped depositions, exhibit enlargements for use before a jury, briefs and memoranda of law on the full range of legal issues—quite simply, thousands of hours of trial preparation, all available by mail for the cost of copying.

Finally, in October 1984, eight months after Judge Lord had urged it to do so, Robins began a campaign for the removal of Dalkon Shields still in use. Robins wrote to doctors and placed advertisements in newspapers, in magazines, and on television urging the removal of the Dalkon Shield and offering to pay the costs involved. In the months that followed, Robins paid for the removal of the Dalkon Shield from more than five thousand women.

2   Judge Merhige

When Robins began its campaign to urge women to remove the Dalkon Shield in October 1984, some 7,700 Dalkon Shield cases had been resolved at a cost of $260 million but another 3,500 cases were still pending. In the wake of Robins's advertising, new cases were filed at the rate of 10 a day. Plaintiffs' attorneys everywhere, emboldened by the events in Minnesota and the ready availability of evidence to support their clients' claims, raised their demands for settlement and were threatening to go to trial. Robins's strategy of fighting individual cases had proved inadequate to stave off overwhelming liability.

Just at this time, the activities of a lawyer in Minneapolis, Joseph S. Friedberg, afforded Robins the opportunity to shape a new strategy designed to consolidate all Dalkon Shield claims in a single proceeding in Richmond, Virginia. In 1982 and 1983 a group of young lawyers in Minneapolis, with more entrepreneurial instinct than legal experience, placed advertisements in out-of-state newspapers offering to represent women injured by the Dalkon Shield. In response, these lawyers were retained by some 1,500 women. At first, they were able to obtain settlements with Aetna merely by sending a demand letter and medical records. In late 1982 Aetna concluded that this approach was encouraging more advertising and more claims, and it adopted a policy of not settling any case unless a suit was filed and prosecuted. Because the young lawyers were not prepared to do this, they entered into agreements with more experienced lawyers under which the latter would litigate the cases in exchange for a portion of the one-third contingent fee. One of these more experienced lawyers was Joseph Friedberg.

Friedberg was born and raised in New York City. In the late fifties and early sixties, he attended college and law school at the University of North Carolina at Chapel Hill. Upon graduation from law school, Friedberg worked for a short period for a corporate law firm in New York. He did not like the life or the pace, and in 1964 Friedberg moved to Minneapolis. After the move, Friedberg did not initially work as a lawyer; he spent a year or so selling encyclopedias door to door. In 1966 he was admitted to the Minnesota bar and gradually began to practice law, representing defendants in criminal cases. Over the years, practic-

23

ing alone, Friedberg established himself as a criminal defense attorney.

In 1982 Friedberg was retained to represent a defendant in a case charging a criminal conspiracy among an adjuster for Aetna, a Minneapolis lawyer, and others to settle Dalkon Shield injury cases for more than their legitimate value. After a lengthy trial, all of the defendants were acquitted. In the process, Friedberg became convinced that there was more money and less work in representing women injured by the Dalkon Shield than there was in criminal law, and he began to look for an opportunity to become involved in Dalkon Shield cases. Before long, he entered into an agreement with the young legal advertisers to handle two hundred of their cases for one-half of the fee.

Usually, plaintiffs in product liability cases file suit in the state in which they reside. Local trials are convenient for the plaintiff and her witnesses, and a local plaintiff pitted against an out-of-state corporation may expect to benefit from the neighborly feelings of the jury. A manufacturer can also be sued in the state in which its business is located, but plaintiffs rarely choose this option. Only a handful of Dalkon Shield cases had been filed in Richmond, and those mostly involved plaintiffs from Great Britain who were unable to sue Robins anywhere else in the United States.

The plaintiffs in Friedberg's two hundred cases did not live in Minnesota, and for this reason their suits could not be maintained in Minnesota over Robins's objection. Nevertheless, in the spring of 1984, in the hope that the company would not object, as it had not in other cases filed in Minnesota for out-of-state plaintiffs, Friedberg filed all his cases in the federal district court in Minneapolis. The cases were assigned to several different judges of that court.

By this time, Robins had had enough of Minnesota. The company immediately filed motions to transfer each of the cases to the plaintiff's state of residence. Friedberg had no basis on which to argue that the cases should remain in Minnesota, but he opposed transfers to the districts in which the plaintiffs lived on the ground that this would "effectively deprive those plaintiffs of meaningful representation," by which he meant he would not be able to handle all the cases. In an effort to keep the cases together, Friedberg asked that they all be transferred to the federal court in Virginia. With the plaintiffs asking that their cases be sent to the defendant's home jurisdiction, there was little basis for opposition, and most of the cases were transferred to Virginia. A smaller number of cases were sent to the plaintiffs' home states.

Some of the cases transferred to Virginia were assigned to the federal court in Alexandria; others, to the federal court in Richmond. Robins then proposed to Friedberg that all the cases in Virginia be transferred to Richmond. The cases in Alexandria had been assigned to Judge Albert Bryan, Jr., whom Friedberg knew by reputation to be unfavorable to plaintiffs in personal injury litigation. Friedberg made contact with Murray Janus, a Richmond lawyer close to Robert R. Merhige, Jr., the federal judge to whom the cases in Richmond had been assigned. Janus had worked for Merhige before his appointment to the bench. Janus, who would become Friedberg's local counsel in Richmond, assured Friedberg that he could expect fair treatment from Merhige. Friedberg then responded to Robins's proposal by suggesting that the cases sent to plaintiffs' home states as well as the cases in Alexandria be transferred to Richmond, and an agreement was reached on this basis. As a result of this unlikely chain of events, in early October 1984 Robins found itself with a large number of Dalkon Shield cases pending in Richmond before Judge Merhige.[1] From that point on, Judge Merhige would dominate and ultimately control the disposition of Robins's liability to women injured by the Dalkon Shield.

Robert Merhige was appointed to the federal bench in Richmond in 1967 by President Lyndon Johnson. He is a judge who prides himself on his ability to solve a big problem and on his willingness to invoke innovative measures to do so. Merhige will decide on a solution, however unorthodox, that seems sensible to him and then shrewdly and effectively use the many tools available to a federal judge to achieve it. According to one reporter: "It is what observers call his pragmatic approach to the facts of a case that draws Judge Merhige both criticism and praise. For once he spots 'the heart of the problem,' they say, little can keep him from trying to solve it."[2]

Before the Dalkon Shield cases, Judge Merhige's best-known effort to solve a big problem through unorthodox measures involved *Bradley v. School Board of the City of Richmond*, the case in which black families sought the desegregation of the public school system in Richmond.[3] When the *Bradley* case was assigned to Judge Merhige in 1970, a "freedom of choice" plan for school desegregation had been in effect in Richmond since the early 1960s. Under this plan, which was the standard remedy in school segregation cases in the decade after *Brown v. Board of Education*,[4] each child could choose to attend any school in the district. The result, in Richmond and throughout the South, was that a small handful of black children braved the psychological, social, academic, and often physical hazards to attend a white school while no white students chose to attend a black school.

In 1968 the Supreme Court issued a series of decisions calling for an end of freedom of choice wherever it had failed to disestablish the segregated system. The Supreme Court ruled that school systems must take "whatever steps might be necessary to convert to a unitary system in which racial discrimination would be eliminated root and branch."[5] In the fall of 1969 the Supreme Court reversed a lower-court decision allowing a school board additional time to comply with this mandate. The Court stated: "[T]he obligation of every school district is to terminate the dual school systems at once and operate now and hereafter only unitary schools."[6] Then, in December 1969, the Supreme Court emphasized that it meant what it had said by reversing a twelve-day-old unanimous decision of all fourteen judges of the United States Court of Appeals for the Fifth Circuit which had allowed school districts from Georgia to Texas to delay the adoption of a unitary system until the fall of 1970. The Supreme Court ordered that unitary systems be in place a few weeks later, at the start of the spring 1970 semester.[7]

In this context, in March 1970 the attorneys for the black children represented in the *Bradley* case filed a motion asking Judge Merhige to require a unitary system in time for the opening of the next school term, the fall of 1970. The Richmond School Board, with 60 percent of its students black, opposed the request. Instead, it proposed, by the limited use of bussing, to eliminate the racial identity of some of the high schools and middle schools, but to do nothing to desegregate the other high schools and middle schools or any of the lower schools. Twelve thousand black children would be left in segregated schools. The plaintiffs submitted a plan involving greater use of bussing that would have desegregated all schools at all grade levels.

Judge Merhige did not think that the time was right for the complete desegregation of the Richmond schools, notwithstanding the explicit pronouncements of the Supreme Court, and he decided not to order it. But instead of saying so and risking an appeal before the fall 1970 term, he delayed announcing a decision until August 17, 1970, just a few days before the schools were scheduled to open. In his decision, Merhige said it was too late to purchase the busses necessary to desegregate the school in time for the fall semester, and he adopted the plan proposed by the school board.[8]

In his decision, Merhige acknowledged that the school board plan did not meet the Supreme Court standards and referred to it as "interim." A few weeks later, in October 1970, plaintiffs asked Merhige to order complete desegregation for the spring 1971 semester. Merhige waited until January 29, 1971, and then announced that he would not do so, again because there was insufficient time to buy the busses and also because it was possible, in a case then pending before it, that the Supreme Court would relax its requirements (which it did not do).[9]

Meanwhile, Judge Merhige was at work on a novel solution to the problem of segregated education in Richmond, a solution that would avoid schools with a majority of black students. The city of Richmond is surrounded by the counties of Chesterfield and Henrico, where only 10 percent of the school children are black. The three systems together would be two-thirds white. During a hearing in the *Bradley* case in June 1970, Merhige asked an expert witness how "optimum desegregation in the Richmond area" could be achieved, and the witness responded by suggesting "the involvement of a larger area than the present boundaries of the city of Richmond."[10]

On July 6, 1970, Merhige wrote a letter to the lawyers in the *Bradley* case in which he said that "[i]t may be that it would be appropriate for the defendant school board to discuss with the appropriate officers of the contiguous counties as to the feasibility or possibility of consolidation of school districts."[11] Two weeks later the Richmond School Board filed a motion asking Merhige to order the consolidation of the city of Richmond school district with the school districts of Chesterfield and Henrico counties. The move was supported by the attorneys for the black children. The Richmond city council was first opposed to it, but when in April 1971 Judge Merhige finally issued an order requiring the city of Richmond schools to open the following fall on a fully desegregated basis, the council changed its position and supported consolidation.[12]

No federal court had ever consolidated neighboring school districts to adjust the racial balance in newly desegregated schools. The county school boards were adamantly opposed to consolidation. They asked Judge Merhige to disqualify himself from ruling on the motion on the ground it was filed at his "invitation or suggestion." Merhige angrily denied the motion.[13]

A fact-finding hearing on the consolidation motion was conducted in August and September 1971. In January 1972 Merhige ordered the three school districts consolidated.[14] The order set forth in detail exactly how consolidation would be accomplished, and it provided that the three separate school boards would go out of existence as of June 30, 1972. In his opinion, Merhige found the state, by such measures as the selection of sites for public housing and the toleration of racially restrictive covenants in real estate deeds, had contributed to the racial segregation in the Richmond metropolitan area, in violation of the federal constitutional rights of black citizens. Merhige held that in these circumstances the state's authority to set geographic boundaries for purposes of administering public education was subordinate to the right of black children to equal educational opportunity and that, in the Richmond metropolitan area, that opportunity could only be secured by a consolidation of the three districts.

Merhige's decision triggered an enormous reaction both locally and nationally. Officials of Chesterfield and Henrico counties denounced the decision as "despicable" and "the death knell of public education." The *Richmond Times-Dispatch* decried the ruling as a "tragedy" that would "serve as a malignant precedent for the final destruction of nearly all powers of local government."[15] School boycotts were urged, and Judge Merhige was afforded round-the-clock protection by the United States marshals' service after he received an anonymous threat on his life.[16]

On the other side, the decision was hailed not only by the city of Richmond officials who had sought it but nationally, as a breakthrough in the elimination of racially segregated education. In a front-page story, the *New York Times* described Merhige's decision as "the first and most far reaching mandate ever issued by a federal court seeking to end classroom segregation by breaking down political boundaries . . . potentially a national landmark."[17] Columnist Tom Wicker predicted: "[I]f it survives appeal . . . [the] decision in the Richmond school case will prove not just historic but cataclysmic, with more and wider practical impact even than the 1954 decision that started school desegregation."[18]

Usually, a decision that is novel and subject to reasonable disagreement will be stayed by the trial judge during an appeal. In this instance, not only was the decision novel and disputable, but its implementation would eliminate the existence of the defendants while the appeal was being considered. But Merhige refused to issue a stay. He explained:

The rights of school children to schooling under nondiscriminatory and constitutional conditions cannot be recaptured for any school semester lived under discriminatory practices . . . The Supreme Court has made it abundantly clear that desegregation matters are not to be delayed.

Merhige added that there was little likelihood his decision would be reversed as it "embodies legal principles long established as the law of the land."[19]

Within a few days the court of appeals stayed Merhige's order pending appeal. In June 1972, by a vote of five to one, Merhige's decision was reversed.[20] According to the court of appeals:

[T]he root causes of the concentration of blacks in the inner cities of America are simply not known and . . . the district court could not realistically place on the counties the responsibility for the effect that inner city decay has had on the public schools of Richmond . . . Whatever its basic causes, it has not been school assignments, and school assignments cannot reverse the trend. A school case, like a vehicle, can carry only a limited amount of baggage.[21]

The Supreme Court agreed to review the case, but on May 22, 1973, the Court announced, without opinion, that the decision of the court of appeals (reversing Merhige's decision) was affirmed by an equally divided court. Justice Lewis Powell, who for many years had served as a member of the Richmond School Board, did not participate.[22] The following year, with Justice Powell participating, the Supreme Court ruled that school districts are not required to bus children across established district lines to achieve desegregation.[23]

Judge Merhige's early decisions restraining the mistreatment of prisoners in the Virginia State Penitentiary are a more successful illustration of his readiness to impose novel remedies. In 1971, at a time when most of the federal courts were following a hands-off policy with respect to conditions in state prisons, Merhige undertook to examine the conditions in the Virginia State Penitentiary to determine its compliance with the Eighth Amendment prohibition against cruel and unusual punishment.[24] After making unannounced nighttime visits to the state prison, he issued a sweeping injunction, hailed by American Civil Liberties Union attorneys as a "bill of rights for inmates," prohibiting bread and water diets, chaining prisoners to their cells, physical punishments, enforced nudity, censorship of mail, interfering with access to courts, and the denial of "good time" reductions of sentences without a due process hearing.[25] Later, Merhige found that the director of the Virginia Department of Corrections had knowledge of and involvement in the mistreatment of three prisoners and ordered that he personally pay $21,265 in damages to the three men.[26]

Other facets of Judge Merhige's approach to his position are suggested by his handling of a celebrated criminal case against the Allied Chemical Corporation. In 1976 Allied was charged with 940 counts of polluting the James River. The company pleaded no contest and came before Merhige for sentencing. Merhige forcefully rejected defense contentions that the pollution had been inadvertent and found that it was done intentionally, "to save money." Merhige imposed a $13 million fine, the largest ever imposed for pollution of the nation's waterways. His action was reported admiringly on the front page of the *New York Times*.[27]

When Merhige imposed the fine, he stated that he would consider reducing it if Allied Chemical could conceive of a way to keep the money in Virginia.[28] Allied was represented by Murray Janus, Merhige's friend and former colleague who years later would serve as Joseph Friedberg's local counsel in the Dalkon Shield cases. Before the fine had been paid, Janus moved for its reduction on the ground that Allied had agreed to contribute $8 million to establish the Virginia Environmental Endowment, a nonprofit corporation intended to improve the quality of the environment in Virginia. Under the documents establishing the endowment, Judge Merhige was given the power to appoint its directors.

The Department of Justice strongly opposed reducing the fine. When the motion came up for hearing on February 1, 1977, William B. Cummings, the assistant United States attorney who had prosecuted the case, argued that the original fine was appropriate since the pollution "was deliberately done . . . in callous disregard" of the environment. Cummings also pointed out that a reduction in the fine equal to the amount of the contribution would reduce Allied's costs because a charitable contribution is tax deductible and a fine is not.

But Merhige told Cummings that "there is nothing un-American about trying to reduce your taxes." As the *Washington Post* described it, "[I]n sharp contrast to the biting comments Merhige delivered when he fined the company for secretly polluting Virginia's James River, the judge went out of his way to praise Allied's executives," whom he hailed as "good boys in my book." Merhige reduced the fine by $8 million.[29] The reduction cost the United States Treasury $12 million (the amount of the reduction plus the amount of Allied's tax saving), saved Allied $4 million, and put $8 million into a fund under Merhige's control. Merhige came to the hearing ready with his appointments of directors of the Virginia Environmental Endowment. These included two close friends, Sydney Lewis, chairman of Best Products Company, and Mr. Lewis's wife, Frances. Merhige also appointed Assistant United States Attorney Cummings.[30]

Several years later the Virginia Environmental Endowment made its largest grant, $150,000, to the law school at the University of Richmond "to establish the Robert R. Merhige, Jr. Center for Environmental Studies."[31] In 1986, McGuire, Woods & Battle, Robins's chief counsel in the Dalkon Shield litigation, donated $7,500 to the Merhige Center.[32]

Merhige was born in 1919 into a Roman Catholic family in Brooklyn, New York. His father was of Lebanese ancestry, his mother of Irish descent. Merhige grew up on Long Island, where his father was a dentist. Although he is only five feet, seven inches tall, Merhige received a basketball scholarship to attend High Point College in North Carolina. After two years in college, Merhige enrolled in the law school at the University of Richmond. He had been a mediocre student in high school and college but liked law and did well in the law school. After he graduated in 1942, Merhige spent three war years in the Air Force, serving as a radar interceptor on combat missions in Europe. He received an "Air Medal with four clusters."

Merhige returned to Richmond and over the next two decades, practicing in a small firm, achieved notable success as a criminal defense lawyer. He was married in 1957 and is the father of two sons. Between his law practice and real estate investments in Richmond, Merhige has acquired substantial wealth. He recently reported a net worth in excess of $3 million.

Merhige entered the public life of his adopted hometown with enthusiasm. He joined the Richmond Citizens Committee and the advisory committee of the County Sanitation District. He served as the appeal agent for the county draft board and held offices in the Richmond Bar Association and the Virginia Trial Lawyers Association. He was an active Democrat and in the 1964 presidential election was co-chairman of Virginians for Johnson.[33]

In 1966 Congress created an additional federal district court judgeship in Richmond, and Merhige undertook to get it. He was able to secure the support of both United States senators from Virginia, of the congressman from Richmond, and of the politically connected family of tobacco tycoon R. J. Reynolds, particularly J. Sargent Reynolds, who would soon be lieutenant governor of Virginia. Merhige was also endorsed by the Richmond-area bar associations. At one point, a delegation of Richmond lawyers that included future Supreme Court justice Lewis Powell traveled to Washington to lobby for Merhige's appointment.[34] Remarkably, at the height of the civil rights movement, when the federal courts were exercising unwelcome authority to reform southern institutions, the political and legal leaders in the capital of the Old Confederacy were virtually unanimous in their support of a criminal defense attorney from New York for the local federal judgeship.

Merhige's selection by President Johnson in July 1967 was greeted with enthusiasm. His swearing-in ceremony was so heavily attended that a loudspeaker system had to be set up in the hallway of the courthouse for the benefit of spectators unable to crowd into the courtroom.[35]

Judge Merhige ardently believes that lawsuits should be compromised, and he has developed a reputation as a judge with an unusual ability to induce litigants to settle.[36] According to Judge Merhige,

[W]hat has been most successful for me is two pots of coffee and Coca-Cola. I've kept those things in here since the day I came on the bench. Getting lawyers to sit down here in this office and have a Coke or a cup of coffee, I think, has accomplished a lot. Once you get the lawyers talking and make them involve their clients, you're on the way to disposing of litigation.[37]

To facilitate this process, and generally in the course of managing litigation in his court, it is Merhige's practice to talk with lawyers outside the presence of their adversaries to urge a particular course of action or to give his reaction to action contemplated by counsel. Merhige has explained that lawyers agree to this unusual policy because they understand that no advantage could be gained by speaking with him informally. "When I talk to lawyers, I learn more from them than they do from me."[38] According to one observer, an entire generation of lawyers in Richmond has grown up with the idea that Judge Merhige should be consulted before any important moves are made in cases pending before him.

The origin of Merhige's renown as a "settling judge" is his handling of a series of consolidated cases against the Westinghouse Electric Corporation between 1976 and 1980. The cases did not settle for four years, and then only after a nine-month trial and a decision on the central issue in the case, but they illustrate Merhige's persistent and unusual approach to the process.[39]

In the early 1970s Westinghouse Electric Corporation agreed to provide more than 50 million pounds of uranium to public utilities across the United States over a period of several years at a price of $8 a pound. By 1975 the market price of uranium was $40 a pound, and Westinghouse, claiming "commercial impracticability," announced that it would not honor its contracts. Thirteen utility companies filed breach of contract suits against Westinghouse in thirteen different United States district courts claiming damages totaling over $2 billion. One of these cases was filed in Judge Merhige's court, and the Judicial Panel on Multidistrict Litigation consolidated all thirteen cases before Judge Merhige.[40]

At the outset Merhige scheduled three days of settlement conferences. In a speech to new federal judges that Merhige happened to deliver in the midst of these conferences, in September 1976, the judge explained his approach.

I also suggested that it might be a good idea if we could sort of get together socially before each of these conferences. Well. I was really surprised at the response I got . . . [T]hey were fairly enthusiastic about it.

So I went home and spoke to the little Irish girl I married and said, "You're going to have three parties, one Sunday night, one Monday night and one Wednesday night."

We started on Sunday and we had about 35 people. The weather was delightful. And the guys were calling each other by their first names. We met on Monday, and the plaintiffs made their presentations, and then we had another party on Monday night. And the crowd came in yesterday, and they made their presentations, and we are going to give it another stab tonight.[41]

These efforts did not result in settlement, however, and a trial, limited to the issue of whether Westinghouse had a legally sufficient excuse not to comply with the contracts, began in September 1977 and lasted until June 1978. During the trial Merhige continued to schedule settlement conferences, sometimes insisting on the presence of company executives or directors, but to no avail. In June 1978, at the close of final arguments, Merhige warned the lawyers for the utility companies that, if they were waiting for 100 cents on the dollar, "they're just damn fools. No other way to say it."[42]

When Merhige did issue his ruling, on October 27, 1978, he did so in a way that did not so much decide the issue of Westinghouse's liability as create further incentive to settle. He ruled that Westinghouse's defense of impracticability did not excuse the company from its contract but that the considerations relating to impracticability would be considered by the court in some unspecified manner to reduce Westinghouse's obligation to pay damages. He added:

The plaintiffs should not be misled by today's holding. The Court is disposed to believe that the plaintiffs are not entitled to anything near the full measure of their prayer for relief.

I expect Westinghouse and the utilities to enter into serious and intense negotiations . . . In the event that the Court's hope in this regard does not reach fruition, then the Court stands ready to issue a decree which insures that Westinghouse pays no more and the utilities receive no less than is fair.[43]

Another of Merhige's techniques to overcome an unwillingness to settle is to create some personal discomfort for the lawyers involved. When settlement proves difficult, Merhige will "place counsel in an uncomfortable position of balancing, at least subconsciously, their personal interest against the interests of the client."[44] Applying this technique to the Westinghouse cases, Merhige threatened to hold conferences on "Saturdays, Sundays, and some days that aren't even on the calendar."[45] During the fall and winter, he set conferences for out-of-town counsel on Sunday afternoons so that the lawyers would miss weekends with their families as well as their favorite football games. The lawyers negotiated while Merhige watched his beloved Washington Redskins in the next room. During the game, Merhige would pop in and out with the ball scores.[46]

Over the months that followed, Westinghouse undertook to negotiate separately with each utility and the cases gradually began to settle.[47] In April 1980 the final settlement was announced.[48]

In the late 1970s Judge Merhige was charged by the United States Attorney's Office in North Carolina with having handled a criminal trial in a manner designed to assure the acquittal of a defendant with whom he had connections. The response of the Richmond Bar is illustrative of its relationship with the judge.

In the summer of 1979, Smith Bagley, a grandson of tobacco tycoon R. J. Reynolds, was charged along with others in federal court in North Carolina with criminal stock manipulation, mail fraud, and conspiracy. The chief judge of the federal court in North Carolina sought a judge from out of the state for the possible lengthy trial, and Merhige volunteered for the assignment. Judge Merhige moved the case to Richmond, and on August 1, 1979, after a two-week trial, a jury acquitted Bagley and his co-defendants on all charges.[49]

On October 5, 1979, H. M. Michaux, Jr., the United States attorney for the Middle District of North Carolina, and Patricia W. Lemley, the assistant United States attorney who had tried the *Bagley* case, sent a lengthy letter to a senior official at the Department of Justice in Washington bitterly complaining of Merhige's "anti-government bias" during the trial. The prosecutors objected to "the court's intemperate comments and outrageous jury instructions," the "circus-like atmosphere" in the courtroom, and the "maniacal trial schedule." With two government attorneys facing nine defense counsel, Merhige had conducted the trial ten to twelve hours a day and had held court on Saturdays and Sundays.

The prosecutors seemed to suggest that the judge had intentionally rigged the trial in favor of the defendants:

In overview, the Bagley trial takes on the quality of a "set-up." Individual incidents which at the time had the appearance of mere intemperance laid the foundation for jury instructions which had the effect of an instruction to the jury to acquit. Only at the time of jury instructions did certain of the judge's exclusionary rulings, unsolicited witness cross-examinations and verbal explosions make sense . . .

During the trial itself, the government was subjected to numerous on- and off-the-record diatribes by Judge Merhige. The judge's views that the government had failed after a week of trial to produce a "scintilla" of evidence as to a conspiracy were repeatedly articulated to the jury . . .

Throughout the course of the trial, the judge displayed a more than merely solicitous attitude toward the jury. He personally served the panel with coffee and donuts on a daily basis and arranged on at least one occasion for them to lunch at his private club. The foreman of the jury was quoted in a local tableaux [sic] as stating the jury had not wanted to let the judge down by its verdict.[50]

The prosecutors' letter did not mention any connections between Merhige and Bagley, but in columns published on November 5 and 6, 1979, Jack Anderson reported that Bagley was a cousin of J. Sargent Reynolds, a close friend of Merhige's until Reynolds's death in 1971, and a key supporter of Merhige's appointment to the federal court. Merhige had met Bagley through Reynolds. When Reynolds died, Bagley was in charge of his funeral arrangements and Merhige served as a pallbearer at the funeral. In his will, Reynolds named Merhige as the co-executor of his estate. Anderson concluded that the "pattern of circumstances . . . gives off a strong whiff of lime."[51]

The issue was taken up by Orrin Hatch on the floor of the United States Senate. On November 2 and 6, 1979, he entered the prosecutors' letter, an Anderson article, and other news stories in the *Congressional Record* and added: "The letter from these two prosecutors is absolutely astounding. No prosecutors would make these criticisms without great consideration and serious reflection."[52] Hatch called for an investigation of the matter by the Department of Justice.

There is no public record of an investigation by the Department of Justice. But on November 8, 1979, the president of the Richmond Bar Association, Wilbur Allen, appointed a committee of Richmond lawyers to investigate the "unwarranted attacks" on Judge Merhige. Allen suggested that the prosecutors were trying to excuse their failure to secure a conviction. The lawyers he named to the committee were John S. Battle, Jr., of McGuire, Woods & Battle, James C. Roberts of Mays & Valentine, and Lewis T. Booker of Hunton & Williams.

Battle, reported to be an "old friend" of Judge Merhige,[53] was the attorney for Westinghouse in the then ongoing uranium litigation. Booker was "liaison counsel" for the utilities. McGuire, Woods & Battle served as counsel to Merhige in matters relating to his personal finances. Both McGuire, Woods and Mays & Valentine represented A. H. Robins in prebankruptcy Dalkon Shield litigation, and James Roberts would be lead counsel in the Robins bankruptcy. Years later, Merhige would sponsor Hunton & Williams, Justice Powell's former firm, for the position of counsel to the $2.5 billion trust established to pay Dalkon Shield injury claims.

In a report issued December 12, 1979, the committee concluded that none of the dozen or so complaints against Judge Merhige contained in the prosecutors' letter had the slightest merit.

Our conclusion can be briefly stated. After a thorough review of the record and an examination of all other available objective data . . . we have reached the unanimous conclusion that Judge Merhige handled the case in a fair and even-handed matter throughout. He showed no bias against the Government and in many instances went beyond his normal function to assist the prosecutors . . . Indeed, our review of the entire record persuades us that this trial was as fair and as error-free as it is humanly possible to make a trial. The short of the matter is that Judge Merhige, in our view, tried this case with exceptional fairness and correctness.[54]

The committee suggested that disciplinary action be taken against the prosecutors for writing the letter.

At the end of a long career, Merhige is comfortable in the role of venerated senior judge in a small southern city. Not scholarly by nature, he enjoys spending time off the bench in casual interaction with members of the local bar. Merhige has reported that his friend Murray Janus had "expressed the view that he wished I wasn't so friendly and read more law."[55] Visiting lawyers report on invitations into chambers, to lunch, or even to Merhige's home, where Merhige will chat easily about the case at hand. Three attorneys involved in the Robins bankruptcy described separate occasions on which they were approached by Judge Merhige in his Wagoneer outside the courthouse following a hearing and insistently offered transportation to wherever they were going.

Merhige takes pride in his courtroom. It is old and elegant, mahogany-paneled, with maroon draperies and carpeting, brass fixtures, and tall windows overlooking the state capitol grounds. At one point late in the Robins bankruptcy, while warning lawyers to be careful with a misfunctioning door, Merhige said that he "would rather see the whole plan go down the drain than hurt anything [in] this courtroom."[56] Merhige enforces courtroom decorum of a style more common years ago. Counsel are admonished not to make any statements to each other; all remarks must be addressed to the bench. Attorneys are not permitted to leave the lectern to hand the judge or the witness a document; a marshal stands by to carry documents back and forth.

Despite these trappings of formality, there is frequent banter in the courtroom between the judge and counsel, the usual theme of which is adulation of the judge. For example, Merhige never tires of pointing out that he, the judge, not any lawyer, gets the "last word." With reference to this precept, Merhige will offer, or a lawyer will obsequiously request, the "next to last word." But Merhige's amiability will quickly turn to anger when his wishes are defied.

Merhige works extraordinarily long hours, and his docket is one of the most up-to-date in the country. The judge boasts that for nineteen years he was in his office for some part of every day he was in Richmond, "Saturday, Sunday, Christmas, New Year's."[57] Merhige was considering retirement when the Dalkon Shield cases came before him in the fall of 1984. He has said that the complexity and challenge of the Dalkon Shield litigation persuaded him to stay.[58]

In assessing its situation in the fall of 1984, Robins concluded that it would be able to meet the costs of compensatory damages in Dalkon Shield cases but that its survival depended on somehow limiting or eliminating claims for punitive damages. Punitive damages are awarded in exceptional cases in which the jury finds that the defendant's conduct is so reprehensible that a penalty, in addition to the normal award of compensatory damages, is warranted to deter future misconduct by the defendant and by others. The amount of punitive damages is determined by the jury at whatever level it considers appropriate to this end. A punitive damage award is frequently many times higher than the award of compensatory damages, and when there are many victims of the same misconduct, punitive damages can be imposed again and again by different juries.[59]

By the fall of 1984 juries in eight Dalkon Shield cases had imposed against Robins a total of more than $17 million in punitive damages. But this was just the tip of the iceberg. Punitive damages were demanded in nearly all of the 3,500 pending cases, and the case for punitive damages was getting stronger as more and more evidence was uncovered. The product liability insurance provided by Aetna did not cover punitive damage awards. It did cover settlements, but the potential for punitive damage awards increased the costs of settlement and threatened to exhaust the remaining insurance coverage while many claims remained unpaid.

On October 22, 1984, just a few days after the Friedberg cases were transferred to Richmond, Robins filed a motion asking Judge Merhige to certify these cases as a nationwide mandatory class action on the issue of punitive damages. Under Robins's proposal, a woman claiming injury from the Dalkon Shield could assert her claim for compensatory damages where and when she chose, but no punitive damage claim could be considered other than in a single class action trial before Judge Merhige. That trial would decide whether there should be any further award of punitive damages and, if so, the total amount. If an award of punitive damages were made, it would be distributed by some formula to all women who asserted Dalkon Shield injury claims.

There is a predisposition against any kind of class action in personal injury cases because of the crucial differences among the cases relating to causation, injury, and damages. Mandatory class actions—in which class members are not permitted to "opt out" and litigate individually—are particularly disfavored in recognition of an individual's right in a matter as important as a personal injury case to choose one's own lawyer and control one's own litigation.[60] There is, however, a provision in the Federal Rules of Civil Procedure that permits a mandatory class in any case in which the prosecution of individual actions would "impair" the interests of other persons.[61] This rule applies "when claims are made by numerous persons against a fund insufficient to satisfy all claims," a so-called limited fund.[62] In that situation, if the claims were adjudicated and paid individually, the interests of those whose claims were reached last would be "impaired" because there would be no money left with which to pay them; a class action permits an equitable allocation of the fund among all those entitled to share in it. Robins relied on the limited fund theory in support of its request for a mandatory class action on punitive damage claims. The company contended that separate litigation of punitive damage claims would "impair" the interests of women whose Dalkon Shield claims were not promptly resolved, because the company's resources would be exhausted before all injured women could be paid even compensatory damages.[63]

Robins's motion to certify a mandatory class for the determination of punitive damages met with the unanimous and vigorous opposition of attorneys representing Dalkon Shield victims across the United States. They saw the motion for exactly what is was—an effort to lower the value of their clients' claims. Whatever truth there was in the suggestion that Robins would eventually run out of money to pay Dalkon Shield claims unless punitive damage awards were limited, the victims' attorneys did not believe this would happen soon enough to affect cases that had already been filed. A ten-member steering committee of plaintiffs' attorneys was formed to oppose the motion. Joseph Friedberg was a member of the committee. Robert Manchester, of Burlington, Vermont, a veteran of the Dalkon Shield battles, was designated as lead counsel.

In 1981 Robins had filed a motion seeking a punitive damages class action on a limited fund theory in a Dalkon Shield case pending before J. Spencer Williams, a federal judge in San Francisco. In the earlier case, Judge Williams had granted Robins's request, but his ruling was overturned by the United States court of appeals.[64] The appellate court based its decision partly on the unwillingness of any plaintiff's lawyer to represent a class and partly on Robins's failure to prove the premise of its request—that, if it were required to pay separate punitive damages judgments as they occurred, its assets would be exhausted before other Dalkon Shield victims could be afforded any remedy.

The legal doctrine of "collateral estoppel" generally prevents a party from reasserting an issue it raised and lost in previous litigation. Judge Merhige was sympathetic to Robins's efforts to limit its punitive damage liability, but he recognized that he would first have to decide whether the company's motion must be denied simply because the issue had been decided in California. In December 1984 the judge asked for briefs and argument on that question.

In the meantime, Robins opened a second front in its effort to consolidate Dalkon Shield nationwide cases before Judge Merhige. In January 1985 Robins filed a motion before the Judicial Panel on Multidistrict Litigation asking that all of the some two thousand Dalkon Shield cases pending in federal courts be transferred to Richmond. (The remainder were pending in state courts and therefore were outside the jurisdiction of the multidistrict panel.) Robins claimed that additional pretrial proceedings were warranted because of the renewed discovery efforts generated by the litigation in Minnesota.

The general rule is that cases are transferred by the multidistrict panel only for consolidated pretrial proceedings, and when pretrial proceedings are concluded the cases are sent back where they came from for trial.[65] But if a case could have been properly filed in the court to which it was transferred, then that court had the authority to keep the case for trial and final decision.[66] Any case against Robins could have been filed in Richmond, and Robins argued that Judge Merhige's authority to keep and dispose of all the cases in one place was a reason to send them to his court. Although Joseph Friedberg had joined the opposition to Robins's class action motion, he had filed a separate motion for a consolidated trial of the punitive damage claims in the cases pending in Richmond, in the event the class action motion was denied. Merhige had granted this request without opposition from Robins, and, in the event of a transfer from the multidistrict panel, Robins expected Merhige to encompass this larger group of cases in such a consolidated proceeding. Indeed, considering Merhige's open-door policy, it seems unlikely that counsel for Robins would have asked the multidistrict panel to transfer two thousand cases to Merhige's court without the judge's knowledge and consent.

There was, however, a major obstacle to Robins's plan to send all federal Dalkon Shield cases to Richmond. The multidistrict proceeding before Judge Theis in Kansas had recently been reopened by Bradley Post and Robert Manchester to seek the production of documents, such as the "secret studies," whose existence had been revealed in the proceedings in Minnesota. If the multidistrict panel were to transfer additional Dalkon Shield cases for consolidated treatment, its procedures dictated adding them to the existing consolidated proceeding before Judge Theis, not creating a second multidistrict proceeding before another judge.

In an attempt to remove this obstacle, in January 1985, just a few days before it filed its motion to transfer with the multidistrict panel, Robins filed a motion in Kansas seeking the disqualification of Judge Theis. After that, Robins argued to the multidistrict panel that additional cases should not be sent to Judge Theis because a motion for his disqualification was pending. The ground for disqualification was that six months earlier Judge Theis had given support to Judge Lord in the judicial misconduct proceeding that Robins had initiated. One of Robins's complaints against Judge Lord was that he had accused the company of evasion in responding to orders for the production of information. Judge Theis filed an affidavit, based on his nine years of experience with Robins, in which he agreed with that assessment.

Robins's elaborate effort to vest Judge Merhige with control of the Dalkon Shield litigation collapsed in the spring of 1985. First, on March 15, Robins's motion to disqualify Judge Theis was denied by the United States court of appeals in Wichita, Kansas.[67]

Then, on May 2, 1985, a jury in Kansas awarded Loretta Tetuan, a childless woman who underwent a hysterectomy at the age of twenty-eight as a result of her use of the Dalkon Shield, $1.5 million in compensatory damages and $7.5 million in punitive damages. Mrs. Tetuan was represented by Bradley Post. The spectacular result in the *Tetuan* case received nationwide attention. A few weeks later, at the Robins shareholders meeting, Claiborne Robins, Jr., reported "a sharp upsurge in the number of new claims related to the Dalkon Shield."

On May 28, 1985, the multidistrict panel denied the company's request to transfer Dalkon Shield cases to Richmond. The panel ruled that there was no need for further consolidated pretrial proceedings.

The next day, May 29, 1985, Judge Theis, in the multidistrict proceeding, ruled that plaintiffs had produced substantial evidence that Robins and its attorneys were guilty of a crime or a fraud in connection with the defense of Dalkon Shield litigation.[68] Normally, communications between an attorney and his client are protected from disclosure by the attorney-client privilege. But when a court finds substantial evidence that the attorney participated with the client in the commission of a crime or a fraud, the privilege is lost. Judge Theis's ruling obviated Robins's objection to the production of sensitive documents from the files of its attorneys, including the still undisclosed "secret studies." Judge Theis appointed two special masters, including one who had originally been appointed by Judge Lord in Minnesota, to supervise the review of the files at McGuire, Woods & Battle.

The final and most devastating blow to Robins came on June 15, 1985, at the argument before Judge Merhige on its motion for a punitive damages class action. Although he did not then issue a formal decision, in his remarks from the bench Judge Merhige made clear that he had concluded that Robins's current motion was the same as the motion it had filed in California and the doctrine of collateral estoppel required him to deny it.

For Robins, only a flicker remained of its hope of consolidating Dalkon Shield litigation before Judge Merhige. Despite his conclusion about collateral estoppel, Merhige had made clear that he believed that a class action was a good way to handle the Dalkon Shield litigation and that he would like to allow it. Robins's attorneys suspected that if Joseph Friedberg, an attorney representing plaintiffs, moved for a class action, Merhige would find that the motion was sufficiently different from Robins's motion in California to allow him to grant it.

Robins's attorneys had found it easier to deal with Friedberg than with most of the plaintiffs' attorneys. Friedberg is an affable fellow, prepared to enjoy life's pleasures. He collects art, has interests in racehorses, and likes to socialize over a few drinks. Irreverent in his attitude toward law, he is not given to drawing moral lines between his efforts and those of his adversaries. Counsel for Robins had been able to reach agreement with Friedberg concerning the transfers to Richmond. They had also agreed on an informal mechanism, administered by the dean of a nearby law school, for the settlement of compensatory damage claims in the transferred cases, and through this procedure Robins and Friedberg had been able to settle many cases at levels the company thought reasonable. Friedberg's motion for a consolidated trial of punitive damages claims in his own cases, to which Robins had agreed, indicated that he did not share the deep-seated abhorrence of most of the plaintiffs' lawyers toward consolidated procedures for the resolution of multiple claims.

On June 24, 1985, Robins's general counsel William Forrest and Alexander Slaughter of McGuire, Woods & Battle invited Friedberg and Murray Janus out to dinner. Forrest attempted to persuade Friedberg to join in Robins's class action motion. According to Friedberg:

I unequivocally refused and set forth a series of reasons for such decision. Whereupon Mr. Forrest requested me to take the evening to reconsider and communicate with him a final answer the next day. On the 25th of June at 1:00 in the afternoon, I met with Mr. Forrest for five minutes during a recess in the settlement process at the Federal Courthouse in Richmond, Virginia and reiterated my refusal to join with Robins' motion.[69]

Disappointed with Friedberg's response, Robins applied some pressure. An hour or two after Friedberg had spoken with Forrest, another Robins attorney told Friedberg that the company would be unable to continue the process of settling his cases "because of a severe crisis in the company's cash flow."[70] A cutoff of settlements would stop the flow of fees and force Friedberg to try each of his cases separately, which would be burdensome, particularly with the plaintiffs and their witnesses in faraway places.

It is possible that Friedberg also received a nudge from Judge Merhige. At the end of this same day, Friedberg was alone in the jury room at the courthouse packing up his papers when Judge Merhige came in and struck up a conversation. According to later accounts by both men, Friedberg mentioned that he was having dinner that evening with Murray Janus at a restaurant near Merhige's home. Merhige invited Friedberg to drive home with him and to arrange for Janus to meet him there.

Friedberg was delighted to do this. He drove home with the judge, and the two men had a drink when they got there. They spent over an hour alone together before Janus arrived. According to a sworn statement filed by Robert Manchester, Friedberg told Manchester on June 27, 1985, just two days later, that while he was at the judge's home Merhige had said that if Friedberg filed a class action motion it would be granted.[71] Both Merhige and Friedberg adamantly denied that there had been any discussion of the Dalkon Shield litigation while they were together on the evening of June 25.[72] What is undisputed is that, by the morning after his visit to Merhige's home, Friedberg had changed his mind about a class action motion and had begun preparing the necessary papers.[73] If a successful class action were maintained in a matter as large as the Dalkon Shield litigation, the attorneys for the plaintiffs could expect to be awarded millions of dollars in fees by the trial judge.

On July 18, 1985, Merhige, Friedberg, Manchester, and Alexander Slaughter met in the judge's chambers to discuss further proceedings in the Dalkon Shield cases. Merhige revealed that he had taken the unusual step of organizing a meeting of federal and state judges who were handling Dalkon Shield cases. The purpose of the meeting, scheduled to take place on August 6 in Wichita, Kansas, was to "discuss some kind of procedure that will take care of these cases so that the last lady doesn't lose out."

Merhige emphasized, however, that he did not want to hold this meeting if Robins was about to enter bankruptcy.

Now I want to talk about one other thing because it concerns me very much. And that is, what is Robins going to do? Now, I keep hearing a poor-mouth situation, "things are tight, things are tight" . . . I don't want to get a bunch of judges together to be talking about other ways of disposing of this thing and then come back and find that Robins has filed a petition for Chapter 11. I want them to be perfectly frank and open with me. If that is going to happen, I want to know it so I don't waste a bunch of judges' time.

Slaughter responded that "we will confirm one way or the other before the meeting."

At least by the time of this conference, Merhige knew of Friedberg's plan to file a class action motion. Before Friedberg had said anything, Merhige volunteered his "initial view . . . that it can work; it can work as a class action." The judge explained what he had in mind:

I think my own idea of the mechanics of the thing is . . . you guys admit that your Dalkon Shield was not what it was supposed to be, and I hope I can talk the plaintiffs in exchange for that into forgetting the punitive damages. And let's see if we can't come to a number to take care of everybody.

Later in the conference, Friedberg confirmed his intention to file a class action motion shortly after Merhige formally denied Robins's class action motion. For his part, Manchester made clear that the group of plaintiffs' lawyers for whom he spoke would oppose a class action, which he described as a "coercive practice."

Four days later, on July 22, 1985, Judge Merhige released his formal decision denying Robins's class action motion on grounds of collateral estoppel.[74] In his opinion, however, the judge expressed his enthusiasm for an omnibus resolution of all Dalkon Shield claims. He exhorted counsel

to devise, within the framework of the law, a procedure which will fairly and expeditiously conclude this massive litigation. The Court stands ready to assist, within its appropriate role, to the end that all litigants receive the benefits of a system of justice which is capable of meeting any challenge. It can, must and will be accomplished.[75]

News of Judge Merhige's decision rejecting the basic element of Robins's plan to stave off financial collapse coincided with the release of the company's financial report for the second quarter of 1985. In April 1985 Robins had announced that it had recorded on its books for 1984 a $615 million charge to cover its estimated Dalkon Shield liability, exclusive of punitive damages. The charge created a large net loss for 1984 and a deficit in stockholders' equity (the company's liabilities exceeded the book value of the company's assets), and caused Robins, for the first time, to suspend the payment of dividends to its shareholders. The report for the second quarter of 1985 revealed that Robins's uninsured Dalkon Shield expenses for the quarter were $39 million, $15 million more than the portion of the reserve allocated to those three months. This necessitated an additional $15 million charge against income and created serious doubts about the adequacy of the reserve. And for reasons unrelated to the Dalkon Shield, the company's operating profits for the quarter were down sharply compared to the second quarter of 1984.[76] The combination was too much for the financial community. Between Wednesday, July 24, and Friday, July 26, on heavy volume, the price of a share of A. H. Robins stock on the New York Stock Exchange dropped almost 50 percent. On July 25, G. E. R. Stiles, the company's senior vice-president for finance, was quoted in the *Wall Street Journal* as saying that reorganization in bankruptcy was one of Robins's "dwindling options."[77]

In the meantime, Judge Merhige had arranged with counsel for Robins to meet privately with Claiborne Robins, Jr., to discuss the company's intentions with respect to bankruptcy before he went to Kansas to meet with other judges. Merhige later explained that he did this because he was dissatisfied with the response to his inquiry that he had received through counsel. Merhige and Friedberg both say that Merhige mentioned the planned meeting to Friedberg privately and that Friedberg had no objection. Robert Manchester was not told that the meeting would occur. To avoid publicity, it was agreed that Mr. Robins would come to Judge Merhige's home.

E. Claiborne Robins, Sr., and Judge Merhige are neighbors in the West End section of Richmond. Although only Claiborne, Jr., was expected, when Judge Merhige responded to the knock on his door at the appointed hour, 5:00 p.m., on August 1, Claiborne, Jr., was standing at the door and Claiborne, Sr., was sitting in a car in the driveway. "I hope you don't mind, I brought a friend," said the younger Robins. Merhige did not mind and invited both men in.[78]

According to Judge Merhige, the Robinses told him that Chapter 11 reorganization was a last resort that the company hoped to avoid. Claiborne, Jr., added, "Judge, you understand we don't know what the situation might be three weeks from now or a month from now."[79] This was apparently enough to satisfy Merhige's concerns, and he proceeded with his plans to meet with other judges.

The following day, August 2, 1985, Friedberg filed a motion for a mandatory class action covering all claims in the Dalkon Shield litigation, compensatory damages as well as punitive damages. As such, Friedberg's motion was better suited than Robins's motion had been to solving the company's problem; Friedberg's motion would foreclose all independent Dalkon Shield litigation. Like Robins, Friedberg relied on a "limited fund" theory for class certification.[80] The goal was to recover a fixed amount that would be allocated among all women injured by the Dalkon Shield.

Thirteen state and federal judges, from among the hundreds then handling Dalkon Shield cases, attended the meeting Judge Merhige had arranged in Wichita on August 6, 1985. Merhige reported that Claiborne Robins, Sr., had told him that the company hoped to avoid bankruptcy, if possible. He distributed copies of Friedberg's class action motion and stated that "the first step of the decision-making process in reference to a national class deals with Robins' financial capabilities."[81] Merhige vowed that he would resolve this issue, which would require determination of both the net worth of the company and the total value of all filed and unfiled Dalkon Shield claims, within sixty days. He said that he intended to stay all other activities in his Dalkon Shield cases in the meantime, and at least implied that he thought it would be a good idea if the other judges did the same.[82]

Merhige then raised the possibility of the transfer of cases to Richmond. According to an order issued a few days later by Judge Walter Skinner, a federal district judge in Massachusetts who participated in the meeting, "Judge Merhige has suggested that it would be useful for him to have as many as possible of the pending Dalkon Shield cases transferred to his district, not only for the purpose of assessing the motion for a class action, but also for facilitating a settlement across the board in the event the motion fails."[83]

On August 7, 1985, back in Richmond Judge Merhige scheduled a conference on the Friedberg motion for August 9. At that conference, Robins supported Friedberg's request for a class action. Merhige reiterated that he would first determine, within sixty days, whether there was a limited fund, because if "Robins can respond to the demands that have been made throughout the country, then I don't think your motion for a class action is going to fly." Merhige also expressed doubts that "there is such a thing as punitive damages available for any case from this point on."

Merhige, Friedberg, and William Cogar, of the Richmond law firm of Mays & Valentine representing Robins, then chatted amiably about the standards that would apply to an examination of Robins's financial situation. The logic of the "limited fund" concept would suggest that the relevant inquiry is whether the amount of the personal injury claims exceeds the amount of the company's net worth apart from those claims. Cogar's comments at the August 9 conference made clear that this is not what Robins had in mind. He suggested that a determination of the available fund be based on the company's cash flow, not "what the company would bring on the market block." The hope, which was carried into the bankruptcy proceeding, was that Robins's liability would be fixed in an amount it could afford without altering the equity interests in the corporation.

Robert Manchester interrupted this discussion to oppose both Friedberg's motion and the procedure Merhige proposed to address it. Manchester described a July 30, 1985, meeting in Chicago of one hundred attorneys representing some four thousand women claiming injury from the Dalkon Shield. He reported that this group was unanimously opposed to a class action. Manchester went on: "We view these lawyers as renegade plaintiffs . . . to be the wrong plaintiffs' attorneys in the case . . . to have chosen a low improper road out of this litigation, not seeking to try cases, but rather to surrender, coming to Virginia to surrender."

Manchester told Merhige that a sixty-day schedule to litigate the complex issues of Robins's worth and of the total value of the Dalkon Shield claims was not acceptable to him and his colleagues. Several cases in which they were involved were set for trial during this period, and the judges in those cases were not delaying those trials on account of Merhige's activities. Manchester asked Merhige to consider first the various legal objections to the proposed mandatory class action, which, if valid, would avoid an extensive factual inquiry. Merhige rejected this plea. "Regrettably, your committee doesn't run this court," he said.

In the days that followed, Robins decided that, despite Judge Merhige's cooperation, time had run out—the company could not wait for a decision on Friedberg's class action motion. The strength and breadth of the opposition expressed by Manchester, and confirmed by letters from plaintiffs' lawyers received daily by the court, made it clear that the creation of a class action would involve a long, hard fight, during which there would be no respite from other litigation. In the preceding months Robins and Aetna had disposed of Dalkon Shield cases at the rate of eight per day, but new cases were being filed at twice that rate; by mid-August 1985 six thousand claims were pending.[84] Three hundred separate Dalkon Shield cases, all claiming punitive damages, were set for trial in the fall of 1985 in courts all over the United States. Robins concluded that it could not properly defend all these cases in so short a time and that it could not accept the risk of a large number of huge punitive damage awards. In addition, the special masters appointed by Judge Theis were physically in the offices of McGuire, Woods & Battle, and documents whose production had long been resisted by Robins at great cost were about to be turned over to plaintiffs' attorneys.

On the afternoon of August 21, 1985, the A. H. Robins Company, Incorporated, filed its petition for reorganization in the United States Bankruptcy Court in Richmond. The filing automatically stopped all proceedings against Robins; all trial dates were canceled, and the inspection and production of documents in Richmond were suspended. In a statement, Claiborne Robins, Jr., explained that the company had filed the petition "because it became evident at a hearing in federal court earlier this month that the necessary cooperation of a majority of plaintiffs' counsel would not be forthcoming." He added that the filing was necessary "to protect the company's economic vitality against those who would destroy it for the benefit of a few."[85]

The day of the bankruptcy filing, Joseph Friedberg was in Richmond intending to propose to Robins a dollar amount at which his proposed class action could be quickly settled so that Merhige could be asked to approve a fait accompli without undertaking a complex inquiry into the limited fund question. After Robins filed its petition, Friedberg told a reporter that he took "no pride in being right," but that he was critical of the plaintiffs' bar for their "lack of foresight and inability to see what is clear to everyone with more than 100 IQ—that Robins indeed has limited ability to pay claims in the normal course of business."[86]

Before the bankruptcy filing, Judge Merhige had scheduled another conference on the Friedberg motion for August 22. At the appointed hour, Judge Merhige convened court to announce that all proceedings on the class action motion were stayed because of the bankruptcy filing. Merhige volunteered that

[h]ad it taken, [the class action] would have been a great thing. But be that as it may, it was fairly obvious it was going to be time consuming when I started get-

ting letters in opposition . . . and I suspect that may have influenced to some extent the actions taken yesterday. Actually, which actions, not knowing more about it than I do, I think were perfectly appropriate. I just don't see how anything else could have been done. I think it is going to turn out to be a service to everybody.

There followed an extraordinary colloquy in which Douglas Bragg of Denver, Colorado, one of the most prominent and successful attorneys representing women injured by the Dalkon Shield, questioned Merhige about his conduct. First, Bragg asked Merhige about reports that he had requested the judges in Wichita to transfer their Dalkon Shield cases to him:

MERHIGE: You have been misinformed. I don't know where you get that information. I was asked specifically by Judge Brown if I had any objection if he transferred them and did I think they could be transferred. I told him I thought they could and I had no objection . . . I have enough work without going out soliciting cases . . . I am a judge, not a huckster. I don't advertise for business . . .

BRAGG: We understand that you said [at the judges' meeting] that it was your belief based on a conversation you had with E. C. Robins Sr., which conversation we understand was ex parte, not in the presence of any lawyers, that the Robins company did not want to file a Chapter 11 proceeding, but that you had concluded based on the conversation with Mr. Robins that there was a limited fund available to pay Dalkon Shield claimants. And we are interested in knowing whether you said that, and if the reports we have back are correct or not.

MERHIGE: Well, I frankly don't think it is any of your business. It had to do with the three hundred cases that were pending in my court. I will tell you, though, just as a matter of being overly generous to a visitor, yes, I did. I did not contemplate a meeting with Mr. Robins, Sr., that was just by accident, I suspect . . . It was true that Mr. Robins attended, and his view was that Chapter 11 was a last resort. Consideration had been given to it, but they hoped to avoid it, that he felt confident with time all of these matters could be disposed of. And that is what I reported to the judges . . .

BRAGG: We understand that Mr. Robins, Sr. is a neighbor of yours, and probably a social friend.

MERHIGE: Well, I wouldn't say social any more than anybody I know. And that, too, is none of your business. But he is a neighbor and a fine man as far as I know.[87]

On this acrimonious note, the Dalkon Shield bankruptcy began.

3 The Law

The United States Constitution grants Congress the power "to establish uniform laws on the subject of bankruptcies," and federal bankruptcy laws have existed from the earliest days of the Republic. The central purpose of bankruptcy law is to provide a procedure that will assure that the creditors as a group recover as much of what is owed them as possible when a debtor is unable to pay its bills as they become due.

In a traditional bankruptcy, known as a "liquidation," a trustee takes possession of the debtor's assets (the "estate") and sells them in a manner designed to obtain the best possible price.[1] The proceeds are then distributed to the creditors according to an established distributional hierarchy.

In general, the distributional hierarchy set forth in Chapter 7 of the Bankruptcy Code, which governs liquidation bankruptcies, is as follows: first, secured claims (such as a loan secured by a mortgage on real estate); second, priority claims as defined by the Bankruptcy Code (these include the costs of the bankruptcy proceeding and certain categories of claims, such as some claims for wages, to which Congress has decided to accord preferred treatment); third, unsecured claims that were filed on time; fourth, unsecured claims that were filed late; fifth, claims for fines or penalties, including claims for punitive damages; and, finally, interest on all claims from the date the bankruptcy began until payment. In the unusual case in which there is money left over after the debt has been paid in full, the remainder is paid to the debtor or, in the case of a liquidating corporation, to its shareholders.[2]

The way the system works, claims at one level of the hierarchy are paid in full before any amounts are paid at the next lower level. At the level at which the available funds run out, each creditor is paid the proportion of its claim equal to the remaining available cash divided by the total amount of the claims at that level. For example, if there are $100,000 worth of timely-filed, unsecured claims and $50,000 is left after higher-level claims have been paid, each of the creditors in this group would be paid 50 percent of the amount it is owed. Creditors with claims at lower levels would receive nothing.

49

This collective procedure is considered more advantageous to the creditors as a group than the alternative of allowing the individual creditors who move most quickly to recover in full while others recover little or nothing. Not only is each creditor in the same class paid the same proportion of its entitlement, but the proceeds of the estate, and consequently the proportion of the debt paid, are likely to be higher if the assets are liquidated in a coordinated manner rather than grabbed piecemeal by individual creditors and sold at distress prices.

In the case of an individual debtor, the portion of the debt that cannot be paid from available assets is "discharged"; the individual is accorded a "fresh start," unburdened by past debt. (The fresh start policy is not applicable to a liquidating corporate debtor because the corporation will be dissolved after completion of the bankruptcy proceeding.)[3]

To enable bankruptcy procedures to work properly, they are mandatory; no creditor is permitted to pursue individual remedies. The filing of any bankruptcy petition automatically operates as an injunction prohibiting any person from initiating or continuing any litigation or procedure to collect on an obligation of the debtor. This is known as the "automatic stay."[4] Each creditor is notified of the bankruptcy and is bound to file a claim with the bankruptcy court and to look solely to the bankruptcy proceeding for payment.[5] Conversely, and equally important, the debtor in bankruptcy is prohibited from making payments to any of its creditors. All the debtor's assets and liabilities come under the supervision of the bankruptcy court, and payments can be made only with the court's approval.[6]

To avoid favored treatment of particular creditors, bankruptcy law sometimes overrides nonbankruptcy law in the process of marshaling the assets of the estate. An example of this is the rule relating to so-called preferential transfers. The trustee may recover payments to creditors that were made by an insolvent debtor, other than in the ordinary course of business, in the ninety days before the bankruptcy filing or, in the case of payments made to persons defined as "insiders," in the year before the bankruptcy filing.[7] The debts for which these payments were made, if valid, are then included among the unpaid claims against the estate.

While bankruptcy rules sometime override nonbankruptcy rules in the course of collecting the assets of the estate, a salient principle—and one crucial to an assessment of the Robins bankruptcy—is that bankruptcy law is not intended to override or modify nonbankruptcy law in assessing the value of a creditor's claim. It may not be possible to pay the claim in full, but its value—for the purpose of totaling the value of all claims in the particular level of the distributional hierarchy and computing the percentage at which each claim in that level can be paid from the available funds—should be unchanged by the bankruptcy proceeding.[8]

There are two reasons behind this principle. One is that the purpose of bankruptcy law—to maximize the debtor's estate and to distribute it in accordance with established priorities—does not include reevaluating the claims of the creditors according to a different set of legal principles. In the words of the Supreme Court: "[T]here is no reason why [property] interests should be analyzed differently simply because an interested party is involved in a bankruptcy proceeding."[9] If Congress or the federal courts decide to alter an existing rule defining obligations—as, for example, those seeking constitutional or statutory limits on the award of punitive damages have urged[10]—there would be no reason to limit the change to the obligations of debtors in bankruptcy. A particular defendant's inability to pay its debts, as they are defined outside of bankruptcy, is already taken into account by the distributional rules of the bankruptcy system.

The other reason to adhere to nonbankruptcy claim values is that otherwise incentives would be created for the debtor or a creditor to precipitate unnecessary bankruptcies to attain the change in value. Because, as we will see, bankruptcy cases are very expensive, as well as disruptive, and consume resources of the debtor that would otherwise be available to pay debts, unnecessary bankruptcies can harm the interests of creditors as a group—the exact opposite of the purpose of bankruptcy.

The A. H. Robins Company did not petition for liquidation under Chapter 7 of the Bankruptcy Code, but for reorganization under Chapter 11. The reorganization provisions of federal bankruptcy law, first adopted by Congress in the 1930s, were designed to increase the payback to the creditors in business bankruptcies by increasing the value of the estate.[11] Sometimes this is their effect, but directors and managers do not petition for reorganization for the satisfaction of paying a higher proportion of the corporate debt before they sail off into oblivion. They do so in an effort to keep their jobs, to retain control of the business, and to salvage some value for the existing shareholders. In reorganizations involving large publicly held corporations, these objectives, particularly that of preserving value for the shareholders that they would not recover in a liquidation, are frequently realized.[12]

The premise of reorganization in bankruptcy is that the liquidation of a financially distressed business by a trustee, even a liquidation that takes the form of a sale of the entire business, may fail to realize its full value. It is possible that a sale at a better price may be arranged in a reorganization proceeding, where existing management continues to operate the business as a "debtor in possession" and where the time frame in which a sale must be arranged is less hurried.[13] The more usual course is a restructuring of the ownership interests in the debtor corporation on the assumption that the business is worth more in the hands of the existing creditors and shareholders than the amount for which it could be sold to a third party.[14]

Restructuring can take the form of a transfer of part or all of the corporate ownership to the creditors, in exchange for the extinguishment of the debt. The transferred stock is distributed among the creditors in proportion to the value of their claims. In effect, part or all of the corporation is sold to the creditors. Alternatively, restructuring can take the form of the infusion of new capital sufficient to pay the debts from a third party in exchange for an equity participation, or through the merger of the debtor corporation with another corporation that is in a position to supply the needed cash. In some circumstances, with the breathing space offered by the automatic stay, a Chapter 11 proceeding may even enable the existing owners to obtain new financing that will permit payment of debt without any change in ownership.

Chapter 11 procedures encourage the parties with an interest in the ongoing corporation—management, creditors (functioning through one or more creditors' committees appointed by the court), and shareholders (usually also functioning through a court-appointed committee)—together perhaps with potential outside investors, to negotiate some arrangement (a "plan of reorganization") that will allocate the corporation's resources. But while negotiation on the terms of a plan of reorganization is emphasized, agreement is not necessary so long as certain statutory requirements are met. The most basic of these—the "absolute priority rule"—prevents any distribution to the shareholders unless the plan of reorganization provides for the full payment of all of the corporation's debts.[15] This is what happens automatically as a result of the distribution rules followed in a liquidation case under Chapter 7.

Frequently, however, the creditors do consent to the retention of substantial value by the equity interests even though the debts will not be paid in full. The creditors do this to avoid delay; they choose to get paid what they can in the near term rather than allow the matter to drag on for months or years. When the managers of the debtor are also substantial shareholders, as is usually the case in small reorganization cases and as was the case in the Robins bankruptcy, another reason for the creditors to waive the absolute priority rule is to secure management's cooperation, or to avoid its obstruction, in the sale or restructuring of the company. The ability to delay, together with existing management's control of the business during the reorganization proceeding, is the shareholders' source of strength in the complicated negotiations that typify large-scale Chapter 11 proceedings. In theory, as "debtor in possession," management stands in the shoes of a trustee as a fiduciary for the creditors, but in practice, management's loyalty is to the shareholders and to itself.

Several attributes of Chapter 11 practice enable management to delay the case if an agreement with the creditors is not reached. For 120 days, the debtor has the exclusive right to propose a plan of reorganization. If it does so, no other plan can be proposed during an additional 60-day period while the debtor seeks acceptance of its plan from the classes of creditors whose rights are impaired under it. Under the terms of the Bankruptcy Code, if a plan of reorganization is not filed by the debtor and accepted within this "exclusivity period" and if the court does not extend the time limits for "cause," a plan of reorganization can be proposed by any creditor or other party in interest.[16] It was Congress's intention in adopting these provisions in 1978 to abolish the practice under the prior law permitting only the debtor to propose a plan of reorganization. Congress found that a permanent exclusive right to file a plan afforded the debtor "undue bargaining leverage, because by delay it can force a settlement out of otherwise unwilling creditors."[17] Nonetheless, there is a widespread disposition among bankruptcy judges to consider first a plan of reorganization proposed by the debtor, and, particularly in large Chapter 11 cases, it is common for bankruptcy courts to extend the period during which management has the exclusive right to file a plan.

The close relationship between the exclusivity period and the length of the reorganization process was dramatically illustrated in the *Texaco Inc.* Chapter 11 case, which was filed in response to a $10 billion judgment imposed against Texaco and in favor of the Pennzoil Company by courts in Texas. After one 120-day extension of the exclusivity period that did not lead to an agreed plan of reorganization, the bankruptcy judge announced that he would allow a plan to be filed by the other major parties without the participation of management. Eleven days later, Texaco management and Pennzoil filed a joint plan of reorganization that was quickly confirmed.[18] In the Robins bankruptcy, as we will see, Judge Merhige extended the company's exclusivity period throughout the proceeding, until a plan of reorganization was confirmed after three years.

Another basis for delay, and one that depends less directly on the cooperation of the court, is litigation within the bankruptcy proceeding. A plan of reorganization to which the creditors have not consented can be imposed through a procedure known as a "cramdown" if the court finds that the plan will pay the creditors in full, in compliance with the absolute priority rule.[19] If the plan proposes to transfer to the creditors a portion of the stock in the corporation, the court must determine the total value of the business to enable it to decide whether the portion offered to the creditors constitutes full payment. The debtor will present expert opinions and other evidence supporting a high valuation of the corporation to justify the retention of a portion of the equity for its shareholders; the creditors will present evidence supporting a lower valuation that would require more or all of the equity to be transferred to them. The issue is complicated, requiring a forecast of future earnings and the conversion of that forecast into a computation of present value. There is no exact answer. When the matter is disputed, its resolution can take a long time. There may also be room for extensive litigation over the validity or the amount of the outstanding debt, as there certainly is in bankruptcies arising out of massive unresolved personal injury claims.

In the meanwhile, time is very much on the shareholders' side. Management is usually able to obtain any new credit necessary to continue normal operations—even though it may have been unable to obtain credit before the bankruptcy—because the Bankruptcy Code grants debt incurred during the case a priority over prepetition debt.[20] (It does this on the theory that the reorganization is for the benefit of the prepetition creditors and that postpetition borrowing is a means to that end.) The debtor in possession is not permitted to pay either its prepetition debts or to issue dividends to its shareholders. As a result, if the company is earning money from operations, its cash position continually improves as the bankruptcy goes on. The A. H. Robins Company, for example, had $26 million in cash and cash equivalents the day it entered bankruptcy.[21] Three years later, still in bankruptcy, the figure exceeded $425 million.[22] The accumulation of cash increases the net worth of the company and strengthens the shareholders' claim to retain value. And unless the right of the creditors to receive interest on their claims for the duration of the bankruptcy is preserved—and often it is not because the creditors ultimately accept a plan that does not provide for the payment of interest—the effective cost of the claims is gradually reduced.

Accordingly, if the creditors insist on their right to payment in full and if this would leave nothing for the shareholders, the shareholders have everything to gain and nothing to lose by delay. The shareholders do not even have to bear their expenses in creating the delay, because these are paid from the assets of the estate, which, by hypothesis, belongs to the creditors. The situation thus creates a powerful incentive for the creditors to reach an agreement with management and the shareholders that compromises the absolute priority rule.[23]

A plan of reorganization that does not comply with the absolute priority rule must be submitted to the creditors for a vote. A "disclosure statement," approved by the court as containing adequate information to permit an informed decision, is sent to each such creditor, with a copy of the proposed plan and a ballot. The plan is considered "accepted" by a class of creditors only if the holders of one-half the number of claims and of two-thirds the value of the claims vote in the affirmative.[24]

Although a class of creditors is permitted to vote to accept a plan of reorganization that reserves value to the equity interests without paying all the debts in full, the Bankruptcy Code provides protection for any dissenting creditor. In expression of the principle that reorganizations are designed primarily to enhance value for creditors, the code provides that no plan of reorganization can be confirmed over the objection of even a single creditor unless the court finds that the dissenter will be paid as much as he would have been paid in a liquidation under Chapter 7.[25] This is known as the "best interests" test. Theoretically, unless the creditors unanimously accept a plan of reorganization, only the extra value of the business (if any) that is realized by use of reorganization rather than liquidation is subject to disposition other than in strict accordance with the absolute priority rule.

In practice, this protection frequently proves specious. To meet the best interests test, the debtor submits a "liquidation analysis" that purports to compare the amount the dissenting creditors would receive under the proposed plan with the amount they would receive in liquidation. The problem is that the crucial numbers relative to liquidation— most significantly, the price the company or its assets would bring in a sale that is not going to take place—are matters of speculation and are subject to manipulation. Management, the proponent of the plan, has available to it expert bankruptcy counsel and investment advisers from Wall Street who are adept at putting together numbers that indicate that the creditors will do better under the reorganization than they would in liquidation. The dissenting creditor, particularly a dissenting creditor who is an individual, does not generally have these resources available. He may not even understand what a liquidation analysis is, much less be able to effectively challenge it. Unless the court is very demanding in its examination of the liquidation analysis—and the court itself may not have the knowledge or skill to do this, even if it has the desire—the best interests test can prove as illusory as the benefits to the creditors of reorganization.

If a plan of reorganization providing for the continued existence of the corporation is confirmed, the corporation's debts in excess of the amounts paid under the plan, including its obligations to any creditor who failed to file a claim in the bankruptcy proceeding, are discharged.[26] The reorganized corporation is said to be afforded a "fresh start," but the function of the fresh start is different than it is in liquidations involving individuals. In the latter case, the discharge expresses the social policy of allowing the individual who has undergone bankruptcy to restart economically with a clean slate. In corporate reorganizations, there are no humanitarian considerations. Discharge of the debt makes it possible to realize the value of the estate by allowing the corporation to be marketed unburdened by its debts or by allowing the stock of a debt-free corporation to be distributed to the creditors in satisfaction of their claims.

If a plan of reorganization cannot be confirmed, the case will be converted to a liquidation under Chapter 7.[27]

The provisions of the Bankruptcy Code were developed to deal with the usual situation in which the creditors are identifiable persons who dealt commercially with the debtor and the debtor's obligation to each is clearly ascertainable. The creditors chose to extend credit to the debtor in the normal course of business, and they assumed, presumably at a tolerable level, the risk of the debtor's insolvency. Bankruptcies triggered by mass liability for personal injuries are different in fundamental respects. The personal injury victims did not choose to extend credit to the debtor or to assume economic risks. If their injuries are substantial, the importance to these claimants of securing compensation is far greater than it is to commercial creditors. The debtor's bankruptcy, with the attendant delay in obtaining compensation and the risk of nonpayment or partial payment, is a burden additional to their physical injuries that may cause real hardship. For the most part, the amounts due to personal injury claimants are not fixed but are in dispute. The debtor may deny any responsibility for particular injuries. Some injured persons have not yet filed a claim and are unknown to the debtor. There are likely to be other persons not yet injured, or not yet aware of their injuries, but who will be in the future. Not only are these "future claimants" unknown to the debtor, they are unknown to themselves.

For all these reasons, the attempt to use bankruptcy reorganization procedures to deal with mass product liability has raised many novel and complex questions. Are persons who have not yet manifested injuries creditors? How can creditors unknown to the debtor or not yet aware of their injuries be notified? Will the rights of unknown personal injury victims who do not file claims with the bankruptcy court be discharged or otherwise affected? How will the debtor's total liability for injuries suffered by identifiable and by unidentifiable tort victims be quantified? How will the debtor's liability for punitive damages be measured? How will the entitlement of each individual claimant be determined for purposes of weighting the votes on a plan of reorganization and for purposes of paying the claims? Can payments be made for urgent medical expenses of the injured persons before the entire matter is resolved? What will be the effect of a reorganization on the tort claimants' rights against persons other than the debtor who may be responsible for their injuries?[28]

In recent years several companies that manufactured asbestos and faced mounting liability for personal injuries resulting from asbestos exposure have filed for reorganization under Chapter 11, most notably the Johns-Manville Corporation.[29] In the Johns-Manville bankruptcy, several of the complex issues arising in mass tort bankruptcies were skirted by a settlement between the principal parties in interest that did not set any near-term deadline for the assertion of personal injury claims, and that did not attempt to determine the value of the personal injury claims or to place a precise limit on Manville's liability.

Specifically, a trust was established that assumed Manville's liability to asbestos victims and undertook to pay their claims for compensatory damages. Claims against the trust could be filed for twenty-seven years. (Asbesteosis, a crippling lung disease, is frequently not manifested for more than twenty years after exposure to asbestos.) When the plan of reorganization was implemented, the trust was funded with $815 million from available insurance and from funds of the corporation. In addition, the trust was granted 50 percent of the stock of the reorganized company and the right to increase its interest to 80 percent of the stock, if necessary, to pay asbestos injury claims in full (although no stock could be sold by the trust for three years). Beginning three years after the implementation of the plan, the company would be obligated to pay to the trust $75 million a year for twenty-four years. In addition, beginning four years after implementation and continuing as long as necessary, the trust could call on 20 percent of the reorganized corporation's profits. Beyond these obligations, Manville was discharged from liability to asbestos victims. Claims for punitive damages were disallowed.

When this plan of reorganization was confirmed, it was hailed by the bankruptcy judge as providing an "evergreen" source of funding that guaranteed full payment of all present and future asbestos claims.[30] By the summer of 1990, however, less than two years after the trust began functioning, the trust was nearly out of cash and no additional funds were due for over a year. More than 150,000 filed claims were unpaid, and it appeared some of these would not be paid for twenty years, which was likely to be after the victims had died from asbestos-related disease.[31] In July 1990, citing a "judicial emergency," Jack B. Weinstein, a United States district judge in Brooklyn, enjoined the trust from paying any additional claims until the trust was refinanced.[32] Judge Weinstein secured the cooperation of the reorganized Manville Corporation in that endeavor by threatening to revise the company's obligations under the confirmed plan of reorganization. In November 1990, Manville and attorneys representing personal injury claimants agreed on a restructuring proposal that provides for the conversion of the trust's stock ownership in the corporation to 80 percent of the common stock, as contemplated by the plan, and for the distribution of special dividends to shareholders over the next seven years that would increase the cash flow to the trust by over $500 million.[33]

The A. H. Robins Company—meaning the Robins family—had very different ideas in mind for its Chapter 11 case. Robins hoped to limit and discharge its liability to women injured by the Dalkon Shield without altering the company's equity structure and without allowing a claimants' trust to call on profits or equity in the future. Robins planned to ask the court to set an early deadline for filing Dalkon Shield injury claims and to establish a limit on its total liability for compensatory damages to those who met the deadline. Robins would be discharged from liability in exchange for a commitment to provide funds to a claimants' trust up to the established limit. Confirmation would be based either on the acceptance of the plan by the Dalkon Shield claimants or on a finding by the court that the plan would allow full payment of Dalkon Shield claims (even though no punitive damages would be paid). Assuming that the court would set the maximum amount of the company's liability at a manageable level, Robins expected to borrow the necessary funds and to repay the loan out of earnings in future years.

Robins's goals were at odds with the right of an injured woman to claim damages at a reasonable time after knowledge of her injuries, to have the value of her claim, including punitive damages, individually determined in accordance with applicable nonbankruptcy law, and to be paid that amount in full, or, at least, in the proportion permitted by the total value of the company. This conflict pervaded the bankruptcy proceeding.

4   Merhige Takes Control

Judge Merhige's efforts to assume control of the Dalkon Shield litigation, begun in the weeks before Robins's bankruptcy filing, accelerated when the Chapter 11 proceeding was commenced. In rapid succession Merhige canceled the normal assignment of the case to a bankruptcy judge and assigned the matter to himself, he enjoined litigation against persons other than Robins alleged to have responsibility for injuries related to the Dalkon Shield, and he ordered the transfer to his court of all Dalkon Shield–related litigation.

Bankruptcy jurisdiction is lodged by statute in the United States district courts.[1] The district courts are authorized—"expected" more accurately reflects the intention of Congress—to refer bankruptcy cases to the bankruptcy courts established within each judicial district.[2] Virtually all the United States district courts, including the district court in Richmond, have entered blanket orders automatically referring all bankruptcy cases to the bankruptcy courts.

On the afternoon of August 21, 1985, when William Cogar, of Mays & Valentine in Richmond, and Penn Butler, Robins's newly retained bankruptcy counsel from the firm of Murphy, Weir & Butler in San Francisco, went to the bankruptcy court on Main Street in Richmond to file Robins's petition for reorganization, they brought with them for Judge Merhige's signature a nine-page document entitled "Administrative Order No. 1." The crucial provision of this order canceled the normal reference of the case to the bankruptcy court and assigned the case to Merhige.

Cogar asked to see Judge Merhige. The clerk of the bankruptcy court, Michael Sheppard, consulted the local bankruptcy judge, Blackwell N. Shelley, and together Sheppard and Shelley walked over the little enclosed bridge that connects the third floor of the bankruptcy court building with the third floor of the United States Courthouse next door, where Merhige's chambers are located, and asked Merhige what to do. (Cogar had already called Merhige's office and ascertained that the judge would be available for a conference.) Merhige said to send the lawyers over. He then met with Cogar and Butler and in the course of the meeting agreed to Robins's request that he preside over the bank-

60

ruptcy. After minor language changes were made, Merhige signed Administrative Order No. 1. In an unusual arrangement, Judge Shelley agreed to sit next to Merhige on the bench throughout the proceeding and to advise him about bankruptcy law.

Later, Judge Merhige attempted to explain his assignment of the Robins bankruptcy to himself on the ground that the law required that the matter be handled by a United States district judge. Merhige said:

My knowledge of the bankruptcy came when the best bankruptcy judge in the country who sits to my left appeared in my office with the best bankruptcy clerk in the country and said, can we see you? There are lawyers over in the bankruptcy court filing a Chapter 11 for Robins and they have an order of retention that they want to bring over . . .

I said [to Judge Shelley], well, is it proper? He said, yes, because this looks like it is primarily a tort case, a case where a [district] judge is going to be required in the majority of it. I have since inquired of him how much of this is [required to be before a district judge]? I think his last estimate was 90 percent and then he changed his mind and said, no, just about all of it.[3]

Judge Merhige was referring to special provisions of federal law that require a decision by a district judge rather than a bankruptcy judge of certain issues relating to the resolution of personal injury claims against a debtor in bankruptcy. The statute provides that a district judge must decide "the liquidation or estimation of . . . personal injury tort or wrongful death claims against the estate for purposes of distribution."[4] ("Liquidation" in this context means fixing an exact value.)

In fact, there were no decisions in the Robins bankruptcy that could not have been made by a bankruptcy judge. The personal injury claims were not liquidated until after the Chapter 11 case was concluded. There was an estimation of Robins's total Dalkon Shield liability but not "for purposes of distribution." An estimation was conducted for purposes of evaluating and confirming a plan of reorganization, an activity within the competence of the bankruptcy judge.[5] And all the hundreds of other issues that arose in the Robins bankruptcy were within the competence of the bankruptcy judge.[6] The Chapter 11 cases relating to asbestos liability, including the mammoth Johns-Manville bankruptcy in New York, were handled, except for appeals, entirely by bankruptcy judges in bankruptcy courts.

Judge Merhige assigned the Robins bankruptcy to himself not because there was any legal imperative for him to do so but because he had the power to and he wanted to. Indeed, as previously noted, several years later Merhige told the *New York Times* that the complexity and challenge of the Robins bankruptcy induced him to remain on the bench.[7]

The morning after the bankruptcy was filed, Merhige defiantly told lawyers who had opposed consolidation of Dalkon Shield claims in Richmond, "You are going to find that 99% of what you all might have any interest in will be in this court." And at the first hearing in the bankruptcy, on September 21, 1985, Merhige said:

There are women who have been injured—they haven't received anything in ten years. Doesn't do people much good to be compensated if you are too old to enjoy it. I am going to put a stop to it. It has been my goal since the case came here. It was my goal when I asked the judges . . . to meet and see if we could come up with something.

For its part, Robins wanted Judge Merhige to have the case because it expected to benefit from the judge's well-known loyalty to the Richmond community and his demonstrated readiness to break new ground to achieve a desired result. Although Merhige had not granted Robins the class action it sought, his eagerness to resolve the problem, together with his usual emphasis on compromise, led Robins's attorneys to believe that he would be supportive of a limitation on the company's Dalkon Shield liability at a level that would permit Robins to survive under existing ownership.

Indeed, despite the judge's denial, there are strong reasons to believe that Merhige had been consulted in advance and had agreed to assert jurisdiction over Robins's Chapter 11 case. Just three weeks earlier, at a private meeting at his home, Merhige had been told by both Claiborne Robinses that they hoped and expected to avoid bankruptcy. Merhige relied on that information in convening a meeting of judges of other courts and urging them to delay any action in Dalkon Shield cases until he had had time to act on Friedberg's class action motion. A month earlier Merhige had requested to be informed of the company's intentions with respect to Chapter 11 and had warned that "I would be very unhappy. I would feel like it was a double bank to wake up one morning and find a petition on my desk."[8] Given these circumstances, together with Merhige's ready availability to counsel and the near absolute control over its future that Robins was about to place in his hands, the inference is compelling that some company representative paid the judge what would be viewed locally as the courtesy of letting him know what was coming.

This supposition is bolstered by the provisions of Administrative Order No. 1. Most of the nine-page order prescribes internal court procedures that would govern the case, things such as the proper heading for pleadings and the room in the courthouse in which documents should be filed. These are matters about which Robins was unlikely to make, or the court to take, suggestions. The inclusion of these provisions in Robins's proposed order indicates that it was prepared in consultation with someone at the court before the case was filed.

Judge Merhige quickly moved to stop all litigation relating to the Dalkon Shield. Under the doctrine of "joint and several liability," two or more persons can have liability for the same injury if the wrongful conduct of each contributed to the injury. The injured person can proceed against all of those responsible for the full amount of her damages until she is paid once in full.

A number of persons and corporations may have been liable, jointly with A. H. Robins, for injuries caused by the Dalkon Shield. These included both E. Claiborne Robinses and other officers and directors responsible for the company's misconduct, the law firm of McGuire, Woods & Battle, which was alleged to have conspired with Robins to destroy or withhold evidence relating to the Dalkon Shield, and, most important in terms of available resources, the Aetna Casualty and Surety Company, Robins's product liability insurer.

Co-defendants were named in approximately half the Dalkon Shield injury suits pending against Robins when it went into bankruptcy. In response to the automatic stay of proceedings against Robins resulting from the bankruptcy filing, several plaintiffs' attorneys took steps to separate the claims against Robins from the claims against other defendants and to proceed with the latter.

On September 25, 1985, Robins asked Judge Merhige to issue an injunction preventing these suits from going forward during the reorganization. The primary reason put forward for this request was that the claims against third parties were actually claims against Robins's assets, either because the judgments would be satisfied through unused product liability insurance (Robins's officers and directors were insured persons under the company's agreement with Aetna) or because Robins's was contractually obligated to indemnify (reimburse) its officers and directors for any liability imposed against them. Robins's unused product liability insurance was an asset of the estate, and if Dalkon Shield claimants could be paid out of insurance proceeds during the bankruptcy, there would be unequal treatment of similarly situated creditors in violation of one of the basic precepts of bankruptcy law. And even apart from the insurance, judgments against Robins's officers and directors that resulted in claims for indemnity against the company provided a mechanism for the liquidation of some Dalkon Shield injury claims but not others outside the bankruptcy process.

The other reason cited by Robins in support of the requested injunction was that ongoing litigation against third parties would divert the attention of key Robins personnel from the reorganization, both in responding to demands for the production of witnesses and documents and, because of the company's obligation to indemnify the defendants for any liability, in the defense of the cases. Robins may also have been interested in assuring that the production of documents from its attorneys' files under Judge Theis's discovery order, which had been shut off by the bankruptcy filing, not be reopened. If Dalkon Shield litigation against co-defendants went forward during the reorganization, there would be pressure for the production of these documents, with possible new damaging disclosures. If it did not, the production of these documents might be avoided altogether by limiting the defendants, the issues, or the scope of discovery in postbankruptcy litigation. At least, production would be postponed until after Robins's obligation for Dalkon Shield injuries had been fixed.

Section 105 of the Bankruptcy Code provides broadly that the "[c]ourt may issue any order . . . that is necessary or appropriate to carry out the provisions of this title." On October 9, 1985, relying on this provision, Judge Merhige granted Robins the injunction it requested. He explained:

> If relief were not granted here, we would have a rush to judgment; we would have 5,000 lawsuits filed throughout the country against anybody counsel thought they had a reasonable chance of obtaining a judgment against. No, these suits are enjoined. As far as I am concerned the law of this case is that all such suits will be enjoined.[9]

Attorneys for women seeking to proceed against co-defendants appealed the injunction, but in April 1986 it was upheld by the court of appeals.[10] Both the reasons for the injunction and its language applied only during the pendency of the Chapter 11 case, but later, in one of the most controversial decisions in the Robins bankruptcy, Judge Merhige entered another injunction that permanently prohibited the assertion of Dalkon Shield injury claims against Robins's co-defendants.[11]

The automatic stay and the injunction issued by Judge Merhige had the effect of stopping all Dalkon Shield–related litigation, but they did not address the question of where these cases would be tried, if at all, after the stay and the injunction were lifted. In 1984, in response to the bankruptcies in the asbestos industry, Congress had enacted a statute providing that bankruptcy proceedings "do not affect any right to trial by jury that an individual has under applicable non-bankruptcy law with regard to a personal injury or wrongful death tort claim."[12]

This statute guarantees a person with a personal injury claim the right to reject any settlement offered under a plan of reorganization and to insist that her claim be resolved in a traditional jury trial. It is possible that the personal injury claimant will not be paid the full amount of the jury verdict, depending on whether the funds in the estate permit the full payment or only the pro rata payment of unsecured claims, but the claimant is entitled to have the *value* of her claim determined by a jury. The statute also provides that, when a jury trial is demanded, the district court in which the bankruptcy is filed shall decide whether the trial will take place in that court or in the federal court in the district "in which the claim arose."[13] The latter is usually the place of the plaintiff's residence and the place where the suit would ordinarily be filed.

Three weeks after Judge Merhige issued the injunction against codefendant litigation, Robins asked Merhige to rule that the eventual trial of Dalkon Shield injury cases could take place only in Merhige's court. Claiming that the centralization of all Dalkon Shield litigation would facilitate the reorganization, Robins also asked Merhige to order the immediate transfer to his court of all of the six thousand pending cases.[14]

Robins intended to propose in the Chapter 11 case that a maximum, but not a minimum, be fixed on its liability to women injured by the Dalkon Shield. If that could be accomplished, the company would have a direct interest in the liquidation of claims at the lowest possible level. Moreover, there was no precedent for the establishment of a maximum on a debtor's liability for a class of personal injury claims before the claims were individually liquidated. If Robins was unable to achieve this, then the amount at which individual claims were liquidated would be of vital concern; liquidations at high levels could consume the entire value of the company.

The highest liquidation values could be expected in jury trials near the homes of the injured women. The transfers requested by Robins would reduce the number of demands for jury trial and would assure that any jury trials that did occur would take place in Richmond. To invoke her right to trial by jury, an out-of-state woman would have to employ a Virginia lawyer and transport herself and all her witnesses to

Richmond. She would lose the advantage of a local jury and would face enormous delays resulting from the necessity to try all the jury cases in one court.

Robins did not notify the plaintiffs in the pending cases of its motion to transfer. At a hearing on Robins's motion on November 9, 1985, representatives of Dalkon Shield claimants argued that each plaintiff was entitled to be notified and given a right to be heard before her case could be transferred. They also argued that Robins's motion should not be granted because (1) the transfer of pending cases was unnecessary for purposes of developing a plan of reorganization, as all the cases were automatically stayed and each plaintiff was required to file a claim in the bankruptcy case, which would be governed by the plan of reorganization; (2) a local jury trial, rather than one in Richmond, was a more accurate reflection of the congressional intent in preserving the right to trial by jury; and (3) the transfer of more than six thousand cases to Richmond—most of which would ultimately be settled without a jury trial—would involve the unnecessary expenditure of more than $1.5 million in attorney fees, copying costs, and court fees.

At the conclusion of the hearing, Judge Merhige granted Robins's request to transfer all pending cases to Richmond. Although the jury trial statute explicitly allows for local trials, Merhige said that "under the whole theory of bankruptcy all of the cases ought to be at the same place. . .under the auspices of the bankruptcy court." He did not mention the issue of notice or of expense. (Throughout the case, the judge would emphasize or ignore the factor of expense depending on whether saving money supported or contradicted his intended course of action.)[15] The judge did add that his predisposition was not to allow any individual jury trials in any event but to conduct a single class action trial. "I think we'll get the cases settled but I am also thinking in fairness if it ever gets tried here it will probably be tried as a class action. I mean, honestly, that is it. That is in the back of my mind, I haven't ruled on it." Whether a class action trial would be consistent with the jury trial statute was never tested. On appeal, the court of appeals ruled that, although Judge Merhige had the right to transfer the cases to his court for trial, each individual was entitled to be notified and to be heard in opposition before her case was transferred.[16] Robins never undertook to give individual notice of its transfer motion, and the transfers never occurred.

Judge Merhige was more assiduous about notice when two motions to dismiss the bankruptcy proceeding were filed in early 1986. Then, he imposed prohibitive notice requirements that prevented these motions from being considered.

One of the motions to dismiss, filed by Douglas Bragg's partner John Baker and others, argued that the bankruptcy petition had not been filed in good faith, but in culmination of Robins's longstanding efforts to force all Dalkon Shield cases into a consolidated proceeding before Judge Merhige in Richmond and to avoid disclosure of documents that could lead to criminal prosecution of Robins officials.[17] The other motion to dismiss, filed by Washington, D.C., attorney Michael Goldberg on behalf of five women he represented in suits filed before the bankruptcy, argued that Robins was not in financial distress and therefore not entitled to the protections provided by the Bankruptcy Code. The Bankruptcy Code does not set forth a requirement of insolvency or any other financial prerequisite for a Chapter 11 filing. The disadvantages of bankruptcy, in terms of cost, adverse publicity, financial disclosure, and court supervision, are thought sufficient to discourage unwarranted petitions under Chapter 11. The courts have, however, dismissed Chapter 11 petitions when they have concluded that the filing was not in good faith. Goldberg argued that a company entering Chapter 11 must be in real need of financial reorganization and not simply invoking bankruptcy procedures as a tactic in civil litigation.

In support of his motion, Goldberg cited Robins's financial statements, which showed that the company's assets far exceeded its liabilities (apart from the Dalkon Shield reserve) and that the company's profits from operations had been substantially in excess of its costs for resolving Dalkon Shield claims in every quarter, even those in which Dalkon Shield costs were at their highest. An affidavit filed with the Robins petition showed that the company had realized net earnings of $35.3 million in the first six months of 1985, after taxes and after all Dalkon Shield expenses, compared to $20.0 million for the comparable period in the prior year.[18] The financial information relied on by Goldberg did not, however, take account of Robins's ability to meet the judgments and settlement that it reasonably anticipated would be imposed in the future. This would be a key ingredient in a determination of the need for reorganization. In denying a similar motion to dismiss the Johns-Manville Chapter 11 case, the court had relied largely on evidence indicating that Manville would be unable to meet its projected liability to asbestos victims.[19]

Judge Merhige did not undertake to determine whether Robins was a proper candidate for reorganization. Instead, he said that he would not consider the motions to dismiss unless their proponents gave notice to each of the almost two hundred thousand women who by then, in response to notices published by Robins, had indicated an intention to make a claim for Dalkon Shield injuries.[20] Bankruptcy Rule 2002 provides that "the clerk, or some other person as the court may direct, shall give . . . all creditors . . . not less than twenty days notice of a hearing on a motion to dismiss." Merhige ruled that each woman who had responded to the advertising was a creditor who must receive notice, and he reassigned the burden of giving that notice from the clerk of court, who was able to do it, to the women seeking dismissal of the bankruptcy, whom he knew were not.

At a hearing in February 1986, Merhige told Goldberg:

I will give you exactly one week. If I don't hear from you in the affirmative that you are going to give notice and the manner in which you intend to do it, then I am going to deny your motion. I am not going to waste any time. You may have, and your clients may have resources, but if they have got $5 million [to pay for notice], they ought not be worrying about what they can get out of Dalkon Shield, they ought to retire.[21]

Rule 2002 equally requires giving notice to all creditors for a variety of other matters, including certain sales of property and applications for compensation in excess of $500. Judge Merhige had not required notice to every Dalkon Shield claimant in these other situations; notice to the official parties was deemed adequate. Goldberg and Baker came back and asked Judge Merhige to permit a more limited form of notice of their motions to dismiss. They offered to mail a notice to the six thousand Dalkon Shield claimants who had a court case pending against Robins when the bankruptcy was filed and to all attorneys for other claimants who had filed requests for notices with the bankruptcy court. They contended that this, together with notice to the official committees, would be adequate and would ensure that all points of view were presented and considered. Alternatively, they asked that the clerk of the court be required to give notice, as provided by the rule. "Requiring the claimants to serve all those registering an injury," the attorneys argued, "in effect prevents anyone from moving to dismiss the proceeding."[22]

Without further comment, Judge Merhige denied the motions to dismiss.

5   Representation of the Women

An important early battleground in the Robins bankruptcy was the selection of the official representative of women injured by the Dalkon Shield.

In Chapter 11 cases, creditors are represented by one or more official committees whose members are appointed by the United States trustee, an official designated by the attorney general in each of various regions of the country to perform administrative functions in bankruptcy cases. The official committees are given broad authority as principal participants in the case. They are entitled to investigate the conduct and the financial condition of the debtor, to raise and be heard on any issue, to participate in negotiations for the formulation of a plan of reorganization, and to communicate to their constituencies their evaluation of any proposed plan of reorganization. Moreover, the official committees are authorized to hire, with the approval of the court and at the expense of the debtor, lawyers, accountants, investment bankers, and other professionals to assist them in these activities. Without official status, and the attendant right to retain expert assistance at the debtor's expense, effective participation in the Robins bankruptcy would not be possible.

As soon as Robins entered bankruptcy, two groups set out to gain recognition as the representatives of women injured by the Dalkon Shield. One group included the traditional leadership of the plaintiffs' bar—Bradley Post, Douglas Bragg, Robert Manchester, and other lawyers associated with them in the prebankruptcy litigation against Robins. The other included Joseph Friedberg and the lawyers associated with him in his effort to maintain a class action against Robins.

After the angry confrontation with Judge Merhige on August 22, 1985, Post, Bragg, and Manchester decided to move quickly. They scheduled a meeting of plaintiffs' attorneys to take place a few days later in Chicago. There, an ad hoc committee of plaintiffs' lawyers was formed, and the names of its thirty-eight members were submitted to William C. White, the United States trustee for the Eastern District of Virginia, for appointment as members of an official committee representing Dalkon Shield claimants. Robert Manchester estimated that the thirty-eight lawyers represented over eight thousand women injured by

69

the Dalkon Shield, including a large majority of the women with suits on file.[1] In an effort to include the entire spectrum of attorneys representing plaintiffs in Dalkon Shield litigation, the ad hoc committee invited Joseph Friedberg, Murray Janus, and two other lawyers associated with them in the class action effort to serve on the committee. All four refused, not wanting to be a minority voice on a committee led by Post and Bragg. On August 28, White filed a motion asking Judge Merhige to authorize him to appoint the thirty-eight lawyers whose names had been submitted as the official committee representing Dalkon Shield claimants. This would be an unusually large committee; although the provision is not mandatory, the Bankruptcy Code refers to a creditors' committee in a Chapter 11 case composed of seven members.[2]

In the meantime, Friedberg tried a different tack. He and his colleagues were in Richmond on August 21, 1985, to meet with Robins's lawyers at Mays & Valentine about a possible settlement of their proposed class action. When they discovered that the Chapter 11 case had been filed, Friedberg's group, which included the author of the leading treatise on class actions, Herbert Newberg, huddled and decided to refile their class action within the bankruptcy proceeding. They did so at 10:16 a.m., on the morning of August 22. Class action proceedings in a Chapter 11 case are permitted by the Bankruptcy Rules but are generally confined to side issues; they have not been used to supplant an official committee in representing the most important class of creditors in the case. On a theoretical level, the concept of a class action in the bankruptcy to resolve Robins's Dalkon Shield liability made little sense. Because of the collective and compulsory nature of bankruptcy proceedings, a Chapter 11 case is in essence a mandatory class action, with the official committee as the representative of the class of creditors but without the necessity of satisfying an additional set of technical and difficult requirements from class action law. But Friedberg saw the class action as a mechanism by which to compete for the right to represent women injured by the Dalkon Shield.

The United States trustee's motion was heard by Judge Merhige on September 21, 1985. Robert Manchester appeared at the hearing as a representative of the ad hoc committee with the attorney chosen by the committee, Murray Drabkin of the well-known New York and Washington, D.C., law firm of Cadwalader, Wickersham & Taft. A native New Yorker and a 1953 graduate of the Harvard Law School, Drabkin had spent nine years working on bankruptcy legislation for the Judiciary Committee of the House of Representatives. For ten years preceding the enactment of the Bankruptcy Code of 1978 (the first major overhaul of federal bankruptcy law since 1938), Drabkin had represented the National Conference of Bankruptcy Judges in connection with the preparation of that legislation. Thereafter, Drabkin worked extensively in corporate reorganizations. A slender, courtly man, Drabkin is astute, knowledgeable, and hard-nosed in the practice of his specialty.

Merhige was enthusiastic about Drabkin's participation.

MERHIGE: I will be delighted to hear from Mr. Drabkin. Delighted to have him. I am very familiar with his reputation. It is no fun having a large case around here unless your firm is in it, Mr. Drabkin.

DRABKIN: Judge, we do our best.

MERHIGE: You do pretty good.

Nevertheless, Merhige expressed his reservations about the size of the committee White intended to appoint. In addition, Merhige was not happy with the prospect of a committee led by lawyers who had militantly resisted his prebankruptcy efforts to forge a consolidated resolution of Robins's Dalkon Shield liability, particularly as Friedberg, Janus, and their associates, who had supported these efforts, would not be members.

I have dealt with Mr. Janus and Mr. Friedberg and Mr. Meshbesher and Mr. Cochrane, because I have had 300 of these Dalkon cases . . . I have found them to be extremely cooperative. One hundred percent cooperative. And I will be disappointed—and I will be looking for their views, because I know they have worked hard to get rid of the cases that we have gotten rid of.

The members of the ad hoc committee did, however, represent the great majority of women making claims against Robins, and despite his misgivings Merhige approved their appointment as the official claimants' committee. The judge made clear, however, that he would accept this committee only so long as he was satisfied with its performance. In discussions with the judge, the leadership of the new claimants' committee had agreed to develop and propose within sixty days a mechanism for the liquidation of individual claims. On September 30, in remarks addressed to John Cochrane, one of Friedberg's co-counsel in seeking a class action, Merhige stated:

Mr. Cochrane, your group has not been forgotten. You were extremely cooperative . . . I want to give the committee a chance, let me put it that way, but we want your input. And I want you to understand that. But we will know in sixty days, as far as I am concerned, whether this claimants' committee is going to work or it isn't going to work . . .

I have not forgotten the class action aspect . . . I have gone along with the committee because it is the trustee's responsibility to appoint the claimants' committee and he has done so. I think he agrees with me . . . that the large number of members borders on the ridiculous . . . These are all lawyers. They will be lucky to elect a foreman . . . But it seems to me that fairness dictates that they be given the opportunity.

In a memorandum filed in early November 1985, Robins made clear that it preferred Friedberg as the representative of the Dalkon Shield claimants by endorsing his proposed class action. Robins said the class action would create a "unified framework for resolving Dalkon Shield claims."

The attorneys for the class action proponents have exhibited initiative, imagination and cooperation in their pre-petition and post-petition proposals to this Court. This approach contrasts markedly with pleas for a continuation of the "business as usual" practices that led to this crisis for the court and litigants alike.[3]

Also in early November 1985, the committee submitted a written proposal to the judge relative to the resolution of Dalkon Shield claims under a plan of reorganization. Merhige was apparently satisfied with this submission, at least temporarily, and he encouraged Robins and the committee to negotiate over its terms. After hearing arguments on Friedberg's class action motion on November 9, 1985, Merhige decided to allow the claimants' committee to continue and to keep Friedberg's proposal in reserve. He said that he would not rule on the motion for class certification until he had the opportunity to assess the progress of the negotiations.[4] Merhige emphasized, however, that "the first time I think negotiations are not moving anywhere, then I am going to do something about it, about putting somebody else in the picture to do it. We have got to have people that will come up with a plan."

Soon after its appointment, the claimants' committee had adopted bylaws, elected officers, and organized itself into an executive committee and several subject matter subcommittees. In December the negotiations subcommittee, together with Murray Drabkin, began meeting with a team of Robins lawyers.

But within the committee there were strong crosscurrents at work in opposition to the whole concept of the Robins Chapter 11 proceeding under Judge Merhige's control. There was substantial sentiment, particularly on the part of Bradley Post and Douglas Bragg, who initially served as chair and first vice-chair, to move to dismiss the bankruptcy and to move to disqualify Merhige. From their perspective of years of battling with A. H. Robins, they were certain that the bankruptcy filing was another in a long series of illegitimate maneuvers designed to frustrate the rights of their clients. And they were equally convinced that Merhige was determined to protect Robins to the detriment of the interests of women they represented.

Drabkin, whose natural habitat is a bankruptcy case and who was not hostile to Judge Merhige or resentful of Robins, counseled against attacks on the bankruptcy proceeding or the judge. He warned that these actions would not succeed and would only make Merhige more difficult to deal with. According to an affidavit filed by Bradley Post, Drabkin advised the claimants' committee at a meeting in Denver at the end of October 1985 that Merhige would be "vengeful" in response to a motion to disqualify and "would likely certify the Friedberg class action, dissolve the committee or take other steps which would be detrimental to the interests of Dalkon Shield victims."[5] The following month, the committee received a similar analysis from George Little, a Richmond lawyer acquainted with the judge who was retained by Drabkin as local counsel for the committee.

Post, Bragg, and others were unconvinced. They were unfamiliar with bankruptcy law, and they overestimated the strength of their objections to Robins's bankruptcy. They also believed that Merhige would not give the Dalkon Shield claimants a fair break, whether or not a motion to disqualify was filed.

Other members of the committee, however, had a different perspective. Post and Bragg are the leading examples of lawyers with a relatively small number of clients injured by the Dalkon Shield, with no reluctance to go to trial and with the determination to secure the best possible recovery in each case. Other lawyers—generally those who had advertised—had hundreds of clients with Dalkon Shield injury claims. They were in favor of an alternative dispute resolution mechanism adopted through a plan of reorganization that would provide a rapid and relatively expeditious means of disposing of cases, even if the dispositions were not at the highest possible value. These two schools of thought on the committee came to be known as the "retailers" and the "wholesalers," with the latter inclined to accept the bankruptcy, to work for its quick conclusion and for an early start on the informal resolution of individual cases.

When it came to a vote, the committee by a narrow margin accepted Drabkin's advice not to challenge the bankruptcy or the judge. It did agree, however, to allow members to raise these issues on behalf of their own clients, and Post and Bragg resigned their leadership positions on the committee to be free to do this.

Although Drabkin had prevailed on these points, the seeds of dissatisfaction with his representation—the feeling that he was unwilling to stand up to Robins or to Merhige—had been sown. The dissatisfaction was compounded by differences between Drabkin and many members of the committee over the manner in which Drabkin should function. The committee members believed that Drabkin should consult the committee and take instructions with respect to issues that arose. Drabkin, not impressed with this disparate band of personal injury lawyers, felt that he was the one with knowledge of bankruptcy law and procedure and that the committee should allow him some independence of action. These different points of view were never resolved. Drabkin engaged in discussions with Merhige, Robins, and others that the committee had not specifically authorized, and he did not keep the members of the committee informed to their satisfaction as to his activities and as to proceedings in the case. The situation degenerated to the point that, at a meeting of the claimants' committee in Florida in January 1986, a motion was made (but not passed) to prohibit Drabkin from engaging in any conversations with the judge, except in the presence of a court stenographer.

An example of the problem between Drabkin and the committee concerned the process of obtaining information from Robins. Members of the committee, on the basis of their experience in the prebankruptcy Dalkon Shield litigation, expected obstruction and evasion from Robins in responding to requests for information. The committee therefore urged Drabkin to initiate formal discovery proceedings to secure from Robins the financial information that would be necessary to develop or evaluate a plan of reorganization. Formal discovery requests establish a time frame in which responses or objections must be filed and provide a record of what has been asked in case a dispute requires resolution by the court. On the basis of his experience in reorganization cases, Drabkin believed that he could better secure the necessary information informally. By the middle of February 1986, no formal requests had been filed.

An unfortunate incident, closely related to a possible effort to disqualify Merhige, led to a final breakdown between the committee and Drabkin. On December 9, 1985, Merhige had written a letter to Richmond counsel for Robins and the official committees revealing certain business connections he had with lawyers involved or interested in the bankruptcy case, including a lawyer at McGuire, Woods & Battle who provided legal services to the judge in matters relating to his personal finances. In the minds of many plaintiffs' lawyers, McGuire, Woods & Battle was liable to women injured by the Dalkon Shield because of its alleged role in destroying documents and covering up information harmful to Robins's defense. Merhige said that he had written the letter "so that you can take such steps as you or [your clients] deem appropriate." The letter was sent to George Little, local counsel for the claimants' committee, but not to Drabkin. Neither Little nor Drabkin mentioned the letter to the committee.

Members of the committee heard reports from other sources about the Merhige letter and, at the meeting in Florida in January 1986, raised the matter with Drabkin. Drabkin said that he knew nothing about it. On February 4, 1986, Mary Beth Ramey, a lawyer from Indianapolis who had replaced Post as chair of the committee, wrote a testy letter to Drabkin stating that she had positive confirmation that the Merhige letter existed and asking that he check his files or obtain a copy from other counsel. In response, Drabkin reaffirmed that he had never seen such a letter but added: "George Little informs me that he believes that there was such a letter. George has undertaken to obtain a copy and mail it directly to each of the members of the executive committee."

On February 13, L. B. Cann III, a member of George Little's firm, sent a copy of Merhige's letter to the officers of the claimants' committee, with a covering letter stating, in part, "In all candor, George did not notice that neither Murray Drabkin nor Mark Ellenberg [a partner of Drabkin's active in the case] were addressees of the letter, and George only discussed the letter with them verbally and did not send them a copy." The Cann letter convinced Post and Ramey and perhaps others that Drabkin had known about the letter and that he and Little had concealed it so as not to fuel the sentiment for a disqualification motion.

In the meantime, on February 12, 1986, Ramey, together with second vice-chair Frederic Bremseth and finance committee chair James Szaller, went to New York City to discuss Drabkin's representation of the committee with the lawyer who represented the asbestos claimants in the Johns-Manville bankruptcy, Ronald Rosenberg of the firm Latham & Watkins. Rosenberg offered an opinion on various matters that was different than Drabkin's. For example, Rosenberg said that the claimants' committee might have been well advised, some months earlier, to oppose the creation of a deadline for the filing of personal injury claims, as the asbestos claimants' committee had done, successfully, in the Johns-Manville case. Rosenberg explained the relationship of a filing deadline to the establishment of a limited fund to compensate Dalkon Shield victims.[6]

According to Ramey, the consultation with Rosenberg, and consultations with other bankruptcy attorneys, confirmed the view that "a significant, serious problem existed in relationship to the committee's representation" and that "a change in counsel was mandated to protect the interests of the claimants."[7] Rosenberg agreed to represent the committee if Drabkin was discharged.

On February 18 and 19, 1986, just after the receipt of the Cann letter and a report from Ramey, Szaller, and Bremseth on their consultations in New York, the members of the claimants' committee were polled by telephone on the question of substituting Rosenberg for Drabkin. Later, some members of the committee criticized this process, contending that those known to oppose Drabkin had been called first and those called later had been told that the vote stood heavily against Drabkin, and that only lukewarm efforts had been made to reach those likely to support Drabkin. Be that as it may, thirty-two of the thirty-eight members were reached, and the vote was thirty in favor of the substitution, one opposed, and one abstention.

On the afternoon of Wednesday, February 19, 1986, Ramey and Bremseth called Drabkin to advise him of this decision. A motion had already been prepared to substitute Rosenberg for Drabkin as counsel, and they asked Drabkin to sign it that afternoon. Drabkin requested a day to reflect on the best way to handle the matter. Ramey and Bremseth, perhaps naively, agreed to do nothing until they called Drabkin back the next day.

Representation of the Dalkon Shield claimants' committee in the Robins bankruptcy was worth millions of dollars in fees to Drabkin's law firm.[8] Whether because of the money involved, the importance of the case, his belief that he could best represent Dalkon Shield victims in the bankruptcy, an unwillingness to be ousted, or some combination of these, Drabkin moved to protect his position. On February 19, 1986, shortly after he spoke with Ramey and Bremseth, Drabkin called Judge Merhige and the same afternoon a conference call was set up among Merhige, Drabkin, George Little, and the United States trustee William White. Drabkin reported that the committee had voted to discharge him. According to a later report from Little, Merhige was "furious" at this news.

Even before the call from Drabkin, Merhige had become increasingly unhappy with the claimants' committee as its members evidenced various forms of resistance to the bankruptcy proceeding. For example, at a hearing on February 14, members of the committee (acting individually) had argued for the dismissal of the bankruptcy case and had bitterly attacked A. H. Robins. They had categorized the bankruptcy as a fraud and accused high company officials of criminal conduct. Twice during the proceedings on February 14, Merhige had expressed his intention to certify Friedberg's class action if a speedy resolution to the Chapter 11 case was not forthcoming. He also mentioned, however, that he was "delighted that we have Mr. Drabkin."

Moreover, Merhige had by now concluded that he did not need the support of the members of the claimants' committee to secure the approval of a plan of reorganization by the Dalkon Shield claimants. By mid-February 1986 almost two hundred thousand Dalkon Shield claims had been filed—largely by women who had no attorney—and hundreds more were arriving every day. Merhige had reluctantly gone along with the appointment of the thirty-eight-lawyer committee largely because these lawyers represented the great majority of the plaintiffs in pending Dalkon Shield litigation. These women now constituted only a small fraction of the total number of Dalkon Shield claimants and would not control a vote on a proposed reorganization plan. Merhige decided that the time was right to get rid of the committee.

As a result of the February 19, 1986, conference call, White undertook to file a motion asking Merhige to dissolve the committee. Merhige told Drabkin that he could not withdraw unless a written motion to withdraw was filed and granted by the court. When Ramey and Bremseth called Drabkin the next day, Drabkin told them, to their surprise and chagrin, that he had already informed Judge Merhige of the committee's action. Drabkin also said that he would file a motion to withdraw in a day or two. Ramey and Bremseth had intended to advise Merhige of the committee's selection of Rosenberg, an experienced and qualified attorney, at the same time that he was informed of the decision to remove Drabkin.

On Monday, February 24, 1986, three motions were filed: White's motion to dissolve the claimants' committee, Drabkin's motion to withdraw, and Ronald Rosenberg's motion to be recognized as counsel to the committee. White's motion said that "the present committee is not a manageable representative in light of the circumstances of the case." Judge Merhige ordered all three motions set for hearing on March 4.

When the hearing began, Judge Merhige made clear that he had already decided to dissolve the committee.

I predicted from the very beginning that we were going to have trouble . . . I said 38, it is an impossible thing. But he [White] assured me it was going to work. And, well I will be quiet until I rule . . .

If you want a committee that won't work, you get more than five or six or seven, and that is what is going to happen . . . I am taking this case back, or taking it now. Period. Because I can see that we are not getting anywhere.

When called upon to support his motion, Mr. White offered only the following:

The record is replete with . . . pleadings with lawyers on the committee taking one position, the committee taking another position. There seemed to be several voices speaking for the claimants. It is my perception that the committee is not negotiating effectively with Robins . . . By my motion I simply seek permission to reform the committee to perhaps seven people, and to a more effective manageable representative group for the claimants.

In fact, there was not a single instance of a committee member filing pleadings in conflict with those of the committee. White did not explain what he meant by "not negotiating effectively" or from whom he had acquired that perception, but the phrase had the unfortunate connotation of "not reaching an agreement with Robins."

White had not anticipated that he would be asked to prove that there was a problem with the committee, and he became flustered when John Davids, a member of the claimants' committee from San Francisco appearing in opposition to the motion, insisted on some evidence:

WHITE: Your Honor, this is not taking the form that I had conceived of . . . I don't advocate a position that the court is not comfortable with . . . If [the court] feels it is fine at thirty eight, that is certainly fine with me.

MERHIGE: I can tell you now it is not fine at thirty eight.

WHITE: It is just things that I have heard and perceptions, most of which I can't present, that led me to bring this motion.

MERHIGE: . . . I have had the same perception, that things were not going as we had all hoped they would. I couldn't put my finger on anything, but I sometimes got the impression of a bunch of loose cannons floating around.

Merhige nevertheless encouraged White to present some evidence, and after a short recess, White called as witnesses two members of the committee who had not favored discharging Drabkin. Neither supported White's assertion that the size of the committee was a problem or that the committee was not negotiating effectively with Robins. The two described instead the disagreements on the committee relative to filing motions to dismiss the bankruptcy and to disqualify Merhige. One of these witnesses was Paul Rheingold, a New York lawyer who had resigned from the committee a few days earlier after he was challenged for violating the committee's policy forbidding its members to advertise for additional Dalkon Shield clients. Rheingold testified:

Your Honor, I feel the committee is unwieldy not largely because of its size, but because of the viewpoints. That there were two camps from the very beginning, indeed even before the bankruptcy, which has carried on to this very moment.

One group arising out of their hatred of A. H. Robins Company was committed in every way to fight . . . the bankruptcy . . . Another group, which has always turned out to be the minority, has as a goal the rapid winding up of the bankruptcy, screening of cases, insuring fair money to the women, but not attacking the bankruptcy.

Rheingold testified that the division he described did not interfere with the effectiveness of the efforts of the negotiating committee. "It was three people and the reports back to us were things were going well, and I don't feel that the division in the steering committee became a handicap in carrying on."

Four members of the claimants' committee testified in opposition to Mr. White's motion. One of these was Judy Rentschler, the chair of the subcommittee designated to negotiate with Robins. She described the process of negotiating with Robins and the decision-making process within the committee.

There have been five negotiating sessions . . . We met with Robins, talked with them, got their ideas, got issues on the table, would go back to the committee and formulate our views by democratic process of discussion and voting of how we would like to see a plan formulated. And then we would go back to the next session with Robins, and discuss those issues, and present our positions. And we would listen to Robins as to the way they viewed it.

I think we were making good progress. Robins has been, their attorneys have been difficult to deal with, at best . . . But overall, I think we were making good progress.

Addressing the question of alleged "disarray" on the claimants' committee, Rentschler testified:

There have been many viewpoints expressed on issues. But as a committee we have come together to reach decisions that I think are solid, sound decisions with the interests of the women at heart. We have a lot of different experiences but the bottom line so far we have put it together with agreement, with a decision, majority decision, with which we can live.

By agreement among the representatives of the committee, Drabkin, and Merhige, the committee did not explain the reasons for its decision to discharge Drabkin. Drabkin said he felt "constrained by the principle of client confidences from commenting." For the committee, Robert Manchester said, "[W]e have mutually agreed to a parting of the ways, we have found other counsel and I do not think it is appropriate to discuss it any further." Merhige concurred: "I am inclined to agree with you. As he so aptly put it, he is constrained. He can't say, and I don't think it is proper anyway."

It all seemed very correct. But a few moments later, in explaining his decision to dissolve the committee, Merhige said that Drabkin had "done his job completely" and emphasized the committee's decision to discharge him. "[The committee asking Drabkin] to resign indicates a lack of being able to work things out. You can't get along with your own lawyer, I don't know how you can get along with each other, to be perfectly frank with you." The only other reason offered by Judge Merhige for his decision concerned the disagreements within the committee. Merhige stated:

I think there is a large divergent view in the committee, which is not necessarily unhealthy, I must admit. But the nature of the differences are such to satisfy me that the committee is not well suited for the purpose for which it was formed. The committee stands dissolved as of this moment.

Merhige instructed United States trustee White to appoint a new committee with between three and seven members. In the meantime, Merhige appointed Drabkin as the "court's expert" representing the claimants until a new committee could be appointed. "Mr. Drabkin," the judge said, "you are still on the payroll."

Judge Merhige ordered the dissolution of the Dalkon Shield claimants' committee at 5:10 in the afternoon on March 4, 1986. Literally five minutes later, Douglas Bragg, Bradley Post, and eight other members of the dissolved committee filed a motion to disqualify the judge on grounds of bias or the appearance of impropriety.

The primary bases for the motion were Friedberg's visit to Merhige's home on June 25, 1985, at which, according to Robert Manchester's account of statements he said Friedberg made to him, Merhige told Friedberg he would grant a class action motion, and the visit of both Claiborne Robinses to Merhige's home on August 1, 1985, at which Robins's plans with respect to bankruptcy were discussed. The motion to disqualify also cited Merhige's statement on August 22, 1985, that Claiborne Robins, Sr., was "a fine man"; Merhige's various financial connections with lawyers involved in the Robins bankruptcy; Merhige's alleged prejudgment of issues in the case; and Merhige's reference to Douglas Bragg as a "wise-ass lawyer" and a "son of a bitch" during conferences in the bankruptcy case.[9] On March 14, in an emotional statement from the bench, Merhige denied the motion.

In response to the motion to disqualify, Friedberg had filed an affidavit denying that he and Merhige had discussed a class action or that he had told Manchester that they had. Merhige also denied the conversation.

If Robins was mentioned—I know it wasn't—the only thing I am not sure about, I am not sure that when we turned the corner I might not have said that is where Mr. Robins lives, I might have done that. Certainly there was no discussion. There might well have been, because I discuss, under the deal we had, I catch them anywhere to talk about settlement. Lawyers gave me the authority to do that. But we didn't even do that.

There was no question that there had been a "discussion" when the Robinses had visited the judge on August 1, 1985. Merhige relied on a technical justification for this meeting. The opponents of Robins's class action motion had been permitted to participate in Friedberg's cases in Richmond only for the purpose of opposing that motion. When the motion was formally denied on July 22, 1985, they were no longer participants in the Richmond cases. Merhige said:

Accordingly, since these interveners were no longer considered "parties" by the Court, I did not deem it appropriate, nor necessary, to get their consent before I met with Robins, Sr. (Consent to meet with Robins, Sr., was of course received from counsel for the class action plaintiffs [Friedberg] and counsel for Robins.)[10]

The Code of Judicial Conduct provides that a judge shall "neither initiate nor consider *ex parte* or other communications concerning a pending or impending proceeding."[11] Judge Merhige's discussion with Robins, Sr., and Robins, Jr., concerned a possible Chapter 11 proceeding and a possible national class action—both "impending" proceedings—and was plainly in violation of the code. Merhige had been ignoring this edict for years, but no one had made an issue of it. In fact, the code contains no exception to its prohibition against *ex parte* communications for those that are consented to, but even if such an exception can be inferred, consent to the discussion between Merhige and the Robinses would have had to come from the thousands of people who would be affected by the impending proceedings.

Merhige made short shrift of other grounds of the motion. Particularly, he dismissed the idea that his relationships with Richmond lawyers could affect his rulings in the case.

Nobody seems to say anything about it, but . . . every lawyer at this bar is a friend of mine . . . They don't expect any breaks around here. And if they did, they wouldn't be my friends. As simple as that . . . There is just not enough money or friendship in the world to make me do anything that I don't think I ought to do as a judge.

Merhige denounced the motion as "frivolous, unfounded and delaying" and added that he would "request that the Chief Judge of this District seek a disinterested judge to review the instant motion and determine whether sanctions should be imposed against movants." There is no indication that such a determination was ever made.[12]

Members of the Dalkon Shield claimants' committee were concerned from the outset about the constant reports of informal conferences or discussions between counsel and Judge Merhige of which no record was made. In many of these discussions, not even all the official parties in the case were represented. Particularly infuriating in this regard was Drabkin's telephone conversation with Merhige and United States trustee White that led to the dissolution of the committee. On March 13, 1986, Bradley Post and Douglas Bragg filed a motion asking that all proceedings in the case be transcribed by a court reporter. Merhige also denied this motion.

Bradley Post then asked the court of appeals to order Judge Merhige to transcribe all proceedings. Twenty-one months later, in December 1987, the appellate court announced that

the district judge has already acted with commendable promptness to allay any possible concern of a possible failure to keep all parties provided with appropriate records by securing a full-time court reporter to provide a full record . . . We commend this action [which] . . . should satisfy any reasonable concerns about the purpose and intent of the district judge to see that this case proceeds with proper regard for the rights of all parties, without any favors or partiality to any party, and accordingly warrants dismissal of the petition for mootness."[13]

Merhige had taken no discernible action with respect to transcription of conferences, and he did not interpret the statement of the court of appeals to prevent off-the-record discussions with less than all counsel, which were a constant throughout the proceeding.[14]

On March 4, 1986, Judge Merhige ordered William White, the United States trustee, to appoint a new claimants' committee. On March 5, Drabkin visited White in his office in Alexandria, Virginia.[15] On March 6, Drabkin and his co-counsel George Little conferred with White in Richmond concerning possible members of the new committee.[16] As it turned out, White appointed a five-member committee composed of two members of the dissolved committee who had not voted to dismiss Drabkin and three Dalkon Shield claimants, two of whom were recommended by Drabkin and Little. In later testimony, George Little explained White's attitude.

In all candor, Mr. White has the highest respect in the world for Mr. Drabkin . . . Mr. White felt that Mr. Drabkin had excellent knowledge of bankruptcy law, had worked with him extensively in the past through the years, and also knew that it would be a lot less costly to the estate if the same counsel were retained.[17]

The two members of the dissolved committee who were reappointed were Gorman King and Judy Rentschler. King, who practices in Fargo, North Dakota, has a master's degree in public health from Harvard University. He was out of the country when the vote to remove Drabkin was conducted, but when he returned on February 26, he wrote to White deploring the committee's action. Then, on March 5, King wrote to Drabkin volunteering to serve on the new committee and stating that he was "pleased that your Firm's excellent representation will continue in this important litigation." Drabkin and Little each recommended King for appointment.[18]

Judy Rentschler practiced law with a medium-sized firm in San Francisco, and she was experienced in the litigation of Dalkon Shield injury claims. Rentschler had distinguished herself on the first committee for her leadership on the subcommittee negotiating with Robins and for her ability not to get embroiled in the disputes among committee members. Rentschler was out of her office when she was called about discharging Drabkin, and, to her annoyance, before she returned the call two hours later, the matter had been decided. She had helped to defend the original committee against White's motion to dissolve, but she liked Drabkin and was not critical of his representation. George Little favored Rentschler's appointment to the new committee. Drabkin initially had doubts about whether she would vote to retain him, but Little persuaded Drabkin to join in recommending Rentschler's appointment.[19] The night before she was inducted as a member of the new committee,

Little invited Rentschler and Drabkin to dinner at his club and urged Rentschler to support Drabkin.[20]

The only other lawyer considered for appointment was Joseph Fried-berg, who was recommended by William Cogar of Mays & Valentine, counsel for Robins.[21] This time, with leadership of the old committee repudiated, Friedberg wanted the appointment, but in an interview, he told White that he would be opposed to retaining Drabkin as counsel and White decided not to appoint him.

The three Dalkon Shield claimants appointed to the committee were Ann Samani, an attorney who was employed as an estate administrator in the bankruptcy court in Lexington, Kentucky, Dr. Helen Clemo, a member of the faculty of the Medical College of Virginia in Richmond, and Nancy Worth Davis, a clinical instructor in bankruptcy law at the George Washington University Law School in Washington, D.C.

Drabkin was acquainted with Samani from before the Robins bank-ruptcy, and he knew that she had filed a Dalkon Shield claim. He called her in Kentucky and asked if she would serve on a reconstituted clai-mants' committee, and she agreed to do so. Drabkin recommended her to White. White then called and offered her the appointment. She was not interviewed.

George Little knew of Helen Clemo and called her to ask if she would serve. When she agreed, Little arranged for White to meet Clemo in Little's office in Richmond. Both Drabkin and Little attended this inter-view. White himself knew Nancy Worth Davis and asked her to serve on the committee. When she wanted to know more about it, he put her in touch with Murray Drabkin. Davis filed a Dalkon Shield claim after she was asked to serve on the committee.

On Saturday, March 22, 1986, the new committee members ap-peared before Judge Merhige to be introduced and to receive his instruc-tions. Merhige spoke of the committee's right to choose its own counsel. Then he called on Murray Drabkin to brief the new committee on the status of the case. After the meeting with the judge, the new committee members gathered with William White. White reiterated that the com-mittee had the right to select its own lawyer, but he recommended that serious consideration be given to employing Drabkin because of his fa-miliarity with the matter. Drabkin acted as counsel for the new commit-tee while it was deciding on permanent counsel.

Gorman King just wanted to hire Drabkin, but Rentschler insisted that others be considered. The committee solicited applications from other lawyers and interviewed three in addition to Drabkin. When the time came to make a selection, it was, in Dr. Clemo's words, "very clear to all of the committee to hire Mr. Drabkin."[22] On April 3, the new committee voted to retain Drabkin and Little.[23]

With this decision, the issue of who would represent Dalkon Shield claimants in the Robins bankruptcy was finally settled. It would be neither the Post-Bragg-Manchester group nor the Friedberg group; it would be Murray Drabkin. The members of the new committee had no desire to control Drabkin's activities and were content to be consulted when he thought it appropriate. With Post, Bragg, Manchester, and their allies safely out of the way and Merhige "delighted" with Drabkin, the judge lost interest in Friedberg's odd proposal to maintain a class action against Robins within the Chapter 11 case.

It was, of course, galling to the leadership of the first claimants' committee that Drabkin should speak for the Dalkon Shield victims when it was their decision to discharge Drabkin that had led to the dissolution of their committee. On May 22, 1986, James Szaller, Bradley Post, and Mary Beth Ramey, for a group of their clients, filed a proceeding seeking to dissolve the new committee on the ground that its members had been selected to assure Drabkin's retention. Szaller, who took responsibility for presenting the motion, specializes in Dalkon Shield litigation as a member of a small firm in Cleveland.[24] He was the chairperson of the finance subcommittee of the first claimants' committee, and he had worked hard to make the committee an effective representative of women injured by the Dalkon Shield.

The legal basis of the motion was a statement in a House committee report on the legislation that was to become the Bankruptcy Code of 1978. The report expressed the intention of eliminating the practice of allowing attorneys who were seeking employment as counsel for a committee to control the process by which the committee was selected.[25] To support his contention that this was what happened, Szaller wanted to take depositions of White, Drabkin, and Little and of the members of the new committee.

In a pattern that would become familiar to lawyers raising issues in the Robins bankruptcy that Merhige did not want raised, the judge upheld Szaller's right to discovery in the abstract but constructed a series of roadblocks and delays that made it impossible to obtain meaningful information. At first, Merhige refused to allow any depositions. Instead, he permitted Szaller to submit written questions to the committee members but not to White, Drabkin, and Little, the three persons with the greatest knowledge of the selection process. Merhige said that these restrictions were necessary to "avoid undue expense on the debtor."[26] Later, Merhige agreed to allow depositions of the committee members (but still nothing directed to White, Drabkin, and Little). Nonetheless, because of various procedural obstacles, after three and a half months, when the matter was scheduled for hearing, Szaller had succeeded in deposing only Gorman King.

On September 4, 1986, the day of the hearing, Merhige offered Szaller a continuance to allow him to take the depositions of the other committee members and to reargue the issue of deposing White, Drabkin, and Little. But Merhige told Szaller that any depositions that were allowed must take place in the courthouse in Richmond. He also told Szaller that, if the challenge to the committee was unsuccessful, he would be required to pay the costs of the depositions, including travel costs and attorney fees.

The prevailing rule in the federal courts is that the losing party is not required to pay his opponent's attorney fees, unless the position he asserted was frivolous. And, unless the court prevents it, depositions can be taken near the residence of a witness, thereby avoiding any issue of travel costs for the witness. (Members of the first claimants' committee who lived near the homes of the members of the second claimants' committee were prepared to take their depositions.) By restricting Szaller to depositions in Richmond and by stating that he would be required to pay travel costs and attorney fees if his motion were unsuccessful, Merhige was threatening Szaller with untold thousands of dollars of additional expenses. Szaller protested:

SZALLER: Your Honor, what would costs include? . . . You mean travel and attorneys fees?

MERHIGE: Yes. Reasonable costs. But I have got to have somebody controlling the depositions or they will get out of hand, and you know it.

SZALLER: I don't know that . . . I can't afford to do discovery under those terms. I am sorry. I want to go forward.

MERHIGE: Go forward. Call your first witness.

Szaller had intended that his first witness be Murray Drabkin. But, although Szaller had written a letter to Drabkin asking him to be in court for the hearing, Drabkin was not present. Drabkin could not be subpoenaed because he lives and works outside Virginia. A few days before, when Merhige learned that Drabkin was not going to have the members of the second claimants' committee present for the hearing, he had told Drabkin, "[T]hat kind of surprises me, to be perfectly frank with you."[27] Now Drabkin himself had decided not to attend.

MERHIGE: Was he subpoenaed?

SZALLER: You know I was not permitted to take depositions.

MERHIGE: I didn't ask you that. I asked if he was subpoenaed.

SZALLER: I must give a full answer, Your Honor. He was not subpoenaed because he was not within the subpoena power of the court. Again, for the record, I was not permitted to take his deposition.

MERHIGE: Just move on with your evidence, will you, Mr. Szaller.

White did testify at the hearing. He acknowledged that he had consulted with Drabkin and Little in selecting the members of the second committee but said he did not consider whether prospective committee members would retain Drabkin. With respect to his decision not to appoint Friedberg, White claimed that the problem with Friedberg was not his opposition to Drabkin but his insistence on naming the lawyer who would be counsel to the committee. White stated that he was "concerned that whoever was appointed to the committee would have an open mind . . . about counsel."

Robins's counsel, William Cogar, testified and contradicted White. Cogar said White had told him, during the period in which he was considering his selections, that Friedberg had conditioned his appointment on the employment of a particular lawyer. Cogar said that he had telephoned Friedberg, who said that this was not true. Cogar called White back and told him, "'Bill, I have just talked with Friedberg and he is not insisting [on naming the lawyer].' I asked Mr. White to call Mr. Friedberg to confirm that. Whether he did or he didn't I do not know."

A few days after the hearing, Judge Merhige issued his decision denying the motion to dissolve the committee.[28] He found that the committee members were selected not because they would retain Drabkin but because of their "excellent credentials." Merhige said that "the membership of the present committee is highly diverse [because] . . . its members . . . reside in the North, the South, the mid-West and on the East Coast." He emphasized that both the court and the trustee had told the committee members of their right to select counsel of their choice. Merhige did not mention that four of the five people appointed were recommended by Drabkin and Little.

Merhige also found that "the complete lack of evidence in support of the movants' motion" warranted the court to consider the imposition of attorney fees and costs on Szaller. Merhige invited the parties to file their views on this question. No one submitted any support for this suggestion, and Merhige let the matter drop. Almost a year later the court of appeals affirmed Merhige's denial of Szaller's motion.[29]

6 Business as Usual

On August 21, 1985, the day the A. H. Robins Company filed its petition for reorganization, E. Claiborne Robins, Jr., summoned the company's executives to the auditorium in the headquarters building on Cummings Drive in Richmond. He explained to his audience, which was stunned by news of the bankruptcy, that the company would continue "business as usual" under the control of existing management. He added that, "when we use the term 'business as usual,' we mean it."[1]

Six months later, on February 18, 1986, a Robins employee, testifying at a routine hearing before Bankruptcy Judge Blackwell N. Shelley, mentioned that the company had recently paid a contractor $100,000 for services performed before the bankruptcy. In response to questions from the judge, counsel for Robins acknowledged that there had been other such payments and that the "numbers are not insignificant."[2] Judge Shelley ordered the company to disclose all payments of prepetition debt, and two weeks later Robins acknowledged that during the Chapter 11 proceeding, without authorization of the court, it had paid millions of dollars in prepetition debt to hundreds of creditors.

The prohibition against the payment of prepetition debt by the debtor is basic to the purpose and functioning of the bankruptcy system. It goes hand-in-hand with the automatic stay of litigation against the debtor. Both serve to maintain the status quo until a distribution can be made that will treat all creditors equitably in accordance with their priorities and in accordance with available resources. There are various circumstances in which prepetition debt can be paid, generally for reasons that relate to increasing or preserving the value of the estate, but this can done only on a specific order of the court, entered after notice and hearing.[3] On August 23, 1986, two days after Robins's bankruptcy began, Judge Merhige had entered an order that expressly prohibited the company from paying "any debt which was incurred prior to the filing of its petition . . . except upon order of the court."[4]

On March 12, 1986, the United States attorney in Richmond, acting on behalf of the Internal Revenue Service, the largest creditor in the bankruptcy, filed a motion asking Judge Merhige to hold Robins in contempt of court for violations of this order and to punish the responsible individuals. The government also asked Merhige to appoint a trustee to run the company.

In Chapter 11 cases, existing management is usually allowed to remain in control of the day-to-day affairs of the debtor corporation, on the assumption that it is best able to operate the business and maximize its value. In case of misconduct, however, the bankruptcy court has authority to appoint a trustee to run the company.[5] When this happens, management loses control over the reorganization process as well. The exclusive period, in which only the debtor can file a plan of reorganization, is automatically terminated. But even more significant, the trustee assumes the power to speak for the corporation with respect to the reorganization. The trustee is able to make proposals or agreements on behalf of the debtor that may be at odds with the desires of preexisting management or of the shareholders.

In fact, in his memorandum in support of the motion for the appointment of a trustee, Assistant United States Attorney S. David Schiller posed the issue as one not only of enforcing the prohibition against the payment of prepetition debt but also of moving the case toward an acceptable plan of reorganization.

After fifteen years of battling, it is clear that counsel for Robins and the IUD claimants have low opinions of one another. The Court has previously commented on the delays and lack of negotiating progress between the two sides and the lingering animosity has no doubt contributed to the standoff. The Court's recent ruling dissolving and reforming the IUD Claimants Committee should help resolve the problem. The Court could complete the process by placing the debtor in the control of a neutral trustee who would not desire to carry on the old battles and who could dispassionately proceed with plan negotiations . . . Perhaps with a new committee and a trustee for the company, the parties will quickly negotiate a confirmable plan. That is, after all, the real goal in this case.[6]

The appointment of a trustee could quickly lead to the simplest and most obvious plan of reorganization and the one consistently advocated by Murray Drabkin—the sale of A. H. Robins at the best available price and the distribution of the proceeds in accordance with the priorities established by the Bankruptcy Code. This possibility led to public speculation that Robins would seek to withdraw from Chapter 11.[7]

Instead, Robins's management gambled that it could avoid the appointment of a trustee by blaming the violations on its lawyers. On

March 20, 1986, eight days after the contempt motion was filed, Robert Watts, Robins's executive vice-president, called Penn Butler in San Francisco and told him that the services of Murphy, Weir & Butler, the bankruptcy specialists Robins had employed to handle the Chapter 11 case, were "no longer desired."[8] On the same day, the company announced that its general counsel, William Forrest—the man accused by Roger Tuttle of ordering the destruction of incriminating documents a decade earlier—was taking early retirement. Robins then claimed that the payments of prepetition debt had been innocently made on the bad advice of its lawyers.

On April 4, Robins moved for authorization to employ the firm of Skadden, Arps, Slate, Meagher & Flom in New York, one of the largest law firms in the United States, to replace Murphy, Weir & Butler as its bankruptcy counsel. In contrast to his attitude toward the decision of the members of the first claimants' committee to replace Murray Drabkin, Merhige did not feel that Robins's inability to "get along with [its] own lawyer" presented a problem, and on April 7, 1986, the request was granted. Dennis J. Drebsky, a forty-year-old partner in the Skadden firm and a native New Yorker, assumed primary responsibility for the matter.

The next day, however, at what Morton Mintz described in the *Washington Post* as a "brief, fiery hearing," an "angry" Judge Merhige instructed Assistant United States Attorney Schiller to pursue vigorously the question of who authorized the unlawful payments. "Get them under oath," the judge said. "They're not going to get away with it." He added, "[T]he law is the law is the law, and no corporation, no person is above it, especially in this Court."[9]

Over the next several weeks, David Schiller and his colleague Robert Jaspen "got them under oath," as the judge had directed. Forty-two Robins executives, employees, and attorneys, including every high-level official except E. Claiborne Robins, Sr., were summoned to the United States attorney's office, made to wait their turn, and deposed.

Merhige conducted hearings on the contempt motion for over twenty hours on June 5, 6, and 7, 1986. In support of their motion, Schiller and Jaspen submitted a ninety-five-page "statement of facts," with 454 numbered paragraphs detailing the evidence of Robins's payment of prepetition debt. In support of the government's motion, Murray Drabkin described the evidence as revealing "a pervasive pattern of conduct under which Robins chose to honor nearly all categories of obligations to its creditors with one exception: the Dalkon Shield claimants."[10]

The evidence showed that Robins had made fifteen hundred unauthorized payments of prepetition debt in the total amount of $7 million after the Chapter 11 petition had been filed. Certain payments were particularly flagrant. With respect to its executives, the company had gone beyond "business as usual" and made payments that would not have been made in normal circumstances. They had begun in the weeks before the bankruptcy.

Robins maintained a Key Executives Compensation (KEC) plan that allowed executives, as a tax-savings device, to defer a portion of their compensation. Under the terms of the plan, deferred compensation could not be withdrawn until the individual left the company's employ, at which time the deferred income with interest would be paid out over a ten-year period. Robins did not segregate the deferred income or pay it into a trust of any sort; its obligations to participating executives were mere unsecured debt with no different status under the scheme of the Bankruptcy Code than the company's obligations to women injured by the Dalkon Shield.

In May and June 1985, in response to the prospect of bankruptcy, several senior Robins executives asked whether they could be paid the balances they had accrued under the KEC plan, without separation from service and in a lump sum. The compensation committee of Robins's board of directors agreed to allow this, and between June 25, 1985 and August 6, 1985, seven present and former Robins executives received $1.2 million in deferred compensation payments.[11]

After the Chapter 11 case was initiated, this process continued; eighteen additional active and retired Robins executives closed out their KEC accounts and received payments totaling almost $1.8 million. This included a payment of $250,000 to William L. Zimmer III on February 25, 1986, a week after Judge Shelley had ordered Robins to disclose all payments of prepetition debt. Zimmer had served as president of the company in the interregnum between the presidencies of E. Claiborne Robins, Sr., and E. Claiborne Robins, Jr. In 1986 he was a member of Robins's board of directors and chairman of the compensation committee, which had approved these unusual payments. In addition to payments of amounts accrued in the KEC plan, Robins had continued to make its normal payments under its Executive Salary Continuation Plan (ESCP), a plan under which retired executives, as additional compensation for their former service, are paid a portion of their former salaries.

The A. H. Robins Company has many wholly owned corporate subsidiaries. Although these are assets of Robins's estate, the separate corporate entities were not themselves in bankruptcy, and they were able to conduct their own businesses without the restrictions or supervision to which a debtor in possession is subject. The evidence showed that several of Robins's prepetition obligations—two in excess of $700,000 each—had been paid by subsidiary corporations. Robins had even used a subsidiary to evade a specific ruling by Judge Merhige. In November 1985 the company asked Merhige to allow it to fulfill a pledge by paying $80,000 to the United Way of Richmond. Merhige had told the company that the payment could not be made. Robins then directed a subsidiary in New Jersey to make the payment.

Robins made no effort to defend the legitimacy of any of these transactions. Its entire defense was that all the payments were innocently made because of bad advice either from Murphy, Weir & Butler or from General Counsel William Forrest. The company claimed that counsel had not informed its key executives of the prohibition against the payment of prepetition debt until the issue was raised in February 1986. Robins officials testified that Murphy, Weir & Butler attorneys had approved the payment of amounts due to its suppliers and had advised that court's approval could be obtained after the fact.[12] In connection with the payments to company executives, Robins produced a memorandum from William Forrest to G. E. R. Stiles, the company's chief financial officer, dated November 18, 1985, confirming advice purportedly received from Penn Butler, "that the company should continue the 1984 Key Executive Compensation Plan and the Executive Salary Continuation Plan, unless and until it is otherwise ordered by the U.S. District Court in the Chapter 11 case." The memorandum included the notation "cc: Penn Ayers Butler, Esquire." Finally, William Forrest testified that he interpreted Murphy, Weir & Butler's advice that the activities of Robins's subsidiaries were not affected by the bankruptcy case to permit Robins to instruct subsidiaries to pay prepetition debt of the parent corporation.

Forrest was a willing foil in Robins's strategy, but Murphy, Weir & Butler was not. That firm specializes in reorganization proceedings involving large corporations and, after being unceremoniously dismissed from its leading role in this highly visible case, had no intention of allowing its reputation to be maligned to save Robins's skin. At the hearing, Penn Butler and other Murphy, Weir & Butler lawyers denied that they ever advised that payments of prepetition debt could be made in advance of court approval and described their repeated admonitions to the contrary. They testified that they were unaware that any such payments had been made.

Penn Butler swore that he had never seen Forrest's November 18, 1985, memorandum and denied ever giving the advice attributed to him in it. (The government contended that "at best, the November 18 memorandum does not accurately reflect what occurred at the meeting. At worst, the November 18 memo and the testimony in support of it are total fabrications.")[13] Butler testified that, after the government filed its contempt motion and before he was fired, Forrest had urged him to lie about his advice concerning payments to executives. Butler said that Forrest implored, "You have to have said it" and that he replied: "Skip, I can't say that I said it. I couldn't have said it. I'm sorry."[14]

The testimony from the Murphy, Weir & Butler attorneys was confirmed by a wide variety of independent evidence. Several Robins employees acknowledged that Penn Butler had explained, at the meeting of company executives in the auditorium at Robins headquarters on August 21, 1985, that prepetition debt could not be paid without prior court approval. The same advice was contained in an August 21, 1985, memorandum from Butler to Forrest that was distributed to Robins's board of directors and in a August 26, 1985, newsletter distributed to a large group of Robins managers.

In fact, the evidence at the hearing indicated that top executives all the way up to both E. Claiborne Robinses had made a conscious decision to ignore the rules. In testimony strikingly reminiscent of Wayne Crowder's efforts in 1971 to convince Robins management to do something about the wicking of the Dalkon Shield tailstring, one middle-level Robins employee, Steven Kirkham, described his efforts to stop the payments to retired Robins executives.

Kirkham was Robins's director of employee benefits. He testified that, shortly after the bankruptcy was filed, he was told by a Murphy, Weir & Butler lawyer, in the presence of G. E. R. Stiles, Robins's chief financial officer, that payments to retired executives under ESCP had to stop. Kirkham informed his superiors, Howard Hall and Richard McCracken, of this advice. A few days later, Hall told Kirkham that "Forrest and others" had decided that payments under ESCP would continue. At the same time, accounting personnel were advised that Stiles had instructed that the payments would continue.

Kirkham memorialized the advice he had received from Murphy, Weir & Butler and the contrary instruction from Hall in a memorandum, a copy of which was sent to McCracken. He also noted his concern in a memorandum that was circulated to Robert Watts, Robins's executive vice-president. In response, both McCracken and Hall advised Kirkham that it was not his job to worry about whether these payments were made and to "drop the issue."[15]

Instead, Kirkham raised the issue with attorneys William Cogar and

Wallace Stark at Mays & Valentine. A day or two later, Stark called Kirkham and told him that senior management had been advised not to make the payments but had decided to make them anyway. Stark's notes showed that he had been informed that "the final call had been made by Robins Sr. and Jr. and is irreversible."[16]

At the hearing, Merhige was critical of the conduct of Robins officials and gave no credence to the claim that the company had not been properly advised. Merhige complained, however, that despite the extensive investigation he did not know who exactly had made the decision to make millions of dollars of illegal payments. Schiller ascribed this to "Robinspeak"—answers of "I don't know," "I don't recall," "I have no present recollection," "we had no definitive discussion," "I probably said," and "I would have said."[17]

Murray Drabkin argued that the evidence required the conclusion that the decision had been made by Claiborne Robins, Jr.:

It wasn't the tooth fairy. It wasn't some vague sinister force. Let's face it, Mr. Townes [Robins's treasurer] and Mr. Stiles were not going to pay out hundreds of thousands of dollars when they had been warned that those kinds of payments were improper, unless they knew from top management that that is what was expected of them. They may be high officials of the company, but they just work there, and there is no need to put their neck on the block unless they knew it was going to please Mr. Robins and that is what happened.

Section 1104(a) of the Bankruptcy Code provides that "the court shall order the appointment of a trustee—for cause, including fraud, dishonesty, incompetence or gross mismanagement of the affairs of the debtor by current management." Schiller and Drabkin argued that the evidence established "cause" and that the word "shall" meant that Merhige was required to order the appointment of a trustee.

Drabkin also argued that the removal of existing management through the appointment of a trustee would facilitate the development of an acceptable plan of reorganization:

We have been told over and over again that a cornerstone of any reorganization plan with this company is that equity will not be impaired . . . And that reflects that the Robins family controls the negotiation . . . and the Robins family has been looking out for its 45% or 48% interest. So I suggest to the court that, far from [a trustee] impairing success in negotiation of a plan, there is probably not going to be a plan with this management because they will not face up to the reality that they may in fact be wiped out.

Merhige disagreed on both counts—that he was required to appoint a trustee or that the appointment of a trustee would be beneficial. On

June 14, 1986, Merhige found Robins in contempt of court but announced that a trustee would not be appointed.[18] Merhige said that the appointment of a trustee would do more harm than good. He emphasized that the company was "making millions of dollars a month" and said he was "very concerned" that if a trustee was appointed "these claimants are going to go down the drain."

Judge Merhige did say that "I have no doubt sanctions are warranted," but he deferred taking any action until August 5, 1986.

I shall issue appropriate sanctions for the contempt that has been found . . . But now is not the time for the Court to pronounce its sanctions. Suffice it to say they will, I hope, be fair and of sufficient severity to impress upon all that the law is the law is the law, and it will be followed.[19]

On August 5, however, Merhige announced that no sanctions would be imposed. Schiller asked the judge to order Stiles, Townes, and Forrest to "show cause" why they should not personally be held in contempt of court, but Merhige said that it would be too costly to pursue the matter further. He suggested that, if these men had violated the law, the government should bring criminal prosecutions. Merhige also refused to order the company to identify the individuals who had made the decisions to authorize the improper payments. "Haven't each one of these people been asked under oath?" Merhige asked Schiller. "What more do you want me to do? Say, Please?"[20]

Judge Merhige did announce that he would order the appointment of an "examiner" to perform various duties in the case, including the oversight of Robins's efforts to recover improper payments of prepetition debt. On August 13, 1986, Ralph Mabey, a forty-two-year-old lawyer from Salt Lake City, was appointed to this position.[21] Mabey had attended law school at Columbia University in New York and then returned to Salt Lake City, where he is an official in the Mormon Church. From 1979 to 1983 he served as a bankruptcy judge in Utah and received national recognition among bankruptcy specialists for the high quality of his performance in that position. In 1986 Mabey was practicing law as a partner in the Salt Lake City office of the New York law firm of LeBoeuf, Lamb, Leiby & MacRae. As examiner, Mabey would play an important role in the Robins bankruptcy, serving as the intermediary for Merhige in a variety of matters, most importantly in the development of a plan of reorganization.

On August 14, 1986, Merhige ordered the company to demand repayment of the money improperly disbursed, plus interest, and to bring suit against anyone who refused repayment. The company sent out hundreds of demand letters to individuals and companies, and most of the money was recovered, including all the payments to past and present company executives. Robins's managers took it upon themselves, however, not to demand repayment in situations in which they believed that doing so would adversely affect a valuable relationship. Even when it was pressed to do so by the examiner, Robins did not demand repayment of over $1 million that had been paid to wholesalers, to promoters of its products, and to research and development institutions.

Finally, in September 1987, the claimants' committee filed a motion to hold E. Claiborne Robins, Jr., in contempt of court because of his company's failure to comply fully with Merhige's order relating to recoupment. (At the August 5, 1986, hearing, Merhige had required Robins, Jr., to personally accept responsibility for any future violations of court orders by the company.)[22] The United States Attorney's office supported the claimants' committee's motion. David Schiller told Judge Merhige: "These people see themselves above the law. They're daring this court to do something about it."[23]

In a bitter response, Robins said that the committee's contempt motion set a "new lower standard" for all the years of Dalkon Shield litigation. It asked that sanctions be imposed against Murray Drabkin for "abuse of authority" and "overstepping the bounds of permissible advocacy." At the same time, however, the company admitted the essential fact that it had not sought to recover more then $1 million that was subject to Merhige's order. Robins said that to demand repayment in all instances would "seriously damage customer relationships" and that, because it intended to pay 100 percent of commercial debt under its plan of reorganization, "any alleged benefit . . . from such circular endeavor . . . truly is more imaginary than real." Robins asked Judge Merhige to terminate the recovery program.

After a hearing on October 12, 1987, Merhige found the A. H. Robins Company in contempt of court for violating his order requiring recoupment and he fined Robins, Jr., $10,000. Merhige said he wanted to end the company's attitude of offering "excuse after excuse after excuse." At the same time, however, the judge relieved the company of any further obligation to recover the improper payments.[24]

That is how the matter ended. In violation of two court orders and at the price of only a token penalty, Robins succeeded in avoiding interrupting payments to its most valued creditors while for years no payments were made to women injured by the Dalkon Shield.

7   The Determination of
       Eligible Claimants

Rule 3003 of the Bankruptcy Rules provides that the court shall fix a date (the "bar date") by which creditors must file their claims. The rule also provides that any person who does not file a claim within the prescribed period "shall not be treated as a creditor." This rule was written in contemplation of the usual bankruptcy in which each of the creditors is known to the debtor and can be mailed a notice of the bar date; it was not written in contemplation of tort-based bankruptcies involving large numbers of potential personal injury claimants who are unknown to the debtor. In the Johns-Manville case, rule 3003 was simply ignored; the court was never asked to fix a bar date, and it never did. In recognition of the long latency period between exposure to asbestos and the manifestation of disease, the Johns-Manville plan of reorganization permits a claim to be filed at any time during the twenty-seven-year life of the trust established to pay asbestos victims.

In contrast, a central element of Robins's strategy for its reorganization involved the strict application of rule 3003—the establishment of a bar date and the exclusion of all claims not filed before the deadline. At Robins's request and without opposition from the claimants' committee, on November 21, 1985, Judge Merhige entered an order providing that "any person that has a claim against Robins . . . but does not file a claim on or before April 30, 1986, shall be forever barred from participating in the Chapter 11 estate."[1]

Women who had asserted personal injury claims against Robins were given written notice of the bar date. Notice to other potential claimants was made by publication, which is allowed by Bankruptcy Rule 2002 if the court finds notice by mail is impracticable. In a different context, the Supreme Court has held that notice by publication to unknown persons of the necessity to act to prevent the loss of a right of action is consistent with due process of law, if the notice is "reasonably calculated, under all of the circumstances, to apprise interested parties of the pendency of the action . . . [and if] the form chosen is not substantially less likely to bring home notice than other of the feasible and customary sub-stitutes."[2]

Robins submitted a plan for publishing notice of the bar date, which Judge Merhige approved with minor changes. In the United States a one-quarter-page advertisement would be published one time on an in-side page of *USA Today* and of 232 local newspapers, and a full-page ad would appear one time in *Time, Newsweek, People, U.S. News & World Report, Jet, TV Guide, The National Enquirer,* and *The Star.* Thirty-second announcements would be broadcast 40 times on network televi-sion and 150 times on cable television, primarily during movies and sit-uation comedies, within a three-week period.[3]

Outside the United States there would be no paid advertising. Notices would be sent to American embassies and to various health authorities in countries in which the Dalkon Shield was used, a press release and a proposed public service announcement would be distributed to forty-eight hundred foreign media outlets, and press conferences would be held by Robins representatives in sixteen foreign cities. The idea was that these efforts would generate news stories that would contain the essential information, including the bar date and the address in Rich-mond where claims should be sent.

The necessary result of advertising the opportunity to file claims, to-gether with a filing deadline, is that a number of persons who would not otherwise have sought compensation will file claims while another group of persons—the size depending on the quality of the notice—who would have sought compensation in due course will fail to file timely claims and be excluded from redress. A higher number of claims could be attracted than excluded by this approach, with a consequent increase in total liability, but Robins accepted this possibility because it thought that the creation of a finite pool of eligible claimants was necessary to attain a limit on the company's liability. Robins believed that only if its liability was limited could it secure the necessary financing and emerge from Chapter 11 with the company's equity structure unchanged. In the Johns-Manville reorganization, where there was no bar date and lia-bility was not limited, the claimants' trust was granted 50 percent of the equity in the company and the right to call on additional stock and cor-porate profits throughout its life.[4]

Robins's decision turned out to be ill advised. The company had an-ticipated that 25,000 to 35,000 claims would be filed. Instead, in re-sponse to the published notice, the bankruptcy clerk in Richmond was swamped with mail, and by the April 30, 1986, deadline, an astonishing 327,064 claims had been filed.[5] (Seven percent of these were filed by husbands or children claiming damages as a result of their wife's or mother's use of the Dalkon Shield. For simplicity, in this book the claimants are usually referred to as women.) As only 4,000 suits were filed against Robins in the year before the bankruptcy, and only 15,000 over fifteen years, quite clearly the vast majority of these claims would not have been filed if they had not been solicited. The resolution of this large number of claims would prove to require far more money than Robins would be able to provide under existing ownership—exactly the opposite of what had been intended.

Robins's managers had failed to understand—perhaps as a by-product of their cherished belief that there was nothing wrong with the Dalkon Shield—that there were large numbers of women injured by the device who had not done anything about it. The bar date procedure overcame barriers that had long inhibited women from filing Dalkon Shield injury claims. The injuries suffered were of the most personal nature and, particularly where infertility was the result, profoundly painful and disturbing. Some women were motivated to fight A. H. Robins for damages, but many more who had suffered serious injuries were reluctant to rehash their pain and would not have filed claims for damages if a final decision had not been forced on them. And, on a practical level, before the bankruptcy, it was necessary to obtain copies of medical records from doctors and hospitals and to convince a lawyer to accept the case. The claim-filing procedure in the bankruptcy made it easier for claims to be filed.

Judge Merhige treated the large number of responses as definitive proof of the adequacy and effectiveness of the notification effort. The following exchange, involving a request from the claimants' committee for approval of fees for media consultants who had evaluated the notice program proposed by Robins, illustrates the judge's attitude.

MERHIGE: Well, Mr. Drabkin, I am going to give you an opportunity to be heard on it, but the first time I heard anything about media consultants from your committee was, I believe, either one, two or three days before the beginning of the campaign and we had a meeting in chambers in which your people came in for the first time, criticized what was proposed to be done, and their great contribution was to point out that we didn't have any newspaper in Arizona, as I recall, and that was it.

DRABKIN: I am sorry . . .

MERHIGE: Let me finish. They were all worried that people weren't going to get notice. My God, we are getting them from Vietnam. Getting them in Chinese. Anybody that says there has not been due process on this notice, they are really going to have a job convincing me with the numbers of claims we have got in here . . . It had to be effective notice. Had to be. Your people didn't help us. And I am not going to approve any money unless you can prove, show me, that it is absolutely necessary . . . Just a boondoggle.

D R A B K I N : Having heard that, I may as well sit down.

M E R H I G E : Saves time. Thank you. Denied. Next.

Although the bar date and notice procedure unquestionably had the effect of including a large number of women who would not otherwise have filed claims, there are serious questions about the propriety of extinguishing the rights of women who did not respond. The most obvious problem concerned the foreign notice.

Less than thirty-two thousand claims were received from outside the United States.[6] This amounted to one of every forty-four foreign women who had used the Dalkon Shield. In the United States one claim was filed for every seven women who used the Dalkon Shield. In some countries the response rate was far lower than the foreign average; in Mexico, for example, it was below one in a thousand. In no foreign country did the response rate come close to that in the United States. Robins spent $750,000 to give notice of the bar date to women outside the United States, less than 25 percent of the amount spent on notice in the United States. An estimated 1.4 million Dalkon Shields were used in foreign countries, 64 percent of the number used in the United States.[7]

In developing a proposal to give notice of the bar date by publication, Robins's advisers were faced with the tension between the legal requirement that the notice be adequate and the company's economic interest in minimizing the number of claims. In justifying the decision not to advertise the bar date outside the United States, Robins stressed the expense of advertising in numerous foreign countries in which the Dalkon Shield had been sold and the prohibition against mentioning contraceptive devices in advertising in Moslem countries. But in 1984, when Robins conducted its campaign urging women to remove the Dalkon Shield and it had no conflicting motivations, the company did advertise in foreign countries in which a large number of Dalkon Shields had been used.[8] More than 90 percent of the Dalkon Shields sold outside the United States had been sold in seven countries—Canada, England, Australia, South Africa, France, Germany, and Mexico; in these countries advertising was "feasible and customary."[9]

Motions to extend the bar date for foreign claims and to require additional notice were filed by the Dalkon Shield claimants' committee and by organizations concerned with women's health issues in Canada, Ireland, and Bangladesh. When the motions were argued before Judge Merhige on June 6, 1986, Mark Ellenberg appeared on behalf of the claimants' committee. Ellenberg, a partner at Cadwalader, Wickersham & Taft, graduated with distinction from the Georgetown Law School in Washington in 1975. Working with Murray Drabkin, Ellenberg played a major role on behalf of the claimants' committee in the Chapter 11 case. In his argument, Ellenberg emphasized the vast statistical disparities between the domestic and foreign response rates.

ELLENBERG: These numbers are so different that it is abundantly clear that the foreign program just did not work . . .

MERHIGE: Of course, you know they were limited by law in certain foreign countries. The Muslim countries, as I recall, they couldn't even mention it.

ELLENBERG: That is another problem . . . But there is also Great Britain and France and Canada and Germany and Mexico. And those numbers are overwhelming. Two tenths of one per cent from France, as opposed to 10% from the United States. Great Britain, one percent . . .

It is an issue of fundamental fairness and common human decency. This company is asking for a discharge of claims from these people. The company is not entitled to that discharge as a matter of right. The quid pro quo is notice . . . The company which wants the discharge should be told to come up with a better program. If it is paid advertising, it is paid advertising.

MERHIGE: You people are a little late with this sort of thing . . .

ELLENBERG: From day one we have questioned the adequacy of the foreign program.

MERHIGE: I think the record will show that you kept it to yourself until a matter of days before the program was kicked off.

ELLENBERG: Your Honor . . .

MERHIGE: Maybe not.

ELLENBERG: Your Honor, from day one and at every hearing we have always said that the foreign program is not adequate. You overruled that. And in the face of that ruling, we went forward.

You also said, and I sat right in your chambers right across from your desk with other counsel present, and we discussed it and you looked at me and said, if when the results come in they don't look right, we will fix it.

MERHIGE: That is right. I recall that.

ELLENBERG: Here we are.

MERHIGE: I am not satisfied that the results look as bad as you say they are.

On June 16, 1986, in a written opinion, Judge Merhige denied the motions.[10] He interpreted the Supreme Court language requiring that published notice be "reasonably calculated . . . to apprise interested parties of the pendency of the action" to mean that the method of providing notice must be reviewed "at the time it was calculated." He said that the "results are insignificant." If a "notice program were subject to hindsight review . . . it would forever be subject to constitutional attack. The Supreme Court must have realized such a preposterous result when it fashioned the test." Merhige found that Robins's notice program was "reasonably calculated" to give effective notice to foreign women because "all parties agreed" to it and because "no one really voiced any objection to the foreign notice until the results of the program were all tolled."

Merhige did go on to address the issue of disparate rates of response, but he did so without mentioning what the disparities were or even the number of foreign claims that had been filed. Instead, he wrote:

> The court finds the results of the foreign notice program not only staggering, but also comprehensive; notice reached women in 81 foreign countries, including women as far away as Bangladesh, Pakistan and Botswana . . . [I]t is the Court's finding that there are many reasons attributable to the discrepancy in the number of foreign and domestic filings, including, *inter alia*, religion, culture, the non-litigious nature of the people, and certain countries' bans on the "advertising" of such women's products or problems.[11]

This ruling was affirmed by the United States court of appeals in Richmond, which also was impressed with the receipt of a few claims from remote lands.[12]

No direct challenge to the domestic notice program was made; its adequacy was treated as a tenet of faith in the bankruptcy. Robins represented that its efforts to advertise the bar date in the United States were "similar" to and "duplicated" the measures the company had undertaken in 1984 to urge removal of the Dalkon Shield.[13] In an affidavit filed with the court, a media consultant employed by Robins estimated that the 1984 advertisements had reached 97 percent of the target audience and suggested "the same 97 percent saturation" would be achieved in the campaign to advertise the bar date.[14]

In fact, the 1986 notification effort fell far short of that of 1984. In 1984 Robins wrote to 185,000 doctors and clinics in the relevant specialties urging them to advise their patients to have the Dalkon Shield removed.[15] According to a Robins document, "[T]his effort to communicate with health professionals and seek their support was a vitally important element of the removal campaign."[16] In 1986 there was no effort to communicate with doctors. Moreover, in 1984 Robins purchased twice the amount of advertising in the print media that it purchased in 1986—half-page instead of quarter-page ads in daily newspapers and full-page ads twice instead of once in weekly magazines.[17]

Even in reference to the 1984 campaign, the 97 percent estimate only purports to reflect the percentage of households that received the television programs, newspapers, or magazines that included the notice, not the proportion of Dalkon Shield users who saw the notice and absorbed the information. No evidence was submitted, and it defies common sense and common experience to believe that 97 percent of the women who used the Dalkon Shield actually knew about the bar date and its significance. If as many 80 percent of the women in this country who used the Dalkon Shield were aware of the bar date, a figure more likely too high than too low, that means that half a million women were not.

By September 1989 more than 10,000 women in the United States had filed claims with the bankruptcy court in Richmond after the bar date and more were arriving daily.[18] Many other women who called the clerk's office were told that the deadline had passed. Robins itself has estimated that, if the filing period was reopened, between 25,000 and 30,000 additional claims could be expected.[19]

The Bankruptcy Rules authorize the court to allow a claim to be filed late "where the failure to act was the result of excusable neglect,"[20] and a relatively small number of women filed motions asking Judge Merhige to allow their claims to be filed after the bar date on this basis. Merhige denied all such motions where the reason stated was that the women had not heard of the bar date. Merhige was firm in the position that Robins's notice campaign constituted legally adequate notice, whether or not any particular individual received notice, and that the failure to file a claim for lack of knowledge of the filing requirement did not constitute excusable neglect.

Over Robins's opposition, a few late claim motions were allowed on narrow grounds. For example, Judge Merhige found "excusable neglect" in the case of fifteen women from Costa Rica whose claims were filed late because their attorney suffered a brain hemorrhage four days before the bar date.[21]

The only requirements for the content of a claim were the claimant's name and address and an indication that it was a Dalkon Shield claim. Most claims were simply letters or postcards containing this information. Judge Merhige's order establishing the bar date directed the clerk of court to send a questionnaire to each person who filed a timely claim. Claimants were told that the questionnaire should be returned by June 30, 1986, and that if it was not "the claim may be disallowed."

The questionnaire was two pages long. It asked for the dates of insertion and removal of the Dalkon Shield, the nature of the injury, and the identification of physicians who performed the relevant services. The questionnaire stated that the claimant did not need a lawyer, and, in fact, most claimants did not have any legal advice. The claimant was not told what to do if she did not know or was uncertain about any of information requested. But directly above the questions relating to Dalkon Shield use and injury, the form stated in large, bold type:

IMPORTANT NOTICE
UNDER FEDERAL LAW, CRIMINAL PENALTIES, INCLUDING IM-
PRISONMENT AND FINE, MAY BE IMPOSED FOR FILING A FALSE
CLAIM OR ONE CONTAINING FALSE OR MISLEADING STATE-
MENTS.

Approximately 180,000 claimants returned the questionnaire by the due date. Robins asked Judge Merhige to disallow the other 147,000 claims for which a timely questionnaire was not returned. Instead, on May 5, 1987, Merhige ordered that a second questionnaire be mailed to claimants who had not returned the first questionnaire. The order stated the questionnaire must be returned by July 15, 1987, and that, if it is not, "the reply will not be processed and the claim will be disallowed."

Another 30,000 questionnaires were received within the extended period, for a total of 210,000. When the time had elapsed, Judge Merhige entered orders disallowing the more than 117,000 claims for which a questionnaire still had not been received.[22] The order stated that "said claimants are barred from ever obtaining compensation arising out of present or future injury" from the use of the Dalkon Shield.

Judge Merhige established a procedure for the reconsideration of the disallowance on account of individual circumstances, and a form to request reconsideration was provided with the notice of disallowance. The claimant was asked to state "the reasons why I believe my claim should be reinstated." Some thirty-six hundred women returned this form. At a hearing on September 21, 1987, Merhige ruled that the strict standard of "excusable neglect" would govern the requests. He explained that reinstatement would be allowed only to a woman who stated a reason beyond her control why the questionnaire was not filed by the deadline.

Merhige appointed William S. White, who by now had left the position of United States trustee and had entered private law practice, as special master to review the written explanations and to make recommendations on whether claims should be reinstated. (The judge later ordered Robins to pay White in excess of $20,000 for this service.)[23] As a result of this process, 368 of the disallowed claims were reinstated, mostly in cases in which the claimant had stated unequivocally that she had not received either questionnaire. By far the largest category of requests for reinstatement that were rejected, over 700, were cases in which women had misunderstood the request to state "why I believe my claim should be reinstated" and, instead of explaining why the questionnaire had not been returned on time, had described the seriousness of her injuries.

Eighty-seven claimants whose requests for reinstatement were denied filed appeals. The cases were consolidated, and counsel was appointed by the court of appeals. The major issue on appeal was whether Judge Merhige was correct in refusing to reinstate claims in which the strict standard of "excusable neglect" had not been met. Counsel argued that the questionnaire was a request for information and that the more lenient standard applicable to the failure to respond to discovery in civil litigation—a standard that would not result in the dismissal of a complaint in analogous circumstances—should have been applied.

In a decision issued December 8, 1988, the court of appeals upheld Judge Merhige's rulings.[24] To do so, Judge Donald Russell—perhaps unwilling to validate the exclusion of 117,000 personal injury claims for failure to respond to a request for information that served no identifiable purpose—engaged in some redefinition. The bar date order, dozens of documents filed in the bankruptcy court, and a prior opinion of the court of appeals[25] had all referred to the responses to the bar date notice as "claims." Judge Merhige had held that responses were "claims" when he refused to consider the motions to dismiss because of the failure to give notice to every claimant.[26] But according to Judge Russell, the responses to the notice were not claims at all; they were "notices of a claim" or "informal claims." The completed questionnaires were not responses to a request for information, as everyone had thought; they were the claims, and as such properly subject to the "excusable neglect" standard.

Judge Russell explained that the responses to the bar date notice could not be the claims, because all that was required was a name and address and a statement that it was a Dalkon Shield claim. The Bankruptcy Rules define a claim ("proof of claim" is the formal term) as a "statement setting forth a creditor's claim," including the "ground of liability."[27] The only information requested by the questionnaire that remotely could be considered a statement of claim or a "ground of liability" is the identification of the injury. Dates of insertion and removal and names of physicians are not a ground of liability. A problem with Judge Russell's analysis is that, required or not, tens of thousands of women—including many women whose claims were disallowed because of their failure to return the questionnaire—had identified their injury (and many had provided a great deal of additional information) in their pre–April 30, 1986, filing. The questionnaire was required and claims were disallowed for failure to return it, regardless of the quality of information actually provided in the original filing. In fact, the principal function of the questionnaire in the Robins bankruptcy was the exclusion of women who failed to return it. The information entered on the questionnaires was never used for any significant purpose.

The 210,000 claims that satisfied the questionnaire requirement were later reduced, through the elimination of duplicates, previously settled claims, and withdrawn claims, to a core of approximately 195,000 eligible claims for which provision had to be made in Robins's plan of reorganization.

8   Future Claims

The rights of individuals who had not yet been injured or who were not yet aware of their injuries—so-called future claimants—were a dominant issue in the Chapter 11 cases in the asbestos industry. A substantial percentage, if not a majority, of the people who would manifest asbestos-related injuries had not yet done so when those reorganization cases commenced. Some were not even aware that they had been exposed to asbestos fibers.

The rights of future claimants were also an issue in the Robins bankruptcy, although it affected a smaller proportion of the universe of personal injury claimants. Future claimants in the Robins bankruptcy fell into three categories. First, some women were still using the Dalkon Shield and were at high risk of injury. A. H. Robins took the position that the number was very small, but the company identified at least 350 such women, almost all in the United States, during the first eight months of the bankruptcy. In the eight months before the bankruptcy, the company had paid for the removal of 5,000 Dalkon Shields.[1] There was no way to know how many women were wearing the Dalkon Shield, but with an estimated 3.6 million insertions, many in Third World countries, where regular gynecological care is not the norm and where Robins did not publish notices urging removal, it is likely that the number was significant.

Another group of potential future claimants were women who had lost their fertility or otherwise suffered injury to their reproductive organs as a result of as yet undiagnosed pelvic infections. These women would not become aware of their condition until they attempted to become pregnant or until their injuries precipitated other problems. The discovery of infertility related to the use of the Dalkon Shield frequently occurred long after the removal of the device.

The third group were women who were currently afflicted with pelvic inflammatory disease related to past use of the Dalkon Shield but whose infection was not yet clinically manifest. Referred to as "silent PID," such an infection can fester at a subsymptomatic level for years after the removal of the device, and then flare up and cause serious injury.[2]

The prospect of future claimants raised difficult legal questions. One question was whether these women had "claims" against Robins, within the meaning of the Bankruptcy Code, before their injuries were manifest. Under usual bankruptcy law principles, claims arising prior to confirmation are extinguished, except to the extent that the plan of reorganization or the order confirming the plan provides otherwise. Claims arising after confirmation of a plan of reorganization can be asserted in traditional litigation against the reorganized corporation.[3]

Under the law of most states, a personal injury claim does not arise, at least not in the sense that the statute of limitations for filing suit begins to run, until the injury occurs or is "discovered." But the result under the Bankruptcy Code may be different. A "claim" is broadly defined in section 101(4) of the Bankruptcy Code as "right to a payment, whether or not such right is reduced to judgment, liquidated, unliquidated, fixed, contingent, matured, unmatured, disputed, [or] undisputed . . . " The interpretive question is whether people exposed to a dangerous product have a "right to payment" from its manufacturer, although "contingent" and "unmatured," before they are aware of or incur any injury. This question had arisen in several asbestos bankruptcies but had never been clearly decided.[4]

If future claims are prepetition claims subject to discharge in a Chapter 11 case, another important question is whether, as a matter of due process of law, the plan of reorganization must provide for the compensation of these claims, even though they are not filed with the bankruptcy court by the bar date. The plan of reorganization in the *Johns-Manville* case discharged the corporation from liability to future claimants but provided for payment of their claims through an independent trust.

The A. H. Robins Company considered it essential that its liability for future claims be discharged in the reorganization process. The uncertainty as to the number of future claims was so great that, if the company remained exposed to this potential liability, it would probably not be able to secure the financing necessary to a successful reorganization. Further, in order to confirm a plan of reorganization, the Bankruptcy Code requires the court to find that "confirmation of the plan is not likely to be followed by the liquidation, or the need for further financial reorganization, of the debtor."[5] The court would have difficulty making such a finding if Robins faced unlimited liability to an unknowable number of future claimants.

From the perspective of the future claimants, the ideal result would be a successful reorganization that did not affect their rights. This would allow them to maintain suit in the normal manner against a reorganized company able to pay their claims. But if Robins's liability for future claims could not be discharged, reorganization would probably not be possible and the company would be forced to liquidate. In that event, future claimants might be left with no recourse—there would be no company left for them to sue when they became aware of their injuries.[6] For this reason, the best practical solution for the future claimants would be the treatment of their claims as prepetition claims eligible for compensation from a claimants' trust when their injuries became manifest, without any preinjury filing requirement. This solution was not inconsistent with Robins's essential interest of separating the liability from the going concern, although the company preferred to discharge future claims without making provision for their payment.

When in September 1985 Robins asked Judge Merhige to establish a bar date, the company proposed that women who had used the Dalkon Shield but who were not aware of any injury be required to file a claim by the bar date in order to preserve their future rights. Several courts had previously questioned the notion that adequate notice of a bar date could be given by publication to persons who had no injury; two courts had called the suggestion "absurd."[7]

At the time, no one had been appointed to represent the interests of future claimants. On behalf of the Dalkon Shield claimants' committee, Murray Drabkin opposed Robins's proposal.

Not only is a bar against future claims unprecedented, it is fundamentally unfair. No matter how minimal the effort required to file a proof of claim, many persons with no present knowledge of an injury are simply not likely to file. Indeed, persons with no present awareness of an injury are not likely to absorb the notice. It would be unconscionable for failure to file a proof of claim during a time of perfect health to eliminate permanently all remedy for what may, in time, prove to be a serious physical impairment.

Judge Merhige straddled the question. His bar date order provided that women who "may have used the Dalkon Shield but not as yet experienced any injury . . . must file" a written claim by April 30, 1986, and that "any person who has a claim against Robins" but who fails to file by the deadline "shall be forever barred" from receiving compensation for a Dalkon Shield injury. These provisions were modified, however, by their reference to another paragraph of the order that stated that the question of "whether persons who may have used the Dalkon Shield but have not yet evidenced any injury" have claims within the meaning of the Bankruptcy Code had not yet been decided.

The published notice of the bar date addressed future claimants as follows:

IF YOU . . . may have used the Dalkon Shield but have not yet experienced an injury . . . and if you wish to assert a claim against [Robins], the United States Bankruptcy Court . . . must receive your claim . . . on or before April 30, 1986 or you will lose the right to make a claim.

The number of women without manifest injury who filed claims in response to the bar date notice was not tabulated, but it was later determined that approximately 35,000 of the 195,000 eligible claimants had checked a box on the court questionnaire indicating that they were in this category.[8]

In the asbestos bankruptcies, the courts had ruled that future claimants were "parties in interest" entitled to representation, whether or not they were "creditors" with "claims" subject to discharge, and had appointed a "legal representative" to speak on their behalf. Such an appointment in the Robins bankruptcy was first suggested in September 1985, but Judge Merhige did not take any action on this matter until after the entry of his bar date order, with its provisions relating to future claims. On December 4, 1985, Stanley K. Joynes III was appointed legal representative of future tort claimants.

Joynes was a young lawyer from Richmond who had begun practice three years earlier in partnership with four other young attorneys. He had attended law school at the University of Tulsa and had then served as a law clerk for a federal judge in Oklahoma. When he returned to Richmond in 1982, Joynes had worked for Judge Merhige for several months on a volunteer basis as an extra law clerk before he opened his law office. Neither Joynes nor his partners had any significant experience in bankruptcy law. When Merhige first mentioned Joynes for this position, Murray Drabkin had suggested that someone with greater experience and expertise should be appointed, considering the complexity and novelty of the issues relating to the treatment of future claimants in a tort-based bankruptcy. In the Johns-Manville bankruptcy, for example, the legal representative of future claimants was Leon Silverman, a prominent attorney with thirty-five years of experience in major litigation and a member of a national law firm. Merhige responded that he would allow Joynes to secure the assistance he needed in fulfilling his responsibilities.

Shortly after his appointment, Joynes took steps to obtain expert assistance. Seeing that all the other parties in the case were represented by teams of bankruptcy experts from major law firms, Joynes contacted Vern Countryman, a professor at the Harvard Law School who is widely recognized as one of this country's leading experts and writers in the field of bankruptcy law. Because of his interest in the issue, Countryman agreed to serve as special bankruptcy counsel to Joynes. On May 1, 1986, Joynes filed an application for approval of his retention of Countryman, reciting Countryman's credentials and stating that Countryman would assist him "with the issue of the Future Tort Claimants' due process rights and the related issues of whether the Future Tort Claimants are 'creditors' and hold 'claims' within the intendment of the Bankruptcy Code."

In his application, Joynes explained that Countryman had agreed to work at a rate of $125 per hour, or whatever lower amount might be set by the court. This is extraordinarily low; large law firms charge more for first-year associates. And, because Countryman would work as an individual and not as part of a law firm with partners, associates, law clerks, and paralegals to involve in the project, his fees for the entire case probably would not have amounted to $50,000.

Joynes's application was quickly denied in an order signed by Judge Shelley. The order stated:

It appears to the Court that Joynes and other members of his firm . . . are lawyers, duly qualified and admitted to practice in this Court and have appeared in this case and that sufficient cause has not been demonstrated to justify this Court authorizing additional counsel, and it further appears that said Future Tort Claimants are currently represented by counsel and there may be a substantial likelihood of unnecessary duplication of effort and expense.[9]

The court's power of the purse is an unusual feature of bankruptcy proceedings. Particularly in a large, complicated case, it enables the court to decide who participates, what issues are raised, and what expenses can be incurred. In the Robins bankruptcy, the court's concern over "unnecessary duplication of effort and expense" did not prevent Robins from retaining one of the largest law firms in the United States, in addition to a major Richmond law firm. During certain months, more than twenty-five lawyers in the two firms did work for Robins, generating bills for the month of several hundred thousand dollars. Ultimately, counsel and other professionals (investment advisers and accountants) for Robins alone would be paid fees and expenses in excess of $28 million. Additional millions were spent on counsel and other professionals for the equity committee, an official committee composed of large Robins shareholders outside the Robins family whose interest in minimizing liability to women injured by the Dalkon Shield was the same as that of the company. Yet cost was cited as the ground to prevent Joynes from consulting with Professor Countryman.

As it turned out, Joynes admirably represented the interests of future claimants on his own. On April 28, 1986, he filed a motion to abolish or extend the bar date for future claimants. The precipitating factor in filing the motion was incorrect information broadcast on NBC's "Today" program. In an interview with Jane Pauley about the bar date in the Robins bankruptcy, Victoria Leonard, the director of the National Women's Health Network, had said that only women who had been injured by the Dalkon Shield should file claims with the bankruptcy court.

In his motion Joynes also challenged the adequacy of the language in the notice. He argued that, if women who had not experienced injuries must file a claim by April 30, 1986, to protect their right to seek compensation in case of future injury, then the prudent thing to do for every woman who had used the Dalkon Shield was to file a claim, because no one could know whether she would later manifest symptoms related to her use of the device. By saying "if you wish to assert a claim" rather than "every women who used the Dalkon Shield should file a claim," Joynes argued, the notice obscured this and suggested that women should have a reason other than mere use of the Dalkon Shield to make a claim. Many uninjured women could be expected to conclude that they did not "wish to assert a claim" without appreciating the risk of future injury or the legal consequences in that event. Even more fundamentally, Joynes argued that "no notification scheme whose objective lies with prompting a response from persons who have no present injury can be made adequate."

On the bar date, April 30, 1986, before any action on his motion was taken, Joynes filed what he described as a "class" claim on behalf of all women who had used the Dalkon Shield but who had not yet experienced or become aware of an injury. Robins promptly challenged the validity of this filing. If this claim were treated, as Joynes intended, as a filing by every woman who used the Dalkon Shield without manifest injury, Robins's plan to extinguish future claims not filed by the bar date would be thwarted.

On June 13, 1986, Judge Merhige denied the motion to abolish or extend the bar date for future claimants. Without explaining why not, Merhige said that the bar date notice was not intended to solicit a response from every woman who had used the Dalkon Shield. "The notice was clear and precise as to [whom] it was addressing," said the judge.[10]

A few days earlier, a motion had been filed that would require Judge Merhige to decide the question he had reserved in the bar date order:

whether women manifesting Dalkon Shield injuries after the bankruptcy filing had prepetition claims against Robins. A California woman named Rebecca Grady was still wearing a Dalkon Shield when Robins filed its Chapter 11 petition. Later the same day, August 21, 1985, Mrs. Grady was admitted to a hospital in Salinas, complaining of fever and abdominal pain. The diagnosis was pelvic inflammatory disease. Her Dalkon Shield was surgically removed on August 28. A few days later her symptoms subsided and she was released. Chronic abdominal pain and fever continued, and several weeks later Mrs. Grady's doctors determined that a total abdominal hysterectomy was required to eliminate the infection. The operation was performed on November 14, 1985. In June 1986 her attorneys asked Judge Merhige to rule that her claim arose after the bankruptcy filing.

Under California state law, Mrs. Grady did not have the right to sue Robins until after she became aware of her injury. Grady's attorneys argued that her "claim," within the meaning of section 101(4) of the Bankruptcy Code, did not arise until she became aware of her injuries because she had no "right to payment" until she had a right to sue under state law. Stanley Joynes filed a memorandum that supported this analysis.

Rebecca Grady had filed a claim with the bankruptcy court before the bar date. At a minimum, she was entitled to the same rights as every other woman who had filed a timely claim. The reason why it mattered when her claim arose was that the automatic stay provisions of section 362 of the Bankruptcy Code do not prohibit lawsuits to recover on claims that arise after the commencement of a bankruptcy proceeding. Mrs. Grady wanted to be free to pursue her case against Robins in the California courts during the bankruptcy proceeding. She also wanted any judgment or settlement she secured to be classified as a postpetition expense that would be paid in full as a priority claim at the conclusion of the reorganization case, even if there were insufficient funds to pay prepetition Dalkon Shield claims in full.[11]

Thus, Mrs. Grady sought not to salvage a claim that would otherwise be barred but to secure an advantage over claimants who had been injured earlier and who had waited longer for compensation. In addition, a ruling in her favor could result in dozens if not hundreds of suits against Robins going forward during the bankruptcy proceeding. Given the prospect of unfair advantage and disruption, it is not surprising that Judge Merhige held that Grady had a prepetition claim.[12]

Judge Merhige ruled that a claim arises, for the purposes of federal bankruptcy law, at the time of the conduct giving rise to the injury, not at the time the injury is manifest, regardless of when state law recognizes a right to bring suit.[13] Under this view, every woman who used the Dalkon Shield had a claim against Robins from the moment of insertion, even though an injury might never occur. In reaching this conclusion, Merhige relied on the broad definition of the word "claim" in the Bankruptcy Code and on language in the House and Senate committee reports on the 1978 act, which express the intention that "all legal obligations of the debtor, no matter how remote or contingent, will be able to be dealt with in the bankruptcy case."[14]

Merhige emphasized that, if Grady's claim were treated as arising at the time of the injury, Robins would be forced to deal with a "continuous flow of piece-meal litigation arising out of the Dalkon Shield" and a viable reorganization would be prevented. "This Court, in the absence of authority mandating such a scenario, will not participate in an obviously futile 'Catch 22' exercise. The result would clearly upset Congress' intent to channel claims towards one forum and allow for a comprehensive plan of reorganization."[15]

The due process clause of the Fifth Amendment to the United States Constitution prohibits the extinction of a valuable legal right for failure to take some action without adequate notice of the necessity to act. Because Mrs. Grady had filed a timely claim in the Chapter 11 case, her motion did not raise the question of whether due process of law permits the court to simply extinguish claims arising after the bar date for failure to meet the filing requirement. This question was raised in May 1987, when Kathryn Glascow of Lynchburg, Virginia, filed a motion asking Judge Merhige to treat her claim, which was filed a year after the bar date, as timely. Unlike Mrs. Grady, Mrs. Glascow was not seeking a priority over other claimants, only a recognition of a claim that would otherwise be barred under the terms of the bar date order.

Mrs. Glascow had used an IUD and had it removed in the early 1970s, before becoming aware of any problem. She did not know the brand name of the device, something that is not uncommon among women who have used an IUD. In the fall of 1986 Mrs. Glascow was diagnosed as unable to conceive. In May 1987 she consulted a specialist in fertility and was told for the first time that her problem could be attributable to her use of a Dalkon Shield. Mrs. Glascow immediately contacted the physician who had inserted her IUD and learned that her record showed that the device had been a Dalkon Shield. Within days Mrs. Glascow filed a claim with the bankruptcy court.

At the hearing on her motion, in July 1987, Mrs. Glascow established that she had no knowledge of the bar date—she does not watch television, and she did not see the single issue of the Lynchburg news-paper or the magazines in which the notice had appeared. Further, she testified that, even if she had seen the notice, she would not have re-sponded because she had no idea that she had worn a Dalkon Shield. In support of Mrs. Glascow's motion, Stanley Joynes argued that due pro-cess of law required a finding that Mrs. Glascow met the "excusable ne-glect" standard for the treatment of a late claim as timely.

Robins argued that the facts of Mrs. Glascow's case did not amount to excusable neglect. The company relied on Merhige's prior rulings in the case—that all Dalkon Shield users had prepetition claims (Grady), that claims for future injuries must be filed by the bar date (Bar Date Order), that notice by publication of the bar date was binding even though some individuals did not receive the information (motion to ex-tend the bar date for foreign claimants), and that the bar date notice was adequate as to uninjured women (motion to abolish or extend the bar date for future claimants). In response to Mrs. Glascow's statement that she had not even known that she had worn a Dalkon Shield, Robins maintained that it was her responsibility to find out. The company la-beled the Glascow motion as "nothing more than a direct attack on the adequacy of Robins' efforts to give notice of the Bar Date."

And Judge Merhige seemed to agree. At the hearing, he told Mrs. Glascow that his "horseback opinion is that you are gone," but he took the motion under consideration.

A few weeks later, another woman, Elena Mallari, with a situation virtually identical to Mrs. Glascow's, filed a motion to be allowed to file a timely claim. Mrs. Mallari had suffered a pelvic infection after the bar date, necessitating a total hysterectomy. She did not know she was wear-ing a Dalkon Shield until her operation. She had not seen any notice of the bar date. At the hearing on the Mallari motion in October 1987, Judge Merhige suddenly changed his position and granted both the Mallari and the Glascow motions. His only explanation was that, if these two claims were not allowed, "there won't be any future claims." Robins immediately asked for reconsideration of these rulings, but Mer-hige took no action on the company's request.

In this unresolved posture, the case approached the determination of Robins's total liability to women injured by the Dalkon Shield—Robins adhering to the position that its only liability was to women who had filed timely claims; Joynes, having appealed the *Grady* ruling, still argu-ing that future claimants do not have prepetition claims subject to dis-charge in bankruptcy but that, if they do, due process of law prevents the discharge of these claims unless adequate provision is made to pay them.

9   Another Source of Funds, Claims against Aetna

Aetna Casualty & Surety Company's potential liability to women injured by the Dalkon Shield was not limited to the remaining coverage under product liability insurance policies it had issued to Robins. Plaintiffs' attorneys contended that, on account of its own conduct, Aetna was directly liable for Dalkon Shield injuries, or at least those that occurred after 1975.

After the *Deemer* verdict in Kansas in 1975, Aetna assumed a major role in the defense of the Dalkon Shield litigation and, more broadly, in Robins's management of the Dalkon Shield issue. It was alleged that Aetna had conspired in the destruction of documents showing Robins's early knowledge of the dangers of the Dalkon Shield, and that it had commissioned and then concealed the negative results of studies of the safety of the device. There were also allegations that Aetna had had a major, if not decisive, voice in deciding not to recall the Dalkon Shield between 1975 and 1984, and had opposed a recall because of the predictable effect of increasing the number and value of Dalkon Shield injury claims. On these grounds, injured women had filed suit against Aetna, claiming that it was liable, jointly with Robins, because their injuries could have been avoided by an honest disclosure of the facts and by prompt recall of the device.

The prebankruptcy Dalkon Shield litigation against Aetna was inconclusive. Aetna had been named as an independent defendant with its own liability in more than one hundred cases, but in none of these had the facts been fully explored. Many of these cases had been settled or were in early stages when Robins's Chapter 11 case began. According to counsel for Aetna, in some three dozen cases the claims against Aetna were dismissed before trial on the ground that an insurer has no duty to consumers to disclose defects in the products it insures, a narrow ground that does not appear to take account of the breadth of the allegations against Aetna.[1]

Early in the Chapter 11 case, the parties had tactical positions on the matter, but no one really had any idea whether Robins's assets would

116

prove sufficient to provide full compensation to women injured by the Dalkon Shield. For this reason the possibility that Aetna, a company many times larger and wealthier than Robins, was independently liable to at least some substantial portion of those women was a potentially important factor in providing full compensation. The crucial questions were whether Aetna's potential liability would be resolved as part of the collective proceeding before Judge Merhige or separately in individual litigation outside Richmond and, if the issue were to be addressed in conjunction with Robins's bankruptcy, who would represent the injured women.

Joseph Friedberg moved first to fill that role. Robins had supported Friedberg's effort to maintain a class action against it within the Chapter 11 case because the company preferred to have Friedberg rather than its traditional adversaries in the plaintiffs' bar represent the interests of women injured by the Dalkon Shield. Merhige kept this prospect alive until March 1986, when the judge solved his problem with the first claimants' committee by dissolving it. When U.S. Trustee White made appointments that would allow Drabkin rather than Friedberg to control the second claimants' committee, the prospect of Friedberg representing the Dalkon Shield claimants in the Chapter 11 case died a quiet death. Not ready to die, however, was Friedberg's hope of acquiring a piece of this massive litigation.

In the course of the prebankruptcy litigation in Richmond, Friedberg had developed friendly relations with some of the lawyers at Mays & Valentine who were active in Robins's defense. Mays & Valentine was also counsel to Aetna in matters unrelated to the Robins bankruptcy.[2] Through this connection, Friedberg came to understand that Aetna would not be resistant to being sued before Judge Merhige in a class action binding on all women injured by the Dalkon Shield. Aetna denied any responsibility for Dalkon Shield injuries, yet the allegation had been made, and Aetna was alarmed at the prospect of remaining exposed to liability to Dalkon Shield claimants after Robins's liability was discharged. Rather than face postbankruptcy litigation of unknown dimension, Aetna preferred to foreclose the issue in connection with the bankruptcy, even at a substantial cost. A mandatory class action—if one could somehow be certified despite the consistent authority to the contrary—would provide that opportunity.[3] And an opponent who had no experience in contested Dalkon Shield litigation and who was disposed to a friendly settlement made the prospect even more attractive.

A potential obstacle to filing suit against Aetna was the outstanding injunction against co-defendant litigation. The principal reason Robins had offered and Merhige had adopted for enjoining litigation against Aetna was that any recovery would reduce the remaining insurance coverage, which was an asset of Robins's estate. This reason did not apply to suits alleging Aetna's independent liability, where recovery would not come out of Robins's insurance coverage. Yet Judge Merhige had stated that the injunction would apply to "all similarly situated persons," and, in one of the eight cases named in the injunction, the plaintiff, Anna Piccinin, was asserting a claim against Aetna based on its own conduct.

Despite this complication, on April 9, 1986, while the government's motion to hold Robins in contempt of court for its payment of prepetition debt was occupying center stage in Richmond, Joseph Friedberg filed suit against Aetna in federal district court in Minneapolis in the name of Glenda Breland and six other women, none of whom lived in Minnesota. The *Breland* suit was framed as a mandatory class action on behalf of all present and future Dalkon Shield claimants. Friedberg filed the suit in association with class action expert Herbert Newberg, St. Paul attorney John Cochrane, and three other lawyers from the Twin Cities with whom Friedberg had been associated in his prebankruptcy and postbankruptcy efforts to maintain a class action against Robins.

Friedberg filed the complaint in Minnesota because he questioned whether the clerk of the federal district court in Richmond would have accepted it without Judge Merhige's approval. Friedberg could, of course, have filed a motion asking Merhige to allow the suit to be filed, but such a request would have engendered opposition from plaintiffs' attorneys, as well as alternative proposals for proceeding against Aetna. Friedberg preferred to file his suit in Minnesota and cause it to be transferred to Richmond before any of these issues were raised. Friedberg filed with the complaint a document entitled "Plaintiffs' Consent to Transfer and Stay" in which he referred to Merhige's injunction against co-defendant litigation and consented to a transfer of the action to Merhige's court.

Eight days after the suit was filed, on April 17, 1986, Friedberg and Cochrane and Thomas J. Collins, an attorney in St. Paul representing Aetna, executed a stipulation asking for the transfer of the case to Richmond. On April 28, 1986, Judge Paul Magnuson of the federal district court in Minnesota, reciting that he was acting "pursuant to the Stipulation of Counsel," granted the transfer to Richmond. Although Aetna had joined Friedberg in requesting the transfer, both Friedberg and John Harkins of the Philadelphia law firm of Pepper, Hamilton & Sheetz, who represented Aetna in the *Breland* action in Judge Merhige's court, repeatedly represented that the case was transferred by the court in Minnesota "sua sponte," meaning on its own without a request from any party.[4] The point, presumably, was to deflect suggestions that Aetna had collaborated with Friedberg in the filing and transfer of the action.

In the meantime, on April 22, 1986, Murray Drabkin filed a motion asking Judge Merhige to authorize the claimants' committee to undertake discovery within the bankruptcy case on the issue of Aetna's independent liability to Dalkon Shield victims. Drabkin stated that "Aetna's liability to the Dalkon Shield claimants might give rise to a claim by the debtor [against Aetna] for common law contribution. This would significantly enhance the assets of the debtor's estate and its ability to satisfy Dalkon Shield claims." ("Contribution" is a doctrine that allows one wrongdoer to require another wrongdoer to share in the cost of paying the injured party's damages.) Aetna opposed Drabkin's motion, and on May 21, 1986, Merhige denied it, citing his desire to avoid the cost of the inquiry.[5]

Aetna's answer to the *Breland* complaint, filed on July 17, 1986, made no reference to the injunction against co-defendant litigation. Aetna denied the allegations of wrongdoing but strongly supported the suggestion that the suit be certified as a mandatory class action. In addition, in its enthusiasm to be sued in a class action handled by Joseph Friedberg, Aetna "stipulated" that, if a class action were certified, it would not contest any individual issues affecting the rights of class members (that is, use of a Dalkon Shield, injury, causation, and damages) and would agree that all such issues be resolved through the trust expected to be established under Robins's plan of reorganization. The purpose of this stipulation was to enhance the prospect of class action treatment by suggesting a mechanism by which the noncommon issues could be addressed without overloading the court with tens of thousands of individual determinations. Nonetheless, in offering this stipulation, Aetna seemed to reveal its expectation that the amount of its financial obligation to the class would be determined by settlement, because Aetna did not agree to allow the trustees appointed in the Robins bankruptcy to determine the total amount of money it owed women injured by the Dalkon Shield, and it is unclear how the court could make this determination without an examination of individual cases. The implication that the case would be settled only served to reinforce the nonadversarial appearance of the *Breland* action. Later, in arguing for the claimants' committee against class certification in *Breland*, Mark Ellenberg categorized Aetna's stipulation as "illusory."

The promise held out by the Breland plaintiffs is that they will obtain a fixed sum of money from Aetna that they will deposit with the estate for distribution under the reorganization plan. Your Honor, Aetna's liability is the sum of its liability to each individual. If that liability is not going to be liquidated in the class action, how will any sum of money be forthcoming from this proceeding? I simply don't understand it.[6]

Aetna never offered an explanation of this point.

Judge Merhige held a conference in the *Breland* case on July 23, 1986. At this conference Merhige made no reference to the injunction against co-defendant litigation. Instead, he directed the two sides, both of which favored a class action, to file briefs in support of the request.

A month later, on August 21, 1986, a group of twenty-three attorneys, most of whom had been members of the first claimants' committee, filed suit against Aetna in the federal district court in Kansas on behalf of 4,200 women claiming Dalkon Shield–related injuries. These attorneys were unwilling to have their clients' rights against Aetna determined in a class action before Judge Merhige led by Joseph Friedberg, and they inferred from the treatment of the *Breland* suit that suits against Aetna based only on its own conduct were not foreclosed by Merhige's injunction. The Kansas lawsuit, styled *Alexia Anderson, et al. v. Aetna Casualty & Surety Company*, was not filed as a class action. The driving forces in filing the suit were John T. Baker, Bradley Post, and Robert Manchester, the attorneys who had led the opposition first to Robins's and then to Friedberg's prebankruptcy efforts to certify a class action against Robins before Judge Merhige.

Aetna's response to the *Anderson* suit was quite different from its response to *Breland*. Scott Street, Aetna's lawyer in Richmond, called the lead counsel for the plaintiffs in *Anderson* and demanded that the case be dismissed. When they refused, Street and James Crockett of Mays & Valentine, representing Robins, went to see Judge Merhige and asked him to hold the lawyers who had filed the suit in contempt of court for violation of the injunction against co-defendant litigation. On August 25, 1986, not long after the friendly conference in *Breland*, Merhige issued an order requiring all twenty-three lawyers for the plaintiffs in the *Anderson* action to appear in his court on September 4, 1986, "and then and there show cause why they should not be found in civil contempt of this court." A contempt citation implies serious misconduct and can jeopardize an attorney's right to continue to practice law.

At the hearing on September 4, 1986, the lawyers in the *Anderson* action argued that Merhige's injunction against co-defendant litigation was inapplicable to suits against Aetna that would not deplete the insurance available to Robins. They also emphasized that, as far as the injunction was concerned, the *Anderson* suit was not different from the *Breland* suit, to which no objection had been raised.

But Merhige was in no mood to listen. Without referring to *Breland*, he stated flatly that under the injunction "all action against Aetna is stayed if it has anything to do with the Dalkon Shield." He made clear that he would find all the lawyers in the *Anderson* action in contempt of court unless they dismissed that action and reimbursed Robins and Aetna for the expenses they had incurred as a result of the filing.

Faced with this choice, Baker, Post, and their colleagues—still smarting from their exclusion from the Chapter 11 case in favor of claimant representatives to the judge's liking, and now threatened with contempt for suing Aetna while Friedberg was permitted to proceed on behalf of their clients—swallowed the bitter pill and, to avoid being held in contempt, agreed to Merhige's terms.

The *Anderson* action was dismissed, but Robins and Aetna and the Anderson attorneys were unable to reach agreement on the amounts of attorney fees and expenses to be reimbursed. The companies then filed motions asking Merhige to approve the amounts they had requested. In response, Stanley Joynes, the former law clerk whom Merhige had chosen to serve as legal representative of future claimants, took it upon himself to file a remarkable memorandum criticizing "the tenor" of the September 4 hearing and suggesting that a "significant unfairness" would result if the lawyers who had been threatened with contempt were required to pay Robins's and Aetna's fees and expenses. Joynes went on:

"Reward your friends and punish your enemies" is a rule of politics, not of law and certainly not of equity. No party to this proceeding in equity should be heard to seek the invocation of this Court's contempt powers depending on the identity and perceived purpose of the opposing party . . . It is palpably inequitable simply to ignore the stay in a case clearly brought in violation of the stay [*Breland*][7] while seeking a contempt citation in a later-filed case which is arguably not stayed by the express terms of this Court's order. This is precisely the situation which Aetna and Robins brought to the court . . . When the defendants filed the *Anderson* action, they had every reason to believe that their conduct was not in violation of the stay.[8]

With a minor adjustment, Judge Merhige granted Robins and Aetna the fees they had requested. In his memorandum, Merhige dismissed arguments based on *Breland*: "*Breland* was not filed to open the floodgate of suits against Aetna. Instead, it was filed with the Court's acquiescence, in an effort to monitor, in the most cost efficient manner, a suit filed by claimants against Aetna."9 This statement, which suggested that Merhige had been consulted and had approved the filing of the *Breland* action, was never explained.

Following the contempt proceeding growing out of the *Anderson* action in Kansas, the battle for control of the claim against Aetna intensified. On September 18, 1986, the Dalkon Shield claimants' committee filed a motion asking Merhige to enjoin the *Breland* action, to appoint a "special counsel" to evaluate the claim against Aetna, and, if it was determined to have merit, to prosecute the claim on behalf of all Dalkon Shield claimants under the supervision of the claimants' committee. In reaction to Merhige citing the factor of cost a few months earlier in denying the claimants' committee's request for authority to investigate Aetna's potential liability, the claimants' committee now proposed to retain special counsel "on a contingent fee basis to avoid any legal fees to the estate in the absence of recovery."

On October 7, 1986, the same attorneys who had brought the ill-fated *Anderson* action in Kansas filed motions asking Judge Merhige to modify the injunction against co-defendant litigation to permit individual actions against Aetna in Kansas and in New Hampshire. In support of their requests, these attorneys argued that the lengthy periods in which suit could be filed in those states would be advantageous to the plaintiffs. They also suggested that any judgments imposed against Aetna would reduce the liabilities of the Robins estate without any offsetting increases, because the law in Kansas and New Hampshire would not allow Aetna to seek contribution from Robins. Both Robins and Aetna filed oppositions to these motions, urging Merhige to prevent all litigation against Aetna except the Friedberg class action.

On October 30, 1986, the issue of how and by whom the claims against Aetna would be handled came to a head. Both Friedberg's motion for certification of the *Breland* suit as a mandatory class action and the motion of the claimants' committee to enjoin the *Breland* action and to employ a special counsel to proceed against Aetna came before Judge Merhige for a hearing. In the background were the requests from members of the plaintiffs' bar for permission to proceed independently against Aetna.

No federal court had ever allowed a mandatory class action for compensatory damages in a personal injury case.[10] In addition, a recent decision of the Supreme Court had strongly implied, if not actually held, that individuals have a constitutional right, as a matter of due process of law, to "opt-out" of a class action for money damages and to maintain their own action.[11] Much of the argument on the class action motion was devoted to technical legal analysis of whether an exception could be made in this instance because of the large number of claims involved, because of the relationship of the claims against Aetna to the Robins bankruptcy, and because of Aetna's "stipulation" that it would not contest issues relating to individual class members.

Although the arguments concerned the intricacies of federal class action law and the practicality of alternative procedures, the real point of contention was Joe Friedberg. Murray Drabkin and his partner Mark Ellenberg did not believe that Friedberg had either the experience or the resources necessary to maintain serious litigation against Aetna, and they had doubts about his will to do so. Most of the lawyers interested in litigation against Aetna, as a matter of principle, would not have been happy with a mandatory class action regardless of who was at the helm, but the idea that it would be Friedberg, who they believed was unqualified for the task and in collusion with Robins, Aetna, and Merhige, brought a special urgency to their opposition. They strongly doubted that Aetna would have been volunteering stipulations to facilitate class certification if the class was to be represented by a lawyer with a track record of fighting and beating large corporations in major litigation.

On the other hand and, as things turned out, far more important, Judge Merhige was comfortable with Joe Friedberg and was favorable toward him and his associates taking the lead in class action litigation against Aetna. Friedberg's background and style is similar to Merhige's, something that cannot be said of any other of the dozens of personal injury lawyers and big-firm bankruptcy lawyers from outside Richmond who appeared in Merhige's court in connection with the Robins bankruptcy. Merhige and Friedberg are both New Yorkers who attended small southern law schools and then took up residence in communities far from home. They both specialized in criminal defense, a typical niche for lawyers outside the local establishment, and they both achieved success, even prosperity, in that line of work.

When Friedberg's Dalkon Shield cases were transferred to Judge Merhige's court in the fall of 1984, he had the good sense to show up with the judge's friend Murray Janus as his local co-counsel. Friedberg established friendly relations with Robins's counsel at McGuire, Woods & Battle and at Mays & Valentine, and quickly established himself as someone who was ready to settle cases without much conflict or difficulty. It could be expected that Friedberg would not present an obstacle when the time came to settle a class claim against Aetna in exchange for Aetna's participation in some way in a plan of reorganization. Whether or not Merhige had actually encouraged Friedberg to file his pre-bankruptcy class action against Robins when they were alone together in June 1985, Merhige clearly appreciated that the filing had been made and was enthusiastic about the possibilities it offered to resolve the Robins crisis short of bankruptcy. And when, in February 1986, Mer-hige's visits with Friedberg and with Messrs. Robins at his home the preceding summer were cited as bases to disqualify the judge from presiding over the Chapter 11 case, Friedberg quickly filed an affidavit that corroborated Merhige's account of both incidents. Merhige liked Friedberg and saw him as a "one hundred percent cooperative" lawyer with whom he could do business.[12]

The divergent assessments of Joe Friedberg were dramatized by Michael Ciresi's unexpected appearance at the October 30, 1986, hearing as the claimants' committee's candidate to be special counsel to pursue the claims against Aetna. Ciresi is the Minneapolis lawyer who had obtained two large jury verdicts against Robins in 1983. Under Judge Lord's auspices, he had then taken the depositions of top Robins management up to and including E. Claiborne Robins, Sr., and ultimately had settled 205 Dalkon Shield cases for over $42 million, an average of more than $200,000 per case. After those settlements, Ciresi had not participated in any further Dalkon Shield litigation, but he had carefully cataloged and made available to plaintiffs' lawyers all the evidence that had been developed against Robins in all of the litigation over a ten-year period.[13]

Ciresi was now lead counsel for the government of India in the litigation seeking damages from Union Carbide following the Bhopal disaster in which more than five hundred thousand people had been injured. Ciresi was also active in litigation against G. D. Searle relating to the Copper 7 IUD, in which he would later obtain an $8 million jury verdict for one woman, followed by unprecedented settlements for many others. Ciresi, backed up by his 200-lawyer firm, had agreed to serve as special counsel to investigate and litigate the claim against Aetna on a contingent fee basis, so there would be no issue of cost to the estate.

Thus, apart from the technical differences between the two proposals, one would vest responsibility for the claim against Aetna in an experienced and remarkably successful mass tort lawyer, backed by substantial resources in terms of money and manpower and widely admired by the members of the plaintiffs' bar, while the other would grant this trust to an attorney with no experience in product liability litigation, sparse resources, and the widespread enmity of the plaintiffs' bar.

Called to the witness stand by Ellenberg, Ciresi explained that his approach would be to investigate vigorously the facts relative to Aetna's possible liability for Dalkon Shield injuries.

CIRESI: [The question is,] what was Aetna's involvement in the perpetration of any fraud which led to infertility, death and other injuries sustained by these women? . . . People don't really get to the table until their feet are to the fire . . . You have an opportunity here to select cases and go forward and start with the discovery against Aetna . . . start finding out what Aetna knew, when they knew it, and what did they do about it and how high up it goes . . .

I know the Minneapolis lawyers. I know they are fine attorneys. I also know they don't have the experience that somebody like me or Doug Bragg or Brad Post would have in Dalkon Shield. Doesn't mean they're not good attorneys.

MERHIGE: Be fair about it. How many Dalkon Shield cases have been tried? Fifty?

CIRESI: Forty-eight, fifty, in that range, yes.

MERHIGE: That is spread over what, ten lawyers or so? . . . The point I am trying to make is I disagree with you that there are any real Dalkon Shield trial experts. I think any good trial lawyer who knows what he is doing can do it, because nobody has tried enough Dalkon Shield cases.

CIRESI: I disagree with you, Judge . . . I was at war with them for seven months in trial, and I disagree on that. If you are saying any good able attorney can learn a case and try it, then I am not disagreeing with you, but there is a distinct difference particularly in this litigation in the defenses that were built up over many years and how you attack those defenses, and what you have to know to get up to speed. There is a dramatic difference.

Ciresi made clear that he was opposed to the certification of a class action until after the claims against Aetna had been fully investigated in a non–class action and, preferably, after Aetna's liability had been established in court. At that point, according to Ciresi, a class could be certified for purposes of settlement without the risk of binding unwilling claimants to an unsuccessful result, the case could be settled on a class basis with solid knowledge of what it was worth, and a good settlement would attract the support instead of the opposition of the plaintiffs' bar.

Following the formal arguments, during which positions were expressed by a dozen lawyers, the discussion continued in Judge Merhige's chambers. Merhige tried to take advantage of Ciresi's expertise without displacing Friedberg or discarding a class action as the vehicle in which to proceed against Aetna. Merhige proposed that a ruling on class certification be deferred until some discovery had been undertaken jointly by the Friedberg group and Ciresi. Addressing Friedberg, the judge said:

What I really have in mind is for you and Mr. Cochrane and whoever and Mr. Ciresi to sit down and work out a plan of operation as to how do we proceed here to determine whether we really have a viable claim . . . I can assure you that if you come back and say "yes," there is going to be a class certified and you will be named as counsel if that is the concern. I am trying to be as practical as I can—it has to be there, Joe.

But neither Friedberg and Cochrane nor Ciresi was happy with this idea. Friedberg and Cochrane were willing to include Ciresi among counsel for the class, but they wanted to be recognized as counsel for the class immediately.

FRIEDBERG: [I]f we certify now . . . it becomes immediately appealable while we are trying to determine whether there is a viable claim, the people will take it up [on appeal], and then we will know whether or not we can have a settlement class . . .

MERHIGE: You look me right in the eye and you tell me why you think it is necessary to have the class certified now.

FRIEDBERG: So that we know.

MERHIGE: As distinguished from two months from now?

FRIEDBERG: So that we know if we proceed the [court of appeals] has already told us that we have a viable instrument . . .

COCHRANE: If the okay came down from the [court of appeals], that discovery would apply to the entire class, Your Honor. That is important.

MERHIGE: Please stop, John, stop. I don't mean to be facetious, maybe it is late in the day. Just be quiet for a minute. We have had lots of cases here. Joe, as always, has been very cooperative. I know him from his work here, you all bear good reputations but the truth of the matter is somehow, and maybe you are not even conscious of it yourself, you guys are afraid you are going to get slipped out somewhere and you are not going to get the fee, and that is as honest as I can be, and I know it is true. I practiced law and I was the most generous lawyer you ever saw, but it always helped when I got paid. And it has to be there in the back of your mind . . .

FRIEDBERG: It is important, there is no doubt about that. But I am not worried that if there is a class certified, somebody else will be class counsel. I am not worried in the least. Nobody else wants it.

For his part, Ciresi reiterated his belief that it would be a mistake to proceed in a class action before Aetna's liability had been established in individual litigation.

The discussion ended without any agreement. On November 4, 1986, Judge Merhige issued an order allowing discovery to go forward in the *Breland* case and, apparently without further consulting Ciresi, directing counsel for *Breland* to cooperate with Ciresi in evaluating the claims against Aetna. A few days later, in a conference call, Merhige asked Ciresi to become associated with Friedberg in the prosecution of *Breland* as a class action. Ciresi said that he would not do this, and Merhige took no further action on the motion for the appointment of a special counsel.

In a brief order dated December 1, 1986, Judge Merhige relied on the pendency of the *Breland* action in denying the motions to allow individual litigation against Aetna to go forward in Kansas or New Hampshire.

> While *Breland*, at present, is not dispositive of the issues presented by this motion, the Court has pending before it in that matter a motion to certify a class action. If *Breland* is so certified, it would appear that the instant plaintiffs might well be members of the certified class. Accordingly, the Court will deny the relief requested, subject to reconsideration if the *Breland* case is not certified as a class action or if certified so as to permit opt[ing] out and plaintiffs choose to do so.

On December 29, 1986, Judge Merhige entered an order in the *Breland* case "conditionally certifying" a class action, "subject to further consideration in light of discovery developments, whether this action should continue to be maintained as a class action, and if so, in what form." Merhige did not specify whether any class he did finally certify would be mandatory or optional, and as a result no appeal from his order was possible.

Joseph McDowell, a lawyer from Manchester, New Hampshire, who specializes in the representation of plaintiffs in personal injury cases, took the lead in an appeal of Merhige's refusal to allow individual suits against Aetna. On September 9, 1987, the court of appeals affirmed.[14] Where Judge Merhige had simply relied on the pendency of *Breland*, Judge Donald Russell, for the court of appeals, concluded instead that an action against Aetna would cause "irreparable harm to the bankruptcy estate . . . That harm would be the burden placed on Robins' officers, directors and employees, which would exhaust their energies and thus interfere with the debtor's reorganization."[15] Merhige had made no findings on this subject and Judge Russell gave no hint of how he knew that litigation against Aetna would "exhaust the energies" of Robins's personnel.

Indeed, McDowell had offered not to seek discovery from Robins or its officials and to rely solely on information already in his possession. Judge Russell concluded, however, that Aetna would be forced to involve Robins in the litigation because "under a system of comparative negligence, the trier of fact must determine Robins' relative fault in order to determine Aetna's relative fault."[16]

In a petition for rehearing, McDowell demonstrated that Kansas and

New Hampshire do not have systems of comparative negligence and that under the laws of those states Aetna would not be permitted to raise the issue of Robins's fault. The petition was denied without comment.

Thus, as the Robins bankruptcy moved toward a plan of reorganization, the only claim against Aetna was squarely in Joseph Friedberg's hands, in the form of an undefined and malleable class action that could provide a mechanism to protect Aetna from future liability in exchange for a contribution to a fund to compensate Dalkon Shield victims.

10   Emergency Fertility
Procedures

In late August 1985, just a few days after Robins entered Chapter 11, an organization known as the National Women's Health Network filed a motion asking Judge Merhige to require Robins to establish an emergency fund during the bankruptcy to reimburse women with unresolved Dalkon Shield claims for the costs of medical procedures related to the restoration of fertility.

Robert Stillman, director of the Division of Reproductive Endocrinology and Fertility and a professor of obstetrics and gynecology at George Washington University Hospital in Washington, D.C., submitted an affidavit in support of the motion. In his affidavit Stillman explained that a frequent reason why women become infertile following pelvic inflammatory disease is that scar tissue caused by the infection blocks the fallopian tubes. Some women with that condition can become pregnant after the surgical removal of the scar tissue, a procedure known as "tuboplasty," or by in vitro fertilization, a procedure that bypasses the fallopian tubes.

Stillman estimated that 5 to 10 percent of the women who were infertile as a result of their use of the Dalkon Shield could benefit from these procedures but emphasized the importance of time.

[There is a] significant decrease in the success rate of infertility treatment . . . as the woman's age increases. In fact, many infertility specialists do not perform surgery in individuals approaching or over the age of 40 years. Many *in vitro* fertilization programs utilize 35 or 40 years of age as upper limits for exclusion. Thus, the younger the reproductive age a women begins and proceeds through an infertility evaluation and treatment, the greater the likelihood of success of achieving pregnancy.

In 1985 most women who had used the Dalkon Shield were in their mid- to late thirties. Because of "the ticking of the biological clock," fertility procedures held promise for these women only if they could be begun quickly. Even for younger women, the likelihood of becoming

129

pregnant after tuboplasty or in vitro fertilization decreased as they became older, so time was of the essence for all potential beneficiaries.

Tuboplasty and in vitro fertilization are recently developed medical procedures and can cost more than $20,000. They are generally not covered by medical insurance. Before the Robins bankruptcy, many women who settled Dalkon Shield claims used the money they received to pay for fertility procedures. This source of funds was cut off by the bankruptcy.

Robins strongly opposed the motion to provide funds for fertility procedures. At the first hearing in the Chapter 11 case, on September 21, 1985, Judge Merhige vowed that checks to injured women "would be in the mail in one year." In response, the Health Network decided not to press the issue.

During the life of the first Dalkon Shield claimants' committee and again after the second claimants' committee was appointed, Murray Drabkin raised the matter of providing funds for medical fertility procedures during the Chapter 11 case with Judge Merhige and with counsel for Robins, but to no avail. The company was unwilling to relieve the pressure on the claimants' committee for a quick settlement that resulted from the urgent need of many of its constituents for funds to pay for fertility procedures. Robins took the position that the claimants' committee could secure funds to pay for tuboplasty or in vitro fertilization by agreeing on a plan of reorganization. Judge Merhige did not press Robins on the matter.

When Ralph Mabey was appointed examiner in August 1986, Drabkin raised the issue with him and Mabey responded favorably. Mabey urged Robins to cooperate in developing a mechanism to provide immediate funds for fertility procedures. With a wide range of matters important to the company affected by Mabey's goodwill, Robins changed its position and, in the spring of 1987, agreed to establish an emergency medical fund.

Under the terms of the agreement, the company would make a total of $15 million available, with no payment for any woman to exceed $15,000. Eligibility for the program was strictly limited in order to select women who were both likely to become pregnant with the help of a fertility procedure and also entitled to compensation under a plan of reorganization. The following were the requirements for participation:

1. a woman must be an eligible claimant in the Chapter 11 case;
2. she must be less than forty years old;

3. she must submit complete certified medical records that would show, to the satisfaction of a panel of medical experts,
    a. tubal infertility due to obstruction of her fallopian tubes from pelvic inflammatory disease,
    b. that a Dalkon Shield had been inserted before the first diagnosis of pelvic inflammatory disease and before the first diagnosis of tubal infertility
    c. proof of ovulation, male fertility, and unsuccessful efforts to conceive for at least twelve months,
    d. an absence of possible causes of pelvic inflammatory disease other than the Dalkon Shield, such as gonorrhea,
    e. an absence of possible causes of infertility other than pelvic inflammatory disease,
    f. no pregnancies following Dalkon Shield use, and
    g. the use of no other IUD; and
4. she must submit an affidavit from her physician stating that her chances of conceiving could be improved by tubal reconstructive surgery or in vitro fertilization.

Under the terms of the program, payments for fertility procedures would be deducted from the amount the woman would otherwise receive under the confirmed plan of reorganization. If, however, a beneficiary of the program was later determined, for some reason, not to be entitled to any amount under a plan of reorganization or to be entitled to an amount less than the amount of the payments that had been made on her behalf, she would not be required to make a refund.

The agreement between Ralph Mabey and A. H. Robins was set forth in a joint motion seeking Judge Merhige's approval. The motion was supported by Murray Drabkin on behalf of the claimants' committee, by Stanley Joynes on behalf of the future claimants, and by Assistant United States Attorney David Schiller on behalf of the Internal Revenue Service. Only the equity committee—the official committee representing Robins's shareholders—opposed the motion. Judge Merhige had undoubtedly been consulted about the matter, and there was little doubt that he would grant the motion.

On May 18, 1987, at the hearing on the motion to establish the emergency fund, there was an air of jubilation. Stanley Joynes captured the general feeling when he said, "It is the best exercise of the court's equitable power I can imagine, and it is the right thing to do, the best thing we have done to date."

But because the emergency fund was opposed by the equity committee, it could not simply be approved by consent. Robins's obligations to the women who would participate in the program constituted prepetition debt of the estate. For Judge Merhige to approve payments to these women, it was necessary to establish a legal basis for deviating from the normal Chapter 11 procedure under which prepetition claims are paid in accordance with the terms of a confirmed plan of reorganization.

The proponents of the emergency fund relied on section 503(b)(1)(A) of the Bankruptcy Code, which defines "administrative expenses" as "the actual, necessary costs and expenses of preserving the estate." Because administrative expenses are said to be incurred for the benefit of the prepetition creditors, the supposed beneficiaries of the reorganization proceeding, these expenses are given first priority in the distribution of the estate.[1] Beyond that, although there is no explicit statutory authority for the practice, administrative expenses are frequently paid during a Chapter 11 case, with the approval of the court. The rationale is that some preconfirmation payments of administrative expenses are necessary to preserve the estate or maintain the going concern. For example, employees would not work and suppliers would not send materials if they knew they would not be paid for several years.

Mabey submitted a statistical analysis designed to show that the disbursements under the emergency program would increase the value of Robins's estate by reducing its liabilities. The analysis showed that, in the two years preceding the bankruptcy, Dalkon Shield cases involving pelvic inflammatory disease *and* infertility were settled for an average of $70,000; cases involving pelvic inflammatory disease *without* infertility were settled for an average of $38,000.[2] Each successful in vitro fertilization or reconstructive surgery would move a woman from the more expensive to the less expensive category and reduce the cost of settling her claim.

Mabey also submitted affidavits from medical doctors in the field setting forth various success rates for fertility procedures. The rates ranged from 20 to 60 percent or higher, depending on how carefully the participants were selected. One calculation, based on an assumed 30 percent pregnancy rate among one thousand participants in the program, indicated that the program would save $9.6 million in settlement costs.[3]

These figures also demonstrated that the proposed distributions were below those that could be expected under a plan of reorganization. Robins and Merhige had consistently pledged that all Dalkon Shield claims would be paid "in full." Even if this proved to be an overstatement, it was nearly certain that a woman whose medical records met the requirements for participation in the program would recover at least

$15,000 under a plan of reorganization. Thus, all or nearly all of the $15 million would be offset against the estate's obligations to the beneficiaries under a confirmed plan of reorganization. Any amount that could not be offset would be far smaller than the savings in settlement costs engendered by the program.

In support of the program, Examiner Mabey also relied on section 105 of the code, which authorizes the court to "issue any order, process, or judgment that is necessary or appropriate to carry out the provisions" of the statute. Mabey cited a recent case that recognized the discretion of the court to authorize preconfirmation payments of prepetition debt on the basis of the exigencies of a special situation.[4]

The equity committee was represented in the Robins bankruptcy by Robert Miller, then a thirty-six-year-old graduate of St. John's Law School in New York. Miller specializes in bankruptcy law as a member of the New York firm of Bishop, Liberman & Cook. Throughout the proceeding Miller presented a hard line, often harder than company management, against the interests of the Dalkon Shield claimants.

At the hearing Miller stated that "as human beings we are completely and fully sympathetic to the goals sought to be achieved by this motion, and our objection does not go to any aspect that touches upon those matters." But he went on to argue that the proposed emergency program was prohibited by Chapter 11 because it called for the payment of disputed, unliquidated prepetition claims before a plan of reorganization was confirmed. Miller emphasized the possibility that payments would be made for the benefit of women who would ultimately be found not to be entitled to compensation. Although that possibility existed, the evidence suggested that overall the program would save money for the estate. Miller did not address this evidence or explain why the equity committee opposed the program. The shareholders were apparently prepared to use the plight of the women who could benefit from fertility procedures, but who could not afford to pay for them, to induce the claimants' committee to make concessions with respect to a plan of reorganization.

Three days after the hearing, on May 21, 1987, Judge Merhige granted the joint motion to establish the fund. Merhige found that a "true emergency exists for these infertile claimants because . . . any further lapse of time could permanently deprive them of an opportunity to bear children." He found that "there is no question" but that women who meet the eligibility requirements of the program will have "a claim for damages [in] . . . a substantial amount" and that, because of the recoupment provisions of the program and the potential for mitigation of damages, the emergency fund "would not deplete the debtor's estate." He also found that his approval of the emergency fund was "necessary or appropriate to carry out the provisions" of the bankruptcy laws and was thus authorized by section 105 of the code.

Judge Merhige refused to delay the program during an appeal, and notices of the emergency fund were immediately mailed to all of the women who had qualified as eligible claimants in the Robins bankruptcy. It is a measure of the need that existed that, within four days of the mailing, 401 telephone calls were received asking for more information and for application forms.

On behalf of the equity committee, Miller quickly filed a motion asking the court of appeals to suspend the emergency program during an appeal. A stay of an order of a district court pending appeal will be issued by an appellate court only if the party bringing the appeal establishes that it will suffer irreparable injury if a stay is not granted and that a stay will not result in substantial harm to other parties. Miller argued that Robins's shareholders would suffer irreparable injury in the absence of a stay because some of the payments from the emergency fund might not be recouped. He argued that the harm to the women who would benefit from the fund should not be considered, because these women "have not yet been determined to hold allowed claims; thus, they are not necessarily entitled to any duty or protection—let alone immediate recovery—from Debtor's estate."[5]

In opposition to the stay, Mabey and others made the court of appeals aware of the evidence indicating that the likelihood was that the program would save money for the estate and benefit the shareholders, and they argued that the relative equities demanded a denial of the stay. In the words of the examiner:

If a stay is granted, the mere passage of time will irreversibly alter the *status quo* for those women who will become ineligible for assistance during the pendency of the appeal. On balance, the prospect that some women . . . will permanently lose the opportunity to bear children if a stay is granted far outweighs the remote possibility of a *de minimis* loss to the estate.[6]

The judges of the United States Court of Appeals for the Fourth Circuit weighed this balance and decided that the potential injury to the shareholders predominated. On July 7, 1987, the court stayed all aspects of the emergency fund program pending an appeal by the equity committee.

Four months later, the court of appeals ruled that the emergency program was unlawful.[7] Writing for the court, Judge Robert Chapman said he could "understand and sympathize with . . . the Dalkon Shield claimants who may desire reconstructive surgery or *in vitro* fertilization" but found that the creation of the fund "violates the clear language and intent of the Bankruptcy Code."[8]

The Bankruptcy Code does not permit a distribution to unsecured creditors in a Chapter 11 proceeding except under and pursuant to a plan of reorganization that has been properly presented and approved . . . The creation of the Emergency Treatment Program has no authority to support it in the Bankruptcy Code and violates the clear policy of Chapter 11 reorganizations by allowing piecemeal, pre-confirmation payments to certain unsecured creditors.[9]

In his opinion, Judge Chapman omitted or misstated the facts and the authorities in conflict with his conclusion. In the face of the strict eligibility requirements incorporated in the program, Chapman asserted that any claimant was eligible for participation if "(a) she is less than 40 years old; (b) she claims infertility; and (c) she is not surgically infertile."[10] The judge did not even mention the evidence indicating that the program would enhance the value of the estate by reducing Robins's liability, or the contention that the program was authorized by section 503(b) of the Bankruptcy Code as a means to reduce costs and preserve the estate. Chapman also failed to note the authority suggesting that a bankruptcy court may authorize a deviation from strict distributional priorities where it is justified by special circumstances and not prejudicial to the rights of other creditors.[11] Thus, the court of appeals never came to grips with the important question of the ability of the Bankruptcy Code to respond to the urgency actually presented.

The court of appeals decision in November 1987 ended all efforts to finance fertility procedures before the completion of the Chapter 11 case. It would be more than two and a half years before funds for these procedures were made available under a confirmed plan of reorganization. By that time, it would be too late for many of the women who might have benefited from the original proposal. In the summer of 1988 Judge Merhige told the *New York Times* that he regretted his decision approving the emergency fund. "I ruled with my heart and not my head," the judge said.[12]

11   The Exclusivity Period

A reorganization under Chapter 11 can take place only under the provisions of a court-approved ("confirmed") plan of reorganization. The Bankruptcy Code grants a debtor-in-possession a period after the filing of the case in which it has the exclusive right to file a plan of reorganization. Initially, this exclusivity period is 120 days but it can be extended by the court "for cause." If the exclusivity period is allowed to expire before the debtor has filed a plan, any party with an interest in doing so may file a plan of reorganization.[1] The purpose of the exclusivity period is to encourage negotiations and agreement on a plan of reorganization. It is limited in duration to prevent the debtor from "starving" its creditors into agreement by preventing consideration of any plan other than its own.[2]

Extensions of the exclusivity period are frequently granted in large Chapter 11 cases, but when there is opposition from the creditors, detailed and persuasive reasons for an extension are usually articulated.[3] In the Robins bankruptcy, Judge Merhige repeatedly extended the exclusivity period, over the opposition of the claimants' committee, for no discernible reason other than to foreclose noncompany plans. Robins did not file a plan of reorganization until April 1987, when the Chapter 11 case was twenty months old. The exclusivity period was then continued while Robins filed six amended plans before it secured confirmation of the last of these, its Sixth Amended Plan of Reorganization, in July 1988. The inability of the claimants' committee to propose its own plan of reorganization at any time was a major factor in shaping the outcome of the Chapter 11 proceeding.

The long delay in the submission, consideration, and approval of a plan of reorganization had significant advantages for Robins and disadvantages for women injured by the Dalkon Shield. For Robins, despite the inconvenience and even the indignity of the bankruptcy proceeding, the interim economic situation was not unattractive. As a result of the automatic stay, Robins was freed from the expense and the pressures of Dalkon Shield litigation. At the same time, because of its status as a debtor-in-possession, the company could not pay dividends to its shareholders. Robins was realizing profits in excess of $10 million a month, and with this money going neither toward Dalkon Shield expenses nor to shareholders, the longer the bankruptcy continued, the stronger and more valuable the company became. In the meantime, women injured by the Dalkon Shield were without compensation for their injuries. And, under the plan of reorganization that was finally approved, the women were not paid interest to compensate them for the delay in payment attributable to the Chapter 11 case, interest that collectively would have amounted to over $1 billion.[4] The result was that, in real dollars, two opposite phenomena were taking place: the assets of A. H. Robins were increasing, and the cost of its debt was declining. The pressure to compromise was squarely on the representatives of the injured women.

The original exclusivity period terminated on December 19, 1985. When Robins filed its first request for an extension, in late November 1985, it had not yet met with representatives of the claimants' committee to discuss a plan of reorganization. In support of its request, the company argued that it could not propose a plan until after the April 30, 1986, bar date, when it would know how many claims had been filed. For the claimants' committee, Murray Drabkin opposed the extension. He argued that Robins had other, better means of estimating its liability to Dalkon Shield victims and that the prospect of competing plans would stimulate action by the company and expedite a resolution of the case.

After a lengthy argument on December 16, 1985, Judge Merhige concluded that Robins should be afforded some additional time, but only until March 31, 1986, one month before the bar date. This was still during the phase in which Merhige maintained that the injured women would be paid by September 1986, one year after the case was filed, and he told Penn Butler, of Murphy, Weir & Butler, Robins's bankruptcy counsel, not to expect any further extension. "Something so horrendous that I don't even want to think of it will have to happen before you get any [further] extension from me. Now I mean it . . . [If] you ask and you don't have a good reason, have your resignation come with it. That is how serious I am. I am not being facetious."

On March 24, 1986—four days after Penn Butler was fired in the wake of disclosures of Robins's payments of prepetition debt—the company moved for an extension of the exclusivity period to June 30, 1986. Murray Drabkin urged Judge Merhige not to grant another extension. "After some three months of negotiations," Drabkin said, "the debtor [has] failed to put even a general dollar amount on the table let alone a complete plan."[5] Without comment, Merhige entered an order extending Robins's exclusivity period to June 30, 1986.

Then, on June 30, 1986, again over Drabkin's objection ("[Robins] has shown not the slightest interest in good faith negotiation"), Merhige granted the company's request to extend the exclusivity period to September 30, 1986, thus formally ending the talk of mailing payments to injured women within a year of the bankruptcy filing. Merhige told the company that he would terminate its exclusive right if he found that it was not conducting "honest and sincere" talks toward resolving the Dalkon Shield claims.[6]

In fact, during the first year of the Chapter 11 case, the parties made no progress toward agreement on a plan of reorganization. In November 1985 the first Dalkon Shield claimants' committee, at Judge Merhige's request, had submitted a proposed framework for the resolution of claims under a plan of reorganization. Under the committee's proposal, Robins's liability to women injured by the Dalkon Shield would not be limited. An independent trust would be established to attempt to settle, or if necessary to litigate, each claim. The proposal included a three-step procedure to simplify and to encourage settlement of claims without litigation. The claims would be paid in the order in which they were resolved from funds Robins provided to the trust. The committee was prepared to negotiate with Robins over the initial funding of the trust and over the proportion of Robins's profits that would be paid into the trust every year until all claims had been paid. If the trust funds were not adequate to pay all liquidated claims at any point, the claims would be paid over time in the order in which they had been liquidated. Because, in the fall of 1985, no one had any idea of the huge number of claims that would be filed, the proponents of this approach did not anticipate that this procedure would entail a long delay in the payment of claims.

The first meeting between Robins and the claimants' committee to discuss a plan of reorganization took place in Richmond on December 3, 1985. Over the next ten weeks, until March 1986, when Judge Merhige dissolved the first claimants' committee and Robins dismissed Murphy, Weir & Butler, four or five additional meetings were held. The early meetings were devoted to procedural issues, but when Robins finally gave its response to the proposal advanced by the claimants' committee, it was distinctly negative; Penn Butler referred to the committee's proposal derisively as the "pay and pay" plan. Robins saw the proposal as not fundamentally different from the prebankruptcy situation. Indeed, the company representatives expressed doubts—and as it turned out they were right—that the operating profits available to pay claims would be sufficient to cover the interest alone on liquidated claims lined up for payment. Robins considered the committee's proposal a prescription for the company forever to devote the lion's share of its earnings to Dalkon Shield claims.

The company did not propose a specific plan of reorganization at these early meetings, but it did emphasize five points it considered essential to any plan of reorganization. The first was that no one, including future claimants, who did not file a claim by the bar date be compensated. The second was that Robins's liability be fixed and limited—that the plan be "closed-end." The company took the position that its reorganization would not be "bankable"—the necessary financing could not be secured—unless there was an immutable cap on its liability. Robins's third essential point was that there be no punitive damages, that only compensatory damages be considered in fixing the amount of its liability. The fourth point was that individuals associated with the company, its officers, directors, and employees, as well as the company itself, be discharged from future liability, a concept that Butler described vividly as a "super discharge." And, lastly, a trust must be created to take on the responsibility of settling and defending claims, with money supplied by Robins in the amount fixed. The company wanted to get out of the business of defending Dalkon Shield injury claims. Except for the creation of a claimants' trust, none of Robins's essential points were acceptable to the committee.

Although in its negotiations with the claimants' committee Robins demanded that its liability be limited, it did not propose a figure. Butler took the position, whether as a negotiating tactic or otherwise, that the company had no basis on which to compute or justify a figure and he invited the committee to suggest a figure. But the committee's position remained that Robins's liability should not be capped, and it was unwilling to make a proposal inconsistent with that position. The result was that, in the negotiations preceding the dissolution of the first claimants' committee, neither side changed its stance on the basic structure of a plan of reorganization and no figure for Robins's total liability was ever proposed. Discussions were at an impasse. Before he was discharged, Butler had drafted a plan for filing on March 31, 1986, that simply committed the company to pay to a trust up to but no more than an unspecified amount to be determined by the court as the total value of all the Dalkon Shield injury claims.

As a result of the government's motion to hold Robins in contempt of court and to appoint a trustee, and the resulting discharge of Murphy, Weir & Butler, negotiations for a plan of reorganization were suspended in the months of March through August 1986. When the parties turned their attention back to the process of developing a plan of reorganization after this six-month hiatus, the situation had changed in several important respects. The original Dalkon Shield claimants' committee, dominated by lawyers who had battled with Robins before the bankruptcy, had been dissolved, and a new committee solidly under Murray Drabkin's control had been appointed. The giant New York firm of Skadden, Arps, Slate, Meagher & Flom had replaced Murphy, Weir & Butler as counsel for Robins, and the Skadden, Arps lawyers seemed to have established stronger footing with management. Joseph Friedberg was no longer competing for the right to represent the injured women in their claims against Robins, but Judge Merhige seemed prepared to designate Friedberg as the representative of the injured women with respect to claims against Aetna. By acquiescing in Friedberg's class action, Aetna had implied that it was willing to make some financial contribution to the resolution of the Dalkon Shield claims in exchange for immunity from further liability. Ralph Mabey, a bright and energetic former bankruptcy judge, had been appointed examiner and had made clear that he intended to play a major role in the development of a plan of reorganization. But the most significant new development, and the one that came to dominate the Chapter 11 case, was the massive, and totally unexpected, number of Dalkon Shield injury claims that had been filed in response to the bar date notice. An open-ended plan, under which Robins would make payments to a trust out of earnings until all claims had been satisfied, could no longer be seriously supported.

Indeed, insofar as Murray Drabkin was concerned, the number of claims filed dictated a sale of the company. Before the bankruptcy, in March 1985, B. Thomas Florence, vice-president of Resource Planning Corporation, a management consulting firm in Washington, had been retained by Robins to develop an estimate of its present and future Dalkon Shield liability for the company's use in taking a charge against profits in its accounting records. Florence limited his analysis to compensatory damage claims of women within the United States. He determined that Robins could expect some eight thousand new claims, in addition to the nearly four thousand that were pending on December 31, 1984, for a total of approximately twelve thousand cases. On the basis of past settlement costs, Florence estimated that it would cost $705 million to settle these cases.[7] Of that amount, $24 million had been allocated to the first quarter of 1985. Robins's actual Dalkon Shield expenses during that quarter were $39 million, which suggested that Florence's total estimate was low.

When more than 327,000 claims were filed in the Chapter 11 case,

Murray Drabkin did some rough calculations. On the basis of the assumption that $705 million was low for 12,000 cases, Drabkin concluded that, no matter what rational method was used to discount the number of claims—for duplicates, for false or mistaken claims, for claims that would be abandoned or withdrawn, for minor injuries—Robins's liability to women injured by the Dalkon Shield substantially exceeded $2 billion. At that time the available estimates of the total worth of the A. H. Robins Company—without its Dalkon Shield liability—were well under $2 billion. Drabkin also concluded that Robins could not finance the Dalkon Shield claims out of its stream of income, because its income—then approximately $120 million a year—was less than the interest on its obligations to Dalkon Shield victims.

Accordingly, Drabkin adopted the position that the only plan of reorganization to which he could agree would involve selling the company at the highest available price, holding the proceeds in some interest-bearing form, liquidating and then paying the Dalkon Shield claims (either in full or on a pro rata basis, depending on the relationship of the proceeds of the sale to Robins's total debt), and then, when that was done, if any money was left over, paying the balance to the shareholders. In other words, Drabkin rejected the idea that the funds available to pay the Dalkon Shield claims should be limited (other than by the worth of the company) before the claims were individually liquidated; he insisted on a distribution in accordance with the priorities established by the Bankruptcy Code. And, if Judge Merhige had ever allowed the claimants' committee to propose a plan of reorganization, this is what Drabkin would have proposed.

This analysis was an anathema to the Robins management, which remained determined, despite the response to the bar date notice, to see the company emerge from bankruptcy as an independent entity with no change in its existing ownership. Management rejected Drabkin's premise that Dr. Florence's report accurately reflected, or even understated, the company's liability to twelve thousand potential claimants. The company had accepted a charge on its 1984 financial records based on Florence's calculations, but it had done so only to satisfy the demands of its accountants. Top management, particularly Messrs. E. Claiborne Robins, did not expect to pay, or claimed that they did not expect to pay, the amount Florence had projected.

Moreover, Robins's officials distinguished between the twelve thousand lawsuits predicted by Florence and the responses to the bar date notice, most of which were only postcards filed by unrepresented women. Despite the overwhelming numbers, management insisted that the bar date responses did not include significantly more claims that were valid than had been assumed in Florence's study and that those that were valid involved a lower proportion of serious injuries than had been the case in the prebankruptcy litigation. Moreover, Robins maintained that substantial savings could be achieved, without reducing net recoveries, by compensating injured women through an alternative dispute resolution procedure established by a plan of reorganization. (Before the bankruptcy, only 37 cents of every dollar spent by Robins on the resolution of Dalkon Shield injury claims was received by injured women. The balance went to lawyers and experts on both sides of the litigation. In his calculations Dr. Florence had assumed that this would continue. An alternative dispute resolution procedure administered by a trust and stressing settlement would vastly reduce the costs on Robins's side. Claims filed by unrepresented women could be settled with no costs on their side for attorneys or experts. For represented women, the need for experts would be reduced or eliminated and there was some thought that the fees paid to their attorneys could be limited by the bankruptcy court to reflect the simpler mode of procedure.)[8]

Accordingly, when negotiations for a plan of reorganization resumed in late August 1986, Robins took the position that the 327,000 Dalkon Shield claims filed in the bankruptcy could be paid in full for less than the $705 million Florence had estimated for the predicted 12,000 claims. If that were true, the company would be able to borrow the necessary funds and to repay the debt over time from its income stream. For that reason Robins refused to discuss the possibility of a sale of the company. For his part, Drabkin refused to discuss anything other than a sale of the company.

As the September 30, 1986, expiration date of Robins's exclusivity period approached with no progress in the negotiations, the attorneys from Skadden, Arps decided that the company should file a plan with a specific figure for Dalkon Shield claims. They reasoned that this would overcome Drabkin's allegations of stonewalling and would set the framework for further discussions and proceedings. They drew up a plan of reorganization that would obligate the company to make available to a claimants' trust up to, but no more than, $700 million over an extended period of time. They proposed to ask Merhige to find that $700 million was sufficient to pay all valid claims in full.[9] Robins's board of directors initially took the position that even this plan was too generous, but after extended discussions it authorized Skadden, Arps to go forward. On September 23, 1986, Robins announced its intention to file a plan of reorganization on September 30, 1986.

The plan was not filed, however. On September 25, 1986, Ralph Mabey, the newly appointed examiner, took it upon himself to file a motion for a five-month extension of Robins's exclusivity period. Mabey stated:

> In the Examiner's view, the process of serious negotiations among Robins and the committees is at a relatively early stage because of numerous earlier concerns with statutory compliance which diverted the attention of the parties. Substantial further negotiations are necessary to determine whether a consensual plan is a realistic possibility. The Examiner believes that premature filing of a plan of reorganization by Robins in order to meet the present exclusivity deadline will not advance these negotiations.

At a hearing on Mabey's motion on September 29, 1986, Dennis Drebsky, speaking for Robins, said that the company had agreed not to file its plan because filing might have served "to inflame tempers and harden positions."[10] Judge Merhige extended Robins's exclusivity period until February 5, 1987. Later, Merhige remarked that he had decided "not to let Robins file their plan." He explained:

> I was concerned that any plan they filed might not really be a fair plan to these women. And I don't mind telling you any plan that is filed, if the court has authority over it, I am not going to let it go out if I don't think it is fair . . . I was satisfied that anything that went out you would have had the numbers [i.e., enough votes to accept the plan], because there are people out there that will take anything.[11]

Notwithstanding Drebsky's comment in court, Robins's strategists were resentful of Mabey's intervention and viewed Merhige's informal rejection of the company's $700 million offer as an ominous sign.

Desultory discussions between Robins and the claimants' committee continued into the fall of 1986, but nothing fundamental had changed and no progress was made. Given his position that the value of the claims exceeded the value of the company, Drabkin would not talk about a limited fund, and, given this, Robins saw no point in making any monetary proposal. Instead of talking about money—the real point of contention—the meetings in the fall of 1986 were devoted to discussions of an alternative dispute resolution process to facilitate the settlement of Dalkon Shield claims once a fund was established.

On January 2, 1987, Judge Merhige sent a letter to the lawyers for women injured by the Dalkon Shield who had made an appearance in the bankruptcy case, emphasizing his determination that a plan be filed on February 5, 1987. He wrote:

As you know, the A. H. Robins plan of reorganization will be filed on or before February 5, 1987. For some time now, the various committees, so I understand, have been meeting in an effort to negotiate a plan and/or a fair and equitable manner of disposing of the myriad of issues involved. The parties, for reasons sufficient to them, have not sought any assistance from the Court . . . Hopefully the parties will be able to reach an understanding on all issues, though the past reports have not been encouraging.

While I recognize that circumstances do arise, which in the interest of justice frequently, as in the past, require adjustments in schedules, I *foresee no*, nor can I conceive of any, *circumstances* which will delay the filing of a plan as *now scheduled*.

I am satisfied that the debtor's counsel knows, from statements both from the bench and at status conferences, that the Court anticipates submission of the most generous plan which will be fair to all creditors. I am also satisfied that the parties do not intend to file a plan which is designed as an opening negotiation proposal; if it is, that would be inconsistent with the Court's view of equitable conduct.

Thank you for your cooperation. I assure you of the Court's *firm* intention not to acquiesce in any further delay.

Nevertheless, unforeseen circumstances did arise, and on February 4, 1987, Merhige entered an order extending Robins's exclusivity period for filing a plan of reorganization for the fifth time—this time, indefinitely. Again, the extension was granted on the motion of the examiner, Ralph Mabey.

Shortly after the court's previous extension of the exclusivity period in late September 1986, Mabey had reached the conclusion that the impasse in the bargaining could be broken and years of litigation over novel issues of bankruptcy law avoided only through the sale of the company. Mabey pointed out to Drabkin that a consensual plan was impossible if he demanded the company's entire value for the claimants. Drabkin agreed that, in the context of a sale that would clearly define the total value of the company, he would accept less than the entire purchase price and leave something for the shareholders, even if the claimants' share was less than the full value of the Dalkon Shield claims. This was the first indication that Drabkin was prepared to support a plan of reorganization that modified the absolute priority rule, in recognition of the power of management and the shareholders to prolong the Chapter 11 case if he did not.

Meanwhile, Alan Schwartz, a partner in the New York investment firm of Bear, Stearns & Company, had analyzed the situation and independently reached the conclusion that an acquisition of the A. H. Robins Company was the only possible solution. He approached several companies he thought might be interested in such an acquisition and eventually found interest at the American Home Products Corporation.

American Home Products is one the nation's largest manufacturers of health care and food and household products, including Anacin, Advil, Dristan, Chef Boyardee, and Woolite. It is a company many times larger than A. H. Robins, with sales in 1987 in excess of $5 billion and profits of $845 million. The aggregate value of its outstanding stock was over $11 billion. In late 1986 American Home Products had over $1 billion in cash. The A. H. Robins Company would be an attractive acquisition for American Home Products if Robins's Dalkon Shield liability could be eliminated. The two companies' product lines were compatible and related, and American Home Products could make good use in marketing its own products of Robins's highly esteemed distribution system. American Home Products authorized Schwartz to explore the possibility of an acquisition.

On January 13, 1987, Schwartz met with Ralph Mabey. In their discussion, the potential buyer was not identified but Mabey made clear that he would support a sale of Robins as a solution to the Chapter 11 case. A possible framework for an acquisition and for a plan of reorganization based on an acquisition was discussed. Schwartz invited Mabey to come to New York on January 21, 1987, and on that date he introduced Mabey to John Stafford, American Home Products' president and chief executive officer, and to Robert Blount, its executive vice-president. The four men spent the day discussing a possible acquisition of Robins by American Home Products.

The next day, without identifying American Home Products, Mabey informed Robins and Murray Drabkin that he was in touch with a prospective purchaser. On January 30, 1987, Mabey met again in New York with Stafford, Blount, and Schwartz and was told that American Home Products was prepared to make an offer.

John Stafford saw an acquisition of Robins by American Home Products as a benign solution to Robins's problem, and he wanted it to have the support of all interested parties, particularly that of Robins's management. Stafford was acquainted with E. Claiborne Robins, Jr., from various industry gatherings, and he expected to be able to do business with him. At Stafford's request, on January 30 Mabey called Robins, Jr., and told him to expect a call from Stafford. Within minutes, a Robins official called back to tell Mabey that Robins, Jr., would not accept a call from Stafford. Mabey was told to tell Stafford that, if he wanted to make an offer for A. H. Robins, he should put it in writing; otherwise, there was nothing to talk about.

Stafford was affronted by this response. Instead of putting an offer in writing at that time, Stafford decided to seek an agreement with Murray Drabkin. Stafford authorized Mabey to approach Drabkin with an offer to pay $1.2 billion in cash into a claimants' trust in connection with an acquisition of Robins by American Home Products. American Home Products and Robins would be discharged from any additional Dalkon Shield liability, but all of the $1.2 billion, plus whatever interest the money earned during the process of liquidating claims, would be distributed to Dalkon Shield claimants, even if the individual claims were eventually liquidated at a lower total figure. In the language of the bargaining over a plan of reorganization, it would be a "closed fund" with no possibility of a "reversion." Unlike the proposals formulated by Robins, the amount of the fund would be a "floor," as well as a "ceiling."

On February 2, 1987, Mabey went to Drabkin's office in Washington and presented Stafford's proposal. The $1.2 billion offered by American Home Products was far more money than Robins had ever considered paying, and the proposal came with Mabey's strong endorsement.

Murray Drabkin's stock in trade is shrewd bargaining. He is known for getting the last possible dollar for his client, not for accepting the opening bid. To Mabey's dismay, Drabkin rejected the proposal.

Shortly after Mabey had left Drabkin's office, he telephoned Drabkin and asked whether Drabkin would meet that evening with representatives of American Home Products. Drabkin agreed, and a meeting was scheduled in an apartment maintained by American Home Products in the Watergate complex in Washington. Drabkin was accompanied by Mark Ellenberg and by Nancy Worth Davis, the chair of the Dalkon Shield claimants' committee. American Home Products was represented by Robert Blount, its second-ranking official, by Charles Hagan, its general counsel, and by Alan Schwartz of Bear, Stearns. Ralph Mabey also participated in the discussions.

Despite Drabkin's conclusion that the Dalkon Shield claims were worth more than the total value of A. H. Robins, he knew, of course, that the price that could be realized in a sale of the company, less the transaction costs and the amounts diverted to pay non–Dalkon Shield debts, placed a natural limit on the amount that could be made available to pay Dalkon Shield claims. Because he was evaluating a possible deal with

American Home Products in terms of the proportion of this natural limit allocated to Dalkon Shield claimants and not in terms of the abstract value of the claims, Drabkin wanted to reach an agreement with American Home Products that would include the amount that would be paid to Robins shareholders. The American Home Products negotiators resisted that suggestion.

The parties bargained (according to Drabkin, "I played poker, Blount played poker"), and by 2:00 a.m., American Home Products' offer stood at $1.7 billion and Drabkin was holding out for more. They recessed for the night and resumed discussions the following morning at Cadwalader, Wickersham & Taft's office in Washington, D.C. Before the morning was out, an agreement was reached on a $1.75 billion closed-end, nonreversionary fund, the entire amount to be paid in cash upon consummation of the plan of reorganization, with the added condition that American Home Products would pay no more than $600 million to purchase the 24.1 million outstanding shares of Robins's stock. American Home Products had adhered to its position that it would not negotiate with Drabkin over the amount to be offered to the Robins shareholders, but it did reveal its intention in this regard and agree to condition its understanding with Drabkin on not going above the stated level. A handwritten memorandum of agreement, dated February 3, 1987, and setting forth these terms, was signed by Blount and by Drabkin. Drabkin agreed to cede to Robins's shareholders almost 25 percent of the total value of the deal because the American Home Products offer would provide far more money for Dalkon Shield claimants than had ever been contemplated, more, indeed, than the estimates he had received of the total worth of A. H. Robins, and because he thought it likely that the announcement of an offer from American Home Products would put Robins "into play" and result in other, higher offers that would enable him to negotiate an even better deal for Dalkon Shield claimants.

With Drabkin's support assured, a formal proposal in the form of a "Dear Claiborne" letter to Robins, Jr., signed by John Stafford, was sent by courier from New York to Ralph Mabey in Washington. Late in the afternoon of February 3, 1987, Mabey caught a ride down to Richmond with Mark Ellenberg and hand-delivered American Home Products' proposal to A. H. Robins headquarters on Cummings Drive. American Home Products offered to pay $1.75 billion in cash into a nonreversionary claimants' trust, to pay all of Robins's other debt in full, and to exchange $450 million worth of its stock for all of Robins's stock (allowing itself a $150 million cushion under the maximum to which it had agreed with Drabkin). The offer was worth $18⁵/₈ for each share of Robins stock. The stock had closed at $10³/₄ on January 30, 1987, the last trading day before American Home Products' approach to Drabkin.

The reaction at Robins headquarters was shock and anger, both at the size of the offer to the Dalkon Shield claimants and that it came with Murray Drabkin's support. Although Robins, Jr., had spurned Stafford's effort to discuss the matter before Drabkin was approached, Robins management now felt that the process was unfair. American Home Products had locked itself into a number with Drabkin without first exploring the company's position on the value of the claims.

With the sixth and supposedly "final" deadline just two days away, Robins's attorneys at Skadden, Arps had been putting the finishing touches on a plan of reorganization that would have established a reversionary trust to which Robins would commit a maximum of $1.09 billion over twelve years. The proposal, which had not yet been presented to Robins's board of directors when the American Home Products proposal arrived, involved an initial cash payment of $450 million and Robins's unsecured promise to pay $45 million each year for twelve years, plus another $100 million if and when needed. Any amounts not needed to pay Dalkon Shield claims would either not be paid to the trust or would be returned to Robins.

A fund payable in installments over a period of time is, of course, worth less than the same total amount all paid at the outset. This economic verity would prove significant in the comparison of the various offers to fund a claimants' trust that were made or considered in the Robins bankruptcy. The "present value" of a series of future payments is the amount it would be necessary to have in hand at the outset in order to make the projected payments, considering the interest that would be earned until the payment dates at an assumed rate. Using a 10 percent interest rate, ignoring the reversion, and treating the "when needed" $100 million in the Skadden, Arps proposal as if it were to be paid at the outset (an unrealistically generous assumption), the present value of the proposal Skadden, Arps had drafted was $857 million, less than half the amount for the payment of Dalkon Shield claims proposed by American Home Products.

For public relations purposes, Skadden, Arps had structured an offer that included a number in excess of $1 billion. Beyond that, Skadden, Arps felt compelled to recommend an increase in real value from the amount that Robins had been prepared to offer in September 1986 because of Merhige's disapproval of the previous proposal and the judge's comments in his January 1987 letter to counsel. However, given the problem Skadden, Arps had had a few months earlier getting the company's approval for the $700 million offer (which itself involved payments over time and was worth less than $700 million), it is uncertain whether its revised proposal would have been approved. In fact, because it knew that Mabey was working on an offer involving a sale of the company, Skadden, Arps had pleaded with Robins management to approve and file a plan early so that it would be in court when the acquisition offer arrived, but to no avail.

The American Home Products proposal put overwhelming pressure on Robins to scrap or at least defer its plan and to entertain the prospect of selling the company. On February 4, 1987, with Robins's agreement, Mabey filed a motion asking Merhige to permit a two-week extension of the exclusivity period. In the motion, Mabey represented that "there is a highly significant, recently presented development in the plan formulation which must and can be promptly explored." After lengthy discussions with counsel on the afternoon of the 4th, Merhige entered his order indefinitely extending Robins's exclusivity period.

Eight days later, on February 12, 1986, to the apparent surprise of everyone involved, Stafford called Robins, Jr., and told him that American Home Products' offer was withdrawn. American Home issued a press release stating ambiguously that the reason for the withdrawal was "uncertainties surrounding the situation [that] have not been clarified to our satisfaction."[12] The price of A. H. Robins stock on the New York Stock Exchange, which had risen from $10 3/4 on January 30 to $25 1/2 on February 5, and then dropped back to $22 by February 11, declined to $15 in the ninety minutes after American Home Products' announcement.

There were various interpretations of exactly what had happened. It is clear that to Robins management, and particularly to Messrs. E. Claiborne Robins, the offer was most unwelcome. Any offer of acquisition would have been unwelcome, as management was far from convinced that the company could not meet its Dalkon Shield liability without yielding its independence. This reaction was aggravated by American Home Products' prior agreement with Drabkin to pay, at the expense of the shareholders, far more in the compensation of Dalkon Shield claims than Robins's principals thought the claims were worth.

Despite their unhappiness with the offer, Robins's management did not feel free to reject it. Management of a debtor-in-possession is legally charged with the fiduciary duty to maximize the value of the estate for the benefit of its creditors. The American Home Products offer would pay trade creditors in full and had the support of the Dalkon Shield claimants' committee. Management also has a fiduciary obligation to the shareholders, and the American Home Products offer represented a substantial premium over the market price of the company's common stock. In fact, after American Home Products made its initial offer, it quickly had agreed to Robins's demand that $550 million, rather than $450 million, in American Home Products stock be exchanged for Robins's stock. This represented almost $23 per share, more than double the pre-offer market price. With this change, Drexel Burnham Lambert, which had been retained by Robins in January 1987 to provide advice about a possible sale of the company, recommended that the offer be accepted. Robins's management reluctantly concluded that it probably had no other choice.

Yet, in what one lawyer close to the case has called an effort "to kill the deal, without leaving footprints," Robins began putting forth a seemingly endless series of demands that did not amount to much in terms of the total value of the deal—certainly not as much as the $50 million that Robins had unknowingly "left on the table"—but that seemed inappropriate to American Home Products. Thomas Morris, of the *Richmond Times-Dispatch*, reported:

The items had far more symbolic than financial meaning and became the proverbial straw . . . The items included retaining E. Claiborne Robins, Jr. at no cut in pay, retaining E. Claiborne Robins, Sr. as a director or consultant at $100,000 per year, and offering three year contracts to more than two dozen members of Robins management . . .

[S]ources indicated American Home balked at being asked to pay the elder Robins more than other AHP directors are paid and being asked to give the Robins executive corps the security of written contracts that no American Home official has. American Home viewed that as an unacceptable sign of distrust . . . Moreover, AHP compromises led not to a deal, but to more demands.[13]

Both Robins and American Home Products denied that demands by Robins relating to compensation of its executives had destroyed the deal. American Home Products issued a statement that "[w]e have nothing but the highest praise for Robins' attitude and conduct."[14] In fact, Robins, in Chapter 11 and under Mabey's watchful eye and Merhige's iron hand, could not have insisted on its demands relating to personnel benefits, and, in due course, it would have had to accept American Home Products' best offer.

What happened was not that Robins's demands had actually caused

American Home Products to abandon the deal but that these demands had given John Stafford and others at American Home Products time and reason to have second thoughts about the entire transaction. Stafford had expected a universally appreciative reaction to his offer. American Home Products sells consumer products, and women are its major customers. Stafford wanted an acquisition of Robins to be a public relations benefit, not a detriment.

Instead of the quick agreement they expected, Stafford and his advisers began to envision weeks of negotiation, trench warfare, and controversy. Robins's management was reluctant, at best. The equity committee saw the American Home Products proposal as diverting to the overpayment of Dalkon Shield claims value rightfully belonging to the shareholders, and it quickly announced its opposition to the acquisition. Robert Miller, the committee's attorney, told reporters on February 5, 1987, that the American Home Products offer to shareholders was "woefully inadequate."[15]

At the same time, some prominent attorneys representing women injured by the Dalkon Shield made public statements that put in question the adequacy of the payment into the claimants' trust. Although it seemed like a great deal of money in the context of the prior discussions, the $1.75 billion figure was a product of negotiation, not of judicial determination; the figure was unsupported by hard data. Even if the limitation on its liability could be made legally binding, American Home Products did not want to face the public relations consequences if the trust proved inadequate to pay all the Dalkon Shield claims. According to one source, John Stafford reported having a "nightmare" over the possibility of pickets outside American Home Products headquarters.

When Stafford withdrew his offer, he made clear that it was not a negotiating tactic and that American Home Products was no longer interested in the acquisition. In fact, Judge Merhige called Louis Hoynes, of Willkie, Farr & Gallagher in New York, lead counsel for American Home Products, when he learned of the withdrawal, and offered his services in overcoming any obstacles to the deal, but Hoynes told him that his client was simply no longer interested.

On February 16, 1987, Merhige conducted a conference, with some participants in his chambers and others on the speaker phone. Merhige strongly expressed his unhappiness over the failure of the American Home Products offer to result in a resolution of the case. At the same time, the judge praised Drabkin for committing himself to a specific number for a closed-end fund, something Drabkin had previously resisted. Drabkin and Mabey argued that the American Home experience demonstrated that a sale of the company was the best hope for a prompt and consensual plan of reorganization and asked that other bids be encouraged. The process had demonstrated that the company could attract a high enough price to meet Drabkin's demands and also provide substantial value to the Robins shareholders.

In reaction to the reports that Robins had discouraged the deal with American Home Products, Merhige directed that any new offers of acquisition be received by Mabey, not by Robins, and that everyone except Mabey refrain from public comment on the situation. In the meantime, the American Home Products offer had changed expectations and made it impossible for Robins to resume its consideration of Skadden, Arps's plan to pay $1.09 billion over twelve years to a claimants' trust. Merhige asked Robins not to file a plan of reorganization until Mabey had had time to look for another prospective purchaser.

The next day, February 17, 1987, Mabey issued a statement saying that A. H. Robins was looking for a buyer and that a prospective purchaser could "expect substantial cooperation from the significant parties in the case and the court." Mabey emphasized that "nobody would be hostile to a sale, that a sale on the right terms would be embraced, with nobody out there trying to torpedo it. The world at large should understand that by making an offer for Robins they're not obligated to wage war."[16]

There was no immediate response to this invitation, and a week later, on February 24, 1987, Mabey wrote to Judge Merhige recommending that the A. H. Robins Company be sold at an auction co-managed by the investment advisers for Robins, for the claimants' committee, and for the equity committee.

Mabey had been advised that management's cooperation would be necessary to attract the highest possible price. In an effort to secure this cooperation and to assure that a sale would lead quickly to an agreed plan of reorganization, Mabey undertook to negotiate with Robins's representatives and with Drabkin over the terms of an auction, particularly over the division of the proceeds between the claimants and the shareholders. One early proposal was that the proceeds of a sale be divided between the claimants and the shareholders in the ratio of 1750 to 550, the ratio of the American Home Products proposal. Drabkin would not agree to this out of concern that the auction price would be lower than the American Home Products offer. After some discussion, it was tentatively agreed that, after Robins's other debts were paid, the first $1.75 billion would go to a claimants' trust and the next $550 million would go to the shareholders. But discussions then bogged down on the question of what would happen to any additional money.

Robins was a reluctant participant in these discussions, as it was still hoping, on its own, to meet its Dalkon Shield liability in an amount set or approved by Judge Merhige. Although the company never ruled out the possibility of an auction, it constantly raised problems and would never agree to a complete proposal.

In the meantime, Alan Schwartz had brought the idea of acquiring Robins to the Rorer Group, another pharmaceutical company but one far smaller than American Home Products. Rorer was interested and entered into discussions with Ralph Mabey. On March 28, 1987, Rorer made an offer for the acquisition of Robins that was similar to the American Home Products offer. Again, Robins resisted. The company claimed that it could not evaluate and respond to the offer in the two-day time period Rorer had specified. Rorer, sensing Robins's hostility, withdrew its formal offer, but unlike American Home Products, Rorer made clear to Mabey that it would still like to go forward if it could secure the necessary cooperation from management. The offer and the withdrawal were not made public.

Frustrated and angry by Robins's refusing to agree to an auction and then thwarting an offer he had worked for weeks to attract, on April 7, 1987, Mabey sent a remarkable letter to the court in which he reported that Robins's exclusive right to file a plan of reorganization was preventing a sale of the company.

Dear Judge Merhige and Judge Shelley:

[T]he American Home Products offer crystallized the positions of the Company and the Dalkon Shield Claimants Committee such that they were able to agree to basic financial terms. A similar or enhanced offer may well reopen these avenues of agreement and provide hope for a largely consensual plan of reorganization in a case whose complexity and emotion otherwise portend the waging of war over novel legal and factual issues which may take many years to resolve.

A sale avoids other awkward problems. For instance, an internally-funded plan might involve payout over a number of years of Company profits or stock into a Dalkon Shield fund; during these years, the Dalkon Shield claimants and the Company would be in an uneasy marriage where each was subject to the other's scrutiny and dependent upon the other's cooperation.

Furthermore, I am informed by the investment bankers that the Company most probably can return much more to its constituents through a sale than through an internally-funded plan. While this fact may not be crucial if the Dalkon Shield claims are of a manageable magnitude, since doubt will persist for a long time respecting the size of those claims, maximum return for the estate is significant. It, for example, spares the shareholders from seeing their stock values depressed because the stock is subject to future call to satisfy Dalkon Shield claims.

In light of the advantages to a sale, the Court instructed me to entertain prospective purchasers and I have done so. But the status quo is entirely unsatisfactory.

The parties have been unable to agree upon, and to cooperate in, the basic procedures necessary for an orderly exposure of the Company to the market. The Company is a recalcitrant participant in a sale. Prospective purchasers are confused . . . Any statements of willingness notwithstanding, I do not believe that the Company desires to step in and entertain purchase proposals—and, in any event, other parties in interest do not trust the Company to do so . . . The reorganization process is dead in the water while tens of thousands of creditors await relief.

Accordingly, I recommend that, while the Company should still have the opportunity to file its plan of reorganization, another entity should be empowered to file a plan of reorganization and, if the entity deemed it appropriate, to pursue the marketing of the Company.

The examiner accompanied his letter with a motion asking the court to grant him authority to arrange for a sale of the company and to submit a plan of reorganization based on a sale. Merhige immediately placed the letter and the motion under seal. The motion was set for argument on April 16, 1987.

On April 8, 1987, the same day that Mabey's letter and motion were received by the court, the Dalkon Shield claimants' committee filed a motion to terminate the exclusivity period and to appoint a trustee. Murray Drabkin said that these measures would assure the necessary cooperation and would quickly result in a plan of reorganization based on a sale of the company. "This would end the case. The time has come."

As a result of these motions, particularly that of the neutral examiner, Robins's management stood at risk of losing control of the case and control of the company. In the days that followed, Judge Merhige made known to the company that, despite Mabey's and Drabkin's preference for a sale, he would be receptive to a stand-alone plan that was as favorable to the claimants as was the American Home Products proposal. With this assurance, Robins's management concluded that its best response to the motions would be to quickly file a plan of reorganization that would make $1.75 billion available to a claimants' trust, without any change in the ownership of the company. Accordingly, on April 16, 1987, a few minutes before the scheduled hearing on the motions of the examiner and the claimants' committee to terminate the exclusivity period, Robins finally filed a plan of reorganization.

Although Robins included the $1.75 billion number in its plan to meet the practical requirements of the situation, the terms it proposed were actually far different in value and in certainty from the deal Drabkin had negotiated with American Home Products. Robins proposed to pay only $75 million in cash into a claimants' trust. The balance of $1.675 billion would be secured by letters of credit issued by a consortium of banks, led by the Manufacturers Hanover Bank in New York. The letters of credit would not be issued unless Drexel Burnham Lambert was successful in raising collateral through the sale for Robins of $800 million worth of high yield (junk) bonds. Payments under the letters of credit to the trust would be made in $25 million installments whenever the trust funds fell below $50 million. The unpaid amount of the letters of credit would earn interest at 5 percent. American Home Products had agreed to pay the entire $1.75 billion in cash at the outset.

In addition, Robins's proposal was for a reversionary trust. Robins firmly believed, as it always had, that the value of the Dalkon Shield claims was far less than $1.75 billion. Under its proposal, if the claims were liquidated at a total value below $1.75 billion, the difference would not be paid. In fact, in connection with obtaining the letters of credit, Robins had submitted evidence to the banks to support its contention that substantially less than the full amount of the commitment would be required. Under the American Home Products proposal the entire fund would have been paid irrevocably to the trust. Any amount above the liquidated value of the claims would have been distributed to the claimants in lieu of punitive damages.

The importance of the reversion was not so much the denial to the claimants of funds in excess of the total liquidated value of their claims—a factor that might not be entitled to much weight if it were assumed that each claimant would be paid the full value of her claim—as its effect on the administration of the trust. The reversion meant that every dollar awarded to a woman injured by the Dalkon Shield would come directly out of A. H. Robins's pocket. This would give the company a strong incentive to keep recoveries to a minimum.

Several provisions of Robins's plan of reorganization reflected this perspective. The plan provided that Robins would select the trustees of the claimants' trust. It also provided that the Virginia two-year statute of limitations (the shortest in the United States) would apply to all claims.

The trust would pay claims under a series of restrictive "options."

- Under option 1, a claimant would be offered $100, in final settlement of her claim, upon signing a sworn statement that she had used the

Dalkon Shield and suffered an injury that has been associated with its use.

- Under option 2, a claimant could receive between $400 and $2,000, depending on the injury, upon submission of medical records verifying Dalkon Shield use and the claimed injury. There would be no inquiry into the question of whether the injury had been caused by the Dalkon Shield.
- Under option 3, a claimant could receive a settlement based on historical values after an in-depth review of all relevant factors. Robins proposed a "downward adjustment" in historical values to reflect the lesser degree of investigation, the waiver of the defense that the Dalkon Shield was not defective, speed in resolution, and lower transaction costs, as well as "to remove the shadow effect of punitive damages."[17] (The latter is premised on the reasoning, favored by the company, that historical values exceed the actual value of the compensatory claims because the risk of an award of punitive damages at trial exercised an upward pressure on the amount of settlements.)

In other words, under Robins's proposal, claims would be settled below the level of prebankruptcy settlements in similar cases. Robins's plan provided that a claimant who rejected a settlement with the trust could elect binding arbitration or exercise her statutory right to have the value of her claim determined by a jury in a suit against the trust. But suit could only be filed in the federal court in Richmond. In a jury trial, all defenses, including the defense that there was nothing wrong with the Dalkon Shield, would be available to the trust but punitive damages could not be recovered.

Drabkin and Mabey were served with copies of Robins's plan of reorganization when they walked into the courtroom on April 16, 1987, for the hearing on their motions to terminate the exclusivity period. Robins then opposed the motions on the ground that it had filed a plan of reorganization and was now entitled to an additional exclusivity period to secure acceptances.[18] The company contended that its plan met "the basic economic terms previously deemed satisfactory by the Dalkon Shield Claimants Committee" and that, unless the court determined that more money was required to pay all Dalkon Shield claims in full, it was irrelevant whether or not a sale of the company would maximize its value, as the examiner and the claimants' committee had suggested.

Robins also argued that the "real purpose" of a Chapter 11 proceeding is the "reorganization of the debtor and its continuance as a going business"[19] and that it had the right, if possible, to pay its creditors by reorganizing its finances without selling the company.

The desire to find an easy, quick solution does not justify ignoring the statutory purpose and depriving Robins of its statutorily-created rights . . . The Examiner's motion is the first step in a transparent attempt to force Robins to agree to a sale of its entire business to an unknown third party. This sale would take place although Robins (1) has been precluded from filing its own reorganization plan; (2) never had the opportunity to solicit creditor acceptance of its own plan; and (3) has been precluded from having the court estimate the claims asserted against it so that it could evaluate whether any sale would make good business sense.

At the hearing, Mabey, Drabkin, future claimants' representative Stanley Joynes, and Assistant United States Attorney David Schiller all expressed opposition to Robins's plan and asked the court to authorize the filing of other plans. In the first public reference to the matter, Drabkin revealed that the Rorer Group stood ready to purchase Robins on terms equivalent to those propounded by American Home Products and suggested that Robins had used the exclusivity period to thwart consideration of the Rorer offer.

Drabkin portrayed Robins's plan as a "Rube Goldberg contraption which would dribble out" payments to Dalkon Shield victims. He questioned the reliability of the letters of credit, noting that Manufacturers Hanover Bank's own credit rating had recently been downgraded. "It's just a letter of credit. Robins says this has the same certainty as cash, but this isn't cash no matter how many times Robins says it is. It's a promise that claims will be paid over time." Drabkin added that the provision for a reversion of unexpended funds and the consequent incentive to Robins to fight the claims were "a prescription for litigation."

But according to the *Wall Street Journal,* Merhige "seemed buoyant as the hearing began" and declared that "this new filing puts us on the road we want to be on."[20] Merhige concurred in Robins's suggestion that, if it could pay the Dalkon Shield claims through borrowing rather than through a sale of the company, it was entitled to do so.[21] He ruled that he would not, at that time, allow competing plans to be filed. Instead, the judge ordered attorneys for all the parties to meet over the next fifteen days in an attempt to reach an agreement on the rules and procedures that would govern the resolution of claims. Although these questions and the issue of whether A. H. Robins should be sold were unrelated, Merhige prodded Robins into concessions on issues relating to claims procedures by implying that he would allow Mabey to file a plan calling for a sale of the company if agreement on these issues was not reached.

A series of meetings followed at which Mabey advanced several fundamental changes in the rules and procedures proposed by Robins, changes that would make the trust procedure more attractive to women injured by the Dalkon Shield. Under the circumstances, Robins felt forced to agree. James Roberts of Mays & Valentine, one of Robins's principal negotiators, told Thomas Morris of the *Richmond Times-Dispatch* that the discussions were conducted "in an atmosphere we felt dictated reaching an accord."[22]

When the discussions concluded in early May, Robins had agreed that

- the trustees would be appointed by the court, not by the company;
- the trustees would fix the payments at all stages of the claims resolution process in lieu of the schedules and standards contained in Robins's proposal. The payment under option 1 would be set at an amount below the cost of reviewing and processing the claim;
- jury trials could take place wherever the plaintiff could sue before the bankruptcy, not only in Richmond;
- the limitations period for suits would be determined by the law of the state in which the case was filed (extended for the length of the bankruptcy proceeding);
- in lieu of punitive damages, $50 million from the funds available to the trust, if not otherwise paid to claimants, would be distributed to women who received compensatory payments. (Apart from this provision, Robins's proposed right of reversion was unchanged.)

These changes had been taken to Robins's board of directors and approved by it on the assumption that they were necessary to convince Merhige to continue his exclusion of competing plans of reorganization. In this way Merhige secured agreement on an acceptable framework for the operation of a claims resolution facility, the essential points of which were carried forward into the final plan of reorganization. But because the changes relating to claims resolution did not address any of the fundamental economic issues with which Drabkin was concerned, they did not alter his strong opposition to Robins's plan.

In response to Judge Merhige's stated preference for a stand-alone plan, Ralph Mabey redirected his efforts during May and June 1987 to revamping the economic provisions of Robins's plan in a manner that would secure Murray Drabkin's support. It was Mabey's theory that, if he and Drabkin could agree on the terms of a stand-alone plan, Merhige would force Robins to accept it.

Mabey met with Drabkin repeatedly in an effort to reach such an agreement. The discussions focused on the changes in Robins's plan that would be necessary to provide a claimants' trust with the present value of $1.75 billion. Combinations of letters of credit and cash payments totaling up to $2 billion over time were considered, and Mabey prepared successive drafts of a revised plan. But while Drabkin participated in these discussions and never precluded his possible acceptance of a stand-alone plan, he continually emphasized his concern over the reliability of the funding of a trust based on letters of credit and, in fact, he would not agree to any set of terms. Just as he had come to realize in April that Robins was not going to agree to an auction of the company, Mabey now realized that Drabkin was not going to agree to a stand-alone plan.

In the meantime, pressure for a sale of Robins continued to build. On May 6, 1987, Merrell Dow Pharmaceuticals, a subsidiary of Dow Chemical, made an offer to purchase Robins's consumer products for $840 million. Robins immediately rejected the offer, stating that "the company . . . has no interest in selling major segments of its operations." In reporting this story, the *Washington Post* quoted an unnamed attorney "familiar with the case" as saying that "a well structured offer would be very difficult to turn down. The Company is in play. It is sitting out there on the auction block."[23]

A front-page story in the business section of the Sunday, May 17, 1987, *Richmond Times-Dispatch* reported that Pfizer, Inc., another pharmaceutical company, was prepared to bid for Robins's consumer products. The article also reported on Rorer's continued interest in an acquisition of the entire company. The story by Thomas Morris made explicit that these approaches were barred by Judge Merhige's refusal to allow competing plans. "A takeover offer or an offer to buy assets is in effect ruled out, unless Robins were to endorse it, for as long as Robins continues being alone in being allowed to file or amend a reorganization plan."[24]

In May and June 1987 the Dalkon Shield claimants' committee initiated discovery proceedings first against Manufacturers Hanover Bank and the other banks that had agreed to issue the letters of credit, and then against the federal and state agencies that regulate those institutions, to inquire into the solvency of the banks. Robins opposed these efforts, contending that it was disingenuous to question the solvency of major American banks and that Drabkin's efforts to do so reflected his personal determination to force a sale of the company. Manufacturers Hanover found the proposed inquiry intolerable and informed Judge Merhige that it would withdraw from the deal rather than provide the requested information. But just at this time, news reports appeared that gave credibility to the committee's concern by describing serious difficulties that were facing major banks, including specifically the Manufacturers Hanover Bank, as a result of bad loans to Third World countries. Although the matter became moot before Merhige made a final ruling, the judge did acknowledge the relevance of the information and appeared ready to order the disclosure.[25]

Apart from questions concerning the reliability of the letters of credit, doubts were expressed in the financial community concerning Robins's ability to meet the condition for the issuance of the letters of credit by selling $800 million worth of junk bonds, and concerning the company's ability to function under the weight of the debt that those bonds would represent. A May 4, 1987, article in the *Wall Street Journal* reported widespread concerns that the company would be unduly burdened by debt as a result of its insistence on remaining independent.[26] It was later reported that even influential members of Robins's management team harbored doubts about the heavy debt that the company would have to assume under its plan.[27] It began to appear that $1.75 billion, even with the provision for payments over time and for a reversion, was simply more money than Robins could afford to commit.

The pressure on Robins to abandon its stand-alone plan was heightened by a fundamental change in the position of the equity committee. Until the spring of 1987 the equity committee had uniformly provided support to the company on the various issues that arose in the bankruptcy, including its efforts to remain independent. But following the collapse of the American Home Products deal, two independent investment groups in New York, one led by Michael Steinhardt and another headed by George Soros of the Quantum Fund, began buying large amounts of Robins stock in the expectation that the company was ripe for takeover. In fact, Robins stock had the largest percentage appreciation of any stock on the New York Stock Exchange for the first six months of 1987, moving from $7 to $28 per share. On May 4, 1987, the Steinhardt group reported ownership of 6.7 percent of the common shares outstanding.[28] The Soros group owned another large block, and together these groups were the dominant voice among the nonfamily shareholders.

Before Steinhardt and Soros came on the scene, the equity committee had proceeded on the theory that Robins's stock was undervalued because of the uncertainty about the company's Dalkon Shield liability, and that there would be substantial appreciation in the price of the stock if the Dalkon Shield liability could be limited at a reasonable level. Steinhardt and Soros did not share this perspective. They were unhappy with the decision of Robins's management to offer $1.75 billion to resolve the Dalkon Shield claims, and they were concerned over the level of debt that Robins was prepared to assume in its quest to remain independent. They wanted to turn a profit on their investment in the short run through a sale of the company.

In mid-May 1987 the equity committee demanded that Robins abandon its stand-alone plan in favor of a plan based on a sale of the company. When the company did not comply, Robert Miller dispatched a letter, dated June 10, 1987, to Robins's board of directors in which he again demanded a sale of the company and threatened reprisals if the demand was not met.

Gentlemen:

The Equity Committee has previously demanded that the Board of Directors, in the best interests of the Company's outside shareholders, abandon the Company's filed plan of reorganization and in lieu thereof attempt to sell the Company for a minimum price of $30 per share. On Friday, May 22, 1987, we were advised . . . that the Board had determined at its May 21st meeting to pursue such a sale, that it was investigating all potential suitors, and that a sale was perhaps 1–2 weeks away . . .

However, nearly three weeks later, no sale has yet occurred. Moreover, we understand that negotiations with Rorer have stalled due to Robins' unwillingness to conclude the deal (specifically, the failure of Mr. Robins, Jr. to speak and conclude the deal with Mr. Cawthorn [chief executive officer of the Rorer Group]) . . .

The Equity Committee wants a sale to Rorer and it wants it now. No more stalling or excuses will be suffered. If the Board does not publicly announce a deal with Rorer by next *Tuesday, June 16, 1987,* the Equity Committee will take the following actions, among other things:

1. Immediately call a shareholders' meeting for the purpose of replacing the Board and, ultimately, the senior officers of the Company.

2. Sue each of the Board members for breach of fiduciary duty to the shareholders. We will hold each of you personally liable for the shareholders' loss of $30 per share.

3. Publicly oppose the Debtor's filed plan and advocate a court-ordered sale of the Company. This will effectively kill any remaining life left in your plan.

4. Oppose the Company's motion to pay the banks' fees, and object to its disclosure statement.

5. Seek to disallow the Robins family's stock interests under any plan.

Robins did not announce a sale by June 16, 1987, and despite these strong words the equity committee neither demanded a shareholders' meeting nor filed suit against the directors. But on June 25, 1987, in its first public break with the company, the equity committee put additional pressure on the situation by joining the claimants' committee in opposition to Robins's motion to pay $20 million in fees to the banks that were to provide the letters of credit under the pending plan of reorganization. In that connection, the equity committee stated that it opposed Robins's plan of reorganization "primarily because it purports to grossly overpay the alleged Dalkon Shield claims." It described $1.75

billion as a "fabricated amount, which reflects only what a failed bidder proposed to pay for Dalkon Shield claims based on a unilateral negotiation."

Late in the afternoon of June 25, the Rorer Group dealt the final blow to Robins's stand-alone plan by submitting a formal offer for the acquisition of the company through an exchange of stock worth at least $30 for each share of A. H. Robins stock—a total of more than $720 million. The offer provided for payments to a claimants' trust totaling $1.75 billion over seven years and for full payment of Robins's commercial debt.

When Robins's board of directors met on June 29, 1987, representatives of the equity committee appeared in support of the Rorer proposal. Committee counsel Robert Miller made clear to the members of the board that they would be sued personally if the Rorer offer was rejected.[29]

Faced with what the *Wall Street Journal* described as a "gathering groundswell" against the company's reorganization plan, Claiborne Robins, father and son, finally accepted the inevitable—the Dalkon Shield, or more precisely their stubborn unwillingness over fifteen years to face up to the problem of the Dalkon Shield, had brought about the end of the A. H. Robins Company.[30] After a few days of discussion with Rorer representatives, on July 3, 1987, Robins's board of directors unanimously approved a letter of intent to merge with Rorer, incorporating the terms of Rorer's latest offer. Judge Merhige set August 21, 1987, as the deadline for filing a revised plan of reorganization.

On August 21, the sixth deadline set by the court for Robins's submission of a plan of reorganization and the second anniversary of the bankruptcy, at a few minutes before midnight, a messenger brought to Judge Merhige's home Robins's Second Amended Plan of Reorganization and Disclosure Statement, reflecting its agreement with Rorer. The new plan made changes in the provisions relating to the financing of the claimants' trust that obviated two of the major objections to the Robins stand-alone plan. First, it eliminated any legitimate question of whether the promised funds would be paid. Rorer proposed to pay $450 million into the trust at the outset instead of $75 million. The balance of $1.3 billion would be paid by the merged corporation over a seven-year period, and the merged corporation would remain directly liable for the payments. In addition, letters of credit guaranteeing the obligation would be obtained from a consortium of indisputably strong banks. These letters of credit were immediately available and were not conditioned on the prior issuance or sale of bonds, as they had been under the Robins stand-alone plan.

The second important difference was that the trust would be non-reversionary. To the extent that the total amount committed was not expended in the liquidation of individual claims, it would be distributed pro rata, in lieu of punitive damages, to claimants who received compensatory payments. Not only did this assure that the full amount would be distributed, regardless of the outcome of the liquidation process, but it eliminated any incentive for Robins (or Rorer) to seek to limit individual awards. Presumably, this would relax and expedite the liquidation process.

The Rorer plan also eliminated a provision of Robins's stand-alone plan that provided that trust funds would be available to indemnify present and former officers and directors of Robins for any Dalkon Shield–related liability that might be imposed on them. The Rorer plan provided instead for the creation of a separate trust, the "Other Claimants Trust," to be funded by the merged corporation with an additional $250 million over four years.[31] The Other Claimants Trust would assume Robins's preexisting indemnification agreements with its directors, officers, and employees. This trust actually provided a double blanket of protection because it was a condition of the plan of reorganization (as it had been of Robins's stand-alone plan) that Dalkon Shield–related claims against persons associated with the A. H. Robins Company would be permanently enjoined in the confirmation order. The Rorer plan provided that monies not spent by the Other Claimants Trust after six years would be paid over to the claimants' trust for distribution to claimants. As it would be unlikely, in the face of such an injunction, that a significant portion of the funds earmarked for the Other Claimants Trust would be used for the purpose of indemnification, the Rorer plan held the promise of up to an additional $250 million in payments to the trust over seven years, on top of the $1.75 billion.

Rorer had not secured Murray Drabkin's support for its proposal but was hopeful that his support would be forthcoming. For several reasons, however, Drabkin opposed the Rorer plan. By agreeing to exchange stock worth $720 million instead of the $550 million offered by American Home Products, Rorer had added $170 million to the deal, none of which would go to Dalkon Shield claimants. Although Drabkin was repeatedly faced with the argument (from Judge Merhige, among others) that he had agreed to accept $1.75 billion for the Dalkon Shield claimants and that he should stand by this agreement, his position was that he had accepted $1.75 billion in a context in which it represented more than 70 percent of the value of the company. When Rorer agreed to pay the shareholders another $170 million, $1.75 billion was a smaller piece of the pie.

This problem was exacerbated by a reduction in the present value of the payments to the claimants' trust. Rorer proposed to make payments to the trust totaling $1.75 billion over seven years. American Home Products had offered to pay $1.75 billion at the outset. Even if it were assumed that the entire $250 million earmarked for the Other Claimants Trust would be paid to the Dalkon Shield Claimants' Trust, the present value of the payments to the two trusts over seven years was $1.55 billion, $200 million less than the American Home Products offer.[32] Thus, the increase for the shareholders in the Rorer plan was made at the expense of the claimants.

Drabkin continued to believe that the value of the Dalkon Shield claims far exceeded the value of the company. By the summer of 1987 his belief was confirmed by advice he received from experts in claim evaluation retained by the claimants' committee. Drabkin was still willing to agree to the diversion of some portion of the company's value to its shareholders but only if the amount diverted was small enough that its loss was preferable to prolonged litigation to enforce the absolute priority rule. In Drabkin's view, the Rorer plan, with more for shareholders and less for claimants than the American Home Products offer, did not meet this test.

By contrast, Robins took the position that the Rorer plan provided far more money than was necessary to pay all Dalkon Shield claims in full. In fact, Robins and Rorer had reserved the right to amend the plan to provide lesser funding for a claimants' trust in the event that the court determined that less money was needed. The lines were drawn for the ultimate court battle in the case—a determination by Judge Merhige of the total amount of money necessary to pay the Dalkon Shield claims.

12   The McGovern Process

A plan of reorganization that reserves value for the equity interests can be confirmed only if each class of creditors votes to accept the plan or if the court determines, through a procedure known as a "cramdown," that the plan provides for full payment of the claims in any dissenting class.[1]

With the claimants' committee opposed to the Rorer plan on the ground that it did not provide adequate funds to pay the Dalkon Shield claims, the only circumstance in which the class of Dalkon Shield claimants might be expected to accept the plan was if they were advised that the court had determined that their claims would, in fact, be paid in full. Thus, whether by appealing to the claimants to accept the plan over their representatives' opposition or through a cramdown, a determination by the court that the Rorer plan would provide full payment was essential to its further consideration. The only alternative was to allow a different plan to be filed that would unquestionably comply with the absolute priority rule or would otherwise be acceptable to Drabkin.

In accordance with a widespread practice among bankruptcy judges, Judge Merhige took the position that Robins was entitled to proceed with its own plan of reorganization if that plan met the requirements for confirmation. Accordingly, instead of allowing competing plans to be filed, Merhige undertook to determine whether the Rorer plan would provide full payment to women injured by the Dalkon Shield by estimating the total value of the outstanding claims.

Section 502(c) of the Bankruptcy Code provides that "[t]here shall be estimated for purpose of allowance under this section . . . any contingent or unliquidated claim, the fixing or liquidation of which . . . would unduly delay the administration of the case." (An unliquidated claim is a claim, such as an unresolved claim for personal injuries, whose value is in dispute.) Both the House and the Senate committee reports on the 1978 legislation state that this provision "requires the estimation of any claim the liquidation of which would unduly delay the closing of the estate, such as a contingent claim . . . This subsection requires that all claims against the debtor be converted into dollar amounts."[2]

165

The draftsmen of section 502(c) were not thinking of Chapter 11 cases based on mass product liability but of traditional bankruptcy proceedings in which there were one or a few unliquidated claims that could be individually reviewed and estimated. Every instance before the Robins bankruptcy in which a court actually used the estimation procedure established by section 502(c) had involved such a situation.[3] Although neither the statute nor the legislative history say so expressly, it is a fair interpretation of the congressional purpose that, in that situation, the unliquidated creditor's recovery may be limited to the amount of the estimate, if necessary to avoid undue delay to the other creditors.[4] Treating a judicial estimate of the value of an individual claim as limiting the creditor's recovery on the claim is quite different, however, from treating an *in globo* estimation of the value of hundreds of thousands of personal injury claims as a basis for a cramdown that would limit the total recovery of the class of personal injury claimants.

A more palpable obstacle to a binding estimate in the context of a mass tort bankruptcy was created in 1984 when, in response to the Johns-Manville bankruptcy, Congress enacted a series of special protections to individuals with personal injury claims against a debtor in bankruptcy, and particularly the provision guaranteeing the right to trial by jury in a nonbankruptcy court.[5] (The rule had been established, in situations not involving personal injury claims, that a creditor who filed a claim in a bankruptcy proceeding lost any right to trial by jury that may have existed outside of bankruptcy.)[6]

The right to a jury trial on a personal injury claim against a debtor in bankruptcy does not necessarily mean that the claimant will be paid the amount of the jury verdict. If the total value of the estate is less than the liquidated value of all the unsecured claims, the jury award will not be paid in full but only in the same proportion as all other unsecured claims. It does seem, however, that the right to trial by jury would be infringed if a personal injury claimant were paid less than the amount of the jury award, not because there were insufficient assets in the estate but because a judge estimated the value of her claim at a lower level.[7]

Although no group estimation had ever been conducted when Judge Merhige undertook the process, in two cases courts had stated, in the course of decisions involving other issues, that section 502(c) of the Bankruptcy Code permits the estimation of a debtor's overall liability to a class of unliquidated personal injury claimants.[8] One of these cases was *A. H. Robins Co. v. Piccinin*, the decision in which the court of appeals reversed Merhige's order, entered early in the Robins bankruptcy, transferring all pending Dalkon Shield cases to Richmond.[9] Although the court ruled that the transfers could not be made without providing notice and an opportunity to be heard to the affected women, it did endorse the goal of centralization of the cases in Richmond. In the course of its discussion the court of appeals volunteered an endorsement of a group estimation of Robins's liability to women injured by the Dalkon Shield.

[E]stimation of the debtor's potential personal injury tort liabilities [is] an incident of the development of a plan of reorganization . . . It is manifest, of course, that the process of estimation will involve some examination of the claims . . . It is unlikely that all 8,000 to 10,000 claims which have been filed would have to be tried before an intelligent estimation of the claims could be made by the bankruptcy court.[10]

The court of appeal's discussion is couched in optimistic references to agreement among the parties following an estimate and does not address the issue of the effect that can be given to a group estimate in the absence of agreement by the class of Dalkon Shield claimants or in the event that an individual claimant demands the right to trial by jury.

It had been Penn Butler's view from the outset that Robins should seek an estimate by the court of the value of the Dalkon Shield claims filed in the Chapter 11 case. Butler believed that an estimate would provide an alternative means of limiting Robins's liability if an agreement with the claimants' committee could not be reached. Robins's management was initially wary of the idea but finally authorized Butler to file a motion asking for a group estimation in February 1986, before the decision in the *Piccinin* case. In his motion, Butler proposed that detailed information be elicited from a representative sample of the claimants, that on the basis of this sample information the company prepare an estimate of the value of all the claims, and that an evidentiary hearing on the company's estimate then be held.

Murray Drabkin strongly opposed the motion because he recognized that an estimate could lead to cramdown, which would deprive the claimants of the power to veto any plan of reorganization that did not guarantee that Dalkon Shield claims would be paid in full before value was paid to equity. Drabkin thought that the risk of an insufficient estimate was particularly acute because Judge Merhige had recently suggested that the payment for Dalkon Shield claims should be measured not by the full value of the claims or by the full value of the company, but by "the largest feasible amount that could be paid to claimants and still keep the company viable over a reasonable period of years."[11] The company would be perfectly viable if it were sold to new owners; Merhige's formulation suggested his inclination to limit Dalkon Shield claimants to a fund that would be consistent with maintaining existing ownership.

At a conference in chambers in March 1986, Drabkin was able to convince Judge Merhige that a formal estimation proceeding would promote litigation over the meaning and application of section 502(c) in a mass tort bankruptcy and over the amount of the estimate, and would impede a consensual resolution of the case. The judge took no action on Robins's motion. Instead, it was agreed that a process of collection of information relative to the value of the claims from a sample of claimants would be initiated to facilitate informal assessments of Robins's total liability by the parties for their use in connection with settlement discussions and, if necessary, to support a formal estimation by the court at a later date. On March 21, 1986, Merhige appointed Francis E. McGovern, a professor at the University of Alabama Law School with experience in facilitating the settlement of complex litigation, to oversee this process. McGovern is a native Virginian and a graduate of the University of Virginia Law School.

On June 26, 1986, with Skadden, Arps now in the case, the *Piccinin* decision in hand, and the threat of the appointment of a trustee eliminated, Robins renewed its motion for a formal estimation of the total value of the Dalkon Shield claims. Robins hoped that an estimate would establish that its Dalkon Shield liability could be met at a figure it could afford and help break the deadlock with Drabkin, who by now was talking about more than $2 billion. Again, Judge Merhige did not act on Robins's request. On August 14, 1986, the day after the appointment of Ralph Mabey as examiner, Robins withdrew its motion. Robins later explained it had done so "at the urging of other parties-in-interest in an attempt to facilitate plan negotiations."[12]

The issue of estimation was not raised again until May 15, 1987, when the equity committee, in furtherance of its opposition to Robins's then pending stand-alone plan of reorganization, filed a motion asking the court to estimate Robins's total Dalkon Shield liability under section 502(c). The equity committee contended that an estimation would show that the $1.75 billion Robins proposed to provide would overpay Dalkon Shield claims at the expense of the shareholders.

On June 5, 1987, Robins filed another estimation motion of its own. Although at odds with the equity committee over the sale of the company, Robins concurred in the contention that the $1.75 billion figure was too high. Alternatively, the company asserted that the number was certainly high enough to pay Dalkon Shield claims in full. Robins argued that an estimate by the court was necessary for the information of the Dalkon Shield claimants in connection with their consideration of the company's plan of reorganization, and, if the plan was not accepted by the claimants, to provide a basis for a cramdown. The company hoped that an announcement by Judge Merhige that he would estimate the value of the Dalkon Shield claims would ward off proposals for its sale, at least until it became clear whether Robins could afford the estimated amount without a sale.

During the hearing on these motions on June 22, 1987, Judge Merhige indicated that he had not previously understood that Robins and the equity committee were suggesting that an estimate serve as the basis of a cramdown and as a limit on Robins's liability to the Dalkon Shield claimants. When Robert Miller for the equity committee and Dennis Drebsky for Robins made clear that this was exactly what they were suggesting, Merhige's reaction was negative. Four days later, on June 26, 1987, Merhige issued an order directing Professor McGovern to release the data he had compiled concerning a sample of the claimants to the official parties for their use "in evaluating the claims in this case," but he still did not make a decision to estimate the claims under section 502(c).

A few days later, Robins accepted Rorer's proposal for its acquisition. When Drabkin announced his opposition to the Rorer plan, the company and the equity committee resumed their efforts to convince Judge Merhige to conduct a formal estimation. Unlike Robins's stand-alone plan, under which the company would have paid no more than the actual liquidated value of the claims (up to a maximum of $1.75 billion), the Rorer plan provided that the amount committed to a claimants' trust would be paid, without possibility of refund, regardless of the total liquidated value of the claims. This difference strengthened the position of Robins and the equity committee that they were entitled to a judicial determination of the total liability. They reasoned that, if the estimate was below $1.75 billion, the commitment to the claimants' trust could be reduced before the submission of the plan to the claimants for a vote, to avoid overpaying the claimants at the expense of the shareholders.

In an effort to move the court away from the idea of a group estimation, on July 14, 1987, Drabkin filed another motion to end Robins's exclusivity period. Drabkin pointed out that the reason stated by the court in April 1987 for continuing the exclusivity period—its perception that Chapter 11 contains a preference for a reorganization that does not involve a sale of the company—was no longer applicable. He argued that the Rorer plan was inconsistent with the absolute priority rule in its failure to guarantee full payment of Dalkon Shield claims and that it could not be confirmed over the objection of the claimants.

Drabkin's motion evoked vitriolic opposition. The equity committee, once again Robins's ally now that $30 per share was in the offing,
called the motion "the most disingenuous pleading yet filed in this very
contentious case." Robins condemned the motion as "a cynical and un-
justifiable effort to sabotage" a reorganization based on a merger with
Rorer. Both contended that the Rorer plan would give the claimants "exactly what their counsel has consistently demanded"—a sale of Robins
and a $1.75 billion nonreversionary trust.[13]

The claimants' committee's motion to terminate the exclusivity
period was heard by Judge Merhige on July 27, 1987. Responding to
Robins's contention that there was not a "scintilla of evidence" that the
funds promised under the Rorer plan would be inadequate to pay
Dalkon Shield claims in full, the claimants' committee presented its expert in the evaluation of the Dalkon Shield claims, Dr. Howard Pifer of
Putnam, Hayes & Bartlett of Cambridge, Massachusetts. Pifer testified,
out of the public view in Merhige's chambers, that his preliminary analysis of the McGovern data indicated that the Dalkon Shield claims were
worth $7 billion. Merhige dismissed Pifer's testimony as ridiculous and
denied the committee's motion.

Judge Merhige had delayed ordering a formal estimation in the hope
that the parties would reach agreement on a figure that he could simply
approve. But Drabkin's opposition to the Rorer plan, together with his
sponsoring testimony that the claims were worth four times the figure he
had earlier agreed to, convinced Merhige that no agreement would be
forthcoming. On July 27, 1987, following Pifer's testimony, Merhige
granted the motions of the equity committee and of Robins to estimate
the total value of the Dalkon Shield claims and scheduled an evidentiary
hearing on the issue to commence November 5, 1987. In his order, Merhige suggested that he was now prepared, if necessary, to rely on an estimate for purposes of a cramdown.[14] Merhige added that the Rorer plan
"will not be confirmed unless the Court concludes that funds available
to the Trust called for in the plan will be adequate to pay the claims, as
estimated by the Court, in full."

All the while, from March 1986 to July 1987, a process of collecting
information that could be used as a basis of estimating Robins's total
liability to Dalkon Shield claimants had been ongoing under the supervision of Professor McGovern.[15] The basic idea of the McGovern process was to create two databases. One would contain information
concerning the injuries and settlement amounts in a sample of resolved
cases. The other would contain injury information from a sample of

pending cases. The information in the resolved case database could then be used to attach values to comparable cases in the pending case sample. The value of the universe of pending Dalkon Shield claims could then be estimated by projection from the value found for the sample. The McGovern process was intended only to produce the databases. Analysis of the data was left to experts representing the different parties in interest.

Robins, the official committees, and Aetna each retained a person qualified in the field of statistical sampling or data analysis to work with McGovern and with each other in the data-gathering process. It was agreed within the group that an effort would be made to resolve the various issues that arose by consensus, and except on a few matters, consensus was achieved.

McGovern secured information concerning a random sample of some 1,600 of the 9,500 cases that had been resolved before the bankruptcy, plus the 100 cases with the highest and the 100 cases with the lowest values. Information about each case in the sample was requested from the plaintiff's attorney, Robins's attorney, Aetna, and Robins. Summaries were then prepared setting forth the relevant information according to an agreed form, and the information from the summaries was keypunched to form the resolved case database.[16]

With respect to pending cases, the McGovern group developed a request for information to be sent to a random sample of claimants. These claimants were asked to submit medical records establishing their use of the Dalkon Shield and describing their injuries. They were also asked to complete and return a questionnaire concerning the claimed injury and other factors relevant to an evaluation of their claims.

Some tension arose among the participants in the McGovern process concerning the construction of the questionnaire. Robins intended to accord no value, or only a minimal value, to the claims of members of the sample who did not respond to the inquiry and to the claims of the corresponding proportion of the universe. Its interest, therefore, was in a low rate of response. To this end, Robins wanted the questionnaire to be long and complicated. Conversely, the claimants' committee wanted to assure that the questionnaire was neither forbidding in its bulk nor discouraging in its content. In matters of the inclusion or exclusion of particular inquiries, McGovern largely sided with Robins on the theory that more information was better than less, and in the end the questionnaire was fifty pages long.

The only questions on which McGovern could not secure consensus were those inquiring into the sexual history of the women in the sample.

Consistent with its position in the prebankruptcy litigation, Robins demanded the inclusion in the questionnaire of a wide variety of questions relating to sexual partners and practices and to personal hygiene. McGovern prevailed on Robins to drop the most offensive of these questions, but Robins insisted on the inclusion of the following:

1. How old were you when you first had sexual relations?
   I was _____ years old.

2. For *each* sex partner you had up to the time you were diagnosed as having an infection, a septic abortion, an ectopic pregnancy, or infertility, provide the following information:
   a. approximate dates of first and last sexual relations:

   First   *Last*

   b. to the best of your knowledge, as to *each* sex partner advise whether or not said partner engaged in sexual relations with others between the dates referred to in (2)(a) above.

The claimants' committee would not agree to the inclusion of these questions, and the matter was brought to Judge Merhige for resolution.

At a hearing in August 1986, a physician employed by the claimants' committee testified that the information sought by these questions would be of no use in evaluating claims and that the inclusion of the questions would bias the sample by discouraging participation. In addition, Mark Ellenberg produced a letter from Thomas Florence, Robins's representative in the McGovern process, to one of Robins's lawyers, categorizing questions concerning sex partners as inflammatory and advising against their inclusion. A physician employed by Robins testified that the information was relevant to the evaluation of the claims, but Robins did not rebut the evidence that the proposed questions would bias the sample. In a written order, stating only that he "deem[s] it proper so to do," Judge Merhige ruled that the questions should be included.[17] Whether the sex questions actually discouraged participation cannot be measured. It is certain, however, that this was their only possible effect on the process, because none of the experts made any use of the answers to these questions in making their estimates of Robins's liability.

A random sample of 2,500 names was drawn from the 327,000 responses to the bar date notice, and beginning in September 1986 the McGovern questionnaire and other instructions were mailed. A cover letter signed by Judge Merhige told the recipients that the completed questionnaire must be returned within thirty days, and medical records submitted within sixty days, or "your claim may be disallowed."

Merhige's letter also contained the following statement concerning counsel:

It is not necessary for you to retain an attorney in order to complete these forms. If you have an attorney, I'm sure that he or she will assist you. If you do not have an attorney and feel you should, the Court suggests you contact an office of the Bar Association or other lawyers' associations in your locality . . .

Judge Merhige had made clear, in connection with the published notice of the bar date, in connection with the two-page court questionnaire, and then again in this letter, his strong feeling that women injured by the Dalkon Shield did not need attorneys to make and process a claim in the Robins bankruptcy and that they should be told as much. Merhige felt that the involvement of attorneys would increase the cost of settling the claims and at the same time decrease the amounts actually received by the injured women. Representation by counsel could also cause the claimants to be less tractable in accepting a plan of reorganization and, ultimately, in accepting the amount of compensation offered in settlement of their claims. In fact, the vast majority of the Dalkon Shield claimants did file their claims without the assistance of counsel.[18]

The claimants' committee was concerned that women in the McGovern sample who were unrepresented by counsel might fail to respond to the inquiry or might make misleading or ill-informed statements that would result in an undervaluation of their claims and a corresponding undervaluation of the universe of claims. Despite Merhige's attitude about counsel, the committee felt entitled, even obligated, to act independently in this regard.

Accordingly, the claimants' committee sent a letter signed by committee member Judith Rentschler to attorneys throughout the United States with experience representing plaintiffs in Dalkon Shield litigation. The letter explained the McGovern process and asked the recipients' permission to include their names on a list of lawyers who were willing, without charge, to assist women in the sample in responding to the McGovern questionnaire. Rentschler stressed the importance of not having overall values "falsely depressed by inadvertent statements or admissions by claimants."

For instance, many questions deal with the statute of limitations and related issues . . . Robins has asked the Court to apply Virginia law, which would bar any claim two years after the first manifestation of injury. Should Robins prevail, a woman responding that her first symptom was "pain" upon insertion of the Shield could well be time barred long before she truly suffered injury.

Forty-nine lawyers agreed to participate.

Rentschler then provided a list of these attorneys and the names and addresses of the women in the McGovern sample to the president of the Association of Trial Lawyers of America (ATLA), who in turn wrote to each member of the McGovern sample informing her of the availability of free, expert legal advice in responding to the questionnaire. The ATLA letter stated, in part:

> The questionnaire is very detailed and many questions have legal implications of which you may not be aware, if you are not a lawyer. To assure that the responses to the questionnaire do not unfairly prejudice you or the Dalkon Shield claimants as a whole, you may wish to give serious consideration to obtaining the help of an attorney to complete this questionnaire.

Enclosed with this letter was the list of participating attorneys. The claimants' committee had informed Professor McGovern, but not Robins or Judge Merhige, of its intention to make these arrangements. McGovern did not endorse the plan, but neither did he raise any objection.

When Robins's attorneys learned that the president of the American Trial Lawyers Association was writing to the members of the sample directing them to free legal advice, they reacted angrily. On October 17, 1986, Robins filed a motion asking Judge Merhige to invalidate the sample, to select a new sample, to require the members of the claimants' committee and their attorneys personally to pay the resulting expenses, and to require Drabkin to explain the circumstances leading to the ATLA letter to the members of the sample. In its motion, Robins accused the claimants' committee of "unilaterally and surreptitiously interfering with the experimental design."

There is no question that Robins was genuinely disturbed over the committee's action, but the company may have also seen an opportunity to rid itself of some troublesome opponents. Judy Rentschler was the only lawyer with significant experience in Dalkon Shield litigation who had survived the dissolution of the first Dalkon Shield claimants' committee. In addition to serving as a member of the second claimants' committee, Rentschler was serving as a representative of the committee in the McGovern process. Rentschler was familiar with the interpretation of medical records of women claiming injury from the Dalkon Shield and with the factors relevant to the evaluation of their claims. Her participation had prevented experienced attorneys representing Robins from dominating the process.

William Cogar of Mays & Valentine was a central figure on Robins's side in the prebankruptcy Dalkon Shield litigation. On October 14, 1986, Cogar made a series of calls to Judy Rentschler in San Francisco, at one point even reaching her in the evening at a friend's home. Cogar demanded that Rentschler come to Richmond for a hearing concerning her letter and threatened her with professional sanctions and even criminal charges.

Rentschler's response was to discontinue her involvement with A. H. Robins and the Dalkon Shield. For the preceding several months, in ill health, she had suffered criticism from her former colleagues on the first Dalkon Shield claimants' committee for accepting an appointment to the second committee and for agreeing to Drabkin's retention as counsel. Now, faced with accusations of misconduct and threats of professional discipline from Robins, and unsure of what Judge Merhige would do, she felt that the price of continuing was too high. On October 15, 1986, Rentschler resigned from the claimants' committee. She, of course, meant this to include her representation of the committee in the McGovern process, but a few days later Merhige recorded his sentiments by entering an order prohibiting Rentschler's further participation in that process.

Robins would have liked to have gotten rid of Murray Drabkin at the same time. Drabkin had frustrated Robins by refusing to discuss a limited fund for Dalkon Shield claims and by pressing for a sale of the company and for the reservation of the entire proceeds to the payment of Dalkon Shield claims until every claim was paid. At a conference in chambers on October 30, 1986, Cogar pressed for a full-scale inquiry to determine responsibility for the Rentschler and ATLA letters, an inquiry that would have shown the involvement of the entire committee, its lawyers, and its experts. Drabkin's partner, Mark Ellenberg, was able to dissuade Merhige from this course by arguing that a public hearing would result in the publication of the Rentschler and ATLA letters in the press and thereby raise questions about a new sample. Merhige chastised Drabkin and Ellenberg, but decided to postpone any effort to look further into the matter. Merhige instructed McGovern to send the questionnaire and the request for medical records to an additional sample of 3,500 claimants and to maintain separately the responses of the two groups. (Drabkin and Ellenberg had decided to protect McGovern by not telling the judge that he had been informed in advance of the committee's action.) Later, the experts concluded that the results from the two samples were indistinguishable and they were treated as one.

Altogether, 6,000 Dalkon Shield claimants, plus an additional sample of 340 claimants whose cases were pending in court when the bankruptcy was filed, were mailed questionnaires and requests for medical records. When the responses to the questionnaires and the medical records were received, the relevant information was summarized and keypunched according to the same system that had been used with the resolved case sample to create the pending case database. Although they had participated in the design of the study, the experts were not given access to the responses until Judge Merhige's June 26, 1987, order.

The 6,340 members of the McGovern sample included more than 2,000 claimants who were no longer eligible, mostly because their claims had been disallowed by Judge Merhige for failure to return the two-page court questionnaire. Of the sample members who were eligible, approximately 65 percent returned the McGovern questionnaire and most of these also submitted at least some medical records. Professor McGovern considers this response rate to be "extraordinary" and has suggested that the "claimants seemed to relish the opportunity to tell their own stories without the indignities often suffered in the formal litigation discovery process."[19]

Nevertheless, the claimants' committee was concerned about the implications that might be drawn about the 35 percent of the eligible claimants in the sample who had not responded. The claimants' committee filed a motion asking Merhige to direct McGovern to supervise a telephone survey of a sample of these women to determine why they had not responded. At a hearing on the motion on September 18, 1987, Dr. Timothy Wyant, a biostatistician retained by the claimants' committee, testified that it was necessary to do this to test the assumption—made by the experts representing all the other parties in the case—that 35 percent of the members of the sample, and a corresponding proportion of the universe of claimants, intended to abandon their claims.

Robins was of the view that the response rate was more than sufficient and adamantly opposed the suggestion that the motivations of the nonresponders be explored. Nevertheless, on October 2, 1987, Merhige entered an order authorizing McGovern to undertake a telephone survey of a sample of nonresponders. The results of this survey showed that substantial numbers of sample members for whom responses had not been recorded stated that they had not received the McGovern materials, that they had completed and returned the materials, or that they had not returned the materials because of difficulties they had encountered securing medical records. The survey findings were reported to the parties on October 20, 1987.[20]

The experts representing Robins, the equity committee, the unsecured creditors' committee, Aetna, and the Dalkon Shield claimants' committee each conducted a separate analysis of the McGovern data and prepared an estimate of Robins's total liability to women injured by the Dalkon Shield. Ironically, considering the time and expense that had gone into the development of the questionnaire, the experts made little or no use of the answers the claimants had provided. Because of its greater uniformity and accuracy, they relied on the information contained in the medical records. The testimony describing their methods and findings was the subject of five days of evidentiary hearings before Judge Merhige from November 5 to November 11, 1987.

13   The Estimation

The estimation hearing promised to be the most important event in the Robins bankruptcy. Judge Merhige's July 27, 1987, order scheduling the hearing, which had been mailed to every woman with a claim pending in the case, suggested that the estimation process could lead to a court-imposed limitation on the funds available to pay the personal injury claims.

The lawyers experienced in prebankruptcy Dalkon Shield litigation—none of whom now had any official role in the Chapter 11 case—were unwilling to stay at home while this matter was worked out among Robins, Merhige, and Drabkin. Apart from their continuing animosity toward Drabkin, the plaintiffs' lawyers were concerned because neither the members of the claimants' committee nor their lawyers had any experience in the evaluation of Dalkon Shield injury claims, and they doubted that the committee representatives would be able to stand up against A. H. Robins's expertise in these matters. In addition, some of the women who had filed claims in the case were interested in participating in, or at least observing, the estimation process.

Section 1109 of the Bankruptcy Code provides that "a creditor . . . may appear and be heard on any issue in a case under this Chapter." This language notwithstanding, Judge Merhige refused to allow any woman with a Dalkon Shield claim or any attorney for a Dalkon Shield claimant to be heard in connection with the estimation process. Indeed, some women who traveled to Richmond in response to the notice were unable even to get into the courtroom.

In his July 27, 1987, order, Judge Merhige appeared to invite broad participation in the proceeding. The order provided that "[a]ny party in interest who wishes to be heard as to any of the issues referred to herein must cause to be delivered to the Clerk's office, on or before October 5, 1987, a written notice of intention to appear." By October 5, almost one hundred notices had been received by the Clerk, almost all from attorneys representing Dalkon Shield claimants. A large group of these attorneys formally designated Douglas Bragg to appear and participate on their behalf. Bragg is among the most knowledgeable and successful lawyers for plaintiffs in Dalkon Shield cases, but as the man who had interrogated Judge Merhige on August 22, 1985, he was also a particular object of Merhige's wrath.[1]

On October 15, 1987, Judge Merhige entered a "Pre-Trial Order" in which he provided that only counsel for the official claimants' committee would be permitted to participate in the estimation hearing on behalf of Dalkon Shield claimants. Merhige added that "counsel for individual claimants are advised to contact counsel for the Dalkon Shield Claimants Committee for purposes of offering such assistance as said counsel deem appropriate."

In the weeks before the estimation hearing, Murray Drabkin and his colleagues at Cadwalader, Wickersham & Taft had made known their intention to call several women injured by the Dalkon Shield as witnesses. The purpose was to give the court a sample not only of cold statistics but also of the actual impact on women's lives of injuries resulting in the destruction of their reproductive systems—the same kind of information a jury would consider in assessing damages for personal injuries. Robins objected on the ground that testimony about individuals was irrelevant to the estimation. In his October 15, 1987, order, Judge Merhige sustained Robins's position:

The Court once again reminds all parties that the Group Estimation Hearing is precisely for the purpose of determining the estimated value of all outstanding Dalkon Shield claims. Evidence as to the value of any individual's claim is, in the Court's view, irrelevant to this issue and a claimant will not be permitted to testify or to offer evidence of an individual claim.

Despite this statement, when the time came for the claimants' committee to present its evidence at the estimation hearing, John Walsh of the Cadwalader firm sought to call a Dalkon Shield victim as a witness. Walsh intended to argue that this testimony was not "evidence as to the value of any individual's claim" but evidence relevant to the evaluation of all Dalkon Shield claims. Judge Merhige was outraged:

WALSH: The claimants committee's next witness is Peggy Louis.
CAROL HEWITT (attorney for Robins): We filed a motion . . .
MERHIGE: Approach the bench.
(At the Bench):
MERHIGE: Are you beginning to put a claimant on the stand? You are not going to do it. By golly, get Rule 11.

Rule 11 of the Federal Rules of Civil Procedure provides for penalties when an attorney files documents for an improper purpose, such as to harass his opponent or to cause unnecessary delay or expense. Merhige went on: "I won't put up with it . . . I don't want to hear any. We talked about it. Mark [Ellenberg] was there. I think Murray [Drabkin] was here. There isn't any question about it, Mr. Walsh. I am sick and tired of this being used as nothing but a money bag. It won't happen."

Not only would Merhige not let injured women testify, he did not even want them in the courtroom. In on-the-record remarks in chambers before the hearing began, Merhige evidenced his disdain toward both the claimants and their lawyers:

Our biggest problem is going to be with these people who represent individual claimants who are going to want time to talk to Murray and Mr. Walsh and what have you. We have given you, Murray, the jury room. I will recess any time you think it appropriate to recess. I certainly will recess after an examination of each witness so that you can go to that room and get the benefit of your co-counsel's advice, which if you follow it might result in an end to this case in a hurry . . .

The same with the ladies. Now, I will try to explain to the ladies, there isn't any need for them to stay around, but I don't think that will chase many of them away until maybe the first recess, and then [they'll] get tired.

The first morning of the estimation hearing, Judge Merhige's courtroom was unable to accommodate the large numbers of claimants who wanted to get in, a situation that could hardly have come as a surprise as almost two hundred thousand notices of the hearing were sent out. Despite their status as "parties in interest," with the legal right to attend the proceedings, the overflow crowd was treated just as curiosity seekers are treated at a sensational trial: they were admitted if there was room. Consistent with his view that there was not "any need for the ladies to stay around," Merhige felt no obligation to make arrangements to hold court in a room with sufficient space to allow the women to observe the adjudication of their rights. United States district judges are authorized to conduct sessions "at such places in the district as the nature of the business may require."[2]

Before the hearing, the clerk of the bankruptcy court, Michael Sheppard, set up a table at the entrance to the courtroom. Initially, only attorneys who had submitted a timely notice of an intent to participate were admitted. Sheppard maintained a sign-up list for all others, and when the hearing commenced, he admitted people from this list to the extent that seats were available. Dozens of women who had come to the hearing were not admitted at any time that day. Discouraged with sitting in a dark hallway, fewer and fewer claimants presented themselves for admission as the hearing continued, and within a day or two everyone who arrived could be accommodated.

At the hearing, estimates of Robins's total liability to women injured by the Dalkon Shield, derived from the McGovern databases, were presented by statisticians or data analysts employed by Robins, the equity committee, the unsecured creditors' committee, Aetna, and the Dalkon Shield claimants' committee. All of these witnesses employed processes of (1) identifying the women in the sample deemed to be entitled to compensation at historic levels; (2) determining the value of the claims of those women, generally by reference to the resolved case database; and (3) projecting this value to the universe of eligible claims. To reach a total estimate, the witnesses added to this base figure various amounts for minimal or nuisance payments to excluded claimants, for potential future claims among eligible claimants, for nonuser claims (husbands claiming loss of consortium), and for costs of administration.

A serious shortcoming with the methodology concerned the identification of the claims in the sample to which historic value would be accorded. Ideally, in statistical sampling the pertinent information is determined concerning the sample and the assumption is made that the same factual pattern will be replicated in the universe. If 25 percent of the homes in a statistically valid sample are tuned to the "Cosby Show," it is assumed that 25 percent of all the homes in the universe from which the sample was drawn are tuned to the "Cosby Show." The comparable methodology for estimating the value of the universe of Dalkon Shield claims would be actually to liquidate the claims in a sample, using the procedures that would be used to liquidate claims under the plan of reorganization, and to project the liquidated value of the sample to the universe.

That was not done. Rather, the parties' experts made assumptions concerning the number of women in the sample who would present their claims for payment, and concerning the criteria by which the claims that were presented would be evaluated and paid. The differences among the estimates depended almost entirely on the differences in these assumptions. The witnesses had no expertise relative to these matters, and no evidence or even opinion was offered in support of the assumptions that were made. The witnesses simply made the assumptions that would support the result favored by their employer.

The clearest example of this concerns the relationship between responses to the McGovern questionnaire and future participation in a claims resolution process. Each witness, except Dr. Pifer for the claimants' committee, assumed that all the members of the sample who failed to return both the questionnaire and medical records documenting an injury related to the Dalkon Shield—that is, more than half of the

eligible claimants in the sample—would not participate in a claims resolution process and, at best, would receive only a token payment. Pifer
assumed the exact opposite—that every woman in the sample would
participate in the claims resolution process, whether or not she returned
the materials requested in the McGovern process. It is plain that neither
assumption was correct.

There are many reasons to expect that there would be a greater rate of
participation in an actual claims resolution process than in the
McGovern sampling process. Thirty and sixty days were allowed to return the questionnaire and medical records in the McGovern process;
fifteen months would be allowed in the claims resolution process. Questions about past sexual activities and partners were included in the
McGovern questionnaire; such questions would not be included in the
questionnaire distributed by the claimants' trust. There were serious
problems with the receipt of mail in the McGovern process; the longer
time frame in the actual process would allow for the correction of these
problems.[3] The McGovern process did not provide an opportunity to
supplement a response that was considered deficient; such an opportunity would be provided in the claims resolution process. There was a
large increase, between the fall of 1986 when the McGovern questionnaire was distributed and the spring of 1990 when the trust distributed
its questionnaire, in the proportion of claimants represented by counsel.
Lawyers have a greater facility for obtaining medical records from recalcitrant doctors, hospitals, and clinics and frequently will advance the
costs of obtaining the records on behalf of the client.[4]

Most important, participation in the McGovern process did not lead
to the receipt of money; participation in the claims resolution process
would. Judge Merhige emphasized the significance of this during the testimony of Robins's expert witness:

MERHIGE: Let me ask. Wouldn't one anticipate that more people would
respond to an offer of money, forget the amount, than they would be to filling out
a 50 page questionnaire? . . .

This isn't very scientific, but my own experience is people respond more to an
opportunity to get cash than they do to wait.

Robins and the equity committee wanted an estimate that would allow a reduction of the $1.75 billion provided in the Rorer plan or, at
least, a finding that $1.75 billion was adequate to pay Dalkon Shield
claims in full. The Rorer plan provided for full payment to the unsecured
creditors, so the unsecured creditors' committee wanted an estimate at

Table 13.1. Summary of Estimates of Party Experts

Party	No. Full Compens.	Aver. Full Compens.	Tot. Full Compens. (millions)	Adjusted Estimate (millions)
Robins	24,426	$40,571	$ 991	$1,215
Equity committee	39,658	24,615	976	1,021
Unsecured creditors	35,496†	41,284	1,465	1,633
Aetna	90,934	27,031	2,458	2,500
Claimants' committee	144,390	40,750*	5,878	7,167

* This figure was computed by the author from Dr. Pifer's exhibit 4.
† This figure was computed by the author. The witness for the unsecured creditors' committee found 45,911 claimants in the universe eligible for full compensation but then transferred 22.7 percent of these to a minimal payment category to account for statutes of limitations defenses. See transcript, November 8, 1987, pp. 796–802.

or near $1.75 billion that would allow speedy approval of that plan. Aetna was unhappy with the Rorer plan because it would leave Aetna exposed to unlimited liability to women injured by the Dalkon Shield. Aetna's purpose was to convince Judge Merhige to adopt a figure above $1.75 billion that Robins and Rorer could not meet, or would not want to meet, without a contribution from Aetna. Aetna hoped to make such a contribution in exchange for a release, through settlement of the *Breland* case, of its Dalkon Shield liability. The Dalkon Shield claimants' committee wanted an estimate above the full value of the company to assure that Robins's entire value would be reserved for the payment of Dalkon Shield claims, unless the claimants agreed otherwise.

The estimates of each of the parties' witnesses mirrored these positions perfectly. They are summarized in table 13.1. (The "total full compensation" column reflects the figure for the group of women estimated to receive compensation based on historic values. The "adjusted estimate" column includes the various add-ons relating to minimal payments to other claimants, nonuser claims, future claims, and costs of administration of the trust.)

Robins's estimate was prepared and presented by Thomas Florence, the man who had done the company's prebankruptcy estimate of Dalkon Shield liability. Florence holds a Ph.D. from Michigan State University in "research design and statistics."

Florence applied a series of five screens or disqualifications, the cumulative effect of which was to eliminate 87 percent of the eligible claimants in the McGovern sample. Only those who were not disqualified by the first screen were subjected to the second screen, and so on. Florence's screens, in the order in which he applied them, were:

- Failed to return the McGovern questionnaire;
- Failed to submit medical records that specify that a Dalkon Shield brand IUD was used;
- Failed to submit medical records that confirm an injury on the list of compensable injuries in Robins's plan of reorganization;
- Injury occurred more than three years before the Robins bankruptcy;
- Medical records indicate a cause of the injury other than the Dalkon Shield.

These five disqualifications applied to the sample and then projected to the universe resulted in the 24,426 compensable claims shown in table 13.1. Florence then categorized by injury the sample members who survived his screens, projected the number in each injury category to the universe, and attributed values to each category based on the average amount paid to resolve cases in that category in the resolved case database. Table 13.2 shows Florence's results by injury category. Florence's total estimate of $1.215 billion included an additional $224 million for future claims, nonuser claims, token payments to excluded claimants, and 10 percent for costs of administration.[5]

As Florence had computed an average historic value not significantly different from that proposed by Dr. Pifer for the claimants' committee, the key to his low estimate was the imposition of his disqualifications to reduce the number of claimants eligible for compensation from more

Table 13.2. Compensable Claims in Florence's Estimate

	No.	Hist. Val.	Total (millions)
Birth defect	145	258,000	$37.4
Sterilizing surgery	2,807	91,800	257.7
Infertility	1,248	63,400	79.1
Septic abortion	488	34,400	16.8
Pelvic infection	14,132	34,400	486.1
Ectopic pregnancy	148	28,800	4.3
Perforation	2,736	25,800	70.6
Abortion	1,674	13,100	21.9
Other	1,048	16,300	17.1
Subtotal	24,426		$991

than 195,000 to fewer than 25,000. Florence's disqualifications were based on several questionable practical, legal, and medical judgments. Most significant, in that it resulted in the exclusion of more than half the eligible universe, was the disqualification, already noted, of all members of the sample who did not return both the questionnaire and medical records documenting an injury related to the Dalkon Shield.

With respect to those who did return the McGovern questionnaire with supporting medical records, Florence disqualified large numbers of claims for reasons that had not prevented injured women from receiving compensation before the bankruptcy. For example, Florence eliminated 43,500 eligible claims on the basis of the number of women in the sample whose sworn statements that they had used a Dalkon Shield brand IUD were not explicitly confirmed by their medical records. Women were excluded on this basis even when the medical records confirmed the use of an IUD but did not identify the brand. Judge Merhige protested this exclusion:

MERHIGE: You are not at all sure that the people who were making the determination might not after putting the women under oath, might not accept her statement that the doctor told me it was a Dalkon Shield . . .

Isn't it really more accurate to say that 40 percent of the people who filled out the form showed no evidence on the form of having worn the Dalkon Shield except their own word?

FLORENCE: [The witness nodded.]

MERHIGE: But the word was under oath?

FLORENCE: Correct.

MERHIGE: I am a little bit disturbed . . . at your disregarding the fact that people swear under oath. I realize that some people don't take it as seriously as others, but hope springs eternal. I assume when they do that, that they are telling the truth. And that disturbs me, Dr. Florence. If you can relieve my anxiety in any way, I would appreciate your doing it.

FLORENCE: I am not sure I can, Your Honor.

In his cross-examination of Florence, Mark Ellenberg identified a claimant whose medical records did not confirm Dalkon Shield use but who had been offered and rejected a $150,000 settlement of her claim prior to the bankruptcy. Judge Merhige asked Florence to prepare an amendment to his report including, instead of excluding, women who swore they wore the Dalkon Shield but whose medical records did not confirm it. Several days later, Florence returned to the witness stand and testified that this change would increase his estimate from $1.22 billion to $1.64 billion.

Florence excluded an additional 11,900 claims to reflect the number of sample members screened out by the requirement that the injury have occurred within three years of the bankruptcy. Under Maryland law, which Florence purported to apply, the limitations period runs not from the date of injury but from the date on which the injured person has actual knowledge, or through the exercise of due diligence should have knowledge, that her injury was caused by the conduct of the defendant.[6] Moreover, Maryland and most states allow suit to be filed after the expiration of the limitations period if it can be proved that the defendant fraudulently concealed facts relevant to its liability.[7] In the prebankruptcy Dalkon Shield litigation, cases in which this contention was made to overcome a statute of limitations defense were regularly compromised by settlement.

Lastly, Florence excluded 21,300 of the 45,700 claims that survived all the other disqualifications on the ground that the injuries of a corresponding portion of the sample, although of a type associated with the Dalkon Shield, were caused by some other factor. In making these determinations, Florence relied on criteria developed by Herbert Sandmyer, M.D., a physician in Robins's employ. The factors identified by Dr. Sandmyer as establishing that the injury was not caused by the Dalkon Shield involved debatable issues of causation and proof. For example, Sandmyer excluded claims of infertility unless a medical record reflected a diagnosis of pelvic inflammatory disease prior to the diagnosis of infertility. Ellenberg identified a case resolved before the bankruptcy involving a claim of infertility with no medical record reflecting an earlier diagnosis of PID that was settled for $710,000.

By use of his disqualifications, Florence had removed from the sample all the cases in which there could be any legitimate dispute about the right to recovery. But in attaching values to the surviving cases, Florence did not use average amounts drawn exclusively from resolved cases that would survive his screens. He used average amounts paid in all cases in the injury category in the settled case database, including cases with no confirmation of Dalkon Shield use, cases with possible statute of limitations problems, and cases with a possible alternative cause of the injury. Assuming that the presence of one or more of these factors reduced the prebankruptcy settlement values, Florence's methodology not only improperly denied compensation to the cases that were screened out but shortchanged the cases that were not screened out by applying all-inclusive averages.

The estimates prepared by the witnesses employed by the equity committee and the unsecured creditors' committee were comparable to Florence's in their methodology. Each applied a series of similar screens to exclude claims from the sample and then used averages drawn from all the cases in the resolved case database to attach values to the claims that had survived this process.

Aetna presented an estimate of $2.5 billion. Apart from any question of its methodology, the mere fact that Aetna presented an estimate at this level fundamentally altered the dynamics of the estimation proceeding. Considering that Aetna is an insurance company not given to the overstatement of the value of claims and that it was alleged to have joint liability with Robins for Dalkon Shield injuries, Aetna's estimate effectively precluded Judge Merhige from granting Robins an estimate at or below $1.75 billion, even though Merhige had previously urged Drabkin to accept that figure. Drabkin could never support, and the claimants could not be expected to accept, a figure below Aetna's estimate. And while Aetna's position technically did not prevent a cramdown of a lesser amount, it did have this practical effect.

Aetna's estimate was presented by Dr. Francine Rabinowitz. Dr. Rabinowitz is a professor at the Schools of Public Administration and Urban and Regional Planning at the University of Southern California in Los Angeles. Unlike the other expert witnesses, Dr. Rabinowitz is not a statistician but an expert in the field of "policy analysis."

Starting with the eligible claims in the sample, Dr. Rabinowitz excluded only women who did not submit a medical record evidencing an injury associated with the Dalkon Shield and women who did not claim to have used the Dalkon Shield. Rabinowitz treated the additional factors that Florence used to exclude claims not as exclusions but as matters bearing on the valuation of the claim. Because of this difference, Aetna attached values to 1,864 claims in the sample, which projected to 90,034 claims in the universe, more than three and a half times the number of claims that received compensation at historic levels under Dr. Florence's analysis.

Rather than attempting to match pending cases against cases in the resolved case database for the purpose of determining value, as did all the other experts, Rabinowitz secured new evaluations of pending cases by the same three Aetna claims adjusters who had settled Dalkon Shield cases before the bankruptcy. She explained:

This reflects the fact that each claim situation is a complex and ultimately unique combination of medical, personal, factual and legal circumstances and characteristics. The approach to resolution that has been employed throughout the history of these claims has applied experienced judgment to each such combination. That is also what the valuation process used herein does.[8]

Dr. Rabinowitz developed nine injury groupings to encompass all the 1,864 claims in the sample she had found to be potentially compensable. She also developed four categories to reflect different levels of problems in the file that would weaken a woman's entitlement to compensation, ranging from an absence of such "complicating factors" up to the most serious complicating factors. In this way she had created a grid with thirty-six cells, to which she allocated the 1,864 cases. Then, because she did not want to ask the Aetna claims adjusters to evaluate all 1,864 cases, she took a sample of the sample. Within cells—so as to assure the representation of all the cells—she selected 272 claims and gave these to the adjusters for evaluation.

When Dr. Rabinowitz received the results, she averaged the values for each cell. She then used these averages within the cells to project the value of all the sample cases in the cell. She then projected this total value for each cell to the corresponding number of cases in the universe. This process, prior to any adjustments, produced a figure of $2.458 billion.

Dr. Rabinowitz subjectively reduced this number to $2.2 to $2.3 billion to take account of potential sources of overstatement, including her failure to consider statutes of limitations. She then added a $100 token payment for every active claim not otherwise compensated—roughly $7.3 million—an arbitrarily determined reserve for future claims from women who had filed timely responses to the bar date notice in the amount of $50 million, and 10 percent for administrative costs. Together, these adjustments left her total estimate at approximately $2.5 billion.

At the hearing, Judge Merhige identified two serious problems with Rabinowitz's methodology, at least one of which tended to understate the value of the claims. The latter concerned the objectivity of the Aetna claims adjusters. Rabinowitz's average value per compensable claim had come out significantly below Florence's average value ($27,000 as compared to $40,000), which was based on the amounts actually paid in the resolved cases. Judge Merhige suggested that insurance adjusters would naturally tend to lower evaluations.

MERHIGE: Their job was to keep the price down. Isn't that what the job of a claims adjuster is?

RABINOWITZ: . . . [The adjusters] were told . . . "what I want to know is not your . . . assessment of this claim as an Aetna claims handler, but what it will take to settle this claim either with a claimant or with a claimant who is accompanied by her attorney." They are being asked to forecast the outcome of the traditional negotiation process in which claims handling is done. So I believe, and did some tests to establish, that they are not providing what you are suggesting are potentially low-ball estimates of these claims . . .[9]

MERHIGE: Then your ultimate conclusion to a great extent is premised on the view of people that you have confidence in, that have training settling cases.

RABINOWITZ: Yes.

MERHIGE: And if they are wrong, everything you have done is wrong . . . The fact of the matter is, there may be a built in bias . . . I really do think there is a distinction between the way [claims adjusters] operate and the way defense counsel and plaintiffs' lawyers operate.

The second problem concerned the reliability of making projections from the small number of cases that were actually evaluated by the Aetna adjusters. One of the thirty-six cells included only one case, another included only two, and in several there were three. Dr. Rabinowitz testified that the data were not susceptible to a statistical test to determine whether the sample sizes were large enough to justify predictions to the universe.[10]

This conceptual problem was highlighted by the fact that the resulting averages for the cells were in many instances counterintuitive, both in that less serious injuries were accorded higher values than more serious injuries and in that, within an injury category, more would be paid for an injury with factors complicating the right to recovery than for the same injury without such complicating factors.[11] Thus, a claim of unwanted pregnancy or abortion with no complicating factors was found to be worth $98,000, but a birth defect or infant death with no complicating factors was found to be worth only $7,000. A claim of infection, surgery, and infertility with no complicating factors was found to be worth $33,000; the same claim with the most serious impediments to recovery was found to be worth $63,000. These incongruities may have been attributable to factors peculiar to the particular cases examined, but they underscored the question of whether averages based on such small numbers of cases could be validly used to predict the value of more than ninety thousand claims.

During her testimony Dr. Rabinowitz was asked to explain why the average values for the various cells did not correlate with the seriousness of the injury and with the strength of the evidence.

RABINOWITZ: I did not expect the simplicity that these were hierarchical. I, in fact, knew from looking at the resolved cases that they weren't going to be logical in that way . . . In history and in some future adversarial or trust-oriented process, a quite complicated series of factors are going to be brought to bear in valuing these cases. Simple logic isn't what happened in history and isn't a good guide to what ought to be used as an estimator for the future . . .

MERHIGE: I've got to ask a question. I'll try not to use logic. But it seems to me that much greater value should be placed on no complicating factors than on serious complicating factors. This doesn't make sense to me.

RABINOWITZ: Well, could I suggest what this range of things looks like when you use all of the cases rather than one cell? . . . It isn't the right concept to expect me to be saying, and I am not saying, that in any specific cell these values are right . . . I am predicting for the whole group, and that logic turns out to be present when you look at the whole group. The compensation being paid to cases with no complicating factors is the highest and the compensation being paid to the cases with very serious complicating factors is the lowest.

MERHIGE: That's not always so, though, on this exhibit . . . It just seems strange.

In fact, even when all 272 cases in the subsample were grouped by complication factor without regard to the injury groups, as Rabinowitz suggested, the values did not conform to logical expectations.[12]

The estimate for the Dalkon Shield claimants' committee was presented by Dr. Howard Pifer of Cambridge, Massachusetts, an economist who had taught statistical decision theory and probability theory at the Harvard Business School.

Unlike all the other expert witnesses, Pifer did not assume that the rate of participation by the sample members in the McGovern process was a valid predictor of participation in a future claims resolution process. He presented an estimate based on the eligible claimants in the sample who had responded to the McGovern questionnaire. But he also presented an estimate based on eligible claimants in the sample who had *not* responded to the McGovern questionnaire. He presented a third estimate based on *ineligible* claimants in the McGovern sample (claimants disqualified for failure to return the court questionnaire) who had responded to the McGovern questionnaire.

Pifer's estimate for eligible claimants who responded to the McGovern questionnaire. Pifer's method had some similarities to the approach utilized by Dr. Rabinowitz. Like Rabinowitz, Pifer did not exclude sample members because of possible obstacles to recovery reflected in their files. But instead of relying on new evaluations by Aetna adjusters, Pifer attributed values to these claims by reference to the amounts Robins had paid in the past to resolve similar claims, with similar obstacles, as reflected by the resolved case database.

Pifer constructed a system for classifying claims that took account of the nature of the injury and the quality of the supporting evidence. He established the following classifications:

1. Sterility—strong support
2. Sterility—some support
3. Sterility—no information

4. Nonsterility group A (perforation, surgery, ectopic pregnancy, septic abortion, and infection)—strong support
5. Nonsterility group A—some support
6. Nonsterility group A—no information
7. Nonsterility group B (pregnancy, breakage, impaired fertility, pain and bleeding, spontaneous abortion, and therapeutic abortion)—strong support and some support
8. Nonsterility group B—no information
9. All the above injury groupings (sterility, nonsterility group A, and nonsterility group B)—no support

Pifer included three additional categories of infrequent but very serious injuries, without breakdowns by degree of supporting evidence:

10. Birth defect
11. Maternal death
12. Infant death

Pifer defined "strong support" as "clear confirmation of the injury, strong evidence of causation, little if any evidence of an alternative cause and a close temporal relationship." "Some support" meant that there was medical evidence that the injury had occurred and no evidence that clearly established a cause of the injury other than the Dalkon Shield. "No information" meant that there was no medical record confirming the injury. "No support" (group 9 above) meant that medical records positively showed that an injury had not occurred or, if one had, that it had not been caused by the Dalkon Shield.

With the help of registered nurses and paralegals, each of the cases in the McGovern resolved case database was placed in one of the twelve categories and an average value for each category was computed.[13] Through this process, it was determined that substantial payments had been made by Robins before the bankruptcy to resolve cases in the "no information" category. Even cases in the "no support" category—cases proved to be without merit by the documents sent by the claimant—had been paid an average of eight thousand dollars.[14] Pifer's methodology assumed that a claimants' trust established by a plan of reorganization would similarly pay claims with no information or with information that contradicted the claim.

After categorizing the resolved cases in this way, Pifer moved to the eligible claimants in the sample who had returned the McGovern questionnaire. He selected those who asserted (without contradiction in their records) that they had worn a Dalkon Shield and who identified an injury that had been compensated prior to the bankruptcy. Pifer's only difference from Rabinowitz in identifying eligible responding sample members to be compensated at historic values is that Pifer did not require a medical record confirming the injury; in the absence of a medical record, he accepted the claimant's description of the injury set forth in her response to the questionnaire. Because of this difference, Pifer's eligible responders entitled to compensation at historic value projected to a universe of 94,188 while Rabinowitz had projected a universe of 90,934 compensable claims.

The claims of the eligible responders in the sample who met these criteria were then allocated to the twelve categories through the same procedure used for the resolved cases. All cases for which medical records had not been submitted were placed in the appropriate "no information" category.

The average value that had been determined for the category by reference to the resolved cases was then assigned to each claim allocated to the category, the values for all the claims assigned to all the categories were added, and the total was projected to the corresponding universe of 94,188 claims. The total value determined through this process was $4.2 billion. The average per case was $44,500. Looking at virtually the same claims, the Aetna adjusters had found an average value of $27,000. This difference in average value, far more than Pifer's small increase in the size of the universe, explained the difference between Rabinowitz's $2.458 billion estimate and Pifer's $4.192 billion estimate for eligible, responding members of the McGovern sample. It also provided some support for the suggestion that the Aetna adjusters had underestimated the case values in comparison to the amounts that had been actually paid when claims were resolved in the real world of impending trial dates, unfriendly venues, insistent judges, demands for information that Robins or Aetna did not want to provide, conflicting interpretations of the medical evidence, aggressive counsel, and so forth.

Pifer's estimate for eligible claimants who did not respond to the McGovern questionnaire. Next, Pifer made an estimate of the value of the claims of the universe of women who corresponded to the eligible sample members who did not return the McGovern questionnaire. On the basis of their responses to the two-page court questionnaire, Pifer identified the sample members who asserted that they had worn a Dalkon Shield and identified a compensable injury. Each of their claims was then assigned the average value for all cases at all levels of support in the appropriate injury category. Support levels within the injury categories were not considered on the theory that the claims of the nonresponders would prove to have the same support, on average, as the

Table 13.3. Compensable Claims in Pifer's Estimate

	Number of Claims	Average Compens.	Total Value (millions)
Eligible McGovern responders	94,188	$44,500	$4,192
Eligible McGovern nonresponders	43,903	33,800	1,483
Ineligible McGovern responders	6,299	32,200	203
Totals	144,390	40,750	5,878

claims of those who did respond to the McGovern inquiry. The values for all the cases in this portion of the sample were added, and the total was projected to the corresponding universe of 43,903 claims. The value for this group determined through this process was $1.48 billion.[15]

Pifer's estimate for ineligible claimants who responded to the McGovern questionnaire. Finally, Pifer estimated a value from the claims of ineligible sample members who responded to McGovern. He found that 156 of the 2,030 women in the McGovern sample who had been disqualified by Judge Merhige for failure to return the two-page court questionnaire had completed and returned the fifty-page McGovern questionnaire. Many of these women submitted medical records as well. Dr. Pifer attached a value to these 156 claims following the same procedure he had used in estimating the value of the claims of the women who had responded to both questionnaires. From the total value he had found for the 156 claims, Pifer estimated a value for a like proportion (more than 7 percent) of the universe of disqualified claimants. Through this process a total of $203 million was assigned to 6,299 disqualified claims. Table 13.3 summarizes Pifer's findings for the three separate groups. When Pifer added amounts for future claims (from among timely claim filers) and expenses of administration, his total estimate came to $7.167 billion.

Judge Merhige reacted to Dr. Pifer and to his estimate with undisguised hostility. Merhige's first contact with Pifer was during Pifer's court appearance in connection with the claimants' committee's July 1987 motion to terminate the exclusivity period. At that time Pifer had given a $7 billion preliminary estimate of the value of the Dalkon Shield claims. This had been an unexpected bombshell, totally inconsistent with the numbers that had been under discussion, and Merhige had immediately dismissed Pifer's testimony. At that time Pifer had been in the case for only a few weeks. When, after three months of further study, Pifer came to the estimation hearing with essentially the same figure, Merhige believed that this was proof that Pifer's testimony was not "credible." [16]

The judge's problem with Pifer was aggravated by Pifer's demeanor as a witness. Merhige takes his role as the presiding officer quite seriously, and he is a stickler for enforcing courtroom decorum and deference to his authority. The witness box in Merhige's courtroom is placed in a most unusual location, midway between where the judge sits and the lawyer stands. After he is sworn in by a booming-voiced bailiff, the witness is sealed into place with a large piece of wood, referred to as a "table," laid across the front of the witness box by the marshal. The witness is in an awkward physical position not only because of this strange restraint but because his chair faces the side wall. The questions from counsel come from his right and the judge is sitting to his left, with the result that, when Merhige interposes a question or a comment during the examination, it comes from behind the witness's head.

The witnesses who preceded Pifer at the estimation hearing were modest, soft-spoken, and deferential. Pifer is a large, gruff, contentious man. He was suffering from a back problem at the time of the hearing, and, rather than sitting down, he stood up in the rear of the courtroom for several days before he testified, undoubtedly to the annoyance of the judge. When Pifer was called to the stand, Merhige commented on his apparent back problem and asked whether he would like a straight-backed chair. Pifer responded that he would rather stand, and Merhige agreed to "try that." The result was that, instead of assuming the customary position in Judge Merhige's witness box, Pifer wandered around the courtroom while he testified, not unlike a professor giving a lecture, with a decidedly negative impact on the judge. Alert to the nuances of Merhige's displeasure, Jim Roberts, in the course of attacking Pifer's testimony in his closing argument for Robins, referred repeatedly to the witness having stood when he testified. [17]

Merhige was particularly bothered by Pifer's insistence that the resolved case database reflected value for cases with no medical records to support the claim, and even for cases where the claim was positively contradicted by the medical records.

MERHIGE: [Y]ou put an estimate of $18,206 on claims [nonsterility group B] on which, as I understand from this, you had no information? Is that correct?

P I F E R: No information meant it was not proven one way or the other.

M E R H I G E: Okay. You estimated the value of that no information claim to be $18,206?

P I F E R: We found that, yes, that is correct.

M E R H I G E: How did you get that?

P I F E R: When we went back through the resolved history, we found a number of those that had no information. They were paid a certain amount of money, and we could not prove that they had the compensable injury, or disprove that. On the average, they received $18,206 . . .

M E R H I G E: You are saying then that they were literally giving it away?

P I F E R: I didn't say that. For whatever reason, that is what they settled for on the basis of the information available at the time they settled it, or at least as it entered into the McGovern process.

There was no evidence conflicting with what Pifer reported on this point, and Merhige himself never examined the records to see if it was true; it just did not make sense to the judge, and he did not believe it. And even if it were true that Robins or Aetna had in the past paid unsupported or unmeritorious claims for whatever reason, such claims would not be paid by a trust functioning under his supervision and Merhige did not want an estimate that assumed otherwise.

Judge Merhige also reacted negatively to Pifer's according value to the claims of women in the sample who did not submit medical records and then projecting that value to an estimate of $1.48 billion for almost 44,000 women in the universe of eligible claimants. The following exchange provides the flavor:

J A M E S R O B E R T S [for Robins]: Have you seen the forms that were used by the court? . . . Do you know whether or not it simply explains to the claimant how to get medical records?

P I F E R: It explains how to go about the process, perhaps not as simply as the question.

R O B E R T S: You know about a "Dear Claimant" letter that was written by Professor McGovern? . . . the part that tells the claimant how important it is that they get their medical records in.

P I F E R: Yes. I will read the underlined part that you have. "It is your responsibility to assure that records showing use of the Dalkon Shield or injury from the Dalkon Shield are provided to the court." And it says, "If you don't request medical records your claim may be disallowed. If you have requested your records, you should follow up to assure they are provided to the court." And subsequently, Mr. McGovern also did a phone survey and found that those records are still coming in, are lost, doctor can't be found, too expensive.

M E R H I G E: Mr. Witness, let's not waste time. The Court has already decided that. I don't know of any efforts, any stronger efforts that could have been made than were made by this Court to help people get records and to ask them to get records. Now, whether it was interfered with, you know, we had one instance of a letter going from one of the claimants committee that may have interfered with it. We don't know. But nobody is ever going to convince me that we did not bend over backwards to try to help. Even to the point of my calling doctors. So there is no need to spend a lot of time on that right now.

The situation further deteriorated when it became clear that Pifer had included in his estimate $203 million for more than six thousand claims that Merhige had specifically disallowed. On the basis of the 156 ineligible claimants in the sample who had returned the McGovern materials, Pifer was undoubtedly correct that some portion of the universe of disqualified claimants would participate in the claims resolution process if given the opportunity to do so. The problem was that Merhige had ruled that they would not be given the opportunity, unless they established "excusable neglect" for their failure to return the court questionnaire under a timetable that had already expired.[18] Under these circumstances, Pifer's estimation of value for these claims smacked of defiance, a point that Robins and its allies played to the full in attacking Pifer's overall presentation.

When the estimation hearing was concluded, Judge Merhige turned his attention not to the esoterics of sampling, statistical projections, and epidemiology but to the practicalities of settlement. If it was possible to do so, Merhige still wanted to avoid making an estimate and simply to approve a figure agreed to by the parties.

Merhige proceeded from the assumption that it would not be possible to secure Drabkin's support for a plan providing less than $2.5 billion, the amount of the Aetna estimate. Merhige undertook to attain an agreement among Robins, Rorer, and Aetna to provide at least this amount. In the past, Merhige had not actually participated in settlement negotiations, but in the first week of December 1987, Merhige presided over a series of meetings in his office attended by James Roberts for Robins, Paul Silverman, a New York attorney, for Rorer, John Harkins representing Aetna, and Ralph Mabey, the examiner.

The plan of reorganization that was on file provided that Rorer would pay a total of $2 billion to the two trusts over a period of seven years. The new discussions focused on a proposal calling for $2.6 billion to be paid over seven years. Rorer's total contribution would be increased to $2.3 billion, and Aetna, in settlement of *Breland*, would provide the difference of $300 million. Robins's management supported this proposal. In an apparent misunderstanding, John Harkins caused the other participants to believe that Aetna was prepared to pay $300 million over time. Rorer approached the equity committee to negotiate a reduction in the value of the Rorer stock that Robins shareholders would receive as part of the deal, in recognition of the increased cost of meeting Robins's Dalkon Shield liability. Merhige thought an agreement was in the offing, and he asked Robins to keep its board of directors available to approve the deal. But at the eleventh hour, on December 10, 1987, Harkins made clear that, other than the cash Aetna owed Robins on account of unused insurance benefits (an amount assumed to be between $50 and $75 million), Aetna would only participate in the form of "excess" insurance, not cash. The insurance proceeds would be payable, if necessary, only after all the other funds had been paid to the trust and exhausted.

Whether Aetna had changed its position or there had been a misunderstanding was a much debated point among the participants in the process. Whichever it was, Merhige made one last effort to put the deal back together. Aetna had done some calculations that indicated that the trust, relying only on payments from Rorer under the schedule under discussion, would run out of cash to pay claims during the third year, and recurrently thereafter. Merhige asked Harkins if Aetna would make the insurance proceeds available at any time that funds were needed by the trust rather than only after all the Rorer payments had been made and spent. Merhige warned Harkins that this might be Aetna's only opportunity to be included, as it wanted, in an overall resolution. Nevertheless, Aetna decided that the cost of this proposal was too high and refused to make the concession Merhige had requested. Rorer was unable to increase its contribution, and the negotiations broke down.

Frustrated and angry, Merhige concluded that he had no alternative but to announce an estimate. On December 11, 1987, Merhige summoned Richmond counsel for the various parties to his courtroom and said that his estimate of Robins's liability to women injured by the Dalkon Shield was $2.475 billion "payable over a reasonable period of time." Judge Merhige did not enter a formal order, and did not then or ever provide any explanation for the conclusion he had reached. Later, the judge explained that his purpose had been to avoid the delay of an appeal and to focus the attention of the parties on reaching an agreement.[19] Nonetheless, even after an agreement among the official parties had been reached, Merhige rejected pleas for an explanation of his estimate, and this omission provided the basis for appeals from the final plan of reorganization.

14   Bidding for Robins

Judge Merhige may have conducted some analysis of the statistical data before announcing his estimate, but his figure clearly was less the result of mathematical computations than another effort to stimulate an agreement among the parties. The figure $2.475 billion was below the $2.6 billion that had proved a bit too high for Rorer and Aetna in the discussions that had preceded the estimate. With this discount, Merhige expected that an agreement among Rorer, Aetna, Robins, and the equity committee that would provide this amount would quickly follow. The question was whether Murray Drabkin's agreement could be secured.

To provide room for maneuvering, Merhige had been carefully vague about the time frame ("a reasonable period of time") in which the estimated amount was to be paid. The day of the estimate, Jim Roberts of Mays & Valentine told newspaper reporters that Merhige's failure to object to the seven-year period that Robins and Rorer had previously proposed meant that that schedule was acceptable.[1] If the seven-year payout schedule contained in the Rorer plan was simply adapted to the higher total figure, the present value of the fund would be only $1.88 billion.[2] With a shorter payout period, the value of the fund could be much more.

On December 11, 1987, the day Merhige announced his estimate, E. Claiborne Robins, Jr., and Robert E. Cawthorn, chief executive of Rorer, issued a joint statement affirming their intention to "work to revise the plan of reorganization. We are hopeful we can satisfy the court." It soon became clear, however, that more would be involved than simply restructuring the Rorer offer to include a contribution from Aetna and to meet Merhige's estimate. The announcement of a judicially determined limit on Robins's Dalkon Shield liability precipitated new interest in the acquisition of the company.

The very next day, December 12, 1987, Robins received an overture from Sanofi, the second largest pharmaceutical company in France. Sanofi was founded in 1973 as a spinoff from Elf Acquitaine, the French oil and chemical giant. Elf, which is owned by the French government, still owned 60 percent of Sanofi and could assist in an acquisition of

Robins. Although a major force in the pharmaceutical industry in Western Europe, Sanofi had almost no market in the United States, Canada, or Latin America. It viewed Robins, with its extensive and successful marketing and distribution system, as a perfect vehicle for the introduction of its products into American markets. An affiliation with Robins, with its popular consumer products, would also strengthen Sanofi's own position in over-the-counter pharmaceuticals in Europe.[3]

Sanofi had shown interest in the A. H. Robins Company the preceding spring, when Ralph Mabey was looking for a purchaser following the withdrawal from negotiations of American Home Products. Robins's treasurer, David Davis, and the company's chief financial officer, G. E. R. Stiles, had traveled to Europe to explore several possible deals and had met with Sanofi representatives. Before any proposal had been made by Sanofi, the Rorer agreement intervened. But Sanofi remained interested.

The merger agreement with Rorer prohibited Robins from soliciting any other offer for the purchase of the company in the period before the consummation of the merger, but it did not prevent Robins from considering unsolicited offers or from accepting an offer that was more valuable than the deal with Rorer. The agreement also provided that it could be terminated by either side if Judge Merhige estimated the value of Dalkon Shield claims at a level above $1.75 billion.

In the summer of 1987, not long after the agreement between Robins and Rorer was signed, Sanofi invited E. Claiborne Robins, Jr., to come to Paris to meet its executives. Robins, Jr., made the trip in late October 1987, accompanied by a member of senior management. He was reported to have told his hosts that all he could do was listen because of the restrictions contained in the agreement with Rorer.[4] On November 16, 1987, between the conclusion of the estimation hearing and the announcement of the estimate, when the general assumption was that Merhige would indeed estimate the value of Dalkon Shield claims above $1.75 billion, David Davis and Arvid Johnson, Robins's general counsel, had lunch in New York with Sanofi representatives, including Dr. B. G. Crouch, Sanofi's vice-president for the United States and Canada. At that time, various forms of arrangements between Robins and Sanofi were discussed.[5]

On Saturday, December 12, 1987, Stiles received a call from Sanofi's investment banker in New York that led to a visit by Sanofi representatives to Richmond the following day. The same day, Dr. Crouch called Arvid Johnson and told Johnson that Sanofi was interested in a deal with Robins on terms that would continue A. H. Robins as a separate entity under existing management, a concept that met with an enthusiastic response at Robins headquarters.

Talks in Richmond between Robins and Sanofi representatives continued through Tuesday, December 15, 1987. On the morning of Thursday, December 17, 1987, René Sautier, chairman of Sanofi, called E. Claiborne Robins, Jr., from Paris and offered to invest $500 million in A. H. Robins and to assume Robins's obligation to fund the claimants' trust in exchange for a controlling interest in the company. Sautier reaffirmed Sanofi's intention to leave existing Robins management in place. In a public announcement of the bid, Robins stated that its board of directors had "instructed management and its advisers to consider the Sanofi proposal" while it continued its negotiations with Rorer.

At a conference on December 17, Merhige granted Robins the exclusive right to file a new plan of reorganization until December 28. Still miffed by Aetna's sudden pullout on December 10, Merhige sought to prod Aetna into active participation in efforts to develop a new plan by volunteering that, if a new plan that included settlement of the *Breland* action was not submitted by December 28, he would set the *Breland* case for trial.[6]

On December 23, 1987, American Home Products unexpectedly reentered the fray. In a letter to E. Claiborne Robins, Jr., chairman John Stafford stated that "[w]e have reconsidered our interest in acquiring your company." Stafford proposed to exchange stock worth $550 million for all of Robins's common stock, roughly $22 3/4 a share, exactly the amount to which American Home Products and Robins had tentatively agreed in February 1987. The preceding day, Robins's stock closed on the New York Stock Exchange at 16 1/2. American Home Products would also pay $2.475 billion into a claimants' trust over seven years.

Ironically, considering Merhige's efforts to avoid making an estimate, the reason that American Home Products resumed its efforts to acquire Robins was the announcement of an estimate by the court after a formal fact-finding proceeding. American Home Products' advisers had been uncomfortable relying on a number negotiated by the parties and simply approved by the court. A judicial determination created a greater sense of security that a fund in that amount would truly dispose of the problem, stand up on appeal, and withstand later challenge.[7]

Beginning on Christmas Eve, 1987, teams of Robins representatives entered separate negotiations in New York City with American Home Products, the Rorer Group, and Sanofi. On December 24, with the exclusivity period set to expire on December 28, Robins asked Judge Merhige to grant a further extension. Mark Ellenberg appeared for the claimants' committee and opposed this request. Ellenberg argued that the offers under consideration did not comply with the court's estimate because they provided that payments to the trust would be spread out over seven years. He urged Merhige to allow the exclusivity period to expire so that the claimants' committee could negotiate with the potential purchasers and so that Robins management would be unable to prevent consideration of proposals that were more favorable to the claimants at the expense of the shareholders. As he always had in the past, Merhige refused to allow a noncompany plan of reorganization; he granted Robins an extension of the exclusivity period until January 6, 1988.[8]

Up to this point, although Robins and Rorer had been talking, Rorer had not made any formal offer in response to Merhige's estimate. On Monday, December 28, 1987, Robert Cawthorn, Rorer's chairman and chief executive officer, sent a letter to Robins, Jr., amending the company's proposal for the acquisition of Robins. Rorer proposed to exchange stock worth $480 million for all of Robins's stock, less than $20 a share. Rorer also offered to pay $2.275 billion to the two trusts over seven years, under a schedule that Aetna analysts had concluded would assure that the trust would not run out of funds before all the Rorer payments had been received. In connection with the Rorer offer, Aetna had agreed, in exchange for the extinguishment of its liability through a settlement of *Breland*, to provide the additional $200 million necessary to meet Merhige's estimate in the form of insurance payable only after all the payments from Rorer had been made and only to the extent it was needed. The new offer involved a $240 million decrease in the value of the Rorer stock to be issued to Robins's shareholders and a $270 million increase in the present value of Rorer's payments to the trusts. Rorer had enhanced its offer for Dalkon Shield claims largely at the expense of Robins's shareholders. To make matters worse, at least as far as the Robins family was concerned, Rorer announced that, if its offer was accepted, it would break up the A. H. Robins Company by selling its consumer product lines, including all of Robins's best-known products—Chapstick, Robitussin, and Dimetapp—to Merrell Dow Pharmaceuticals for $950 million.

On December 30, 1987, shortly before a 6:00 p.m. deadline set by Robins, Sanofi put its offer in writing. Unlike American Home Products and Rorer, Sanofi proposed to recapitalize Robins, not to acquire it. Robins would be merged into a small United States subsidiary of Sanofi. The Sanofi subsidiary would then change its name to the A. H. Robins Company. Sanofi proposed to invest $600 million (up from the $500 million offered verbally on December 17) into the reconstituted A. H.

Robins Company. The board of directors of the "new" Robins would consist of the six members of the board of the "old" Robins, plus six additional members selected by Sanofi. Sanofi's holdings of common stock in the "new" Robins would increase from 17 percent to 58 percent over five years through the conversion of preferred stock issued in exchange for the capital investment. Robins's present shareholders would own the balance. Although it was not a term of Sanofi's written offer, the concept included maintaining the same location (Richmond), the manufacturing and selling of the same products, and, at least in substantial part, the same management. The Robins family would retain a significant, although reduced, interest in the company; E. Claiborne Robins, Jr., would head its operations.

Sanofi proposed to fund the claimants' trust with an initial $100 million contribution from the new A. H. Robins and a letter of credit provided by Sanofi and backed by Elf Acquitaine, against which up to $2.375 billion could be drawn, with the limitation that no more than 50 percent be drawn in the first two years and no more than 80 percent in the first four years. Sanofi threatened to revive a previously settled controversy by proposing, as Robins had done in its original plan, a reversionary trust, under which only funds actually needed to pay Dalkon Shield claims would be provided up to the limit of the letter of credit. This provision had originally drawn adamant opposition because it would provide Robins with an incentive to oppose and delay payments from the trust, and because the size of the fund would constitute a ceiling but not a floor on payments to meet Dalkon Shield claims. Neither the American Home Products nor the Rorer offer included a right of reversion; any money left after all claims were liquidated and paid would be distributed to the claimants in lieu of punitive damages.

Late on December 30, 1987, before Robins's board of directors met to consider the three proposals, both American Home Products and the Rorer Group improved their offers. American Home increased its offer to Robins shareholders from $550 million worth of stock to $575 million. It also reduced the timetable for payments of the $2.475 billion into the claimants' trust from seven years to six years. Under the payment schedule incorporated in American Home Products' offer, the present value of these payments was increased to approximately $1.97 billion.

In addition, American Home Products introduced a new concept beneficial to the Dalkon Shield claimants. In connection with American Home Products' offer, Aetna had agreed, in settlement of *Breland*, to provide $150 million in "excess" insurance to be available if the other monies in the trust were exhausted, and another $100 million in "outlier" insurance to pay claims that were ineligible to collect from the trust. Unlike Rorer, American Home Products proposed to use Aetna insurance not to meet Judge Merhige's estimate but to insure against the possibility that it was too low and also to compensate injured women who would otherwise be left without redress as a result of the bar date and questionnaire requirements. The insurance, together with the higher level of funding for the trust, alleviated John Stafford's concern over a shortfall in trust funds that had contributed to American Home Products' sudden withdrawal the preceding February. (At this point, Aetna was negotiating with both Rorer and American Home Products to assure it would have a role if either of these companies were successful.)

For its part, on December 30, 1987, Rorer topped the American Home Products offer to Robins shareholders by increasing its offer of stock from $480 million to $600 million. But Rorer made no improvement in its two-day-old offer with respect to payments for Dalkon Shield claims, which was worth $150 million less than the American Home Products offer, without considering the insurance component of either offer.

On December 31, 1987, during the deliberations by the Robins board, American Home Products denied Rorer its one small advantage by matching Rorer's offer of $600 million in stock to Robins shareholders, approximately $24.50 per share. At this point, the Sanofi offer could not be objectively evaluated because both the price at which shares in the "new" A. H. Robins Company would sell and the timing and amount of payments to the claimants' trust were uncertain. The best available predictions in the New York financial community were that the "new" Robins shares would sell at between $15 and $20.[9]

The Robins board of directors met for five and a half hours on December 31, 1987, and for six hours on New Year's Day to evaluate the three offers. The equity committee and the two largest shareholders outside of the Robins family, Michael Steinhardt and George Soros, appeared before the board and urged it to accept the Rorer proposal. None of the proposals had the support of Murray Drabkin, who insisted that the full amount of Merhige's estimate be paid in cash upon the confirmation of a plan of reorganization. On the evening of Friday, January 1, 1988, Robins announced that its board of directors had accepted the Sanofi bid. In a formal statement, E. Claiborne Robins, Jr., said "the board believes that the Sanofi proposal best serves the interests of Dalkon Shield claimants, other creditors and the company's stockholders."

Both the claimants' committee and the equity committee immediately announced their opposition to a reorganization plan based on the Sanofi proposal. The general reaction was that the board had chosen a proposal "that allow[ed] Robins to exist and keep themselves in power, despite having a superior offer in hand."[10] If that were true, and even assuming that the Sanofi offer would meet Robins's bankruptcy-law obligations by fully satisfying the claims against the estate, the decision would constitute a breach of the directors' fiduciary obligations to the company's shareholders and expose them to personal liability for the resulting loss. Michael Steinhardt, who by now had an 8.6 percent stake in the A. H. Robins Company, said "it strains credulity to say that the Robins board really thought Sanofi was better for financial reasons."[11]

On Sunday, January 3, 1988, Rorer issued a statement expressing its continued interest in the acquisition of Robins and its doubt that the court would approve the Sanofi deal. When asked to explain why Robins had chosen Sanofi, Robert Cawthorn of Rorer said:

It goes back to what Claiborne Robins told us the first time we met. He wanted to keep the company independent if at all possible and provide a reversionary trust. Sanofi's offer is closer to these objectives than either of the other two. But what it doesn't do is satisfy the Dalkon Shield claimants or the stockholders. I was very surprised that the Board came to this conclusion, but it was obviously a conclusion Robins' management wanted to reach.[12]

The breadth of the opposition to Robins's decision suggested that the deal with Sanofi was a way station and not the final destination. In the face of resistance from Robins's management, American Home Products decided to continue its effort to acquire the company by securing the support of the claimants' committee and the equity committee. On January 4, 1988, American Home Products began a series of meetings with Murray Drabkin concerning a revised proposal. Although they did not then reach an agreement, American Home Products was able to ascertain exactly what Drabkin wanted. It concluded that it was willing to make the necessary concessions to secure the support of the claimants' committee when the time was right.

On January 5, American Home Products met with the equity committee. The same day the equity committee conducted separate meetings with Rorer and Sanofi. According to Robert Miller, attorney for the committee, "All three of the bidders indicated that they were willing to improve and enhance their proposals in order to obtain our endorsement." Miller referred to the Sanofi plan that Robins had accepted as a "lame-duck plan."[13]

Nevertheless, on January 6, 1988, in time to meet Merhige's deadline, Robins filed its Third Amended Plan of Reorganization, based on the proposal from Sanofi. In a statement announcing the filing, E. Claiborne Robins, Jr., claimed that the Sanofi proposal would best allow Robins "to meet its obligations fully, [and] emerge from Chapter 11 as economically sound as possible and with the ability to go forward competitively in the marketplace."

In fact, the final round was just about to begin. Flushed with victory, Jean-François Dehecq, vice-chairman of Sanofi, had proclaimed that, based on its relationship with Robins, Sanofi intended "to become a major presence in the U.S. market."[14] This possibility provided American Home Products with an additional incentive for the acquisition of A. H. Robins. On January 12, 1988, Robins announced that it had received an improved offer from American Home Products.

American Home Products had secured the support of the equity committee by meeting its demand for an exchange of stock worth $700 million at current prices. This amounted to $29 per Robins share, or over $4 per share more than its December 31 offer.[15] At the same time, American Home Products made a major move toward the Dalkon Shield claimants by offering a lump sum payment of $2.15 billion. This offer was worth $153 million more than American Home Products' previous offer of $2.475 billion over six years. It was the first time since the original American Home Products offer in February 1987 that any proposal to the claimants had involved a lump sum payment, and it served to underscore the importance of evaluating proposals in terms of present value. Under the revised offer, the trust could count on hundreds of millions of dollars of earned interest before the funds were disbursed. Despite the major increase in value represented by American Home's new offer, Drabkin maintained his demand that the claimants be paid the full amount of the estimate at the outset.

The American Home Products offer had the desired effect of reopening the competition for A. H. Robins. Robins's general counsel Arvid Johnson told the *Washington Post* that "it's interesting sitting here at a bankrupt company and seeing the bidding go up." He added that the Robins board is "anxiously waiting to hear" from Sanofi.[16] Robins scheduled a board meeting for Monday, January 18, 1988, and invited Sanofi, Rorer, and American Home Products to make new presentations.

The denouement was at hand. On January 18, 1988, Jean François Dehecq for Sanofi and John Stafford for American Home Products appeared before the Robins board in Richmond. Robert Cawthorn for

Rorer was scheduled to appear, but weather grounded his flight from Philadelphia and he spoke with the board by telephone.

Dehecq improved the terms of Sanofi's prior agreement with Robins in two respects. In response to shareholder concerns over the value of the "new" Robins stock, Sanofi promised to pay Robins shareholders the difference in cash if the value of that stock did not exceed $50 at the end of five years. This guarantee was seen as giving the new stock a present value of $31 a share.[17] Dehecq also agreed to increase by 5 percent the percentages that the claimants' trust could draw against its letter of credit to 55 percent in the first two years and 85 percent in the first four years, if needed to pay Dalkon Shield claims that had been liquidated.

Cawthorn topped the most recent American Home Products proposal to Robins shareholders by increasing to $750 million, or $31 per share, the value of the stock that Rorer would exchange for Robins shares. But Cawthorn made no improvement in Rorer's proposed seven-year payout to the claimants' trust or its reliance on $200 million worth of insurance from Aetna to meet the amount of the estimate. Moreover, a provision of Rorer's proposal continued to be a sale of Robins consumer products to Merrell Dow, a proposed dismemberment of the company to which the Robins family was bitterly opposed. Rorer's offer found no support in any quarter.

When it was his turn to speak to Robins's board, John Stafford made the dramatic announcement that American Home Products had reached an agreement with Murray Drabkin. Minutes before, in a telephone call placed from Robins headquarters by American Home Products' executive vice-president, Robert Blount, Drabkin had agreed to accept either of two alternative proposals—a lump sum payment of $2.375 billion, including a $75 million cash contribution from Aetna in discharge of its obligation to Robins for unused insurance, or a lump sum payment of $2.3 billion, reserving to the claimants' committee the right to proceed against Aetna for the recovery of the unused insurance. In either event, Aetna would provide the $150 million excess insurance and the $100 million outlier insurance previously discussed, in settlement of *Breland*.

American Home Products made no change from its January 12, 1988, offer of stock worth $700 million to the shareholders, and even though Rorer was now offering $750 million, American Home Products retained the support of the equity committee, simply because the deal could be done with Drabkin's support and could not be done without it. By this time, Aetna had abandoned its neutrality and was also supporting the American Home Products proposal. American Home Products sought to secure the support of the Robins family and the board by re-affirming its intention to maintain the A. H. Robins Company as "a substantial presence" in Richmond and its intention not to sell any parts of the Robins business to finance the acquisition.

Despite the clear superiority of the American Home Products offer, the Robins board resisted, hoping to find a way to accept Sanofi's proposal. Board members openly questioned Stafford's representation that he had reached agreement with Drabkin, commenting resentfully that it was impossible to do so. The next day, while still debating the matter, the board placed a call to Louis Hoynes at Willkie, Farr & Gallagher in New York, American Home Products' outside counsel, and over a speaker phone carefully questioned him about his "level of confidence" in Drabkin's support. Hoynes said he was highly confident. The board then demanded something in writing signed by Drabkin. Hoynes said that he would arrange for this, and shortly thereafter a facsimile of a letter from Drabkin to Robert Blount confirming the terms of his agreement arrived at Robins's headquarters in Richmond.[18]

American Home Products had anticipated resistance from Robins and had made the decision to go forward with its proposal over the company's opposition, if necessary. The equity committee had agreed to file a motion to end Robins's exclusivity period and to submit a plan of reorganization incorporating the American Home Products proposal if an agreement with the company could not be reached. In fact, Hoynes and Robert Miller had already drafted a plan and a disclosure statement. In his January 19, 1988, telephone conversation with the Robins board, Hoynes revealed this and predicted that Judge Merhige would, if it came to that, confirm a plan of reorganization incorporating the American Home Products offer over management's objection.[19]

Robins was left with no choice. All the escape routes had been sealed. Later the same day, January 19, 1988, the company announced that the American Home Products proposal had been accepted. Both Rorer and Sanofi issued statements indicating that the American Home Products bid was too high for them to meet and that they would not improve their offers.

Forty frenetic days after Judge Merhige's estimate of Robins's liability, the shareholders had recovered approximately what they would have received under the preestimate Rorer plan, while the value of the funds available to pay Dalkon Shield injury claims had increased by at least $750 million.[20] Through skillful bargaining and patience, Drabkin had secured for the claimants far more than what Merhige had intended in his estimate. Almost the entire amount of the estimate would be paid in cash rather than "over a reasonable period of time," and the insurance issued by Aetna in connection with a settlement of *Breland* would be "excess" coverage, or "outlier" coverage for otherwise uncompensated women, rather than a component of the funds to meet the estimate.

The spectacular escalation from July 1987 to January 1988 in the price a purchaser was willing to pay to acquire the A. H. Robins Company was attributable to a combination of factors: competition; Robins's strong business performance; the agreement among the principal parties; the deductibility for tax purposes of the payment to the trust;[21] the perception that the judicial estimate reduced the risk of any Dalkon Shield liability surviving the Chapter 11 case; and the reduced risk of unsatisfied claims that is the natural result of a larger trust fund.

15   The Plan of Reorganization

Robins announced its agreement with American Home Products on January 19, 1988. The next day Judge Merhige canceled a hearing that had been scheduled on Robins's motion for authorization to sign an agreement with Sanofi and directed that Robins file an amended plan of reorganization by February 1.

Although all the parties had agreed on the basic financial terms of the settlement, there remained many areas in which further agreement was necessary before a consensual plan could be filed. The most important of these were the identity of trustees of the claimants' trust; the settlement of the *Breland* action; the personal liability of Robins's officers, directors, and attorneys; and the rights of future claimants. Between January 19 and February 1, 1988, intense negotiations took place among the parties in an effort to put together all the pieces of a deal. During the last five days, and continuing into the early morning hours of Monday, February 1, 1988, these discussions went on day and night at the offices of Willkie, Farr & Gallagher, the New York law firm that represented American Home Products.

Perhaps the most intractable issue involved the selection of the trustees. From the earliest suggestion that an independent trust be created, Murray Drabkin had emphasized the claimants' committee's concern over this matter. This concern was heightened when, in the negotiations in April 1987 led by Ralph Mabey concerning the rules and procedures to be used for the resolution of claims, conflicts between Robins and the claimants' committee on a variety of important matters—such as the amount of the payments that would be offered under options 1 and 2— were not resolved but were deferred for resolution by the trustees. The claimants' committee was determined to assure that women would be included among the trustees and that the trustees would be committed to an open, expeditious, and friendly process for the consideration and payment of claims, wholly unlike the situation that had transpired before the bankruptcy. And mindful of Judge Merhige's appetite for control and his generally unsympathetic attitude toward individual claimants in connection with the bar date, the court questionnaire, and otherwise, the claimants' committee wanted to assure that the trustees would make their own decisions and not simply function as staff for the judge.

Robins's first plan of reorganization, filed on April 16, 1987, provided that Robins would choose the trustees, subject to approval by the court. Drabkin strenuously objected to the company having any role in this matter and insisted that the trustees be selected by the claimants' committee. Judge Merhige took the position that he would not approve any plan that did not give him the power to name the trustees. In the course of renegotiating the claims resolution procedures in the days following the filing of its first plan, Robins had agreed to relinquish any role in the selection of the trustees. Thereafter, Robins provided in its various plans of reorganization that the trustees would be appointed by the court.

On June 5, 1987, the day Robins filed its plan based on a merger with Rorer, Merhige and Drabkin had dinner in Richmond to discuss this issue. Drabkin stressed the importance the claimants' committee attached to the choice of trustees. He argued that, inasmuch as the trust was for the benefit of the claimants and the money in the trust belonged to the claimants, the claimants' committee should select the trustees. He also ventured that it would not be seemly for Merhige to appoint people who would appear before him frequently as litigants.

Judge Merhige said that he was unwilling to allow the claimants' committee to choose the trustees, because he had the responsibility of assuring that the trustees were responsible people. In reconciliation of these points of view, Merhige and Drabkin agreed that the claimants' committee would nominate trustees and that Judge Merhige would select trustees from among the committee's nominees.

Beginning in the summer of 1987—long before there was any agreement concerning the economic terms of a plan of reorganization—the claimants' committee under Drabkin's leadership began a search for potential trustees. In their interviews with candidates, Drabkin and the members of the committee stressed that the trust was intended to be independent of the court. As the committee agreed to nominees, the names were sent by Drabkin to Judge Merhige. The claimants' committee decided that one of its members should serve as a trustee, for "continuity," and the name of committee member Ann Samani—a Dalkon Shield claimant who Drabkin had originally recommended for appointment to the claimants' committee—was among the nominees sent to Judge Merhige. Samani agreed to withdraw her own claim in order to serve as a trustee.

Merhige interviewed some of the nominees, including the former mayor of New York, John Lindsay, but did not approve any of them. On October 6, 1987, Drabkin and Merhige had dinner again to discuss the situation. Throughout this meeting, Merhige was noncommittal on the appointment of trustees.

He was emphatic, however, on another matter. According to Drabkin:

Judge Merhige stated to me with great force and emphasis that the Trust had to be located in Richmond. He said he wanted the Trust to employ Richmond people, to place its money in Richmond banks, and to give its legal business to Richmond law firms. He mentioned specifically Hunton & Williams . . . He stated that locating the Trust in Richmond would benefit the Richmond economy.[1]

Hunton & Williams, the former law firm of retired Supreme Court Justice Lewis Powell, was the only large firm in Richmond that had not yet played any role in the Robins bankruptcy. Representation of the claimants' trust, which would exist for many years and have a substantial need for legal services, was a choice piece of business. Drabkin challenged Merhige: "Why are you taking this position? You are a federal judge. You are not the Richmond Chamber of Commerce, you are not a local judge."[2] But Merhige was adamant.

In his interviews with the nominees of the claimants' committee, Merhige reiterated that the trust must be in Richmond. He also expressed the hope that Michael Sheppard, the clerk of the bankruptcy court in Richmond, would be employed as the director of the trust. As clerk of court, Sheppard had responsibility for the complex job of maintaining the files in the Robins bankruptcy and he had worked with Robins employees in establishing computer-based systems for keeping track of the large number of individual claims. Sheppard was close to Merhige, and he conferred with the judge to receive instructions almost on a daily basis during the Chapter 11 case.

Sheppard had, however, in the interests of efficiency, taken several positions antagonistic to the interests of the injured women. For example, because of the burden on his office staff of reading postmarks, Sheppard had argued that claims received after the bar date should be disallowed, regardless of when they were mailed, a position that would have excluded thousands of claims. Sheppard's position was rejected when Robins agreed to include claims postmarked by the bar date, but at Sheppard's continued urging, Merhige did rule that the court questionnaires would be considered timely only if they were received in the

Clerk's office by the due date. Sheppard had been obstructive in connection with the efforts of an organization of Dalkon Shield claimants to secure the names and addresses of other claimants.[3] And Sheppard shared with Judge Merhige the penchant for telling welfare-lady-in-the-Cadillac stories—such as the oft-repeated tale of a claimant who supposedly said she had taken two Dalkon Shields a day. In short, Sheppard was an unlikely choice for the position of director of the claimants' trust if the matter were left to trustees selected by the claimants' committee.

In the meantime, in the fall of 1987, Merhige selected office space for the trust a block or two down Main Street from the federal courthouse in Richmond, negotiated the terms of a lease, asked for and got Robins's signature on the lease, and ordered the transfer to this space of all the claimants' files, under Sheppard's continued supervision.

On November 25, 1987, Merhige entered the following order:

Having sought nominations for Trustees of the contemplated trust from the Claimants Committee, and having over a period of months received only the names of three suggested persons, it is hereby requested that all parties, excepting the Debtor and the Equity Committee, forward to the Court the names of persons deemed qualified to act as Trustees in the event the contemplated Trust shall become a reality.

According to Drabkin, six names were submitted, not three,[4] but whichever figure is correct, it is apparent that Merhige had changed his mind about choosing trustees from among persons approved by the claimants' committee.

On December 10, 1987, in the midst of the last-minute efforts to reach an agreement before Judge Merhige announced an estimate, Drabkin telephoned the judge in an effort to clarify this matter. In this conversation Merhige confirmed the withdrawal, implicit in his November 25 order, of the committee's right to choose those who would be considered for appointment. According to Drabkin, "[T]he judge seemed to backtrack completely, saying he was going to appoint the trustees and seemed to be saying he wasn't going to pay much attention to the nominees of the committee." Rather, the claimants' committee would be given an opportunity "to talk him out of" anyone. Merhige took the occasion to reiterate that he wanted Hunton & Williams retained as counsel to the trust.[5]

When, on January 18, 1988, Drabkin gave his endorsement to American Home Products' acquisition proposal, his support for a plan of reorganization was conditioned on resolving his disagreement with Merhige over the issue of the selection of the trustees. On Saturday morning, January 30, 1988, Drabkin met with Judge Merhige and with Bankruptcy Judge Shelley, who continued to act as an adviser to Judge Merhige, to discuss this matter. They talked all morning, but no agreement was reached. Drabkin went out to meet his wife for lunch. Recognizing the importance of this matter, both the examiner, Ralph Mabey, and American Home Products' counsel, Louis Hoynes, had left the meetings in New York and flown to Richmond. They met with Merhige while Drabkin was at lunch and urged him not to allow the issue of control over the appointment of trustees to block the filing of a consensual plan that it had taken two and a half years to achieve.

These pleas apparently were effective. When Drabkin returned from lunch, an agreement was reached. Merhige agreed to appoint three trustees who had been recommended by the claimants' committee: committee member Ann Samani, Barbara Blum, and Gene Locks. Blum, an old friend of Drabkin's, was president of the Foundation for Child Development in New York. She had served for five years as commissioner of the New York State Department of Social Services and had held other executive and administrative positions in and outside government. Locks was a lawyer in Philadelphia who had served in important roles on the side of the personal injury claimants in five Chapter 11 cases in the asbestos industry. He had originally been recommended by Professor McGovern but was subsequently endorsed by the claimants' committee.

The other two trustees would be individuals whom Merhige had suggested: Kenneth Feinberg, a Washington, D.C., attorney who had served as a special master in the Agent Orange litigation in New York, and Steven Saltzburg, a professor at the University of Virginia Law School. According to Drabkin, "Judge Merhige, Judge Shelley and I shook hands as a token of agreement."[6]

Drabkin appeared to have gotten what he wanted, at least with respect to a majority of the trustees. But Merhige was unhappy with this resolution and resented Drabkin's power to marshal the pressure necessary to achieve it. The judge harbored his unhappiness and resentment, and in time was able to achieve a very different resolution of the matter.

Another major area in which agreement had to be reached between January 19 and February 1, 1988, when Robins's amended plan of reorganization was due to be filed, concerned the claims against Aetna. The agreement that Aetna had reached with American Home Products was conditioned on the settlement of the *Breland* case as a class action and of the claim filed by Robins against Aetna relating to unused insurance coverage. The value of the latter was clouded by various offsetting claims that had been filed by Aetna against Robins, but it was understood by both sides that the balance of these required a payment by Aetna into Robins's estate in the range of $50 to $75 million.

There had been little activity in the *Breland* case in the year following Judge Merhige's tentative certification of a class action in December 1986. At the hearing on class certification, referring to the inference of collusion that might be drawn from his client's support of Joseph Friedberg's efforts to represent a mandatory class, Aetna's counsel John Harkins had promised that, when the issue of Aetna's liability came up for decision, "[there was] going to be a strong fight indeed."[7] But Aetna's plan for the *Breland* case was not a fight, strong or otherwise; it was a settlement attached to the Robins reorganization that would avoid a thorough inquiry into the facts and protect it from future litigation.

The cooperation between Harkins and Friedberg that had led to the class certification order continued in the proceedings that followed. Merhige's order authorized Friedberg to investigate the case against Aetna through the discovery procedures established by the federal rules. These rules authorize written demands for the production of documents and other information, and the interrogation of witnesses under oath before a court reporter. In response to Merhige's order, Harkins suggested to Friedberg that, instead of commencing formal discovery, he and his colleagues review a large number of documents relating to Robins and the Dalkon Shield that Aetna had assembled in Hartford. Friedberg agreed, and over the next several months lawyers associated with Friedberg visited the Aetna facility, read the documents made available by Aetna, and copied and digested those of interest.

By June 1987, Friedberg and his colleagues had completed their review and analysis of these documents. Satisfied that they had learned enough to assess the strength of the case against Aetna, on June 30, 1987, Friedberg and two of his co-counsel traveled to Philadelphia to meet with Harkins and to propose a settlement.

At this meeting, Friedberg suggested a settlement with a cash value of $300 million, without offering a rationale for this figure. Harkins told Friedberg that this was a good deal more than Aetna intended to pay and added that Aetna wanted its participation mostly to be in the form of insurance rather than cash. Friedberg said that he was agreeable to an insurance component of a settlement package but emphasized that he would only value the insurance at its actual cash value and not at the face amount of the policies. Although Friedberg and Harkins seemed to be far apart on the terms of a settlement, they telephoned Judge Merhige from Harkins's office and told him that the *Breland* case "had a potential for settlement" in connection with a consensual plan of reorganization. Friedberg and Harkins also agreed that fees for Friedberg and his colleagues would be paid by Aetna in addition to the amount of any settlement.[8]

After Judge Merhige announced his estimate, Murray Drabkin resisted the integration of a settlement in *Breland* into a plan of reorganization. Drabkin did not want a payment or insurance from Aetna to reduce Robins's obligation to Dalkon Shield claimants as defined by the estimate. On December 24, 1987, Drabkin and Friedberg met and agreed that—contrary to proposals that had been forthcoming from Aetna, Robins, and Rorer—any funds or insurance provided by Aetna in settlement of *Breland* would have to be on top of and not part of the funding necessary to meet Merhige's estimate. According to Friedberg, "[T]hat way Drabkin felt that anything from *Breland* would have real value to claimants as opposed to value to the acquiring party."[9]

Within a day or two after the Robins board had voted to accept American Home Products' offer, John Harkins reached an agreement with Friedberg for the settlement of *Breland* on the terms Aetna had already reached with American Home Products. Aetna would make a $75 million payment to the claimants' trust. It would also issue $150 million in excess insurance to supplement the trust fund, if necessary, and $100 million in outlier insurance to pay injured women who were not eligible claimants in the Chapter 11 case because they had not met the bar date or questionnaire requirement. Aetna would also pay attorney fees to Friedberg and his colleagues in an amount to be determined after final approval of the settlement.

Things hit a snag when Murray Drabkin balked at this agreement. Drabkin had agreed to treat $75 million from Aetna as a component of Robins's obligation to the trust, on the theory that these funds represented unused insurance benefits that were an asset of Robins's estate. The *Breland* case did not involve unused insurance benefits. It involved allegations that Aetna was itself liable to women injured by the Dalkon Shield, and Drabkin felt that he had agreed with American Home Products, as well as with Friedberg, that any payment produced by a settlement of *Breland* would be on top of and not part of the $2.375 billion. The cash component of the proposed *Breland* settlement added nothing to what Drabkin had already been promised by American Home Products: $2.3 billion in cash plus rights against Aetna relating to unused insurance, for which Drabkin expected to receive $75 million.

In fact, transferring Aetna's payment to the *Breland* settlement rather than treating it as a direct commitment to the trust could wind up reducing the funds paid to the trust. The settlement of a class action is subject to the approval of the court. The court must find that the settlement is adequate and not the product of collusion. A decision of a district court approving a class action settlement could be, and in *Breland* undoubtedly would be, appealed. By channeling Aetna's payment through a settlement of *Breland*, $75 million that Drabkin expected to be paid unconditionally would be contingent on judicial approval of that settlement. Drabkin had always doubted the bona fides of the *Breland* case and was unwilling to take this risk. For its part, Aetna was unwilling to do more than pay $75 million and write the two insurance policies, in exchange for a settlement of all outstanding claims, regardless of competing explanations for the payment.

Coincidentally, on January 26, 1988, just as this disagreement surfaced, Ralph Mabey relayed the word that Judge Merhige, in a reversal, now wanted a plan of reorganization that was independent of a settlement in *Breland*. Merhige believed that an agreement that would meet his estimate and that would have Drabkin's support was now possible without Aetna's participation, and he wanted to avoid the difficulties and uncertainties of a plan of reorganization that was conditioned on a settlement of *Breland*. The judge was also resistant to the pressure to approve a *Breland* settlement—he spoke of a gun being put to his head.

Drabkin was glad to proceed separately. He had always been uncomfortable about involving a settlement of *Breland* in a plan of reorganization, and the present situation, in which a *Breland* settlement was proposed that added nothing to the money for which he had bargained, and could take some away, only reinforced this concern.

The next morning, however, January 27, 1988, Louis Hoynes called Drabkin and told him that, despite Judge Merhige's feelings on the matter, American Home would not go through with the acquisition without a settlement of *Breland*. Hoynes explained that his client required "global peace" relating to the Dalkon Shield. Publicity adverse to the A. H. Robins Company, as well as discovery requests to the successor corporation generated by future litigation against Aetna, would undermine the value of acquisition to American Home Products. In addition, American Home Products insisted on the insurance that Aetna had agreed to provide, both to protect against a shortfall in the trust and to provide a remedy for women who were excluded from the bankruptcy process. American Home Products did not want to step into a situation in which thousands of injured women were precluded from recovery by technical rulings in the Chapter 11 case. Drabkin told Hoynes that he could not support the plan of reorganization if the $75 million he was expecting from Aetna for unused insurance coverage was conditioned on a settlement of *Breland*.

Drabkin then called Friedberg in Minneapolis and advised him of the situation. Friedberg was, of course, glad to hear that American Home Products insisted on a settlement of *Breland*. He and Drabkin discussed various possibilities for getting the deal back on track. Drabkin insisted that, if the Aetna cash was to be funneled through *Breland*, there must be some other enhancement of the deal.

In the meantime, on January 27, John Harkins had gone to Louis Hoynes's office in New York, where Charles Hagen, American Home Products' general counsel, William Bailey, the Aetna executive in charge of the matter, Dennis Drebsky and Jim Roberts, counsel for Robins, Stanley Joynes, the legal representative of future claimants, Ralph Mabey, the examiner, and Mark Ellenberg, counsel for the claimants' committee, had gathered in an attempt to hammer out a revised plan of reorganization. As soon as Harkins arrived, he and Hoynes telephoned Friedberg.

Harkins asked Friedberg if he would follow through on his agreement with Aetna regardless of Drabkin's position. Friedberg said he would not. Friedberg was unwilling to be lined up with Robins and Aetna against the claimants' committee, as well as the plaintiffs' bar, when the *Breland* settlement came before the court for approval. Harkins responded angrily, contending that Friedberg was reneging on the agreement they had reached several days earlier. Friedberg replied that their agreement had assumed a consensual plan of reorganization.

Hoynes asked Friedberg what he thought it would take to regain Drabkin's support, and Friedberg agreed to explore the matter. Friedberg then called Drabkin in Washington. By this time, it was the evening of January 27, 1988, and Drabkin was at home. Drabkin said he wanted $100 million in additional excess insurance. They agreed to ask for $125 million, and Friedberg conveyed that proposal to Harkins in New York.

Aetna was unwilling to go beyond its previous offer to meet this demand, but the idea of additional excess insurance, which would provide a further margin against a shortfall of trust funds, was attractive to American Home Products. In discussions between them, American Home Products agreed to pay Aetna a premium of $32 million for an additional $100 million in excess insurance. They also agreed not to mention that American Home Products was paying for the additional insurance, so that Drabkin or Friedberg or both could claim credit for it and so that the apparent value of the *Breland* settlement would be enhanced. Hoynes and Harkins called Friedberg back and offered to increase the excess insurance by $75 million. They did not contradict Friedberg when he commented that they must have decided on $100 million because they knew Drabkin would insist on having the last word.

Friedberg called Drabkin and told him of the offer of $75 million in increased insurance. Drabkin said he would only accept $100 million. Friedberg called Harkins and Hoynes in New York and announced that they had a deal. The $75 million cash would be paid as part of the *Breland* settlement. The total excess insurance would be increased to $250 million; the $100 million dollars in outlier insurance would remain the same. The excess and outlier policies would "spill over" to each other to the extent that they were not used for their primary purpose. The premium that American Home Products had agreed to pay Aetna was not mentioned.

Two nonfinancial issues remained to be addressed in connection with the settlement of *Breland*. In December 1986, when Judge Merhige had tentatively certified a class action in *Breland*, he had deferred deciding whether to create an opt-out class, which would allow individual women to exclude themselves from any settlement and proceed against Aetna separately, or a mandatory class, which would prevent this. One question for the parties was whether the settlement agreement in *Breland* would be conditioned on Merhige's certifying a mandatory class action. The other question concerned the effect on the plan of reorganization of the possible disapproval of the *Breland* settlement—whether the plan of reorganization would be written so that it would go forward even if the *Breland* settlement was disapproved, or whether the two settlements would stand or fall together. Unusual and complex compromise agreements were reached on these issues, so complex in fact that there was considerable confusion among the parties as to their terms in the proceedings that followed.

Aetna, of course, preferred that a class be mandatory and thereby prevent all future Dalkon Shield litigation against it. But there was no precedent for a mandatory class action for compensatory damages in a personal injury case, and it was plain that it would be vigorously opposed by members of the plaintiffs' bar. Aetna was sufficiently satisfied with the proposed settlement in *Breland* that it agreed not to jeopardize it with the condition that the entire case be treated as a mandatory class action. Aetna concluded that plaintiffs' lawyers were motivated to invest the time and money necessary to prepare major litigation by the prospect of punitive damage recoveries and that the preclusion of punitive damages, together with the available remedy from the claimants' trust, would reduce the intensity and frequency of Dalkon Shield litigation to a tolerable level. Accordingly, it was agreed that the settlement of *Breland* would be conditioned on Judge Merhige's certifying a mandatory class action with respect to the claim for punitive damages but not with respect to the claims for compensatory damages.[10] Aetna would ask Judge Merhige to certify a mandatory class on all issues, but the settlement agreement would stand, and Aetna would provide all the cash and insurance that it called for unless Merhige refused to certify a mandatory class for punitive damages.

A similar arrangement was made with respect to the connection of the *Breland* settlement to the plan of reorganization. Aetna wanted final approval of the *Breland* settlement to be a condition of the plan of reorganization because of the pressure for approval that such a provision would create. American Home Products had demanded a settlement of *Breland* as a condition of its participation, but it was wary in going too far with this, particularly as it seemed to be very possible that there would be no appeal from the order confirming the plan of reorganization while protracted appeals from the *Breland* settlement were a virtual certainty.

The following compromise was reached. The plan of reorganization (and the merger agreement between Robins and American Home Products) would be conditioned on approval of the *Breland* settlement in the district court but not on appeal. In the event that there was no appeal from confirmation of the plan of reorganization, the merger and establishment of the claimants' trust would not be delayed by the appeal in *Breland*. If the *Breland* settlement was overturned on appeal, Aetna would not pay the $75 million to the trust and its obligation to provide insurance would be reduced from $250 million of excess insurance and $100 million of outlier insurance to $50 million in each category. Aetna would provide this reduced insurance, regardless of the outcome in *Breland*, in settlement of the Robins claim against it for unused insurance.[11]

The only remaining problem was the judge, who had asked that the plan of reorganization be unconnected to a settlement of *Breland*. On January 30, 1988, in the same session in which they implored Judge Merhige to reach an agreement with Drabkin on the identity of the trustees, Louis Hoynes and Ralph Mabey explained to the judge that a plan of reorganization that did not include linkage to a settlement in *Breland* was not possible. After some discussion, Merhige acquiesced.

The *Breland* settlement addressed Aetna's liability for Dalkon Shield– related injuries. There remained to be resolved the question of the effect of the reorganization on the rights of women injured by the Dalkon Shield to seek damages from other persons potentially liable, particularly present and former officers and directors of the A. H. Robins Company and the law firm of McGuire, Woods & Battle.

The only legal proceeding relating to A. H. Robins and the Dalkon Shield that had not been stayed by the Chapter 11 case was an investigation by the Department of Justice of allegations that criminal laws had been broken by officers and directors of the company and by lawyers at McGuire, Woods & Battle. A grand jury was impaneled in Wichita, Kansas, to assist in the investigation. In denying a motion by Robins to quash a subpoena issued by the grand jury, a United States district judge in Kansas had found that there was substantial evidence that "Robins and its employees and officers participated in the commission of crimes and fraud during the promotion, marketing and sale of the Dalkon Shield, and used its attorneys to perpetuate and cover-up [this conduct] through the commission of frauds on the court, obstruction of justice, and perjury."[12]

The very fact of the criminal investigation and of the court in Kansas making this finding underscored the potential civil liability of these same people for these same acts. Civil liability attaches on less evidence of wrongdoing than is necessary for a successful criminal prosecution. Before the bankruptcy, individuals associated with Robins who were named as co-defendants in Dalkon Shield injury cases were represented by Robins attorneys. When the cases were resolved, the judgments were paid by Robins or by Aetna from Robins's insurance coverage. With Robins discharged from liability, Robins's co-defendants would be exposed to Dalkon Shield injury claims unless these claims could be foreclosed through the reorganization process.

The A. H. Robins Company was controlled and its actions determined by the two individuals with the greatest potential exposure— E. Claiborne Robins, Sr., and E. Claiborne Robins, Jr. From its first meetings with representatives of the claimants' committee in December 1985, the company had insisted that an essential term of any plan of reorganization was a "super discharge," a release of liability of all potential co-defendants. Such a release, backed up by a permanent injunction prohibiting efforts to litigate against co-defendants, was a provision of Robins's first plan of reorganization filed in April 1987 and of every succeeding plan.

This provision was just as consistently opposed by the claimants' committee. Section 524(e) of the Bankruptcy Code provides that the "discharge of a debt of the debtor does not affect the liability of any other entity on . . . such debt," and the courts had uniformly rebuffed efforts to relieve individuals of liability to creditors in connection with a corporate reorganization.[13] The right to sue responsible individuals would provide a valuable alternative means of redress for women injured by the Dalkon Shield. It could provide a speedier and more individualized remedy, considering that the claimants' trust would have the responsibility to process 195,000 claims and would provide a source of recovery in the event that the funds paid to the trust proved insufficient. The right to sue defendants other than the A. H. Robins Company would also provide an opportunity to seek punitive damages, a right that was denied under the plan of reorganization.[14] As the Robins family was scheduled to receive more than $300 million in American Home Products stock following the reorganization, these rights of action were potentially of great value.

Beyond the economic considerations, the venality of the actions that had been taken in the marketing of the Dalkon Shield and in defense of the ensuing litigation, together with the continuing insistence of the men who ran the A. H. Robins Company that there had been no wrongdoing, caused the members of the claimants' committee and their attorneys, as well as others outside the bankruptcy structure who undertook to speak for the women injured by the Dalkon Shield, to believe that it would be a great injustice to release the responsible parties from liability.

When the agreement on the major economic provisions of a plan of reorganization was reached among the principal parties in January 1988, the issue of the personal liability of potential co-defendants remained unresolved. Just as it had with respect to the settlement of *Breland*, American Home Products insisted that litigation against Robins's officers, directors, and attorneys be foreclosed. American Home Products took the position that, regardless of the merits of claims against these individuals, it was paying for everybody by not only meeting but going beyond Judge Merhige's estimate of the amount necessary to pay all Dalkon Shield claims in full. This stance was certainly welcomed by those who stood to benefit by it, but American Home Products' interest was not in the protection of these individuals but in the reduction of hostilities surrounding the A. H. Robins Company and the Dalkon Shield. Drabkin and the claimants' committee did not like it, but they decided that the value of the overall agreement justified this major concession.

Under the agreement that was reached, E. Claiborne Robins, Sr., and E. Claiborne Robins, Jr., while continuing to deny any liability, would personally make a combined payment of $10 million toward the funds to be used to pay Dalkon Shield claims. In exchange, the claimants' committee agreed that all claims against the Robinses relating in any way to the Dalkon Shield would be released and enjoined. In addition, without payments from any other persons, claims against all other potential co-defendants would be released and enjoined. This release of third parties proved to be one of the major grounds for objection to the plan of reorganization lodged by attorneys representing individual injured women.[15]

There remained the thorny question of the rights of women who would manifest Dalkon Shield–related injuries in the future but who did not file claims prior to the bar date. Robins's early plans of reorganization did not allow for compensation of women with future injuries who did not file timely claims. Stanley Joynes, the legal representative of future claimants, had opposed these plans and steadfastly maintained that due process of law prevented the application of the bar date to cut off the rights of these women.

In the negotiation of the American Home Products plan of reorganization between January 19 and February 1, 1988, several changes were made that granted limited rights to nonfiling future claimants. One change was the *Breland* settlement, which would provide one $50 million outlier policy on the effective date of the plan and another $50 million outlier policy on the seventh anniversary of the effective date of the plan. And there was the possibility of additional outlier insurance (up to $250 million) to the extent that the "excess" insurance was not needed by the trust to pay eligible claims.[16] Ineligible claimants, including future claimants, could be paid from these policies to the extent that they met the filing deadline later established in the *Breland* case, September 30, 1989. It was doubtful, however, that the Aetna insurance, and particularly the $50 million available during the first seven years, would allow compensation at the same level as payments to eligible claimants from the trust.[17]

Another change that enhanced the rights of nonfiling future claimants was the addition of a provision that unpaid late claims would be paid by the trust if funds remained (apart from the excess insurance) after all timely claims had been paid. This provision provided another possible source of compensation to ineligible future claimants but only after a delay of many years.

The most significant change benefiting ineligible future claimants was the addition to the plan of reorganization of a procedure for the reclassification of late-filed claims as timely on grounds of "excusable neglect." Under language adopted in the negotiations with American Home Products, the trustees would make an initial determination of "excusable neglect," subject to final decision by the court. The factors to be considered included "whether the late claim is based upon injuries which first became manifest after the commencement of the case or the bar date" and "whether the holder of the late claim had actual knowledge of the bar date."

Although these factors were to be considered, when the American Home Products plan was filed on February 1, 1988, it did not mandate that post–bar date injury and lack of knowledge of the bar date would cause a claim to be reclassified as timely. In a subsequent amendment that secured Stanley Joynes's support for the plan, the following language was added: "Appropriate evidence of a first manifestation of injury subsequent to April 30, 1986, and either lack of actual knowledge of the bar date or lack of knowledge of Dalkon Shield use shall constitute 'excusable neglect.'"[18] The rights of women who suffered post–bar date injuries but who *were* aware of the bar date and of their use of a Dalkon Shield were not explicitly defined.[19] The changes in the plan relating to the reclassification of future claims would have the effect of enlarging the pool of claimants eligible to claim from the trust, but no increase was made in the funding of the trust.

The parties concluded their negotiations early during the morning of February 1, 1988, the day the plan of reorganization was due to be filed. That evening the documents were ready. Dennis Drebsky flew from New York to Richmond in an American Home Products jet. He was met at the airport by an A. H. Robins limousine and driven to Judge Shelley's home in time to deliver Robins's Fourth Amended Plan of Reorganization just before midnight.[20]

16   Disclosure

A plan of reorganization can take effect only if it is confirmed by the court, after classes of creditors and shareholders whose rights are altered by the plan have been informed of its terms through a disclosure statement and given the opportunity to file objections and to vote to accept or reject it.[1] After a hearing on March 21, 1988, Judge Merhige approved the language of a disclosure statement describing the plan of reorganization based on the acquisition of Robins by American Home Products, and ordered that the statement be mailed to the class of Dalkon Shield claimants and to Robins's shareholders, together with ballots and with letters in support of the plan from the claimants' committee and the equity committee.

Although the formalities of the confirmation process were observed, there was never any doubt that Judge Merhige would confirm this plan of reorganization. In every respect except technically, Merhige had been a party to the agreement in support of the plan that had been reached among the official participants in the case. To the extent that the judge was dissatisfied with any of the particulars in the document that Robins filed on February 1, 1988, he had sought and obtained, or agreed to forego, the changes he wanted long before the plan came before him for formal approval.

At a conference held on February 6, 1988, Judge Merhige expressed his dissatisfaction with several provisions governing the proposed claimants' trust. The plan as drafted left it up to the trustees to select the location of the trust. Merhige had already leased space for the trust in Richmond, and he flatly stated that he would not approve the plan of reorganization unless it specified that the trust would be located in Richmond.

Judge Merhige's other concerns related to his authority over the operation of the trust and over the trustees. For example, the trust agreement did not authorize the court to remove a trustee, except on the motion of another trustee or on a motion filed by five attorneys representing one hundred claimants, and then only on a finding of serious misconduct by the trustee to be removed. And, in the event of a vacancy, the agreement authorized the remaining trustees to appoint a new trustee. Merhige in-

224

sisted that he be given authority to remove a trustee on his own motion, merely upon a finding of "good cause," and the authority to appoint successor trustees.

Each of the changes that Judge Merhige demanded eroded the concept of an independent trust that was central to the claimants' committee's support for the plan. As Murray Drabkin later described this process, "[W]hat the Committee was faced with was . . . the Judge . . . trying to renegotiate the plan from the position of the power of the bench with respect to matters that had been negotiated, compromised and resolved."[2] At the conference on February 6, 1988, Mark Ellenberg voiced his opposition to Merhige's proposals, particularly the one to locate the trust in Richmond. Ellenberg cited adverse tax and other regulatory consequences that would result from locating the trust in Virginia, and contended that the trustees should be free to choose a location that would afford favorable tax and legal treatment and that would be convenient to the claimants and their attorneys. Merhige was unyielding. Five days later, without consulting the claimants' committee, Robins filed an amended plan of reorganization (its Fifth Amended and Restated Plan of Reorganization, February 11, 1988) that provided that the trust would be located in Richmond and made the other changes Merhige had demanded.

In the weeks that followed, Judge Merhige proposed several other changes in the rules governing the operation of the trust and the processing of claims. The most significant of these constituted a restriction on the right of a claimant to turn down a final offer of settlement from the trust and to proceed to trial in her local court. The plan already provided that Merhige had the power "to stay the commencement of any trial upon a showing by the Trust of undue prejudice due to the multiplicity of ongoing trials." Merhige wanted to add a provision that would afford him authority to limit and control discovery in cases filed against the trust. Examiner Mabey acted as intermediary between Drabkin and Merhige, and these questions were resolved mostly by acceding to Merhige's position. In a letter to Ellenberg on March 12, 1988, Mabey stated that all Merhige's concerns had been resolved and that no additional changes would be requested.[3]

A few days later, Judge Merhige demanded and received a significant change in the plan of reorganization from American Home Products and Robins. The plan as filed provided that, if an appeal delayed its consummation, Robins would "deposit $10 million in cash into the Claimants Trust to fund administrative expenses of the Trust and to prepare for distributions to be made from the Trust." This money could not be used during the appeal to pay any claims. On March 16, 1988, Robins's motion for authority to sign the merger agreement with American Home Products was heard by Merhige. Arguing for Robins in support of the motion, Dennis Drebsky began by stating that "no party has a problem" with the agreement.

"I have a problem," Merhige shot back. By this time substantial opposition to the plan had been expressed by lawyers representing women injured by the Dalkon Shield. Referring to the likelihood of an appeal ("You know it's coming; I know its coming"), the judge said that he would not tolerate further delay in the compensation of Dalkon Shield victims. "I cannot approve it. I'm telling you that right now . . . These women have waited and waited . . . They can't wait any longer."[4]

Merhige asked that Robins make a "start-up" payment of $100 million instead of $10 million if an appeal was filed. Merhige wanted the claimants' trust to use this money during an appeal to pay women willing to accept option 1—the option designed to pay an amount (later set at $725) less than the cost of evaluating a claim, on receipt of a simple signed statement. Women who would accept option 1 were not, of course, the women who had "waited and waited." They were women with minor or insupportable claims who had responded to the bar date advertising.

The hearing recessed for three hours while the attorneys for Robins and for American Home Products discussed Merhige's demand and conferred with their principals. There was some concern that the availability of funds to pay any claims would reduce the pressure on the plaintiffs' bar not to take an appeal. But before the day was out, Robins and American Home Products returned to court and agreed to Merhige's demand. Merhige then authorized Robins to sign the merger agreement.

On April 4, after Judge Merhige had approved the disclosure statement but before it was printed, he telephoned Mark Ellenberg and said he wanted to increase the number of trustees from five to seven. Just three weeks earlier, Ralph Mabey had assured Drabkin and Ellenberg that Merhige would not demand additional changes, and when Mabey heard of Merhige's proposal to increase the number of trustees, he told Ellenberg that it constituted a breach of faith and that he would resign as examiner if Merhige insisted on it. The claimants' committee conferred the same day and decided not only not to agree to the change but to inform the judge that the committee would oppose the plan of reorganization if the change was made. When he heard this, Merhige was livid, but because American Home Products had made clear that it would not participate in Robins's reorganization unless the plan was supported by the claimants' committee, he did not press the issue.

This incident convinced Drabkin that Merhige was determined to regain control over the selection of a majority of the trustees and that he could not trust the judge to appoint the five individuals upon whom they had previously agreed. Mabey had advised Merhige that identification of the trustees in the disclosure statement was necessary for adequate disclosure, and Merhige had committed to announce the names of the trustees in time to do this. But as the scheduled date for printing the disclosure statement approached, the judge had not acted. Drabkin refused to provide the letter of support for the plan from the claimants' committee, which was to be mailed with the disclosure statement, until the trustee appointments were announced.

Finally, as he had in January, American Home Products' counsel Louis Hoynes appealed to Judge Merhige to make the appointments so the matter could move forward. Merhige acceded, and on April 11, 1988, announced the appointment of Samani, Blum, Locks, Feinberg, and Saltzburg in accordance with his January 30, 1988, agreement with Drabkin. The trustees' names and biographies were added to the disclosure statement, and Drabkin submitted the claimants' committee's letter of support for the plan. Thus, for a second time Drabkin managed to frustrate Merhige's efforts to control the selection of the trustees.

Because of his involvement in the development of the plan of reorganization, Judge Merhige approached the formal approval process not as a disinterested arbiter but as a strategist seeking to assure that the plan was not derailed in his court or on appeal. A vote of the class of Dalkon Shield claimants against Robins's plan of reorganization would have created serious obstacles to confirmation, because confirmation would then have been possible only through the "cramdown" procedure.[5] In that event, Merhige would have had to make a formal finding that the plan would pay the "allowed amount" of each personal injury claim in full. This requirement would raise three difficult questions. The first question would be whether any estimate of the total value of all unliquidated personal injury claims could be treated as the allowed amount of all such claims, particularly considering the right of each claimant to a jury determination of the amount of her claim. Assuming that it could, the second question would be whether Judge Merhige's estimate was adequate to this purpose. This would force the judge to write detailed findings setting out the various legal and factual assumptions underlying his estimate, all of which would be subject to appellate review. Merhige was reluctant to prepare findings of that sort. The third question would be whether a plan of reorganization that denied personal injury claimants the right to seek punitive damages could be treated as providing for the full allowed amount of their claims, even if the compensatory damage components of their claims were paid in full. All these questions were novel and controversial, and no one could be confident of their resolution on appeal.[6] If opponents of the plan prevailed on any one of these questions, the plan would fail. On the other hand, if the Dalkon Shield claimants voted to accept the plan, none of these questions would have to be decided.

In this context Judge Merhige undertook to ensure that the claimants would vote to accept the plan. He did this by refusing to weight the votes of the claimants according to the value of their claims, by refusing to include in the disclosure statement information that would give a claimant some idea of the amount she could expect to be paid, and by preventing any statement in opposition to the plan from reaching the claimants.

Section 1126(c) of the Bankruptcy Code provides that a plan of reorganization is deemed "accepted" by a class if votes in favor are cast by creditors "that hold at least two-thirds in amount *and* more than one-half in number of the allowed claims in such class" (emphasis added). The reason for this dual requirement is to assure that the holders of the largest claims, who have the most at stake, are not outvoted by a majority with relatively little at stake.

The policy behind the statutory requirement of weighted voting had particular force in the Robins bankruptcy. The vast majority of the women eligible to vote within the class of Dalkon Shield claimants—some 94 percent according to a study performed for Robins—had not and would not have made a claim against the company outside of bankruptcy.[7] Many had only minor or insupportable claims, and would be glad to accept a plan that offered them a quick, albeit small, payment without proof of Dalkon Shield use or injury.[8] An estimated 35,000 of the eligible voters—potential future claimants who responded to the notice—did not even claim to have suffered an injury. At the same time, other women, mostly those with cases pending when Robins entered bankruptcy, had suffered serious injuries and had claims of great value. If the votes were weighted according to the worth of the claims, a relatively small proportion of the women, holding claims worth more than one-third of the total value, could block acceptance of the plan. This was a real possibility because women with large claims had the most to lose from a low estimate and because they were the most likely to be represented by counsel who would provide a source of information and advice other than the official mailing. If the votes were not weighted, women with large claims would not have this veto power.

When the estimation hearing was scheduled, Judge Merhige included among the issues to be considered the question of how the 195,000 unliquidated Dalkon Shield claims should be valued for voting purposes. At the estimation hearing in November 1987, Robins took the position that each claim should be given equal value because there was no reliable way to evaluate the claims short of a case-by-case examination that would take many years. Robins cited the precedent of the *Johns-Manville* bankruptcy, where the votes of the asbestos claimants had been given equal weight.[9] The claimants' committee, at that time facing the prospect of a vote on a plan it opposed, suggested that the court assign values to each injury category based on the historic averages used in the estimation process and then require the claimants to identify their injuries on their ballots. The claimants' committee acknowledged that the system would be imperfect, because the categorizations would be rough, because invalid claims (for example, claims by women who did not use a Dalkon Shield) would have no value regardless of the injury category, and because of the possibility of misreporting injuries, but argued that these imperfections in applying the statute were preferable to ignoring it altogether.

On March 21, 1988, Judge Merhige entered an order providing that the votes of all Dalkon Shield claimants, including those who filed as "future claimants" with no manifest injury, would be treated equally. Merhige found that "there is no reliable information that would allow the Court to weight the voting of the Dalkon Shield claims based on the nature of the injuries alleged by the holders of these claims." He added that a rule that grants an equal vote to each claimant vote was necessary to "allow . . . this case to move swiftly towards the confirmation of a plan of reorganization."

Before ballots can be mailed to creditors, the court must find that the accompanying disclosure statement provides "adequate information" concerning how each class of interests will be treated under the plan. Before the hearing on March 21, 1988, more than sixty objections to Robins's proposed disclosure statement were filed on behalf of Dalkon Shield claimants, many directed to its self-laudatory tone, its one-sided presentation of the facts, and its selective inclusion of information.

A major objection to the disclosure statement related to Judge Merhige's failure to issue findings in support of his $2.475 billion estimate of

Dalkon Shield claims. The disclosure statement repeatedly asserted that more funds were provided by the proposed plan than the amount estimated by the court as necessary to pay all claims in full, but it offered no information of the amount that was supposed to constitute full payment for any particular injury. The concept of full payment of an unliquidated personal injury claim is highly subjective. Before the bankruptcy, the amounts collected by different women for the same type of injury varied enormously.

An objection to the disclosure statement was filed on behalf of Rosemary Menard-Sanford and other claimants by Alan Morrison, the director of the Public Interest Litigation Group, an organization in Washington, D.C., associated with Ralph Nader. Morrison, a 1966 graduate of the Harvard Law School and a part-time member of the faculty at Harvard, is one of the best known and most successful public interest lawyers in the United States. Morrison argued that the claimants would not be able to reach a conclusion to support or oppose the plan without some information as to how much money they could expect to be paid:

At a minimum, the notice should disclose the court's estimate of the number of women with valid claims, the percentages of claimants who will select each of options 1, 2 and 3 and those who will go to trial, the average amounts estimated for typical claims under each of the options. This information is vital to a claimant's determination as to whether the amount found by the Court will in fact be adequate to pay all claims. It is the irreducible minimum required in order to cast an intelligent vote on the plan. Without it, we have the most serious doubts that the vote is lawful and may properly be the basis of an approval of the plan.

The argument presumed—probably incorrectly—that Merhige's announced estimate was the result of a calculation he had performed concerning the number of valid claims and the average values to be paid rather than of a tactical maneuver he had designed to break the logjam in the negotiations. In any event, the information Morrison demanded was exactly the information Merhige had decided not to provide. Without this information, the injured women could only fantasize about how much money constituted payment "in full." The inclusion of data that would give women some idea of the amounts that would actually be paid for each type of injury might lead them to vote against the plan.

At the hearing on March 21, 1988, several attorneys for Dalkon Shield claimants argued that adequate disclosure required a statement of the basis for the estimate. Merhige was clearly uncomfortable with the situation and reacted impatiently, if not angrily, to these arguments. At one point he abruptly instructed Dennis Drebsky, attorney for

Robins, to remove from the disclosure statement any reference to the court having "decided" and to substitute instead that the court had "stated" that $2.475 billion would be sufficient to pay the Dalkon Shield claims in full.[10] Merhige said he had no intention of explaining his estimate "unless necessary." The court's unexplained conclusion that the plan provided sufficient funds to pay all claims in full would be used to solicit acceptances from the Dalkon Shield claimants. And if the plan was accepted, it would be confirmed on the basis of the vote, without any explanation of the conclusion of full payment.

In another way, the disclosure statement prevented the injured women from knowing what to expect in terms of payment. Nowhere in the fifty-six closely printed pages is there a statement of the number of claimants eligible to share the funds paid to the trust, a number that at least would have allowed a calculation of the average amount per claim. (The average was between twelve and thirteen thousand dollars.) The disclosure statement was full of irrelevant numbers relating to claims— the number of claims excluded for failure to return the questionnaire, the number of excluded claimants who had requested reinstatement, the number reinstated by the court, and so forth. The one number that would have placed the total amount reserved for Dalkon Shield claims in some meaningful context—the number of eligible claimants—was omitted.

A closely related issue also raised at the March 21, 1988, hearing on Robins's disclosure statement was whether opponents of the proposed plan of reorganization would be permitted to communicate their views to the Dalkon Shield claimants. From early in the bankruptcy proceeding, there had been controversy concerning communication with and among the women who had filed claims.

In December 1985 Robins asked Merhige to prohibit public access to the names and addresses of the claimants for the reason that they might otherwise be contacted by and retain attorneys. Robins said:

Presumably, such representation would be undertaken on a contingency fee basis. Such an arrangement necessarily tends to reduce the actual recovery by any such claimant and to increase monetary demands. Such inflationary pressures would not only harm Dalkon Shield claimants, but Robins' other creditors as well. Accordingly, for the best interests of all creditors in this Chapter 11 case, the list of Dalkon Shield claimants should be impounded.

Robins's motion was opposed by the claimants' committee, and, on First Amendment grounds, by the *Washington Post* and the two Richmond newspapers. On January 10, 1986, Judge Merhige denied

Robins's request. Merhige recognized the right of lawyers to advertise for cases in a nondeceptive manner and stated that he would not assume that any lawyer would "accept employment that is going to increase the cost to their client without a commensurate benefit." Merhige said that "people can come in and pay for copies" of the list of claimants that Robins was required to file.

In July 1986 six Dalkon Shield claimants in the Northwest founded a nonprofit organization called the International Dalkon Shield Victims' Education Association (IDEA). The purpose of the organization was "to help Dalkon Shield victims by informing them of developments in the bankruptcy proceeding, providing an open forum for discussion of the issues, offering medical and legal referrals and providing moral support."[11] The need for information was real, as there was no other mechanism in place to inform the claimants of what was happening in the bankruptcy.

Beginning in January 1987 the members of IDEA began mailing monthly newsletters to small groups of Dalkon Shield claimants whose names were available to it from private sources. In the spring of 1987 Rosemary Menard-Sanford, president of IDEA, asked Michael Sheppard, the clerk of the bankruptcy court, for a list of the names and addresses of all Dalkon Shield claimants so that a broader mailing could be conducted. Inexplicably, in light of Judge Merhige's denial of Robins's impoundment motion, Sheppard refused the request, stating that Merhige had instructed him to keep the list confidential.

In May 1987, shortly after Robins filed its first plan of reorganization, IDEA retained Alan Morrison to file a motion asking Merhige to direct Sheppard to provide access to the names and addresses of the claimants. Bankruptcy Rule 1007(a) requires the debtor to file with the clerk of court "a list containing the name and address of each creditor." In his motion, Morrison relied on section 107(a) of the Bankruptcy Code, which provides, with certain inapplicable exceptions, that "paper[s] filed in a case under this title . . . are public records and open to examination by an entity at reasonable times without charge." He cited *Collier on Bankruptcy*, the leading treatise in the field, as authority for the proposition that one reason the debtor is required to file a list of creditors is to ensure that it cannot monopolize communication to the creditors and thereby control the reorganization process.[12] Morrison also relied on Merhige's earlier refusal to prevent public access to the list.

Robins opposed the motion, arguing that the list of claimants should be kept confidential to "avoid potential embarrassment to, or harassment of, Dalkon Shield claimants who understandably wish to retain privacy and confidentiality in this sensitive matter and to avoid improper contacts of such claimants by attorneys." Robins referred to "the extreme damage that could be inflicted to the progress of this case if the plan confirmation process is delayed by improper solicitation."

In an opinion issued on June 10, 1987, Judge Merhige granted IDEA's motion. Merhige found that "the asserted privacy interest of claimants is not sufficiently compelling to outweigh the broad interest in public access." He also rejected the suggestion of improper solicitation. "The Court . . . cannot order a prior restraint on IDEA's speech based on mere conjecture about possible future conduct." Merhige said that a representative of IDEA could inspect the list without charge in the clerk's office or could apply to Michael Sheppard for an estimate of the cost of obtaining a copy of the list of claimants. Merhige declined to authorize release of the information in the form of a computer tape.

IDEA's next newsletter hailed Judge Merhige's decision, referring to "his well deserved reputation for protecting First Amendment rights." The celebration proved to be premature, however. IDEA would not obtain a list of claimants.

The federal courts charge 50 cents per page for copies of public records. If Robins had filed its list of creditors on paper, with twenty names and addresses on a page, the cost to IDEA of purchasing a copy of the list of eligible claimants would have been less than $5,000. But because of the large number of claimants involved, Robins did not file a printed list. It was decided between Robins and the court that it would be more economical for the names and addresses to be filed on computer tape. In fact, the court imposed on Robins the cost of purchasing the hardware and software—almost $1 million—necessary to set up a computerized system to enable the clerk of court to maintain information concerning the Dalkon Shield claims and to communicate efficiently with the claimants.

On July 18, 1987, Morrison wrote Michael Sheppard asking for an estimate of the cost of a list of the names and addresses of the some 130,000 claimants for whom personal addresses rather than attorney addresses had been submitted. In response, Sheppard stated that the following charges would apply:

Setup charge for computer	$1,200
Mailing labels(130,000 @ $.01 each)	1,300
Per-name charge (130,000 @ $.25 each)	32,500
"User fee" (5% of cost of entire system)	47,877
Total Fee	$82,877

Of this amount, $57,185 would be paid to Robins, the balance retained by the court. The basis for this division was not explained. What was clear was that the first two items, totaling $2,500, represented the cost of providing a list of claimants. The balance represented recoupment of a portion of the expenses already incurred in setting up the system. IDEA's total income from its inception, derived from membership fees and a single $5,000 grant, amounted to $13,000.

On August 14, 1987, Morrison filed a motion asking Merhige to limit the charge to $2,500. He said:

> Movants agree that it is fair for them to pay out-of-pocket costs, but not costs that have been previously incurred and that would have been incurred regardless of whether the movants sought access to the list of Dalkon Shield victims . . . In essence, the proposed charges constitute a penalty to the movants because, for the convenience of the debtor and others, no creditors' list was compiled.

Robins opposed the motion.

> The Clerk is in the best position to determine a charge that, upon consideration of hard costs, increases in work load and inconvenience, approximates the self-sustaining level. This Court has gone the extra mile to accommodate IDEA. The request for a free or substantially subsidized ride should be rejected.

Merhige did not act on Morrison's motion.

In the meantime, the law firm of Cadwalader, Wickersham & Taft, counsel to the claimants' committee, was inundated with telephone calls and letters from women who had filed claims requesting information about the case. On September 10, 1987, the claimants' committee filed a motion asking for authority to mail a letter to all claimants describing the status of the case and responding to the most frequently asked questions. The proposed letter was mostly a simple description of what was going on, but it did include the following comment on Robins's then-pending plan of reorganization based on a merger with Rorer:

> The Committee has a number of serious concerns about the Robins plan. Our most serious concern is that there is no assurance that the Dalkon Shield claimants will be paid promptly and in full. At the appropriate time, the Committee will send you its recommendations as to how your interest as a Dalkon Shield claimant can be served.

Judge Merhige immediately placed the motion and the proposed letter under seal. Strident oppositions to the motion were filed by Robins and by the equity committee, both of which claimed that because of the quoted passage the letter constituted an improper solicitation of votes against the pending plan prior to the issuance of a disclosure statement.[13] The equity committee asked that the claimants' committee be held in contempt of court for filing its motion in the public record. Merhige did not act on the claimants' committee's motion, but he told Mark Ellenberg that he was concerned about the cost of mailing a letter to the claimants, at an estimated $91,586. In his memorandum in support of the request to mail the letter, Murray Drabkin reported that, in a single month during the Chapter 11 case, the "Office of the President" of A. H. Robins had spent $302,000 for "dues and subscriptions."[14]

In early October 1987, while IDEA's motion for a reduction in the cost of the list and the claimants' committee's motion for authority to send a letter to claimants were quietly languishing, Ralph Pittle, an attorney practicing in Seattle who served as general counsel of IDEA and who was co-counsel with Alan Morrison in the efforts to get the list, learned that Dr. Pifer, the claimants' committee's expert, had been provided with a copy of the computer tape that included the names and addresses of all claimants in connection with his preparation for the estimation hearing. Pittle secured an affidavit from an official in Pifer's consulting firm stating that a copy of the names and addresses printed on gummed labels could be provided to IDEA at a cost of $2,200. Pittle filed a motion asking Merhige to authorize Pifer to do so. This, Pittle pointed out, would avoid any cost to or burden on the clerk of court's office. On October 27, 1987, Merhige denied this motion without providing reasons.

On behalf of IDEA and individual claimants, Ralph Pittle and Alan Morrison filed numerous objections to Robins's proposed disclosure statement and to the plan of reorganization. At the hearing on March 21, 1988, Ralph Pittle asked Merhige to authorize the inclusion of a dissenting statement in the official mailing to the claimants. Referring to Robins's intention to mail the disclosure statement and the ballots with letters from the company, the equity committee, and the claimants' committee all endorsing the plan and recommending an affirmative vote, Pittle said: "There is an impression of unanimity. The claimants should be aware of the dissenting view that not enough money is provided to pay all claims in full. The Court should allow the inclusion in the mailing of a letter opposing confirmation of the plan." Merhige responded, "It's not going to happen, Mr. Pittle."

Judge Merhige denied all the objections to the disclosure statement asserted by a long line of attorneys for claimants at the March 21, 1988, hearing. At the end of the day, the disclosure statement was approved.

Considering the letter from the claimants' committee in support of the plan; the exclusion of any dissenting statement; the representation that the court had found that all Dalkon Shield claims would be paid in full; the absence of any potentially troubling information as to how much money an individual claimant could actually expect to be paid; the equal weighting of the votes; and the preponderance of claimants with small claims and no lawyers, a vote in favor of the plan was a foregone conclusion. For insurance, Judge Merhige added to the packet of materials to be sent to the claimants his own letter, in which he recited that he was prohibited from making any recommendation as to how anyone should vote, but then proceeded to describe the plan in laudatory terms:

The plan is a product of negotiations between the debtor, the official committees, and others under the Court's supervision. The plan has the approval of the court-appointed examiner as well as the official committees. The plan provides for payment by the debtor of $2,255,000,000 into the Dalkon Shield Claimants Trust for distribution to Dalkon Shield claimants and for costs of administration of the trust . . . Money in addition to the $2,255,000,000 may also be made available by people or entities other than the debtor for paying Dalkon Shield claimants and trust expenses . . .[15]

A majority of the named trustees were taken from a list of persons selected by the Dalkon Shield Claimants Committee. One of the members of the Dalkon Shield Claimants Trust is a member of the Claimants Committee and was a Dalkon Shield user who filed a claim which will be withdrawn.

The disclosure statement, the ballot, and the various endorsement letters were sent to the eligible claimants in late April 1988. The votes and objections to confirmation were due in early July. The hearing on confirmation was scheduled for July 18, 1988.

On May 31, 1988, Judge Merhige authorized Robins to send another ballot to the claimants who had not yet responded, together with a letter over the name of the Dalkon Shield claimants' committee extolling the plan of reorganization and urging a favorable vote. In seeking authority for the additional mailing, Robins said that it was concerned about "accidentally discarded" ballots and that it wanted "to expend every possible effort to give each claimant an opportunity to vote." The cost to the estate was not an obstacle to this mailing.

17 Confirmation

The traditional leadership of the plaintiffs' bar—most notably Bradley Post and Douglas Bragg—opposed Robins's plan of reorganization. But many lawyers representing Dalkon Shield claimants decided to join the claimants' committee in supporting the plan. These lawyers agreed that it was conceptually wrong for upward of $700 million to be paid to Robins shareholders and for the liability of other defendants to be extinguished while it was still uncertain whether the trust would have sufficient funds to compensate fully all Dalkon Shield victims. Yet, more money would be provided to pay Dalkon Shield claims than they had expected, and even if it might not be enough to pay their clients' claims at prebankruptcy levels, the plan supporters concurred in Murray Drabkin's judgment that it was doubtful a larger amount could be obtained within an acceptable period of time.[1]

The decision by some lawyers to support the plan may also have been influenced by their own economic interests. Some attorneys who represented Dalkon Shield victims before the Robins bankruptcy had few other clients. The automatic stay of litigation against Robins resulting from the bankruptcy filing meant a near-total suspension of their income, and several were forced into substantial debt to keep their offices open. At the same time, because the notice campaign created a sixtyfold increase in the number of women asserting claims against Robins, many lawyers with experience in the field acquired far more Dalkon Shield clients during the bankruptcy than they had had before.[2] The result was that, if the plan was not confirmed, there would be an additional extended period during which these lawyers would make no money. If the plan was confirmed and the claimants' trust began operations, their income would not merely resume, it would reach new heights. Several lawyers had a one-third interest in a thousand or more cases, an interest that could quickly turn them into millionaires, regardless of whether full payment or 75 percent of full payment would be available from the trust.

By contrast, lawyers who did not confine their law practices to Dalkon Shield cases and who did not represent large numbers of claimants did not feel either the pinch of the Chapter 11 case or the prospect

237

of a bonanza upon its conclusion, and they were able to focus on the highest possible recoveries for their clients. To a large extent, the division among plaintiffs' counsel concerning the plan of reorganization was a continuation of the wholesaler-retailer conflict that had marked the deliberations of the first claimants' committee. The difference was that during the Chapter 11 case the ranks of the wholesalers had grown and the weight of their opinion had been enhanced by Judge Merhige's decision to accord an equal vote to every claim, regardless of the severity of the injury.

The support of a substantial proportion of the plaintiffs' bar, including those with the most clients, together with the near-monolithic support for the plan among unrepresented claimants, resulted in an overwhelming vote of approval. When the confirmation hearing began on July 18, 1988, Dennis Drebsky was "happy and proud to report" that the vote of the Dalkon Shield claimants was 131,761 in favor and 7,844 opposed. The only surprise was the substantial number of dissenting votes—a number large enough to leave open the possibility that the holders of two-thirds of the value of the Dalkon Shield claims had not voted in favor of the plan.[3] Nonetheless, assuming the validity of the equal-voting rule adopted by Judge Merhige, the plan of reorganization had been accepted by the class of Dalkon Shield claimants. A cramdown, with a formal finding of payment in full, would not be necessary.[4]

Notwithstanding the vote, however, another requirement of the Bankruptcy Code relative to the level at which creditors would be paid—the "best interests" test—still had to be met. Section 1129(a)(7) provides that a plan of reorganization cannot be confirmed over the objection of even a single creditor unless the court finds that the creditor will receive "property of a value . . . that is not less than the amount that such [creditor] would receive . . . if the debtor were liquidated under Chapter 7."[5]

This provision might be thought to afford inordinate weight to the views of one creditor, but it is essential to the conceptual underpinnings of reorganization as a legitimate alternative to liquidation. A debtor is permitted to reorganize on the theory that this will increase the value of the estate. Under the absolute priority rule, the creditors are entitled to the benefit of the increase up to the full amount of their claims, but the Bankruptcy Code allows them, by a proper vote, to yield part or all of this added value to the equity interests to expedite the proceeding or for any other reason. On the other hand, each creditor is legally entitled to the amount he would receive in a liquidation and, regardless of the sentiments of the other creditors, cannot be forced to take less because the debtor has chosen to reorganize.

The debtor has the obligation to establish, as a prerequisite to confirmation, that the dissenting creditors are not disadvantaged by the reorganization. This is done by means of a "liquidation analysis" that compares the amounts that would be available to the dissenters under a hypothetical liquidation with the amounts to be provided under the proposed plan. Despite the statutory mandate and the conceptual importance of the best interests test, in practice—at least in major Chapter 11 proceedings—the requirement is usually treated as a meaningless ritual. Once the debtor's plan of reorganization is accepted by the requisite vote of the creditors, the court's interest in confirming the plan and concluding the proceeding "successfully" becomes so great that the debtor's liquidation analysis is accepted uncritically. That was certainly the case in the Robins bankruptcy.

Robins's plan of reorganization did not provide for payment of interest to Dalkon Shield claimants. This was no small matter, as interest on $2.3 billion for the fifty-two months between the Chapter 11 filing and the consummation of Robins's plan of reorganization would exceed $1 billion. The Bankruptcy Code provides that in a liquidation creditors are entitled to be paid interest on their claims for the duration of the bankruptcy proceeding, before any payments are made to shareholders.[6] Accordingly, even if Dalkon Shield claimants would be paid their compensatory damages in full by a trust funded in accordance with Merhige's estimate, the claimants would be paid more in a liquidation, where they would also receive interest, unless a liquidation would not provide sufficient funds to make any additional payments to Dalkon Shield claimants.[7] It was this question to which Robins's liquidation analysis was addressed. Robins submitted the analysis shown in table 17.1.

Under the plan of reorganization, approximately $2.356 billion would be paid to the unsecured creditors (Dalkon Shield claimants and unsecured commercial creditors) and stock then valued at $700 million would be issued to Robins's shareholders.[8] By contrast, Robins's liquidation analysis purported to show that, if the company's businesses were sold, somehow only $1.611 billion would be available for the unsecured creditors and nothing would be left for the shareholders. Almost $1.5 billion had disappeared.

The main reason for this is that Robins's analysis was premised on the

Table 17.1. Summary of Robins's Liquidation Proceeds
Computation (dollars in millions)

(1) Total proceeds from liquidation	$2,272
Reduction in sales value:	
(2) Net tax cost	−53
(3) Cost of selling the businesses	−94
(4) Net liquidation proceeds available	$2,125
(5) Secured and unsecured priority claims	−110
(6) Administrative costs for Dalkon Shield litigation	−404
(7) Net proceeds available for unsecured claims	$1,611*

* Robins' Sixth Amended Disclosure Statement, Annex 8, pp. LIQ-2–LIQ-3. All of the numbers in the table are from Robins's liquidation analysis except line 2, which is the net of Robins's figures for tax liabilities and tax benefits resulting from a sale. The breakdown of the secured and priority claims is omitted.

assumption that the proceeds from a liquidation of the company would be only $2.272 billion. The dust had barely settled in a bidding war among American Home Products, the Rorer Group, and Sanofi in which each would-be acquirer had made offers for Robins worth more than $3 billion. The total value of the American Home Products proposal was in the neighborhood of $3.2 billion. Remarkably, the $2.272 billion figure in Robins's analysis was lower than the liquidation value for the company set forth in the Rorer plan of reorganization, filed in August 1987, before competitive bidding had driven up the price of the company by at least $750 million.[9]

Without regard to any other number in the liquidation analysis, if the $2.272 billion figure was valid, the best interests test would be satisfied, because with proceeds from the liquidation of $2.272 billion, the unsecured creditors obviously could not have been paid more than the $2.356 billion provided in the plan of reorganization. The question was how Robins had arrived at $2.272 billion. At the confirmation hearing on July 18, 1988, testimony in support of this figure was provided by Alexa Wilson, a 1982 graduate of the business school at Stanford University with the title of vice-president at Drexel Burnham Lambert, Robins's investment adviser.

Ms. Wilson said that in calculating the figure she had paid no attention to the values actually offered for Robins by American Home Products, the Rorer Group, and Sanofi in January 1988. Instead, she had relied on two technical evaluation procedures that involved the computation of values for Robins based on ratios between common-stock prices and earnings, and between acquisition cost and earnings, of other publicly traded companies. From values derived in this way, Ms. Wilson deducted "risk adjustments" of $100 million to $125 million—principally to reflect the supposed uncertainties regarding a buyer's possible exposure to future Dalkon Shield liability. (In fact, it is clear that a Chapter 7 trustee can sell assets of the estate free of any of the debtor's liabilities.)[10] The average of the results of her two approaches was $1.872 billion, which came to $2.272 billion when Robins's $400 million in cash was added.

Ms. Wilson offered the following explanation of why the value she came up with was so much lower than the values actually offered by American Home Products, Rorer, and Sanofi:

There were several reasons. The first was that . . . we assumed that the offers that had come in and the AHP offer that was outstanding went away in order to get to a Chapter 7 liquidation. So that was one reason.

Secondly, the American Home Products offer itself contained a number of conditions, such as consensus. There were injunctions, releases, a number of conditions which it was unclear would have been available in Chapter 7.

Thirdly, I think American Home Products had previously made an offer, and it had been withdrawn. So there were, again, no assurances in a Chapter 7 that American Home would be there. And then finally, we, Drexel, felt that American Home Products . . . was a very strong bidder . . . economically as well as financially among bidders for the company, and therefore they were best able . . . to use some of the economic and tax benefits available here. It is not clear that other bidders could reach that same type of range.

There was no further, or deeper, exploration at the confirmation hearing of Ms. Wilson's assertion that the three recent offers for the acquisition of the company were not relevant to its evaluation. Nor was Ms. Wilson asked to document the price/earning multiples or the acquisition cost/earnings multiples she had used in her analysis, or to explain why Drexel's evaluation of Robins had declined from the time the Rorer plan was prepared. Her assertion that the proceeds from a liquidation of Robins would be $2.272 billion was accepted without question.

A half a year earlier, in the liquidation analysis accompanying the Rorer plan, Robins had contended that its liquidation value was below (although not nearly so far below) the value of the Rorer offer of acquisition. At that time Ralph Mabey, the court-appointed examiner, who had discussed possible buy-outs of A. H. Robins with several potential purchasers and knew what he was talking about, objected to this valuation:

The Examiner disagrees with Robins' view that the overall value of Robins' business would be significantly less than the value offered by Rorer pursuant to the plan. The Examiner believes that no discount should be applied; a chapter 7 trustee would be able to obtain approximately as much for Robins' business as would be obtained under the Rorer offer.[11]

The Dalkon Shield claimants' committee, which was opposed to the Rorer plan, concurred: "[T]here is no reason that a Chapter 7 trustee would not realize at least what Rorer offered, or perhaps even more."[12] If the claimants' committee had not been supporting the American Home Products plan of reorganization, it presumably would have presented testimony at the confirmation hearing from an investment banker in opposition to Ms. Wilson's analysis. But with all the official participants in the bankruptcy—the only parties with access to the money necessary to employ a witness with the appropriate expertise—supporting Robins's plan of reorganization, no effective opposition could be presented.

In fact, although it did not prove necessary to explain or quantify them at the confirmation hearing, there were tax considerations that would tend to reduce the price A. H. Robins would attract in a transaction that took the form of a sale of assets rather than a corporate merger. At most, however, these considerations would account for only a small portion of the $930 million price reduction reflected in Robins's liquidation analysis.[13]

Robins reduced its "total proceeds" figure of $2.272 billion to only $1.611 billion available to pay unsecured debt through a series of questionable deductions. The most significant of these was the $404 million for costs of litigation (table 17.1, line 6). This involved a double count. The costs of liquidating the claims, including legal fees, were included in the $2.255 billion American Home Products would pay to the claimants' trust under the plan of reorganization. A proper comparison would require that these costs also be included in the funds available to pay Dalkon Shield claims in a hypothetical liquidation. If there had been a liquidation, the bankruptcy court would have had to establish a mechanism for the resolution of the 195,000 claims, and there is no reason why that mechanism would look any different or cost any more than the claimants' trust established under Robins's plan of reorganization.

The fragility of Robins's liquidation analysis can be demonstrated simply by assuming that the total proceeds from liquidation (line 1) would be $2.9 billion ($300 million less than the value of the American Home Products deal to account very generously for the lesser tax benefit to the acquiring corporation), by omitting the duplicative deduction for costs of litigation (line 6), but otherwise retaining Robins's figures. This is done in table 17.2.

Table 17.2. Modified Liquidation Proceeds Computation
(dollars in millions)

(1) Total proceeds from liquidation	$2,900
Reduction in sales value:	
(2) Net tax cost	−53
(3) Cost of selling the businesses	−94
(4) Net liquidation proceeds available	$2,753
(5) Secured and unsecured priority claims	−110
(6) Administrative costs for Dalkon Shield litigation	Included in trust payment
(7) Net proceeds available for unsecured claims	$2,643

This compares to approximately $2.356 billion paid to all unsecured creditors under the plan of reorganization. If a proper analysis had shown that $2.643 billion, or any amount above $2.356 billion, would have been available in a liquidation, then the Dalkon Shield claimants were penalized by the reorganization and the plan of reorganization did not satisfy the best interests requirement for confirmation.

Notwithstanding the support for the plan by the claimants' committee and the vote, strong opposition to the plan was voiced at the hearing by several attorneys representing claimants. Judge Merhige's colloquy with Ralph Pittle provides the flavor.

MERHIGE: Give me an alternative, Mr. Pittle. Tell me what you would do. If we take 100% of the profits, assuming that Robins made the highest amount that they made so far, it will be 30 years [before claimants are paid]. And Robins wouldn't be viable. What is the alternative to getting these women paid?

PITTLE: Thank you for giving me that opportunity, Your Honor. I think there are a couple of possible alternatives.

MERHIGE: As shown by the evidence, of course.

PITTLE: I understand. I am not convinced that either American Home Products, Rorer or Sanofi would not be willing to put in as much or close to as much as they are putting into this deal if all of the money went to claimants instead of $700 million going to the shareholders, or at least if it went to the claimants until such time as the value of the claims was determined . . .

MERHIGE: I am not so sure either. I am not so sure they are not going to walk away. I am not sure of anything except that if we get this money, I am sure as I can be that these ladies are going to get paid, and paid in full . . .

PITTLE: I am certainly convinced that Your Honor sincerely and genuinely believes that the estimation figure would result in full payment for the claimants. I certainly hope that is true. My problem is, and the reason why I am concerned about the injunction that would prevent claimants from bringing actions against wrongdoers other than Robins, which would not be necessary if $2.475 billion results in full payment, my problem is, what if it doesn't? I was here in this same courtroom with Your Honor during the five days of the estimation hearing from opening statement to closing argument, and heard all of the witnesses that Your Honor heard. And the difference between the estimates that were offered by the various parties all turned on various assumptions that were made regarding the degree of participation that would take place by the claimants. And I am fearful that there isn't a clue of what will actually take place.

MERHIGE: The problem with your suggestion, Mr. Pittle . . . is we can't make American Home Products negotiate the way you and I might want them to, or to come to terms that perhaps you and I might want. They said they want peace. And they are not going to put up over $2 billion and be involved in any way whatsoever even peripherally in litigation.

PITTLE: . . . The reason one cannot [know] what American Home Products would be willing to pay is that . . . claimants were never in a position to negotiate with American Home Products in their own right, because the debtor had the exclusive period. So, any plan had to come through the debtor and then seek the consensus of the claimants.

MERHIGE: Mr. Pittle, I suspect it is understandable, over a three year period, that counsel and the court will disagree. And some of the disagreements that the court has had with Mr. Drabkin, if people didn't know us they would think that we were enemies. We have had knock down, drag out. Angry as I may get with him, as angry as he may get with me, if there were any more money, Murray Drabkin would have gotten it. He did everything but ask me to chip in.

PITTLE: The plan itself, Your Honor, has another $700 million in it which isn't going to the claimants.

The only Dalkon Shield claimant who attempted to participate in the confirmation hearing was Karen Hicks, a woman from Bethlehem, Pennsylvania. In 1984, seven days after her wedding, Ms. Hicks suffered a massive attack of pelvic inflammatory disease as a result of her use of the Dalkon Shield and was forced to undergo a total hysterectomy. She organized the Dalkon Shield Information Network, a group, like IDEA, intended to foster communication among women injured by the Dalkon Shield, and she had been visible during the course of the Chapter 11 proceeding in opposition to Robins's efforts to limit and discharge its liability to women injured by the Dalkon Shield.

At the appropriate point in the hearing, Ms. Hicks sought recognition to make a statement in opposition to confirmation. Merhige ruled that she could not do this, even though she was a claimant and entitled to represent herself without counsel, because she had notified the court that she would appear at the hearing on behalf of her organization, the Dalkon Shield Information Network; she did not say that she would appear on her own behalf. Because the date he had set for notification had passed, Merhige would not allow Ms. Hicks to change her notification and speak on her own behalf.

> MERHIGE: I am sorry, ma'am. You gave notice you were going to appear on behalf of a corporation, ma'am. The law requires that only somebody who is counsel at law may do so. Very sorry . . .
>
> HICKS: May I address the court?
>
> MERHIGE: No, ma'am, you may not.
>
> HICKS: You have told us that we don't need lawyers.
>
> MERHIGE: Marshal! Ma'am, you will have to be seated. The law says only attorneys may represent people.
>
> HICKS: I did—what is different—
>
> MERHIGE: You gave notice that you were representing the corporation. I can go no further than I have gone. I will ask you to be seated. Thank you, ma'am.
>
> [Ms. Hicks remained standing.]
>
> MERHIGE: You will be seated or be removed. I am sorry. Escort the lady out of the courtroom, Marshal.

As a deputy United States marshal pulled Ms. Hicks out of the packed courtroom, she called out, "We haven't had a voice in three years." The few other women with Dalkon Shield claims in attendance at the hearing followed Ms. Hicks out.

Murray Drabkin spoke at the confirmation hearing in favor of the plan of reorganization and explained the decision of the committee to accept the plan as an appropriate compromise, despite the undesirable features identified by Pittle and others. But when Drabkin referred to the selection of "an acceptable group of trustees" and to their approval by the court, Merhige reacted angrily:

> MERHIGE: Well, now, in fairness, under duress. I am not going to let you get by with that. Under duress. I was told that either we approved it or you would, two days before the company was to send it, you would withdraw consent. And American Home said they would not do it unless there was a consensual plan. I don't want to hear any more about that because that was duress.
>
> DRABKIN: Duress went both ways. I would remind the court that an agreement was reached with counsel in the presence of the court and Judge Shelley with respect to the five trustees who were named some time ago, and it was only the attempt to change that which resulted in what the court alluded to at the present moment.
>
> MERHIGE: The court thought there should have been seven trustees. And the court was told without any consideration whatsoever, as a matter of fact the trustees, at least [all but] one of them, had been suggested by your committee,

that they either took it or you withdraw your consent. And that would have blown it. And I had in my mind, two hundred thousand women who had been waiting ten years. So I don't want it to go by that the court just eased along with it, Mr. Drabkin.

Beyond this expression of anger, in the days before the confirmation hearing, Judge Merhige had laid the groundwork to gain a larger measure of control over the operation of the trust.

The plan of reorganization provided that the court would be available to resolve disputes concerning the interpretation of the documents governing the trust, to decide whether to grant nonsubordinated status to late claims, and to review periodic reports from the trust reflecting its financial situation and its progress in disposing of cases, but the basic idea, as stated in the plan of reorganization, was that "nothing contained [herein] is intended to confer jurisdiction upon the Court, or grant authority to monitor, the day-to-day operations of the Trusts or the Claim Resolution Facility."[14] In seeking independent status for the trust, Drabkin and the claimants' committee were motivated by the desire to assure that the trust was run by the trustees they had approved and not by Judge Merhige. In the weeks following the submission of the plan of reorganization, Merhige had succeeded in gaining additional control over the trust, but the idea of an independent trust was still operative, at least in Murray Drabkin's mind.

A week or so before the confirmation hearing, attorneys for Robins submitted to Judge Merhige ex parte a draft of a lengthy confirmation order containing all the numerous provisions contemplated by the plan of reorganization. In response, Merhige told Dennis Drebsky that he wanted to add a paragraph to the confirmation order granting him certain additional powers relating to the administration of the trust. Merhige had drafted the following:

All payments made or promised . . . in connection with the administration of the Trust and the Claims Resolution Facility, shall be subject to the approval by this Court, and the retention by the Trust of attorneys, accountants, other professionals or para-professionals shall be subject to prior approval of this Court.

Drebsky added this language as paragraph 44 and circulated the revised version to all counsel. Murray Drabkin immediately made known his opposition to granting Merhige these powers.

A conference was held in Judge Merhige's chambers on Sunday, July 17, 1988, the afternoon before the confirmation hearing, to try to reach an agreement on this matter. Merhige's posture was not conducive to agreement, as he demanded still other powers over the trust. He said he wanted the power to invest the trust funds and to remove trustees at will. (The earlier amendment had granted him the authority to remove trustees "for cause.") To everyone's astonishment, Merhige also stated that he might not appoint as trustees the five persons previously agreed on, even though their names were in the disclosure statement and he had emphasized the role of the claimants' committee in selecting the trustees in his letter to the claimants.[15] The meeting ended acrimoniously with nothing decided.

Section 1129(a)(11) of the Bankruptcy Code requires, as one of the conditions to confirmation of a plan of reorganization, that the court find that "confirmation of the plan is not likely to be followed by the liquidation, or the need for further financial reorganization of the debtor . . . " The purpose of this condition, referred to as the "feasibility requirement," is to assure that the assets of the estate and the earning power of the debtor are sufficient to meet the commitments of the plan and to support the continuation of the business. Because of the prospective acquisition by American Home Products, there could be no doubt along these lines in the case of Robins's plan of reorganization. Nevertheless, in his comments at the confirmation hearing the following morning, Judge Merhige repeatedly suggested that he could not find that the plan of reorganization was "feasible" if he did not have the powers of supervision over the operations of the trust that he had demanded. For example:

The court is being asked to permit the transfer of two and a half billion dollars to five people . . . without any supervision whatsoever. And I am not sure that is feasible . . . I think this court has an obligation . . . to protect a $2 billion sum, to be sure it is utilized the way it is supposed to be. And I agree, whoever the trustees are, they have the say as to what shall be paid on each claim. I don't know as the court has anything to do with that, except to be sure that there is going to be enough money to pay all of them. The court has got to watch the investment. There can be no doubt about that. It is not feasible otherwise.

Judge Merhige backtracked from his threat of the previous afternoon not to appoint as trustees the persons who had been publicly designated, but he referred to them as "initial trustees" and suggested that they might not remain in office.

I might add that the court intends in the order of confirmation to appoint, because I think fairness dictates it, as initial trustees those whose names appear in the disclosure statement, that is what people expect. I must say, without in any manner subtracting from the efforts that will be made by the trustees, I would feel more comfortable if we had more plaintiff-oriented trustees, and that may ultimately come to pass.

The powers Judge Merhige was seeking over the employment of professionals and other expenditures by the trust, in Ralph Mabey's words, were "not in contemplation of the negotiating parties," and several of the attorneys tried to lead the judge gently away from this battle. Louis Hoynes, counsel for American Home Products, who did not otherwise participate in the confirmation hearing, rose to urge Merhige not to disturb the agreement that had been reached.

HOYNES: As I have said to Your Honor on many occasions, our principal interest is in maintaining the spirit of that consensus and cooperation, and I wish to join Mr. Drabkin's remarks to the extent that he has indicated to Your Honor that this plan and all of its accompanying documents, including the trust agreements and the Claims Resolution Facility and the rest, were carefully negotiated and represent very intricate tradeoffs and balances . . . With regard to Your Honor's suggestion, which I know is intended to be for the benefit of the claimants, and for which I have considerable sympathy, I would like to say that that suggestion can only be implemented by a modification of the plan.

MERHIGE: I don't think it requires that. I am not asking you to modify your plan at all.

HOYNES: I appreciate that, because we are not in a position, as I think you understand, to modify the plan.

MERHIGE: I must tell you in honesty . . . I think the law requires that we have this. That is not modifying your plan one iota.

Judge Merhige issued his order confirming the plan of reorganization and an accompanying memorandum seven days after the confirmation hearing, on July 25, 1988.[16] The memorandum is made up of a summary description of the proceeding and a series of short paragraphs asserting that each of the statutory prerequisites to confirmation has been met. In reference to the best interests test, for example, Merhige simply stated that "each holder of a claim or interest will receive under the Plan property of a value . . . that not only is as much as the amount that such holder would receive if Robins were liquidated under Chapter 7 of the Bankruptcy Code but substantially more."[17] The memorandum made no reference to any of the objections.

In an effort to resolve the impasse over paragraph 44 and to avoid an appeal over this issue, Ralph Mabey had come up with the idea that Merhige not include the disputed language in his confirmation order but say something in his accompanying opinion to the effect that the "feasibility" of the plan required that the trust obtain court approval of expenditures and of the employment of professionals. There was apparently a misunderstanding that this suggestion would satisfy Drabkin, and Merhige adopted it. Merhige made no reference to the matter in the confirmation order, but in his opinion explaining the order he stated:

A fair reading of the Plan discloses that the feasibility of same is premised on continuing supervision by the Court of each of the Trusts. Feasibility of this plan and the law requires this supervision to assure the accuracy of the Court's estimate [and], the full payment of all Dalkon Shield personal injury claims . . . Court supervision of the Trusts is sufficient under the facts of this case in that the Court is empowered under the law to approve all payments by the Trusts for services, costs and expenses in connection with the administration of the Trusts and to approve the employment by the Trusts of professionals and administrators, and to otherwise supervise the Trusts as provided for or allowed by the Plan and applicable law.

Referring to the language of the plan quoted above, Merhige added:

The supervision by the Court of payments for services or for costs and expenses in connection with the administration of the Trusts and of the employment by the Trusts of professionals and administrators is not supervision of the day-to-day operations of the Trust.[18]

The conflict between Merhige and Drabkin over the status of the claimants' trust remained to be resolved.

With the confirmation of the plan of reorganization, Robins's exposure to punitive damages—the specter that had driven the company into bankruptcy—was quietly eliminated. The plan stipulated that all claims for punitive damages would be disallowed. By voting to accept the plan, the class of Dalkon Shield claimants had consented to this provision, and punitive damages were disallowed in the confirmation order.[19] The question of whether punitive damages could have been disallowed if the plan had been rejected by the claimants did not have to be decided.[20]

18   Release of Aetna

Unlike most lawsuits, which can be settled simply by the agreement of the parties, a class action can be settled only after an elaborate procedure involving notice to the class of the terms of the proposed settlement and of the right to object, a hearing at which the fairness of the settlement and the validity of the objections are addressed, and a formal determination by the court that the settlement is fair and reasonable. This procedure is designed to ensure that the rights of absent class members have been adequately and faithfully represented, and that the named plaintiffs or their attorneys have not obtained a settlement beneficial to themselves at the expense of the members of the class.

Before notice of the proposed settlement in the *Breland* case could be mailed, it was necessary for Judge Merhige to specify the nature of the class action. Judge Merhige's tentative class certification in December 1986 had not resolved the issue of whether the class action would be mandatory or optional, that is, whether women in the class would be permitted to "opt-out" and pursue their independent actions against Aetna. The agreement for the settlement of *Breland* was conditional on Judge Merhige's certifying a mandatory class with respect to the claim for punitive damages. If he refused to do so, the settlement agreement (and the plan of reorganization) would be void. But if the judge did certify a mandatory class for punitive damages, the agreement would stand and all of the relief Aetna had agreed to provide—the net $75 million in cash, the $250 million in excess insurance, and the $100 million in outlier insurance—would be forthcoming, whether or not a mandatory class was certified with respect to compensatory damage claims.

The terms of the settlement agreement left class counsel no choice but to join Aetna in seeking a mandatory class for the punitive damage claims. Without it, there would be no settlement. Equally clearly, the terms of the settlement would lead class counsel and Aetna to opposite positions on the question of whether the compensatory damages claims should be included in a mandatory class action. Aetna would want to discharge as much of its potential liability as possible in exchange for the insurance and cash it was providing, and it would be expected to ask Judge Merhige to go beyond the minimum requirement of the settlement and certify a mandatory class on all claims. Equally, class counsel would be expected to ask Judge Merhige to allow class members the right to opt out and to seek compensatory damages from Aetna in independent litigation, because the benefits of this choice could be afforded to the women they had undertaken to represent without lessening in any way the benefits of the settlement to class members who did not opt out.

As it happened, Aetna took the expected position but class counsel did not. On February 5, 1988, four days after the settlement agreement had been signed, Aetna filed a memorandum asking the court to certify a mandatory class covering all the claims in *Breland*. The only thing odd about this was that Aetna titled its memorandum "In Support of Plaintiffs' Motion for Mandatory Class Certification," when the plaintiffs had not yet taken a position, at least not publicly, on the nature of the class that should be certified in light of the settlement. Then, on February 11, 1988, Joe Friedberg filed a memorandum dated February 5, 1988, supporting Aetna's effort to prevent the women he represented from opting out and suing Aetna separately for either compensatory or punitive damages.

Until the *Breland* case, efforts to maintain a mandatory class action for compensatory damages in a personal injury case had been unanimously rejected by the federal courts.[1] Friedberg put forth two practical arguments in support of a different result, neither of which related in any way to the requirements of the federal rule governing class actions. First, he asserted that an all-mandatory class in *Breland* was a condition of Robins's plan of reorganization and a condition of the settlement with Aetna. ("The proposed class-certification is a non-waivable condition and indispensable component of the merger of A. H. Robins and American Home Products and, therefore, of the successful Chapter 11 reorganization of Robins . . . [P]ermitting opt-outs will threaten resolution of this action and the Robins reorganization.")[2] In truth, the merger agreement, the plan of reorganization, and the *Breland* settlement agreement all provided that they would be undisturbed if Judge Merhige allowed class members to opt out and separately sue Aetna for compensatory damages.[3]

Friedberg's other argument was that an opt-out right would deny due process of law to Aetna, because Aetna would be prevented by the plan of reorganization from bringing Robins into any future action and claiming that Robins was responsible for the plaintiff's damages. This argument was also plainly wrong, if only because Aetna had agreed to an opt-out class for compensatory damage claims and to the restrictions on its rights against Robins (or American Home Products) contained in the plan of reorganization. But what was remarkable was that the argument was an assertion of Aetna's interests, not those of the women Friedberg had undertaken to represent.

In its memorandum supporting mandatory class certification, Aetna did not refer to either of Friedberg's arguments. Instead, Aetna made an argument based on rule 23 of the Federal Rules of Civil Procedure, which defines the circumstances in which class actions can be maintained. The two provisions of the rule that have been applied to class actions seeking money damages were plainly unavailing. Subpart (b)(3), the provision of the rule most clearly applicable when a large number of people claim damages as a result of the same conduct, allows class certification when common questions of law and fact predominate, but the rule explicitly provides that in such a case each individual must be given the right to opt out and pursue his own claim.[4] Subpart (b)(1)(B) permits a mandatory class action when individual actions could "impair" the rights of nonparties, that is, if the defendant's assets are less than the value of the claims against it (a "limited fund").[5] But that clearly was not the case with respect to Aetna.

John Harkins, counsel for Aetna, devised a novel theory based on another provision of the class action rule, subpart (b)(1)(A), which allows a mandatory class action when "the prosecution of separate actions . . . would create a risk of inconsistent or varying adjudications . . . which would establish incompatible standards of conduct for the party opposing the class." This language was intended to allow a single adjudication where "a large number of persons are in a position to call on a single person to alter the status quo, or to complain if it is altered, and the possibility exists that [the] actor might be called upon to act in inconsistent ways."[6] According to one major decision, this provision "must be interpreted to [refer to] incompatible standards of conduct required of defendants in fulfilling judgments in separate actions."[7] The possibility that a defendant might be found liable to one person and not to another on account of the same completed conduct does not meet this standard. "[A] judgment that defendants were liable to one plaintiff would not require action inconsistent with a judgment that they were not liable to another plaintiff. By paying the first judgment, defendants could act consistently with both judgments."[8]

In an attempt to fit within this subpart, Harkins argued that the question of whether Aetna was liable to women injured by the Dalkon Shield turned on whether a product liability insurer has a duty to inform its insured's customers of potential dangers of which it has knowledge. If one court held that Aetna had a duty to women using the Dalkon Shield to warn them of its dangers, Harkins argued, and another court held that it had a duty to Robins not to give such a warning, "incompatible standards of conduct" for Aetna would be established. This argument oversimplified the theories of liability that had been asserted against Aetna, in that it ignored claims that Aetna had assumed the decision-making role in handling the Dalkon Shield litigation, had concealed or destroyed (not simply failed to disclose) information that would reveal the dangers of the Dalkon Shield, and had prevented a recall of the product at a time when a great deal of human injury and suffering could have been avoided. Harkins's argument also assumed that the hypothetical court that ruled in Aetna's favor would find not only that Aetna was not obligated to warn Dalkon Shield users but that it was obligated to Robins not to, a speculation at best. And since the rule is concerned with inconsistent standards for future conduct, not with inconsistent liability on account of past events, Harkins's argument also assumed that Aetna would face the same situation in the future—knowledge of an insured's coverup of a product defect—another speculation. And even if it did, the inconsistent decisions in the Dalkon Shield litigation would reflect inconsistent legal rules; they would not constitute judgments directing Aetna's future conduct. Aetna would be in the same position as any other product liability insurer.

The complaint in the *Breland* case defined two classes: class A, comprising eligible claimants in the Robins bankruptcy, and class B, comprising all other women with Dalkon Shield injury claims, that is, women who did not comply with bar date or questionnaire requirements in the Robins bankruptcy. Class A members would benefit from the cash and the excess insurance Aetna had agreed to provide. Class B members would benefit from the outlier insurance.[9] Although the claims of class B members were expected to be administered by the claimants' trust, these women would not have the right granted to eligible claimants by the plan of reorganization to reject the final offer of the settlement and take their cases to court.

In a telephone conference with Harkins and Friedberg on February 12, 1988, Judge Merhige expressed his concern about the effect of a mandatory class on eliminating individual rights of action. In response, on February 17, 1988, Harkins wrote to the judge suggesting that class A be certified as a mandatory class with respect to all claims and that class B be certified as mandatory for claims for punitive damages and optional for claims for compensatory damages. Referring to the right of

Breland class A members under the plan of reorganization to sue the trust and obtain a jury trial, Harkins wrote:

> If Class A is mandatory, all that the claimants are being denied is the right to pursue duplicate claims for the same compensatory purpose, thereby burdening the court system with needless litigation. Surely the orderly process constructed by the reorganization plan and the guarantee of full and prompt compensation is ample justification to require those who are eligible to take from the trust to do so, and thereby avoid wasteful, and in this context fruitless, litigation.

By speaking of a fictional "guarantee of full and prompt compensation," Harkins's argument ignored the reasons a woman injured by the Dalkon Shield would proceed separately against Aetna—the uncertainty as to the adequacy of the funding of the trust and the prospect of unacceptable delays in processing claims before the trust. It also obscured Aetna's independent liability for its own misdeeds; Robins's bankruptcy provided no basis for protecting Aetna from that liability. Further, separate suits by members of class B created the potential for so-called inconsistent standards, the avoidance of which was supposed to provide the legal basis for the request that class A be made mandatory.

Some one hundred attorneys representing women injured by the Dalkon Shield opposed mandatory class certification in *Breland*. Most if not all of the opposition to the *Breland* settlement could have been dissipated if Merhige had simply allowed the objectors to opt out and proceed independently against Aetna. Without a right to opt out, women dissatisfied with the settlement had no recourse other than to oppose it. Nevertheless, despite his earlier vacillation on the point, Merhige had become strongly attracted to the idea of bundling up the rights of women injured by the Dalkon Shield in one package under his supervision and preventing independent litigation. On April 12, 1988, he issued an order certifying the class in the manner Harkins had suggested: members of class A would have no rights to opt out; members of class B would have the right to opt out with respect to claims for compensatory damages but not with respect to claims for punitive damages.

In his accompanying opinion, Judge Merhige mentioned in passing Harkins's argument relating to incompatible standards but placed primary reliance on the misstatement, traceable to Friedberg's memorandum, that the failure to treat class A as mandatory for both compensatory damages and punitive damages "would effectively nullify the *Breland* class settlement . . . and render Debtor's Plan of Reorganization voidable." He wrote:

The American Home Products and A. H. Robins merger is dependent on settlement of Breland on a class basis which, in turn, is dependent on Aetna's ability to be relieved of the danger of masses of individual suits stemming from its association with Robins.

The effect of permitting Class A members to opt out, thus triggering such contingencies as are contained in the *Breland* settlement and the American Home Products–Robins Merger Agreement, coupled with the loss of Aetna's contribution to the Plan of Reorganization, would be entirely inconsistent with the Bankruptcy Code . . . as well as with accepted class action jurisprudence.[10]

Even if it were true that the elimination of the individual rights of almost two hundred thousand women to bring actions for compensatory damages against Aetna was a condition of Robins's plan of reorganization, it is not apparent why this would constitute a legal basis for a mandatory class action rather than an infirmity in Robins's plan.

Notice of the terms of the proposed *Breland* settlement and of the right to object was mailed to members of class A (eligible claimants in the Robins bankruptcy) in the same envelope as the disclosure statement, the ballot, and other materials from the bankruptcy case. Class B members who were known to the court because of their unsuccessful efforts to assert a claim against Robins were mailed a notice of the proposed settlement, including a statement of their right to opt out with respect to claims for compensatory damages. Because class B in *Breland* included women who had never made their identity known to the court in the Robins bankruptcy, a notice relating to the settlement was also published in early May 1988 in newspapers throughout the United States.[11] The hearing on the fairness of the *Breland* settlement was scheduled for July 7, 1988.

The role of lead counsel for the objectors to the *Breland* settlement was assumed by Joseph McDowell, the lawyer who had played the major role in the efforts to sue Aetna outside Richmond during the bankruptcy.[12] McDowell, a man in his forties, was a partner in Cullity, Kelley & McDowell, a small law firm in Manchester, New Hampshire. McDowell is a big, curly haired, plain-speaking, friendly man. Because of his personal style, he had not provoked quite the same degree of ire in Judge Merhige as had some of the other attorneys representing women injured by the Dalkon Shield.

McDowell wanted to develop two related arguments in opposition to the settlement. One was that the settlement was collusive, or at least not the result of a true adversarial process. The other was that counsel for the class in *Breland* had not sufficiently explored the merits of the claim against Aetna to make an informed judgment of its worth for purposes of settlement. To support these contentions, it was necessary for McDowell to obtain information from Joseph Friedberg and John Harkins, lead counsel for the settling parties, and perhaps from others, concerning the circumstances surrounding the filing of the *Breland* case, the nature of the investigation of the facts that had been conducted, and the details of the settlement negotiations.

Whether class members who oppose a proposed settlement are entitled to gather information in support of their position through formal discovery procedures is a matter left to the discretion of the district court considering the circumstances of the case.[13] The circumstances in *Breland* were that it was one of the largest personal injury class actions in the history of the federal courts; the case was filed in violation of an outstanding injunction but was warmly embraced by the defendant; lead counsel for the class had no experience in the trial of personal injury cases or class actions and had acted over the near-universal objection of the attorneys retained by the class members; the case had been settled without any formal investigation of the facts; counsel for the class had requested an unprecedented and unnecessary mandatory class certification that would extinguish the rights of action against the defendant of the women he had undertaken to represent; the exact nature of the relief obtained in the class action was unclear both because other claims and obligations of the defendant had been settled in the same package and because the defendant had been paid separately for insurance that was represented to be part of the settlement; and the amount of attorney fees that would be paid by the defendant to class counsel remained to be settled between them after final approval of the settlement. If circumstances ever warranted a thorough exploration of a settlement, this was the case.

Judge Merhige never actually ruled that McDowell would not be allowed to secure information from Harkins and Friedberg. Rather, in the manner familiar to James Szaller from his efforts to obtain discovery to support his challenge to the second claimants' committee, and to Alan Morrison from his efforts to obtain the claimants' list for IDEA, Merhige dealt with McDowell's discovery requests in a manner that assured that no useful information would be forthcoming.

On April 22, 1988, just ten days after Judge Merhige had certified a mandatory class, McDowell served a motion seeking authority to direct discovery to Friedberg and Harkins. To assure adequate time before the scheduled fairness hearing, McDowell called the clerk of court's office and asked for the earliest possible hearing. The motion was not scheduled until May 26, 1988.

On that date, McDowell had difficulty convincing Judge Merhige of the need for discovery. Merhige was particularly resistant to allowing McDowell to take discovery about possible collusion.

MERHIGE: Do you have a scintilla of evidence that there is collusion between the plaintiffs' representative and the defendant Aetna? . . .

MCDOWELL: It is very curious that everyone else in this country was stopped from pursuing Aetna except for the Friedberg group . . .

MERHIGE: Why is that a sign of collusion? They filed a suit.

MCDOWELL: Oh, yes, and so did we. We ended up down here [facing contempt charges] in front of Your Honor . . .

MERHIGE: Didn't file them here.

MCDOWELL: Neither did Mr. Friedberg. He filed his in Minnesota . . . Friedberg agreed to transfer his case here to the State of Virginia. We want to know why that happened and how that happened . . .

MERHIGE: Why what?

MCDOWELL: We want to know why that action was transferred from Minnesota to Virginia.

MERHIGE: Why don't you ask them. Or why don't you ask the judge that transferred it? If he is dumb enough to answer you.

MCDOWELL: It was done by agreement.

MERHIGE: Then you know the reason.

MCDOWELL: Well, Your Honor, we think it is very curious that the lawsuit was transferred by agreement . . . as a class action to this state, and want to know why. And we also want to know when the settlement was reached, when settlement discussions began, that is what we want to know.

MERHIGE: Have you asked them?

MCDOWELL: No.

MERHIGE: Why don't you try that, Mr. McDowell?

In an apparent tactical maneuver that drew adverse comment from the judge, neither Friedberg nor Harkins attended the May 26, 1988, hearing on McDowell's motion. Merhige instructed McDowell to sit down with Scott Street, counsel in Richmond for Aetna, and with Theodore Brenner, Murray Janus's associate who appeared at the hearing for the *Breland* plaintiffs, to see what they would agree to provide voluntarily. Merhige told McDowell to come back to him if he was not satisfied with the result.

MERHIGE: I want you to chat with them.

MCDOWELL: I am happy to do that.

MERHIGE: And follow up with an affidavit for anything you really want. They are high class gentlemen.

Merhige added, however, that he would in no event permit McDowell to depose Friedberg.

I am not fixing to have lawyers subjected to eye ball to eye ball depositions. There has been too much animosity in this case. It is shocking. I have been at it over 21 years and never seen anything like it. People calling each other liars. It is disgraceful.

Five days later, on May 31, 1988, McDowell filed an affidavit reporting on his conversations with Street and Brenner. Neither had agreed to provide any information except copies of documents that were already part of the public record. In his affidavit, McDowell listed twenty-three categories of information that he wanted. Despite Merhige's comment, McDowell asked for depositions of the principal participants in the settlement.

Judge Merhige issued an order relating to discovery on June 1, 1988. He ordered Friedberg to provide to McDowell, within twenty days, a summary of the discovery conducted, a summary of Friedberg's opinion on the merits of the case against Aetna, his estimate of the time necessary to prepare the case for trial and to try the case, and a copy of the time sheets of plaintiffs' counsel "if available." Merhige also directed Friedberg to respond to the statement attributed to him, in an affidavit submitted by Douglas Bragg, that "there was no way the case would ever be tried; that he was going to settle it." (Friedberg later explained that the statement was an expression of his opinion that "the case, like ninety-nine percent of all class actions and ninety-five percent of all cases, was in all likelihood going to settle.")

On June 8, 1988, Merhige issued an opinion explaining his refusal to allow additional discovery. He branded McDowell's discovery request as a "fishing expedition," and stated that he had allowed the discovery that would aid the court in reaching its decision and that would "not be disruptive of counsels' preparation for the fairness hearing." He stated that "not a scintilla of evidence" of collusion had been presented and that he would not, at present, allow discovery on that issue. He added, however, "Movants are invited to supply the Court with such evidence, if any they have, as might lead to a conclusion of collusion or bad faith on the part of class plaintiffs' counsel."

In response to this invitation, on June 16, 1988, McDowell filed a motion for discovery on the issue of collusion. What made the situation a particularly delicate one for McDowell was that the circumstances that he thought gave rise to an inference of collusion directly implicated the judge. McDowell wrote:

The Friedberg group was the only group of plaintiffs' lawyers who would bring a mandatory class action in Virginia against Aetna . . . It is suggested, with respect, that this honorable court is one of the few courts in the Country that would entertain a mandatory class action against Aetna . . . Aetna orchestrated, with the District Court's acquiescence, the filing and pursuit of the *Breland* matter in this Court . . . The automatic stay and the Court's injunctive power have been used as a shield by Aetna and Robins to select the legal counsel who were willing to play ball with them in "their" ball park, and to exclude the lawyers who were not.

McDowell attached to his motion the affidavit from Robert Manchester, originally filed in February 1986 in support of the motion to disqualify Judge Merhige, in which Manchester quoted Friedberg as stating that on, June 25, 1985, when he visited Merhige's home, the judge had told Friedberg that he would grant a request for a mandatory class action against Robins.[14]

On June 20, 1988, in response to Merhige's June 1 order, Friedberg sent McDowell a copy of sections of the brief he planned to file with the court in support of the settlement, in which he described his discovery efforts in general terms. This material did not specify the documents that had been examined or the witnesses who had been interviewed. Friedberg did not provide copies of records showing the time he had spent on the Breland case, stating that these were "only available in raw form." The next day, McDowell filed a motion asking Merhige to enforce his June 1 discovery order.

Both McDowell's motion for discovery on the issue of collusion and his motion seeking enforcement of the June 1 order were considered at a hearing before Judge Merhige on June 28. This time Harkins and Friedberg were in court. Merhige was outraged by McDowell's motion.

MERHIGE: I have got some affidavits that are not factual. It is typical of what has been going on since the beginning of the case, the effort to bust it up in some way. That has been the goal of some of these lawyers who think they are representing their clients. And they have done more harm to some of these claimants. The next big thing will be malpractice, and it ought to be.

HARKINS: Your Honor, we are somewhat disappointed in some of the things we saw filed.

MERHIGE: Well, they are ridiculous. They are either incompetent, or— well, I can't fathom the reasoning. Certainly doesn't help their clients. But they haven't helped their clients from the first day.

HARKINS: Our hope is we can start getting money flowing.

When Friedberg addressed the court, he and Merhige discussed the Manchester affidavit:

MERHIGE: You are the one that is going around telling Manchester that you are a regular customer at my house or something.

FRIEDBERG: Apparently not only told him that, told him that the case was fixed, and everything else, according to that affidavit.

MERHIGE: I don't know about that, but I want the record to show—and you correct me—I think you were in my home once some three or four years ago, and I was giving you a ride to a restaurant in the west end. That was long before I ever heard of Mr. Manchester or any of these folks. Am I right or wrong?

FRIEDBERG: Absolutely correct, Your Honor. In fact, there is an affidavit I filed a long time ago when this issue was first raised, traversing Mr. Manchester's affidavit . . . and Mr. Manchester's affidavit is incorrect to the point that it could not be accidentally incorrect.

What Merhige said to Friedberg and what Friedberg said to Manchester in June 1985 cannot be established, but the suggestion that Friedberg's visit to Merhige's home preceded Manchester's involvement in the Dalkon Shield litigation in Richmond, and that this discredits Manchester's affidavit, is demonstrably untrue. In the affidavit to which Friedberg referred, he fixed the date of his visit to Merhige's house as June 25, 1985, and he corroborated Manchester's statement that, on June 27, 1985, in Richmond, Friedberg discussed with Manchester the matter of a class action against Robins.[15] Manchester first appeared before Merhige in opposition to Robins' motion for a punitive damages class in January 1985.

Notwithstanding Merhige's reaction, McDowell pressed for the right to take discovery on the issue of collusion. Merhige responded by suggesting that McDowell had waited too long in making his request:

MERHIGE: What do you want to do? It is kind of late in the game.

MCDOWELL: That is not my fault.

MERHIGE: The hearing is coming up on Monday or Tuesday? Well, it is your fault.

MCDOWELL: That is not my fault . . .

MERHIGE: [Y]ou waited until May 26 to file anything for discovery, Mr. McDowell.

MCDOWELL: No, no I didn't. I filed it earlier in May.

MERHIGE: But didn't bring it on.

MCDOWELL: I tried. The first hearing they would give me was May 26.

MERHIGE: Well, you know, nobody—you can't control that.

MCDOWELL: I am not pointing fingers . . .

MERHIGE: When you talk about discovery, you say on collusion. I don't know what you want. Do you have any evidence of collusion?

MCDOWELL: I said it in my motion, Your Honor, the motion of June 16 . . .

MERHIGE: All right. Everything depends, I guess, on these affidavits . . .

MCDOWELL: I went a little further. I think I mentioned one of the Honorable Court's orders about *Breland* being filed with the court's acquiescence, and it is our position that collusion takes many forms, including if it has been decided *Breland* will go forward . . . and hold the rest of us at bay with stay orders. I think we are entitled to know about that and go into what has gone on and the machinations that went on in establishing that legal theory and the rationale beyond it, and who thought it out and who joined in the process of implementing it . . .

MERHIGE: I can't let you go on a fishing expedition . . .

MCDOWELL: I know. I want to depose Mr. Friedberg, with due respect, and that is what I would like to do. I will do it anytime you tell me to . . . I would like to do more, but if that is what you give me, I will do that. Your Honor said, if we have got any evidence show it.

MERHIGE: That is right.

MCDOWELL: So I did.

MERHIGE: Where is it?

MCDOWELL: You may not like it, but that is my evidence.

MERHIGE: It is not a question of liking it. It is just not so. Assuming that Friedberg said that, then he told an untruth.

MCDOWELL: The point is, I am not asking Your Honor to accept it as a fact. The point is, it is sufficient evidence to justify us to go to the next step and take discovery . . .

MERHIGE: Why don't you sit down with Mr. Friedberg?

MCDOWELL: I will. In all fairness—wait a minute now—

MERHIGE: You might be happy. You may ask him, and he may give you the things you have[n't] got from him already.

MCDOWELL: You called me—told me to call the guys up. I did. I talked with Mr. Friedberg. I talked with Mr. Harkins.

MERHIGE: You didn't get satisfied?

MCDOWELL: I haven't asked Mr. Friedberg the questions I asked Mr. Harkins because I was waiting for the discovery materials, which I still haven't gotten. You can scoff all you want. We are hamstrung on our side. Whatever you want to say, we have been hamstrung by the injunction. And we haven't been able to participate. Right or wrong, or indifferent, whether you agree, that is the way we look at it. We think we have been denied due process. With respect, we are upset about that. This case has been settled out from under us, and we object.

MERHIGE: What injunction?

MCDOWELL: Issued by the Court.

MERHIGE: You mean the stay?

M C D O W E L L: The stay. Stay or injunction, whatever . . .

M E R H I G E: Would you please chat with Mr. Friedberg and see how far you can get into your collusive theory? I have already helped you by telling you part of your dependence is gone because it is not factual.

M C D O W E L L: Right.

M E R H I G E: But you are free to ask him about it.

Merhige refused to order additional discovery, except that he instructed Friedberg to identify the documents on which he had relied in assessing the case against Aetna. Friedberg said that he had an index of "crucial documents" that he would copy and give to McDowell. After more than two months of trying to obtain discovery, McDowell had received only a copy of Friedberg's brief in support of the settlement, a list of documents, and the court's encouragement to "chat" with Friedberg.

McDowell finally got his chance to cross-examine Friedberg at the fairness hearing. First, he approached the question of Friedberg's credentials to represent more than two hundred thousand women in a personal injury class action.

M C D O W E L L: Mr. Friedberg, how many civil cases have you tried? . . .

F R I E D B E R G: Mr. McDowell, I usually say none, but the truth of the matter is that I did try one once . . .

M C D O W E L L: Okay. Was it a tort case?

M E S H B E S H E R [Friedberg's co-counsel]: I object as outside the scope of this hearing.

M E R H I G E: Well, it is certainly outside the scope of the affidavit. But you go ahead. I am going to tell you now, I know he is qualified to try a case such as we are talking about. Because I have had him here . . . His reputation precedes him, Mr. McDowell, and that is the only way we can tell. Nothing special about this. This is not a products liability case. It is more conspiracy, if anything. And that is what I am really interested in.

M C D O W E L L: Your Honor, I realize the examination of Mr. Friedberg is how much—

M E R H I G E: No, I won't let you fish. I told you that. If you wanted discovery, you could have come in long ago and gotten it. You came in late.[16] You asked for what you called a shopping list. The court did the best it could to give it to you. And that is it . . .

M C D O W E L L: I think the ability of Mr. Friedberg is certainly, as class counsel, is an issue.

M E R H I G E: Well, put evidence on that he is no good, if that is what you are insinuating.

M C D O W E L L: I—listen, I don't want to stand here and jaw with the court.

M E R H I G E: You are not going to.

MCDOWELL: I know. I don't want to. Please don't think I do.

MERHIGE: Ask the next question.

MCDOWELL: Mr. Friedberg, my question was, have you tried a products liability case?

FRIEDBERG: I have not.

McDowell next probed the extent to which the matter of Aetna's liability had been investigated before the settlement was reached.

MCDOWELL: Mr. Friedberg, it is fair to say that discovery is not complete, isn't that correct?

FRIEDBERG: There would have to be more discovery prior to trial, yes . . .

MCDOWELL: Let me ask this. Were any depositions conducted by your group as part of the *Breland* action?

FRIEDBERG: None.

MCDOWELL: There were no requests to produce [documents] filed, were there?

FRIEDBERG: There were none.

MCDOWELL: No interrogatories sent out?

FRIEDBERG: There were none.

MCDOWELL: Now, with regard to the inspection by your group of Aetna documents, how did that come about?

FRIEDBERG: I had a discussion with Mr. Harkins very early on trying to set out a timetable to file requests for production. He suggested that documents had been collected, and that he would give us access to the depositary. And that why didn't we look at all they had available there, and then go back and make any additional requests for production that we wanted.

MCDOWELL: Who assembled those documents?

FRIEDBERG: Aetna.

MCDOWELL: You never filed any formal motion to produce with this court concerning those documents?

FRIEDBERG: That is correct.

MCDOWELL: How do you know if they were complete?

FRIEDBERG: Don't.

MCDOWELL: Aetna told you they were. Aetna told you these were our documents, come look at them, and you looked at what they gave you?

FRIEDBERG: Right.

MCDOWELL: You relied on your opponent to tell you these were the documents they would let you inspect?

FRIEDBERG: At that phase, yes.

MCDOWELL: You never . . . followed up with your discovery to verify these documents were in fact properly assembled?

FRIEDBERG: Not—we did not; that is correct.

A peculiar feature of the procedure for the approval of a settlement of any class action is that counsel for the class, who earlier was charged with proclaiming the liability of the defendant, is now called upon to downplay the defendant's liability to justify the amount of the settlement. McDowell next moved to the question of Aetna's liability.

M C D O W E L L: Sir, what is the total exposure of the Dalkon Shield claims against Aetna Insurance? If you tried the case and won it, what would you expect the verdict to be for compensatory damages?

F R I E D B E R G: The way we evaluated it, we believed, speaking of compensatory damages, that were we to try the case, that our upside potential was approximately $500 million . . .

M C D O W E L L: And your theory on that is that Aetna only became liable [late] . . . in the seventies?

F R I E D B E R G: Correct . . .

M C D O W E L L: And the earlier you can prove liability against Aetna, the greater Aetna's exposure becomes?

F R I E D B E R G: That is certainly true.

M C D O W E L L: For example, if you can prove Aetna was aware of and participated in document destruction in 1975, the exposure of Aetna would increase greatly, would it not?

F R I E D B E R G: . . . If they participated in document [destruction], it might very well make them liable. I saw absolutely no evidence of that, and no possibility of it arising.

McDowell handed Friedberg a document that had come from the Aetna depository.

M C D O W E L L: That document that you have in front of you is handwritten notes concerning something that occurred in February of 1975 . . . and it discusses document destruction, isn't that correct?

F R I E D B E R G: . . . it discusses "purging files . . . so in future will not be as vulnerable."

M C D O W E L L: That was the result of the *Deemer* verdict in Kansas, isn't that so?

F R I E D B E R G: I believe that is correct, yes. This was after the *Deemer* verdict. And it is obvious from the discovery that everybody involved was concerned about what happened.

M C D O W E L L: Now, the generation of these notes took place as a result of a meeting not only of Robins people and McGuire, Woods people, but also of Aetna insurance representatives, isn't that so? . . .

F R I E D B E R G: Yes, this is the document we refer to as the Fazio memo.

M E R H I G E: Who wrote this, can you tell?

F R I E D B E R G: I believe this was notes taken by an Aetna employee named Fazio . . .

M C D O W E L L: It is clear from that documentation that you have in your hands that Aetna was aware of that document destruction and the purging of files in February of 1975? . . .

F R I E D B E R G: The statement that refers to the issue we are discussing is "purging files to be sure that for future trials not be as vulnerable." I interpret this to mean that Mr. Fazio wrote down something that Mr. Forest said about purging files. That is all I can tell you from this . . .

M C D O W E L L: Certainly one of the items you would want to look into upon further discovery?

F R I E D B E R G: Yes . . .

M C D O W E L L: It would be important, sir, would it not, to find out whether Aetna knew or participated in the document destruction?

F R I E D B E R G: Yes, I would like to know that.

M C D O W E L L: You can't evaluate any claims prior to 1978 without taking those depositions, can you?

F R I E D B E R G: Mr. McDowell, I can say that I see no evidence anywhere that Aetna participated in document destruction. I don't even see a hint of it.

M C D O W E L L: February 1975 you have documentation that Aetna is sitting in a meeting where it is discussed, document destruction took place, purging of files.

F R I E D B E R G: The note says what it says . . .

In support of the settlement, Aetna executive William Bailey and Aetna attorney John Harkins testified that they believed there was virtually no risk of liability being imposed on Aetna as a result of its conduct in connection with the Dalkon Shield. Harkins testified that, prior to the bankruptcy, Aetna had obtained the dismissal of thirty-six cases alleging that it was liable for Dalkon Shield injuries and that no court had upheld such a claim.[17] He explained that Aetna had agreed to the settlement not out of any fear of liability, but because Aetna preferred to see its money go to the injured women rather than to defense counsel.

H A R K I N S: If one out of ten [of the Robins claimants] sued, [and] . . . if you look at the Robins experience where it cost more than ten thousand dollars per claim to pay just defendants' lawyers, you were looking at $300 million of defense costs. I think if you read Mr. Bailey correctly, he decided ultimately he would much rather give that money to women than to pay a bunch of defense lawyers. I say defense lawyers because he didn't expect plaintiffs' lawyers to get much . . .

M C D O W E L L: What I am trying to get at is this was not, this is not a liability case from your point of view, is it?

H A R K I N S: It is a no liability case, that is correct.

M C D O W E L L: You are paying what we call in my neck of the woods, when you pay the legal cost of defense, it is called a nuisance value, isn't that right? Three hundred million dollars worth of nuisance?

HARKINS: I don't think that is a proper way to characterize a sum like this, but the thought process in fact was not a heck of a lot different, Mr. McDowell.

Despite Harkins's efforts, Aetna's agreement to the *Breland* settlement could not be reconciled with the contention that Aetna faced no risk of liability. If the claim against Aetna could not be won, Aetna would not get sued thirty thousand times. After a few failed efforts, plaintiffs' lawyers working for contingent fees would get the point and not file additional actions. Aetna might have had to pay defense costs in a handful of cases, but not thirty thousand and probably not even one hundred. As a matter of corporate governance, Aetna's decision to commit large amounts of money to the settlement of *Breland* can only be justified as an effort to protect itself, not from thirty thousand unfounded lawsuits, but from the risk of greater liability to women injured by the Dalkon Shield.

Judge Merhige issued his opinion approving the *Breland* settlement on July 26, 1988, the day after he issued his decision confirming the plan of reorganization.[18] Merhige stated that "the maximum value [of the settlement] . . . is $425 million, the total of the cash [$75 million] and the policies [$350 million]."[19] This was a substantial exaggeration, considering that $100 million of the Aetna insurance would be provided whether or not the *Breland* settlement was approved and that American Home Products had purchased another $100 million of the insurance for a cash premium of $32 million. (American Home Products' agreement to pay this premium to Aetna was revealed at the hearing on July 7, 1988.) Only $150 million of the Aetna insurance could be attributed to the *Breland* settlement, and even this could not properly be valued at its face amount, even assuming it would be paid out, because the payments would not be made for many years.

Judge Merhige concluded that all the standards for approval of a class action settlement had now been met: "eminently qualified" class counsel, adequate discovery, and "no evidence of collusion."[20] He found that the claims against Aetna were "factually and legally flawed," and endorsed Aetna's contention that it had agreed to settle not because of the risk of liability but only to avoid the separate litigation of thirty thousand cases.

[T]he Court finds that plaintiffs have a weak case on all counts. Indeed, it is Aetna's position that there is no case against it. Recognizing the defense costs of numerous, even if meritless, cases against it would be substantial, Aetna decided that it would prefer to make funds available to claimants rather than attorneys and consequently agreed to settle.[21]

In the *Breland* settlement, Aetna had agreed to pay attorney fees to Friedberg and his colleagues, above the consideration for the settlement, in the amount "awarded by order of the Court." The settlement agreement provided that "[i]n advance of the hearing at which final approval by the Court of the Settlement is sought . . . plaintiffs shall file petitions for allowance of their litigation expenses, including attorneys' fees and costs."[22]

Friedberg did not file such a petition in advance of the fairness hearing. On June 20, 1988, when he told Joe McDowell that he would not produce the documents showing how much time he and his colleagues had expended in the litigation, because they "are available only in raw form," Friedberg added, "Since counsel anticipates a separate hearing on the issue of counsel fees in the event that this settlement is approved, those will be available prior to such hearing."[23]

At the fairness hearing, John Harkins explained Aetna's position on Friedberg's fees:

MCDOWELL: Now, who is going to pay the Friedberg group's legal fee . . . ?

HARKINS: Aetna will pay such amount as Judge Merhige orders, if anything. And that was one of the things I learned in class actions long ago. Don't bargain on a fee because I believe that is a conflict. What you do is you say, we will settle the case and let the judge decide what the fee is. We simply said that whatever fee the judge decides to set, we will pay that separately so it doesn't diminish that which is going to the claimants, and it won't take money away from them.[24]

The *Breland* settlement became final on December 6, 1989, after it had been upheld by the court of appeals and review of that decision had been denied by the Supreme Court. On December 9, 1989, Friedberg filed a petition asking Merhige to approve an agreement he had reached with Aetna by which Aetna would pay Friedberg and his colleagues $8.575 million.

The proceedings in *Breland* had been quite limited, and the services performed by counsel for the plaintiffs hardly seemed to justify a fee of $8.575 million. The case had been stayed for much of the twenty months it was pending before the settlement. Until the settlement, all the pleadings filed in the case fitted into a single file folder in the clerk of court's office. While the *Breland* case was pending, Friedberg was twice admonished by Judge Merhige for failing to attend relevant proceedings.[25] Friedberg did not even go to New York in January 1988 to attend the meetings at which the final agreements were reached. The *Breland* case was settled by telephone. After the settlement was approved, counsel for the class did not file a separate brief in the appeal, instead joining in the brief filed on behalf of Aetna. The major activity of plaintiffs' counsel in the litigation was examining the documents Aetna had made available in Hartford.

Friedberg did not submit in support of his petition any records or itemized listings of the time expended by the attorneys for the class or of the nature of the work they had performed. Instead, each of nine attorneys in the seven law offices that formed the Friedberg group submitted affidavits setting forth the total number of hours that he had worked on the case, often in round numbers, and a statement of his customary hourly rates.[26] The hours of work reported in the various affidavits came to a total of 20,210 hours, the equivalent of twelve years full time for one hard-working attorney. The hours spent in preparing the class action that Friedberg filed against Robins on August 2, 1985, and again in the bankruptcy proceeding on August 22, 1985, were included.[27] The rates claimed ranged up to $300 per hour.

All of these hours multiplied by the hourly rates claimed by each attorney came to $3.755 million. Aetna did not question the number of hours or the rates. To the contrary, it agreed to multiply $3.755 million by a factor of 2.2 in consideration of the "very high risk" of the litigation, to reach a total of $8.261 million. (The extra $314,000 was for expenses and to cover future legal services in the case.) Of the total, $1.25 million was allocable to Judge Merhige's former law firm in Richmond for the services as local counsel rendered by the judge's friend Murray Janus and his associate Theodore Brenner.

On December 9, 1989, the same day Friedberg's petition was filed, Judge Merhige signed an order finding that the fees requested were fair and reasonable, and approving their payment.

19   The Appeals

The question of whether to appeal the confirmation
of the plan of reorganization was the subject of intense, even bitter, controversy among lawyers representing women injured by the Dalkon
Shield. The structure of the plan of reorganization provided powerful
disincentives to an appeal. If no appeal was taken, forty days after confirmation American Home Products would acquire A. H. Robins and
pay $2.255 billion into the claimants' trust. As quickly as the trust could
organize to do so, it would begin processing and paying claims. If an
appeal was filed, the acquisition would be delayed and only the $100
million start-up payment would be made until the appellate process was
concluded. During this period, no claims, other than claims for nominal
payments under option 1, could be paid.

The delay would have particularly serious consequences for women
who hoped to benefit from medical procedures to enhance fertility. The
plan of reorganization directed the trustees to give priority consideration to claimants seeking funds for fertility procedures, but no disbursements to pay for these procedures could be made until the plan of
reorganization was final and the trust was fully funded. An additional
delay of a year or more as a result of an appeal would put another group
of women past the age at which candidates are accepted for these procedures and would reduce the prospects for success of those who would
still be eligible for treatment.

There was another disincentive to an appeal. For the duration of an
appeal, the claimants' trust would lose the interest that would otherwise
be earned on $2.155 billion (the difference between $2.255 billion and
the $100 million start-up payment). This loss (computed at 8 1/2 percent)
could exceed $500,000 per day, or $185 million a year. Under the terms
of the plan of reorganization, interest that was earned on trust funds
would all be paid to injured women, either as part of their compensatory
payments or, if funds remained after all timely and late claims had been
paid, in the form of a distribution in lieu of punitive damages.

Finally, the merger agreement provided that, if Judge Merhige's confirmation of the plan of reorganization was reversed, or even if appeals
were still pending one year after the order was entered, American Home

Products was free to abandon the transaction. There was no assurance of what action American Home Products would take after a year, or that a better plan of reorganization could be obtained even if an appeal did overturn the existing plan.

Most of the attorneys for the Dalkon Shield claimants, including some who had opposed confirmation, concluded that the costs and risks of an appeal were too great. They believed that it was time to accept the plan and to allow the process of paying the claims to begin. They were reinforced in that view by the long line of decisions of the court of appeals in the Robins bankruptcy adverse to the positions asserted on behalf of the claimants, which indicated that it was unlikely that an appeal would expand the rights of their clients.[1] But despite the majority sentiment, any attorney representing a Dalkon Shield claimant could file an appeal. Alan Morrison, working with Bradley Post, Douglas Bragg, Ralph Pittle, and others, had taken the lead in opposing confirmation of the plan of reorganization, and it was generally understood that, if an appeal was taken, it would be taken by this group. Morrison and the others were implored by many lawyers, including lawyers who knew and had worked with Bragg and Post for years in connection with Dalkon Shield cases, not to pursue an appeal. A few even threatened to seek penalties, sanctions, and damages against Morrison and his colleagues in the event of an appeal.

In the end, despite these pleas and warnings, Morrison, Post, Bragg, and Pittle, together with Frederic Bremseth and Joseph McDowell, decided to appeal on behalf of their clients. In reaching this decision, these lawyers focused on what they saw as the interests of their own clients, not on the interests of the group of 195,000 women. They believed that the trust fund was too low, or, at least, that it was very likely it would prove to be too low, and that the amounts the trust would offer to their clients would be below the level of the settlements they had been able to obtain before the bankruptcy. Further, they anticipated obstacles in taking a case to trial and in collecting the amount of the jury verdict if the trust's offer of settlement was rejected.

The lawyers who filed the appeal discounted the significance of the interest income that would be lost to the trust, because any increase in their clients' recoveries as a result of interest earned from the earlier receipt of American Home Products' money would be small—even if a direct correlation between interest earned by the trust and the payments to any individual could be assumed.[2] On the other hand, if the appeal was successful, and, for example, if actions were permitted against Messrs. E. Claiborne Robins for compensatory and punitive damages, there would be a vast increase in the recoveries they could obtain and perhaps even an increase in the speed with which they could obtain them.

Apart from the issue of lost interest income, Morrison and his colleagues did not accept the assumption that an appeal would result in substantial delay in the resolution and payment of serious claims. During an appeal, the trustees would be in place. The $100 million start-up money would be available to employ experts and staff, and, presumably, the work necessary to organize the trust and to prepare for the evaluation of individual claims would go forward. The attorneys concluded that it would take the trust the same or nearly the same amount of time to reach the point of paying the most serious claims (option 3), whether or not there was an intervening appeal.[3]

Lastly, the lawyers who appealed, and at least some of their clients, felt that it was simply improper to allow the men responsible for the Dalkon Shield tragedy not only to walk away without being made to account but, in the case of E. Claiborne Robins and his son, to walk away with hundreds of millions of dollars while 195,000 of their victims queued up and hoped for the best from Judge Merhige's trust. These lawyers believed that an appeal could lead to a better economic result, but central to their thinking was that what was happening was wrong and should not be accepted while avenues of protest remained open.

Notices of appeal were filed on behalf of some seven hundred women in late August 1988. The appeal was known as *Rosemary Menard-Sanford, et al. v. A. H. Robins Co.*, after the president of the International Dalkon Shield Victims' Education Association, who was the first-listed appellant. At the request of the parties, an expedited schedule was established by the court of appeals under which all briefs would be filed before the end of November and the appeals would be argued during the first week in December 1988.

The appeal was limited to three issues: (1) whether it was unlawful to accord equal weight to the vote of all Dalkon Shield claimants, when section 1126(c) of the Bankruptcy Code requires that a plan be accepted by the holders of two-thirds of the value of the claims; (2) whether, by referring to a judicial finding of full payment, without including any statement of how that finding was arrived at or of what was contemplated in terms of the average payment or range of payments for particular injuries, the disclosure statement failed to provide "adequate information" to Dalkon Shield claimants, as required by section 1125 of the code; and (3) whether the release of persons other than the A. H. Robins Company from liability for Dalkon Shield injuries violated section 524(e) of the code, which provides that "discharge of a debtor does not affect the liability of any such other entity on . . . such debt."

In contrast to the dispute over an appeal of the plan of reorganization, there was no opposition among claimants' attorneys to an appeal of the settlement in *Breland*. Under the agreements that had been reached, an appeal of the *Breland* settlement (without an appeal of the plan of reorganization) would not have delayed the merger or American Home Products' full contribution to the claimants' trust. All the attorneys who appealed the plan of reorganization, plus several others, joined in the appeal from the *Breland* settlement. The issues raised in the *Breland* appeal were (1) whether the refusal to allow members of class A (women eligible to claim from the trust) to opt out of the class action and sue Aetna individually violated the due process clause of the United States Constitution or the federal class action rule; and (2) whether Judge Merhige had erred in finding that the settlement was fair and reasonable.

The United States Court of Appeals for the Fourth Circuit hears appeals from the federal district courts in Maryland, West Virginia, North Carolina, South Carolina, and Virginia. It holds sessions on the fourth floor of the United States Courthouse and Post Office in Richmond, directly above Judge Merhige's courtroom. The court of appeals chamber is elegant with five tall windows overlooking the grounds of the State Capitol, once the capitol of the Confederacy. Various touches of the southern tradition are preserved. A tray with a silver pitcher of water and a crystal goblet is placed on the bench, at each judge's chair. Oil paintings of old southern gentlemen who served as the judges of the court adorn the walls. The Fourth Circuit is the only federal appellate court in which, at the conclusion of the arguments in each case, the judges stand up, walk in a procession down to counsels' tables, and shake hands with each attorney.

There are eleven judges on the Fourth Circuit, but, as in all of the United States courts of appeals, cases are heard and decided by panels of three judges. The judges assigned to hear the appeals from Robins's plan of reorganization and from the *Breland* settlement were Donald S. Russell, H. Emory Widener, Jr., and Robert F. Chapman. Both Russell and Chapman were born and educated in Spartanburg, South Carolina, where the University of South Carolina is located. Widener is from Abington, Virginia, and attended law school at Washington and Lee

University in Lexington, Virginia. Russell and Widener were appointed to the court by President Nixon, Chapman by President Reagan. Their ages at the time of the argument ranged from sixty-four to eighty-two. All are staunchly conservative and were unlikely to find merit in arguments asserting individual rights that Judge Merhige had rejected.

In fact, with the exception of one panel member in two cases, each of the twelve earlier appeals arising out of the Robins bankruptcy had been decided by the same three judges. Most of these appeals involved complex and unsettled questions of bankruptcy law; yet in each of the ten appeals brought on behalf of Dalkon Shield claimants, this panel had affirmed Judge Merhige's ruling.[4] In the two instances in which the panel heard appeals from Robins or the equity committee, Merhige's rulings had been reversed.[5]

The oral arguments in both the appeal from the plan of reorganization and the appeal from the *Breland* settlement were heard on December 6, 1988. Every seat in the courtroom was occupied, mostly by lawyers and officials associated with Robins, American Home Products, or Aetna. The first case to be argued was the appeal from the plan of reorganization. Alan Morrison argued for the appellants.

The judges were openly skeptical of Morrison's proposal for the weighting of votes according to the self-identification of injuries. Judge Widener suggested that claimants would indicate major injuries to increase the weight of their votes. Morrison pointed out that the ballots were signed under oath, but Widener responded, "[Y]ou will be prosecuting people for perjury until the end of time." Judge Russell referred to the *Johns-Manville* case, where the bankruptcy court had not weighted the votes, 95 percent of all the asbestos claimants had voted in favor of the plan, and the United States court of appeals had ruled that any error in the procedure that was adopted was "harmless."[6] Morrison contended that the error in this instance could not be assumed to be harmless and referred to a mathematical analysis that he had included in his brief that showed that the 7,844 votes against the plan, if they were assumed to have come from the women with the most serious injuries, were enough to reject the plan under a system of weighted voting.

A successful oral argument in an appellate court usually depends on making quick, clear impressions on judges with little knowledge of the details of the case and short attention spans. The judges' negative reaction to Morrison's proposal for weighting the votes and their obvious belief that the plan had the overwhelming support of the Dalkon Shield claimants no matter how the voting was conducted appeared to carry over to Morrison's argument that Judge Merhige was required to explain his estimate, as if the only reason for an explanation of the estimate was to allow weighting of votes.

In fact, Morrison had emphasized the importance of an explanation of the estimate in connection with meaningful disclosure.

Our principal objection is that the Dalkon Shield claimants were not told the only thing they cared about from this reorganization—the amounts of money they could reasonably expect to receive under the plan . . . When Robins and the district court said that they estimated that all claims would be paid in full, they each had in mind a range of figures for each different type of injury, i.e., numbers that would constitute payment in full. It would be nothing short of miraculous, however, if those numbers were the same as those in the mind of a typical claimant.[7]

In support of his challenge to the discharge of persons other than the A. H. Robins Company from liability, Morrison relied on decisions in three other United States courts of appeals that had prohibited, as part of a corporate reorganization, the discharge of corporate insiders from liability to creditors that they shared with the corporation.[8] But Judge Russell declared that claims against Robins officers, directors, or attorneys were without merit, and asked, "Isn't it easier just to enjoin them?"

Sensitive to the milieu, Robins chose James Roberts of Mays & Valentine in Richmond to make its argument in preference to its bankruptcy law experts from New York. Roberts said that Merhige "had tried mightily, had tried desperately," to weight the votes but ultimately found that it was impractical because of the unreliability of injury information reported by the women and the great variations in recoveries within injury categories before the bankruptcy. Roberts did not actually defend the legality of unweighted voting, but he echoed Judge Russell's sentiment that any error was harmless in light of the overwhelming vote to accept the plan.

An underlying theme in both appeals was the denial of individual determinations in favor of a mass solution to the Dalkon Shield problem. If the rights of more than 195,000 individuals, or at least the parameters of those rights, can be adjudicated in one case to conserve judicial resources, one would expect the judges in the consolidated proceeding to be particularly attentive and well prepared. It was an early indication that this would not be the case when Judge Widener fell asleep during Roberts's argument and dozed off and on for the remainder of the morning. At one point, Widener woke up and suddenly asked Roberts whether the case involved a cramdown (the approval of a plan of reorganization that has been rejected by a vote of an impaired class of creditors). Roberts was in the midst of defending the vote in favor of the plan. He negated Widener's suggestion as politely as possible.

The "Special Note to Women Who Used the Dalkon Shield," printed in the front of the disclosure statement, reported that, following the estimation hearing, the court had found that "the total amount of money necessary to pay all Dalkon Shield claims and all expenses of the Trusts in full was $2.475 billion." Nevertheless, in defending the omission of any explanation of Judge Merhige's estimate, Roberts pointed to other language that acknowledged the possibility that Merhige's estimate may prove too low and argued that there had been no representation of full payment. He also argued that, because claim values would be set by the trust, they were unknown and could not have been revealed in the disclosure statement. During Roberts's defense of Merhige's failure to explain his estimate, Judge Russell compared Merhige's decision to an assessment of damages by a jury, and, surprisingly—because judges are supposed to explain their decisions and juries are not—Roberts responded, "That's about right."

In support of the plan of reorganization's release from liability of persons associated with the A. H. Robins Company, Roberts relied on section 105 of the Bankruptcy Code, which authorizes the court to issue "any order . . . necessary or proper to carry out the provisions of this title." Roberts maintained that the release of other potential defendants was appropriate "to ensure a cessation of the long, tragic and painful hostilities over the Dalkon Shield and to ensure a fair and lasting peace."

In recognition of the technical procedural issues involved, the opponents of the *Breland* settlement retained Irving Panzer, a former law professor at Catholic University Law School in Washington, D.C., to argue the challenge to the mandatory feature of the class action against Aetna. Relying on *Phillips Petroleum Company v. Shutts*,[9] the recent case in which the Supreme Court of the United States had held that due process of law requires that state courts permit nonresidents to opt out of class actions for money damages, Panzer argued that due process equally required the right to opt out in federal class actions for money damages. In fact, the court of appeals had specifically interpreted *Shutts* in this way in an earlier appeal in the Robins bankruptcy.[10] And citing the unanimous body of federal appellate decisions prohibiting mandatory class actions in mass tort cases unless there is proof of a "limited fund," Panzer argued that Merhige's refusal to allow class members to opt out violated the federal procedural rule governing class actions.[11] Joe

McDowell argued that the *Breland* action was collusive and that class counsel had entered into settlement without adequate exploration of the facts.

In his argument, John Harkins for Aetna relied on the theory he had presented to Judge Merhige—that the *Breland* case was different from the other personal injury cases in which federal courts had refused to allow mandatory class actions, because of the risk of "incompatible standards" governing Aetna's future conduct with respect to the disclosure of defects in products that it insures.[12] With respect to the constitutional argument based on the *Shutts* case, Harkins emphasized the right of each member of class A to a trial by jury in an action against the trust and the right of each member of class B to opt out and try their claim for compensatory damages separately against Aetna. He said that the only issue before the court was whether punitive damages are a constitutionally protected form of property, because that is the only right that had been denied to individual claimants in the *Breland* settlement.

More than six months after the oral arguments, on June 16, 1989, the court of appeals released its decisions affirming Judge Merhige's rulings in both cases. The opinion in the appeal from the confirmation of the plan of reorganization was written by Judge Widener.[13]

Following the approach of the court of appeals in the *Johns-Manville* case, Widener declined to rule on the legality of unweighted voting on the ground that it was "at most harmless error." He relied on the 94 percent vote in favor of the plan and rejected Morrison's invitation to assume that women with the largest claims had voted against the plan.

Next, Widener rejected the argument that the claimants were entitled to an explanation of Judge Merhige's estimate so that they would know what was meant by "paid in full."

There is no requirement in case law or statute that a disclosure statement estimate the value of specific unliquidated tort claims. In fact, with so many various unliquidated personal injury claims which vary so much in extent and nature of injury, medical evidence and causation factors, any specific estimates may well have been more confusing than helpful and certainly would be more calculated to mislead.[14]

Widener went on to say, however, that "the care the district court took in arriving at its estimate deserves mention."

[T]he district court's figure was within the range of the second highest estimation—that of Dr. Francine Rabinowitz, the expert for Aetna. The district court repeatedly rejected the credibility of the expert for the Dalkon Shield Claimants, the only expert with a higher estimation than Dr. Rabinowitz.[15]

This approach, which also found favor with Judge Merhige, is based on the assumption that the witnesses at the estimation hearing were unbiased scientists rendering objective opinions rather than exponents for the points of view of the parties who employed and paid them. If Merhige had allowed attorneys representing Dalkon Shield claimants to present evidence at the estimation hearing, as they had requested, there would have been other estimates higher than that of Dr. Rabinowitz. If Merhige had not allowed Robins's allies (the equity committee and the unsecured creditors' committee) to present estimates, only Robins's estimate would have been lower. That the estimate for the claimants' committee was the only estimate higher than Rabinowitz's is no indication of whether it was right or wrong. And Merhige's oft-stated disdain for Dr. Pifer's "credibility" did not mean that he thought Pifer was lying on the witness stand but that he did not approve of Pifer's methodology in analyzing the data.

Widener went on to describe Dr. Rabinowitz's estimate without reference to its pitfalls, which Judge Merhige had identified during the estimation hearing.[16] He concluded, "[W]e think the district court would have been quite justified in accepting Dr. Rabinowitz' testimony, so appellants may not complain about the district court's arrival at a somewhat higher figure."[17]

With respect to the challenge to the injunction prohibiting Dalkon Shield–related suits against third parties, Judge Widener dreamed up the idea that the settlement in *Breland* prevented women included in the class action "from further prosecuting their Dalkon Shield claims other than pursuant to the terms of the settlement." He went on: "Given this bar from pursuing compensation for their Dalkon Shield injuries, other than pursuant to the order, the injunction has no real effect on the rights of [these class] members."[18] In fact, the *Breland* settlement said nothing about the right of class members to file suit against anyone but Aetna. The only prohibition of suits against Robins's officers, directors, and attorneys was the provision in the confirmation order that was challenged in the appeal.

Judge Widener went on to uphold the prohibition as to women who were not included in the *Breland* settlement (that is, members of class B who exercised their right to opt out), and who were therefore not subject to its imaginary provision barring suits against third parties, on the basis of another manifestly false premise—that "[n]o party challenges the adequacy of the outlier policies to pay the class B claims." Widener continued:

We are therefore entitled to and do assume that the claims of all class B claimants who wish to have the merits and amount of their claims ascertained by the Claims Resolution Facility will be fully satisfied . . . Since they have chosen to opt-out rather than payment in full, they may have no complaint about a restriction on their ability to sue others.[19]

The amounts and timing of the outlier policies were fixed in negotiations between American Home Products and Aetna, not as a result of any effort to evaluate the claims of the women ineligible to recover from the claimants' trust. There had been no hearing on this subject in the district court, and Judge Merhige had made no finding. In the appeal from the *Breland* settlement, Joseph McDowell had specifically challenged the adequacy of the Aetna outlier policies to satisfy the class B claims. He wrote: "[T]he record is devoid of substantial competent evidence determining the numbers of members of Class B and the total funds which may be necessary to pay the claims of Class B members."[20] In the spring of 1991, a study of this question was conducted under the auspices of the *Breland* trust. It was determined that the first $50 million outlier policy was sufficient to pay only 15% of the value of the claims of the class B members who had not opted out.[21]

The opinion upholding the *Breland* settlement with Aetna was written by Judge Russell.[22] Russell devoted thirty-nine pages of his opinion to a discussion of the potential utility of class action procedures in mass tort cases, without drawing the crucial distinction between mandatory class actions and class actions in which individuals are permitted to opt out and maintain their own suits. When he turned to this issue, Russell ruled that the *Breland* case satisfied the requirements for a mandatory class action established by subpart (b)(1)(A) of the federal class action rule: "[T]he prosecution of separate actions . . . would create a risk of . . . incompatible standards of conduct for the party opposing the class."[23] Russell made this finding without reference to Harkins's argument concerning hypothetical future situations in which Aetna could face conflicting obligations. For all its factual and logical fallacies, Harkins's analysis at least represented an effort to fit within the intended scope of subpart (b)(1)(A)—situations in which one court demands that a party take some action and another court forbids it.[24] Instead, Russell said that the mere possibility that the courts in some states would find that Aetna is liable to the injured women, while courts in other states would conclude that it is not, was sufficient to satisfy the "incompatible standards" provision of the rule.

That threat of conflicting legal standards and results could well create a chaotic situation in this case. There are over 300,000 claims and possibly the same number of suits . . . It would be intolerable that whether liability could exist might vary from state to state . . . The likelihood of conflicting decisions and varying standards of liability based on the standards of law applied to identical facts by different courts provide the very conditions contemplated in Rule 23(b)(1)(A) for class certification herein.[25]

Varying standards of liability in cases brought under state law in different states is inherent in the federal system, and these differences had always been considered an obstacle to, rather than a reason for, class action treatment.[26] If possible inconsistency of result was sufficient basis for a mandatory class action in tort cases, every defendant facing mass liability could do what Aetna did: enter into a friendly settlement of a suit filed in a hospitable forum, pay an agreed sum, compensate plaintiffs' counsel handsomely for their cooperation, and never hear about the matter again.

Turning to the contention that due process of law, as construed by the decision of the Supreme Court in *Phillips Petroleum Co. v. Shutts*, guarantees each potential class member the opportunity to opt out of a class action for monetary damages, Judge Russell accepted Harkins's argument that it was not necessary to decide whether this is a correct construction of the *Shutts* decision because such a requirement "is satisfied in this case."

[T]he Trust created by the parties for the resolution of all Class A claims on individual causation and damages does not in express terms include an opt-out provision but in effect it does. The Plan gives every such class member the right to elect to have her claim settled in a trial with all the procedural rights normally attaching to a jury trial. That is everything that an express opt-out provision could give a class member if such right is required by due process.[27]

After he resolved the class action issue, Judge Russell strongly endorsed the *Breland* settlement and made short shrift of the challenges to its approval. He began with two errors of fact: that the adequacy of the trust fund to compensate all claimants fully was conceded, and that the failure to approve the *Breland* settlement would invalidate the plan of reorganization.

The Robins Plan of Reorganization and the *Breland* settlement are intended to provide full payment to all Dalkon Shield claimants who have properly filed claims. The plan creates a Trust Fund which will be sufficient to achieve this goal. Neither the appellants nor anyone else has asserted that such fund is insufficient . . . Failure of approval of either the Plan of Reorganization or the *Breland* settlement would derail hopelessly the carefully negotiated and crafted Plan and Settlement and leave the Dalkon Shield claimants to the vagaries, expenses and delay of further extended litigation.[28]

The essential premise of both appeals was that the trust fund might be insufficient, as the appellants repeatedly emphasized in their arguments in the court of appeals. And, by the express terms of the controlling documents, disapproval of the *Breland* settlement by the court of appeals would not have upset the plan of reorganization.[29]

Turning to the settlement itself, Judge Russell was positively exuberant in his praise for the efforts of Joe Friedberg and his colleagues. The judge said that "[c]ounsel for the *Breland* plaintiffs aggressively and at great expense appear to have investigated every possible avenue for relevant evidence that might support the *Breland* suit" and that counsel had "zealously developed and analyzed" the relevant factual record."[30] According to Russell, despite this remarkable effort there was no evidence "that Aetna took part in any decision not to recall the Dalkon Shield"; "no evidence, either direct or circumstantial . . . to indicate that Aetna knew of or participated in [the destruction of documents]."[31]

Judge Russell dismissed the allegation of collusion without mentioning any of the grounds on which it was based.

Nor did the appellants offer any evidence or point to any fact in the record which established or indicated collusion between counsel for the *Breland* plaintiffs and Aetna. *Breland* counsel aggressively pursued this case. They did so at great expense. After this exhaustive review of the Robins and Aetna records, it is obvious that they recognized they had found no "smoking gun" but it was not because they had not tried relentlessly to discover one.[32]

The losing party in a case before a United States court of appeals has ninety days after the judgment to seek further review in the Supreme Court of the United States. The decision of the court of appeals in Richmond rejecting the appeal from the plan of reorganization set off a new round of debate within the ranks of attorneys for Dalkon Shield claimants as to whether to seek review in the Supreme Court of the United States or to abandon further challenges to the plan. The appeal had caused a year's delay with nothing to show for it.

This time, not only did Morrison receive calls and letters from lawyers entreating him not to further delay implementation of the plan of reorganization, he received handwritten letters from Dalkon Shield victims themselves. One woman, who was impatiently awaiting funds for a medical fertility procedure, wrote:

PLEASE HELP ME!

TO—Alan B. Morrison,

I am writing you this letter to ask, NO, beg of you to please leave this reorganization plan alone.

I was 14 years old, in June of 1971, when I was forced by my parents to have an *Abortion*. June 3, 1971, I had that abortion and had that crab, ugly, horrifying IUD (Dalkon Shield) inserted into my body. I put all my trust in the doctor's hands, I was told that Crab (Dalkon Shield) was very safe.

I am now 33 years old and still no children (no baby)! When I was a little girl I would play with my dolls as if they were real. I couldn't wait to grow up so I could take care of a real baby, my own baby. My whole life revolved around being a mother. I always told my mother I was going to have 10 kids. Now I can't have any. So please, Mr. Morrison, find it in your heart to think more about me and the *thousands* of other women that are in this nightmare situation and do what is right. Let us have a chance to get pregnant while we can.

I beg you not to appeal. Please have mercy on our souls.

Another woman wrote:

Dear Mr. Morrison,

I am writing you in regards to your continuous appeals. Now I understand that you are doing your job, but my message is not one of your job, but of the human element involved and the criminal act that took place in the use of the Dalkon Shield. I will start with my personal story.

When I was eighteen, seventeen years ago, I became pregnant with the Dalkon Shield still in my uterus. The baby fell out in the toilet. In fear and ignorance I said nothing. In fact, I wasn't absolutely sure about what happened. 24 hours later I was rushed to the hospital near death and in incredible pain. The Dalkon Shield was removed and another one put in.

Now I am a nurse and I know about the sterile field. I'm sure the inventors of this device *knew* you can't put something in a sterile place with a lead from a non-sterile place. This was criminal.

I spent years of hemorrhaging, spontaneous abortions and chronic infections.

Now seventeen years later I married a wonderful man. I've received an abdominal laparoscopy, where they took slides of my tubes. They are completely blocked, with many lesions on my ovaries and uterus. I decided against surgery and thought *in vitro* fertilization would be safer.

I have been very patient for five or more years now with the hope that before it was too late I would be able to give my husband at least one healthy child. This is both of our first marriage and we have no children anywhere else.

Now I'm told that you're appealing *again* to the Supreme Court. What is your motive in preventing justice to be done for my self and thousands of others. I am appealing to you. One human being to another. *Please* stop holding up progress. The clock is ticking. I am getting older.

Another:

I feel at this point further appeals will only hamper our efforts at getting a fair and equitable settlement, and will only add (although I know that is not your intent) to the injustice we have experienced at the hands of A. H. Robins. It seems strange that your zealousness to aid our cause could have the same results as A. H. Robins' complete indifference to our welfare—further injustice and more suffering. What irony.

Stanley Joynes had long played the role of the honest witness in the Robins bankruptcy, earning respect and admiration for his willingness to act independently of Judge Merhige, who had appointed him. While the issue of seeking review in the Supreme Court was still under consideration, Joynes wrote to Morrison to add his plea to let the plan go into effect.

Among the counsel who participated as principal players in the bankruptcy proceeding, I undoubtedly have spoken with more injured women than any other . . . Simply stated, the victims' preeminent concern is delay . . . To the prospect of a shortfall in the trust's funding, they respond that the assurance of something now is better than the possibility of more later.

Joynes also emphasized the risk that American Home Products would exercise its right to abandon its proposed acquisition of Robins if review by the Supreme Court further delayed the matter and expressed doubts that an equally attractive offer would be forthcoming from other quarters.

Joynes commiserated in Morrison's unhappiness with the decisions of the court of appeals, referring to them as a "disaster," but concluded: "I urge you to hold your nose and forego the filing of your petition in the interests of the claimants. Bad law unquestionably—but I think the claimants want it over now."

Morrison and his colleagues looked for some way to continue at least their challenge to the injunction prohibiting suits against officers, directors, and attorneys of A. H. Robins without further delaying implementation of the plan. On June 28, 1989, Morrison wrote to counsel for Robins and for American Home Products proposing a compromise—the Supreme Court would be asked to review only the legality of the injunction barring suits against third parties, and Robins and American

Home Products would consummate their merger and fund the trust without further delay. Morrison's proposal amounted to an invitation to his opponent in combat to lay down its arms while the battle continued. Robins's major argument, indeed its only plausible argument, in support of the injunction was that it was necessary to the plan—that American Home Products would not have entered into the agreement without "global peace." If the merger was consummated and the plan of reorganization implemented while the legality of the injunction was under consideration by the Supreme Court, this argument would be negated. On July 13, 1989, in a letter to Morrison from Jim Roberts and Alesia Ranney-Marinelli of Skadden, Arps, Robins rejected the proposal.

On September 16, 1989, Morrison, Pittle, Bragg, Post, and McDowell filed a petition in the *Menard-Sanford* case asking the Supreme Court to grant review.[33] In taking this action, they reasoned that, should the Supreme Court refuse to take the case, only a short additional delay would result. The plan of reorganization could not in any event have been consummated until the expiration of the ninety-day period in which Supreme Court review could be requested. A decision from the Supreme Court to grant or deny review could be expected within seven weeks after the petition was filed. Morrison and his colleagues also believed that American Home Products would not walk away from the deal, at least not because of delay attributable to Supreme Court review. During the ninety-day period after the court of appeals decision, the one-year deadline contained in the merger agreement had expired, and Robins and American Home Products had extended it until the end of December 1989. The attorneys believed that, if the Supreme Court accepted the case, the deadline would be extended again.

The losing party in the court of appeals is not obligated to present every issue to the Supreme Court and frequently does not. There is a right to appeal from a district court to a court of appeals, and the court of appeals will normally rule on every issue properly presented, regardless of its significance or novelty. Review by the Supreme Court is discretionary. The Supreme Court must be convinced that the issue presented meets certain criteria that it has developed to limit the number of cases it hears to a manageable level. The possibility that a case has been wrongly decided by a federal court of appeals is not a ground on which the Supreme Court will grant review. At a minimum, it is necessary to establish either that the same question of law has been decided differently by different courts of appeals (a "conflict in the circuits") or that the legal

question presented is of major importance. Some 2,500 petitions for review are filed with the Supreme Court each year (not including handwritten petitions from prisoners); approximately 140 of these are granted.

In the *Menard-Sanford* case, despite Robins's rejection of the proposed compromise, counsel were undecided about whether to limit the petition to the legality of the injunction against third-party litigation or whether also to include the issues relating to the approval of the plan of reorganization. Morrison drafted and circulated a petition including both sets of issues, but ultimately it was decided that the issues relating to the approval of the plan—whether the unweighted voting was "harmless error" and whether the information in the disclosure statement was "adequate" without an explanation of Judge Merhige's estimate—were too fact-specific to gain Supreme Court review.

Accordingly, the petition for review was limited to the issue of the legality of the injunction. All the opposition to Robins's plan of reorganization, expressed in the district court over a period of three years in hundreds of motions, objections, arguments, and appeals, had boiled down to the single question of whether the rights of women injured by the Dalkon Shield against persons other than A. H. Robins Inc. could be snuffed out.

Morrison's main argument in support of a grant of review was that there was a conflict in the circuits. Within the last few years, three United States courts of appeals had ruled that a bankruptcy court is without authority in a Chapter 11 proceeding to discharge or to enjoin claims against insiders of the debtor corporation as distinct from claims against the corporation itself.[34] One of these courts had even rejected the contention, on which Robins was relying, that an injunction barring litigation against officers is acceptable when such litigation "will adversely affect the corporate debtor's reorganization."[35]

The opposition to the petition filed for Robins by Skadden, Arps emphasized that American Home Products had demanded the injunction as a condition to its acquisition of Robins and that the district court had "found that such provisions were necessary to ensure a successful implementation of the plan." Robins attempted to distinguish the conflicting decisions on the grounds that the plans of reorganization in those cases did not make provision for the full payment of the debt or that the injunctions in those cases were not a condition to confirmation, but these factors did not alter the undeniable fact that three other courts of appeals had held that an injunction such as that issued by Judge Merhige was beyond the power of the court. Moreover, it was unknown whether Robins's plan actually made provision for the full payment of its debt, or merely claimed that it did.

In addition to the opposition for Robins, briefs in opposition to a grant of review were filed by the unsecured creditors' committee, by the examiner, and, most dramatically, by a group of eighteen plaintiffs' lawyers or law firms on behalf of "18,136 Dalkon Shield Claimants." The last brief described the petitioners as "a tiny minority" of "disgruntled claimants," represented by attorneys "in quest of substantial punitive damages."[36] These additional briefs stressed Judge Merhige's findings relative to full payment, the sentiments of the large majority of the claimants, the consequences of delay, and the risk that the entire plan of reorganization might collapse if review was granted. They also urged the Court to deny review in *Menard-Sanford* and allow the plan of reorganization to go into effect, even if the Court were to grant the separate petition for review in *Breland*.

There was never any question or controversy about seeking Supreme Court review in *Breland*. The petition in *Breland* was also prepared by Alan Morrison, working with Joe McDowell. The contention that Judge Merhige should not have approved the settlement in *Breland* was not included in the petition because of its factual nature, and only the issue of the mandatory class certification was presented to the Supreme Court for review. In a different legal context, it was the same question as that presented in the petition in the *Menard-Sanford* case—whether as a result of Robins's bankruptcy, rights of action against other potential defendants could be eliminated.

Morrison argued that the decision of the Fourth Circuit upholding the mandatory certification of the class A compensatory damage claims on the ground of possible inconsistent results on identical facts was in conflict with decisions of five other courts of appeals.[37] Alternatively, Morrison argued that review should be granted because the mandatory certification violated rights to due process of law as construed by the Court's own decision in *Phillips Petroleum Co. v. Shutts*.[38] Contradicting the court of appeals' theory that all claimants had been given the functional equivalent of the right to opt out, Morrison emphasized the various practical restrictions on the right to sue the trust, including the limitation on available funds and the potential long delay before suit was authorized.

In his opposition for Aetna to the petition for review, Harkins ascribed to the court of appeals his own analysis relative to potential court decisions in Dalkon Shield litigation creating "incompatible standards" governing Aetna's future conduct and argued that none of the cases said to conflict with the Fourth Circuit decision involved a similar risk.

Petitioners are unable to adduce a single case where multiple adjudications would have created a risk of incompatible standards under substantive law such that compliance with the law of one jurisdiction might violate the law of another. In none of the opinions cited by petitioners did the court of appeals have occasion even to discuss some particular substantive area of law to see whether multiple adjudications would create such a risk.

Nor was this issue discussed in the opinion of the court of appeals in *Breland*.

On Monday, November 6, 1989, the Supreme Court denied the petitions for review in both the *Menard-Sanford* and *Breland* cases. Justice Byron White noted his dissent from this action in both cases.[39]

On Friday, December 15, 1989, at 3:00 p.m., in signing ceremonies held at the law offices of Mays & Valentine in Richmond, the merger agreement between American Home Products and the A. H. Robins Company took effect and the plan of reorganization was consummated. By this time, American Home Products had told both E. Claiborne Robins, Sr., and E. Claiborne Robins, Jr., and most of the senior officials of A. H. Robins that their services would no longer be required. On the date of consummation, American Home Products accepted the resignation of the entire Robins board of directors and appointed one of its own officials as chief executive officer of the subsidiary corporation into which the A. H. Robins Company had been merged. Within days, American Home Products announced the layoff of 370 additional Robins employees in Richmond.[40]

The Robins family had lost their company, but there was a bright side for the family and for the company's other shareholders. The merger agreement did not actually provide that American Home Products stock worth $700 million would be exchanged for all the A. H. Robins stock, as was so widely believed. Rather, the merger agreement contained a formula based on the price of American Home Products stock for the thirty days preceding the merger that, if implemented when it was written in January 1988, would have resulted in the issuance of $700 million worth of stock. By December 1989, because of a substantial appreciation in the market price of American Home Products shares, the formula resulted in the issuance of $916 million of American Home Products stock. Of this amount, $385 million went to the Robins family. As an exchange of stock, the transaction was tax-free.

20   Control of the Trust

The conduct of the trustees of the new claimants' trust following the confirmation of the plan of reorganization quickly confirmed Judge Merhige's apprehension that this group would not operate the trust as he wanted. Within weeks, Merhige removed from office the three trustees who had been proposed by the claimants' committee.

The first sign of conflict occurred on July 25, 1988, the day the confirmation order was entered. Judge Merhige had asked the trustees to come to Richmond to meet with him and Judge Shelley.

The trustees were Kenneth Feinberg, a Washington, D.C., lawyer who had served as a neutral in other mass tort litigation; Stephen Saltzburg, a professor at the University of Virginia Law School; claimants' committee member Ann Samani; Barbara Blum, a New York foundation executive, and Gene Locks, a Philadelphia lawyer active in behalf of the personal injury victims in the asbestos bankruptcies. The Feinberg and Saltzburg appointments originated with Judge Merhige; Samani and Blum had been proposed by the claimants' committee; Locks had been first suggested by Professor McGovern and had later been recommended by the claimants' committee.[1]

At the meeting with the trustees on July 25, 1988, the judge read from his confirmation memorandum and said that he expected to be kept informed of all significant decisions. He emphasized that all major expenditures and commitments, including the retention of counsel or other professionals, were subject to his approval. Ann Samani, as a member of the claimants' committee, had participated in the decision to oppose the assertion of these powers by the judge. When Merhige asked for comments or questions, Samani spoke up and disputed the judge's statement of his supervisory authority. Gene Locks voiced support for Samani's position. Witnesses differed as to Samani's actual words and demeanor during this exchange, but there is no question about Merhige's perception: he thought she had been rude and defiant. He also understood her to say that Murray Drabkin had told her that she did not have to follow the judge's orders. Merhige told Samani that he had the power to remove her as a trustee and suggested that she consider resigning. Samani said she did not intend to resign.

287

Under the terms of the plan of reorganization, Robins was not scheduled to make its $100 million start-up payment until thirty days after confirmation, but Judge Merhige had arranged for the company to advance $200,000 on the date of confirmation to enable the trust to cover its immediate expenses. Merhige had planned to have the trustees sign signature cards at this meeting and to place the $200,000 in an account subject to their control, but following his contentious exchange with Ann Samani, the judge did not circulate the cards and later ordered Robins to pay the $200,000 to the clerk of court.

The uneasy situation was exacerbated on August 5, 1988, when the trustees, by a vote of three to two, with Samani, Locks, and Blum in the majority, employed Drabkin and his firm, Cadwalader, Wickersham & Taft, as counsel to the trust. The three trustees and Drabkin made the decision to enter into this relationship with knowledge that at least some of the principal participants in the Chapter 11 case would disapprove of the Cadwalader firm serving as counsel to the trust and despite warnings that there was an actual conflict of interest between Drabkin's representation of the claimants' committee and his representation of the trust.

During the negotiation of the plan of reorganization in January, Louis Hoynes, counsel for American Home Products, had told Drabkin that his representation of the trust would be inconsistent with the purpose of creating an independent trust, which was to put the task of liquidating and paying individual claims in the hands of new people with no prior involvement in the battles and the hard feelings that marked the Robins bankruptcy. On May 4, 1988, the examiner, Ralph Mabey, met with the trustees-designate and told them that the trust was intended to be free of the conflicts that had marked the Chapter 11 case. To this end, Mabey advised the future trustees to retain a law firm that had no previous connection with the Robins bankruptcy.

On June 18, 1988, when the trustees first discussed retention of counsel among themselves, Kenneth Feinberg suggested criteria for the selection of counsel, the first of which was "the immediate elimination of any firm that has a real or apparent conflict." Feinberg made clear his view that this would exclude Drabkin, and, except for Ann Samani, the other trustees seemed to concur in this. Drabkin had originally brought Samani into the Robins bankruptcy by recommending her appointment to the second claimants' committee. As a member of the committee, Samani had worked with Drabkin for more than two years. She believed that his representation of the trust would assure its independence and generally would be in the best interests of the Dalkon Shield claimants.

She saw no difference between Drabkin serving as counsel to both the claimants' committee and the trust, and her own membership in both entities, to which everyone had agreed and which Judge Merhige had emphasized in his letter to Dalkon Shield claimants that was distributed with the disclosure statement and ballots. At Samani's urging, Drabkin was included among the lawyers to be interviewed.

After spending three difficult years championing the rights of women injured by the Dalkon Shield, culminating in the creation of a fund far larger than anyone had anticipated, Drabkin welcomed the opportunity to see the process through to its conclusion. Drabkin was certain that, because of his background in the case, he could perform the job of counsel to the trust better and more efficiently than anyone else. He also felt that his involvement as counsel would prevent Judge Merhige from encroaching on the independence of the trust, because he was conscious of Merhige's predisposition in this direction and, as he had demonstrated, he was ready and able to resist it. And, as any lawyer would, Drabkin saw an opportunity to secure for his firm a substantial client that would have need for legal services over a period of many years.

Although Drabkin was aware that Judge Merhige and others, such as Hoynes and Mabey, would probably be displeased by his employment, he believed that an independent trust had been established and that it was free to choose its own counsel. As he saw no conflict of interest, Drabkin did not anticipate that he would be prevented from serving, or that the decision to retain him would provide Merhige with a basis for the removal of the trustees sponsored by the claimants' committee. This proved to be a major miscalculation.

Lawyers from seven law firms—six large Washington firms and Hunton & Williams, the firm in Richmond that Merhige had repeatedly suggested—were interviewed by the trustees on July 7, 1988. Drabkin was, of course, totally informed about every aspect of the situation whereas the other attorneys knew little other than what they had been able to gather from newspaper accounts. Some of the trustees, struggling to get a handle on the complicated matter confronting them, saw Drabkin's familiarity with the case as a major advantage.

Drabkin was questioned during his interview, particularly by Barbara Blum, about the issue of conflict. Drabkin said that the possibility of a conflict of interest had been analyzed within the Cadwalader firm and the conclusion had been reached that no conflict existed. Drabkin explained that the trust was a successor in interest to the claimants' committee in that both had the responsibility to protect the interests of the claimants. Drabkin was also questioned about reports of his acrimonious relationship with Judge Merhige. This was before Drab-kin had opposed Merhige's effort, through proposed paragraph 44, to assume additional powers over the trust and before Merhige's angry words at the confirmation hearing. Drabkin responded that he and the judge had had their differences but that they respected each other, and he did not see this as a problem.

At the conclusion of the interviews, the trustees took a preliminary vote. Samani, Blum, and Saltzburg voted for Drabkin; Locks and Fein-berg voted for other candidates. The trustees then decided to postpone any final decision until the plan was confirmed and the trust was cre-ated.

By Sunday, July 17, 1988, the day before the confirmation hearing, when Judge Merhige met with the principal attorneys in the Chapter 11 case in an effort to resolve the disagreement over paragraph 44, Merhige was aware that the trustees were considering the retention of Cad-walader, Wickersham & Taft as counsel. An awkward situation had de-veloped because the provision in dispute directly related to Merhige's control over the retention of counsel and Drabkin, who was adamantly opposing the recognition of this control, was seeking the position of counsel. According to Drabkin, during the session Merhige "took me aside at one point, I think toward the end of it, and said, with respect to representation of the trust, which he brought up, that as far as he was concerned, Cadwalader had no conflict."[2] Later that day or the next day, Merhige said the same thing to Mark Ellenberg.[3] Whatever may have been Merhige's purpose in offering this assurance, it did not cause Drabkin to alter his opposition to paragraph 44.

The question of the retention of Drabkin by the trust came up again at the meeting among Judges Merhige and Shelley and the trustees on July 25, 1988. Despite the angry exchange between Merhige and Drab-kin at the confirmation hearing the week before and the indications at this meeting, through Samani's remarks, that the conflict over Merhige's supervisory powers would be continuing, the judge told the trustees that he saw no problem in retaining Drabkin as counsel to the trust. (Accord-ing to Stephen Saltzburg, the judge said, "[Y]ou want to hire Murray, hire Murray.")[4] But later, after the two judges had left the room, Mer-hige returned and backtracked by saying that Judge Shelley thought there might be a conflict if Drabkin was retained. Saltzburg later com-mented that "the judge didn't do us any favors" in giving this mixed message.[5]

When the issue came up for a decision by the trustees on August 5, 1988, Saltzburg, perhaps sensing Judge Merhige's real feelings on the matter, had changed his mind and now opposed Drabkin's retention.

Feinberg was emphatic in his view that not only was there a conflict between Drabkin's role as counsel to the claimants' committee and the
position of counsel to the trust but that by retaining Drabkin the trust
would be causing itself severe, perhaps disabling, problems. Feinberg
said selecting Drabkin would be "suicide, unnecessary and a dangerous
mistake."[6] Samani, fresh from her brush with Judge Merhige, was
equally firm in Drabkin's favor. Locks, who had previously expressed
his preference for other counsel, now had changed his mind and supported Drabkin. Feinberg and Saltzburg later suggested that Locks had
changed his position and voted to retain Drabkin "purely to provoke
confrontation," "to fight the judge."[7] Locks said that he had voted for
Drabkin because Drabkin could meet the short-term needs of the trust
"better, faster, cheaper, more efficiently and capably than anybody else,
not because [of] anything else."[8] Voting last, Barbara Blum listened for
five minutes to a final expression of Feinberg's strong opposition, but
then cast the deciding vote in Drabkin's favor.

After the vote, Locks was designated to call Merhige and inform him
of the decision to retain Drabkin. Merhige reacted coldly. He referred to
Judge Shelley's opinion that Drabkin had a conflict and said that, while
he had an open mind, the matter might have to be addressed.

A week later, acting on Drabkin's advice, Locks, Blum, and Samani
voted to reject Merhige's recommendation that Michael Sheppard, the
clerk of the bankruptcy court in Richmond, be employed as director of
the trust. For several months before the actual establishment of the trust,
Judge Merhige at every opportunity had suggested Sheppard's employment as director. At Merhige's urging the trustees had invited Sheppard
to meet with them in Washington, D.C., on July 9. In fact, the invitation
was relayed to Sheppard by Merhige, and Sheppard understood that the
meeting would include both a discussion of the status of the records of
Dalkon Shield claims and a discussion of his possible employment. At
the meeting, some conflict developed between Locks and Sheppard concerning record keeping, and the meeting ended without anyone mentioning Sheppard's employment.

In late July, Stephen Saltzburg was in Richmond and he talked with
Sheppard about the possibility of his employment by the trust. Sheppard
was earning $72,500 as clerk of the bankruptcy court, but, because he
would lose his pension benefits if he left that position, Sheppard wanted
a five-year contract at $120,000 a year, plus benefits valued at 40 per-
cent of this figure. In a memorandum to his fellow trustees dated August
4, 1988, Saltzburg recommended that Sheppard be employed on these
terms.

The trustees discussed the matter at their meeting on August 5, 1988, but did not make a decision. Although there was no doubt that Sheppard was the best person in terms of familiarity with the files of the claimants (ironically, the same sort of advantages that Drabkin offered), doubts were expressed about making a long-term commitment to Sheppard, partly because the trustees had not decided on a structure for the trust. Consideration was being given to hiring someone with experience as a top executive in business to manage the trust. In addition, there was a feeling on the part of some trustees that Sheppard's loyalties ran to Judge Merhige and that the trustees should be given time to consider independent candidates.

Sheppard was invited to attend the next meeting of the trustees, on August 12, 1988. This was the first meeting after Drabkin's retention, and it was held at the Cadwalader offices in Washington, D.C. Again, record keeping was discussed, but the matter of Sheppard's employment was not. (Saltzburg was not present when Sheppard met with the trustees.) After Sheppard left the meeting, Drabkin told the trustees that he was opposed to hiring Sheppard and, according to one report, described him as "inflexible."[9] The trustees then voted, by the same three to two vote, against offering the job to Sheppard, at least until other organizational decisions had been made.

Next, the trustees selected a bank in New York City for the deposit of trust funds, despite Merhige's expressed preference for the use of a bank in Richmond. Beginning in June 1988, the trustees had carefully evaluated possible banks for the deposit and investment of trust funds. A questionnaire was developed and sent to thirteen banks of national stature and to six additional banks in Washington, D.C., and Virginia. On the basis of the responses, several banks were interviewed and the trustees ultimately decided that Bankers Trust in New York offered the most advantageous terms.

When Judge Merhige learned of this, he telephoned Feinberg, who had taken the lead in the process of selecting a bank, and asked him to come to Richmond on August 17 to interview local banks. At the August 12 trustees meeting, Feinberg complained of Merhige's "continued interference," but on August 17 Feinberg, accompanied by Locks, met with Merhige in his chambers. Merhige walked them over to a meeting he had arranged with the Crestar Bank. The judge told the bankers that they would get the trust's account if they offered the best terms, and he left. The terms offered by Crestar at this meeting were not as advantageous as those offered by Bankers Trust, and the trustees adhered to their decision to use Bankers Trust.

The proverbial last straw was the decision of the claimants' committee to file an appeal objecting to the statements in Merhige's confirmation opinion asserting authority over the retention of professionals and over expenditures by the trust, and the decision of a majority of the trustees to support that appeal. On August 5, 1988, the day he was retained by the trust, Drabkin told the trustees that the claimants' committee had tentatively decided to file this appeal. This decision was both unusual and surprising. Unusual, because the claimants' committee had supported confirmation of the plan of reorganization and courts of appeals generally do not review statements in opinions by lower-court judges, only the correctness of judgments and orders that have been issued. Surprising, because Merhige had deleted the controversial statements concerning his authority from the confirmation order and placed them in his opinion on the basis of a report he had received from Examiner Mabey that a compromise had been reached and that the claimants' committee would not appeal if this change were made.[10]

By August 12, 1988, the decision to appeal was definite and Drabkin told the trustees that he was obligated to follow through with it. When Saltzburg suggested that Drabkin could not represent the trust if he represented the claimants' committee in the appeal, Drabkin agreed that this was true, unless the trustees supported the appeal. A vote was then taken, and by the usual three to two vote—Locks, Blum, and Samani in favor, Feinberg and Saltzburg opposed—the trustees voted to support the appeal "in principle." Ann Samani participated in both the vote of the committee to file the appeal and the vote of the trust to support it.

On August 17, Drabkin met in New York with Louis Hoynes, counsel to American Home Products. Drabkin hoped that American Home Products would not voice opposition to his employment as counsel to the trust and that it would proceed with the acquisition of Robins despite the claimants' committee's appeal, if no broader appeals were filed. (No other appeal had been filed at this point.) Drabkin received a negative response on both counts. Hoynes reminded Drabkin of their conversation the preceding January, which he felt had resulted in an understanding that Cadwalader would not represent the trust. Drabkin did not feel that he had made such a commitment or that American Home Products should have any say with respect to the identity of counsel for the trust. He told Hoynes that, as a result of his involvement in the negotiation of the agreement, he was in a better position than anyone to assure that the trust was administered in the manner intended, in accordance with "the music as well as the words." But Hoynes said that his client preferred to have the trust advised by an attorney who would only rely on the words constituting the trust documents. American

Home Products had hoped that the trust would be the solution to the Dalkon Shield problem, not a continuing course of controversy, and Hoynes expected a constant battle with Judge Merhige if Drabkin was counsel to the trust.

Turning to the appeal, Drabkin emphasized that the claimants' committee would not seek to overturn the plan of reorganization and that he would "stand on his head" if necessary to make that clear to the court of appeals. Hoynes told Drabkin that an appeal was inconsistent with their deal for the committee's support of the plan, that the issue of Merhige's authority over the trust was one for the trust to pursue at the appropriate time if it felt unduly restricted by the judge.

On August 23, 1988, Drabkin filed notice of the claimants' committee's appeal. Although the committee's decision to appeal was not dependent on other broader appeals being filed, in fact, by this time, notices of appeal had been filed by Alan Morrison and others.

Robert Miller, counsel for the equity committee, learned of the trustees' decision to employ Drabkin and of the claimants' committee's appeal on August 23, 1988. Miller called Louis Hoynes and asked whether Hoynes had agreed to Drabkin's representation of the trust. Hoynes said that he had not. Miller replied, "Well, I think it stinks and I'm going to do something about it." Hoynes said, "Go ahead."

On August 24, 1988, Miller filed with Judge Merhige a motion to enjoin Robins from making the $100 million start-up payment to the trust until the examiner had conducted an investigation of the selection of counsel by the trust and of the circumstances surrounding the selection of the trustees themselves. By this point, Merhige needed no prodding. He immediately signed an order directing Ralph Mabey to conduct the investigation requested by Miller and set Miller's motion for an injunction for hearing at 11:30 the next morning, August 25, 1988.

When the hearing began, Miller attempted to explain why the equity committee had an interest in whom the trust retained as counsel.

MILLER: Your Honor, the equity committee has filed its motion because it believes that a serious cloud has been created over the plan of reorganization . . . and that cloud may well adversely affect the chances for success on appeal of that plan . . . The equity committee believes that . . . Cadwalader has a very serious conflict of interest, or at the very least a serious appearance of impropriety in purporting to represent the trust at the same time that it purports to represent the claimants committee . . .

We are afraid, Your Honor, that this conflict may well be seized upon by opponents of the plan in order to try to overturn this Court's confirmation order. That, indeed, would be a tragedy and would be something that would inflict damage and harm upon our clients and everybody else . . . We believe that the equity committee has standing to raise these issues . . .

M E R H I G E: That is really sort of academic, because the Court, Judge Shelley and I have raised it, and had it not been raised in this manner, the Court would have *sua sponte* brought this matter on for hearing.

Miller saw a conflict of interest in two respects. First, in defending suits brought by claimants who rejected offers of settlement, the trust would be obligated to assert Robins's defenses, "the same defenses that Cadwalader and the claimants committee have decried for several years now as being bogus defenses." Second, as counsel to the claimants' committee, "doubtless Cadwalader has received confidential information from individual claimants from time to time." Miller continued:

And I think that it would just be a travesty if any of the professionals that have labored very long and hard in the process—and I don't mean to demean anybody's involvement here—wind up as being paid by, representing, working for, involved with the trust. It makes the whole thing look shabby in our view.

Louis Hoynes was in court and told Judge Merhige that American Home Products supported Miller's motion.

We believe that the trust can only properly be served by counsel who in fact are unconnected with the past deliberations and conflicts . . . [I]t is in the best interests of the trust and certainly in the best interests of my client, that the trust, like Robins, begin anew, with a fresh start, and that fresh start should be accompanied by counsel who are beginning anew in this matter as well.

John Walsh, a partner at Cadwalader, argued that there was no conflict and stressed that the claimants' committee and trust took the same position with respect to the appeal.

W A L S H: The court should know that the trust and the trustees have voted to support that appeal.

M E R H I G E: The trustees? And that is not a conflict?

W A L S H: That removes any notions that the position we take in the Fourth Circuit. . .on behalf of the committee would be adverse to the interests of the trustees. The trustees have voted to support that appeal . . .

M E R H I G E: Unanimously?

W A L S H: Again, not unanimously. But majority and this is trust action.

M E R H I G E: Three to two perhaps?

W A L S H: That is a majority, Your Honor.

M E R H I G E: Well, it is.

After the argument, Merhige announced that he would enjoin Drabkin and his firm from rendering legal services to the trust, pending the examiner's investigation of the matter and another hearing. Without referring to his numerous expressions to the contrary, Merhige now found that the retention by the trustees of the Cadwalader firm, "in the court's view, is a clear appearance of a conflict of interest." He went on:

The court's own records show that the Cadwalader firm almost singlehandedly through its committee, the claimants committee, chose the trustees that we now have. It is true that the formal order was entered by this court. But the exercise of the veto power was always present as evidenced by the fact that the court concluded that two additional trustees would be helpful, and when advising Mr. Drabkin's firm of that was told within the hour that if any additional trustees—this is after the other five had been selected—were appointed, they would withdraw their consent to the plan. I will never forget that as long as I live.

Merhige instructed Ralph Mabey to determine, as part of his investigation,

whether the Cadwalader firm encouraged people to appeal . . . I don't mean just the people they represented but outside people . . . I want to know if there were any commitments by the trustees before they were chosen by the Cadwalader firm . . . I want to know what has been going on. Because if it will not work, I will bite the bullet.

Merhige ordered Robins to make the $100 million start-up payment to the clerk of court, and the next day Michael Sheppard invested these funds through a bank in Richmond in short-term government bonds.

The trustees did not attend the hearing, but they gathered that afternoon in Ken Feinberg's office in Washington to receive a telephone call from the judge. Merhige informed the trustees of his actions. The judge was asked whether the matter could be resolved by canceling Drabkin's retention as counsel. Merhige said that it could not, that the suitability of the trustees themselves was now in question. He referred to the decision of the trustees to support the claimants' committee's appeal and added: "I must tell you that I am looking very, very seriously at whether Mrs. Samani can properly remain as a trustee . . . You heard what she said about her intention not to follow court orders."

During this conversation, Merhige also emphasized the importance of issuing an option 1 offer as quickly as possible. "I just think we've got to get moving on that—my priorities—if I were running—if I were king of the whole world, I would be doing something about option 1 . . . I think it's the single most important thing you have to do. But that's my view now. I'm not running your damn trust yet."

In the days following August 25, 1988, in apparent reaction to Judge Merhige's actions and comments, the trustees took several steps to accommodate the judge's wishes. On September 8, 1988, by a three-to-two vote, with Barbara Blum voting with Feinberg and Saltzburg, the trust employed Michael Sheppard as its director under a three-year contract at $150,000 per year, plus substantial benefits, more than double his compensation as clerk of the bankruptcy court. The Crestar Bank improved its previous offer to the trust and bested the terms offered by Bankers Trust. The trustees then agreed to use Crestar, and in mid-September the start-up payment was transferred to the Richmond bank. The trustees retained Charles Goetz, a well-known economist at the University of Virginia whom Judge Merhige had recommended, to advise them with respect to option 1. Merhige's authorization to employ Goetz was requested and secured.

On September 9, 1988, Ralph Mabey filed his report on the disqualification of Drabkin and the Cadwalader firm. Mabey absolved Drabkin of the most serious of Merhige's imputations. He found that there was no evidence to support the suggestion that Drabkin had secured a commitment from any prospective trustee for the retention of his law firm by the trust. Nor did he find any evidence that Drabkin or anyone at the Cadwalader firm had encouraged others to appeal the confirmation order. To the contrary, Mabey learned that Drabkin and Mark Ellenberg had done all they could to discourage appeals.

Mabey did, however, recommend the disqualification of Drabkin and the Cadwalader firm, largely because of the claimants' committee's appeal. He said that the issues on appeal "are of more direct concern to the trustees and their prospective attorneys than they are to the body of Dalkon Shield claimants, whose principal interest is to be compensated quickly and fairly." Mabey suggested that, in the event that the appeal delayed the funding of the trust or even derailed the plan of reorganization, "the claimants may well perceive that the Committee's decision to appeal was based on advice from a law firm whose loyalty might appear to be divided between its existing client, the Committee, its new client, the Trust, and its own financial and professional self-interest."

Apparently in recognition of his now-blatant hostility to Drabkin, Judge Merhige asked another United States district judge, Albert Bryan, Jr., to decide the equity committee's motion to disqualify the Cadwalader firm. Judge Bryan heard arguments on September 22, 1988. The examiner and counsel representing the equity committee, Robins, American Home Products, and Aetna all argued in favor of disqualification. Stanley Joynes supported Cadwalader in its opposition.

During the hearing, Bryan rejected the argument that the claimants' committee's appeal, or the trustees support for it, created a conflict. He noted that other appeals had been filed that would have prevented consummation of the plan of reorganization and the funding of the trust. When Ralph Mabey argued that the claimants' committee's appeal might cause the plan of reorganization to be set aside, Bryan responded: "You don't think that. No one thinks that."

But Bryan did indicate that he was troubled with the Cadwalader firm representing the trust in the liquidation of claims after representing the claimants, and when he filed his decision five days later, on September 27, 1988, he disqualified Cadwalader on this basis. Bryan concluded that "it is inconceivable that Cadwalader will not be involved to some extent in the decision of processing and payment of claims."

The Court is not persuaded by the argument of Cadwalader . . . that it has only represented [claimants] "generically" and had no individual claimant as a client. This is an unrealistic view of the matter. Cadwalader fought for and obtained substantial benefits for the claimants, and commendably so. To now say that they didn't really represent those claimants is sophistry.[11]

The disqualification of Murray Drabkin, the hiring of Michael Sheppard to run the trust, and the selection of a Richmond bank reversed three major decisions of the trustees of which Judge Merhige disapproved, but the judge's control over the trust still had not been established. The claimants' committee's appeal from Merhige's assertions of supervisory authority over trust expenditures was still pending, and the three trustees selected by Drabkin and the claimants' committee were still in place. Further, by the end of September 1988 the trustees had not heeded Merhige's plea to issue an option 1 offer.

Merhige had tried to move the matter along by preparing a draft of an option 1 proposal, which he had Michael Sheppard mail to the trustees on September 12, 1988, just before Sheppard left his position as clerk of court to become director of the trust. In his letter, Sheppard said: "Judge Merhige hopes that [this] will be of help to you in proceeding along on the Option 1 payment."

Sheppard enclosed a four-page letter to the claimants for the trustees' signatures setting the option 1 payment at $750, and a two-page form by which a claimant could accept option 1 or withdraw her claim. In April 1987, Robins had proposed an amount for option 1 ($100) to which the claimants' committee had objected. As a compromise, it was agreed that the trustees would fix the amount. The relegation of decisions such as these to the trustees was the reason Drabkin had been so insistent on a dominant role for the claimants' committee in the selection of the trustees. In the course of defending his authority over the administrative affairs of the trust, Merhige had frequently acknowledged that this did not include the amounts to be paid to claimants.

On September 20, 1988, on behalf of the claimants' committee, the Cadwalader firm filed an "emergency motion" asking the court of appeals to order Merhige "to discontinue interfering in the operation of the Trust" until the appeal questioning his supervisory powers was decided. Citing Merhige's submission to the trustees of a draft of an option 1 proposal, the motion asserted that the claimants would be irreparably injured if the judge were not prevented from continuing to interfere in the administration of the trust.

To protect the interests of the claimants, [the committee] negotiated for a trust to be administered by independent trustees. Under the district court's findings and conclusions—and, more importantly, under the district court's post-confirmation actions—[the committee] has received, instead, a court-run trust . . . Every notion put forth by the district court—whether by command or suggestion—is a diminution of the independence of the trustees. Each day that such activity continues is an irreparable loss to the claimants of the benefit of the trust terms that were negotiated.[12]

On September 23, 1988, a group of five lawyers from California, led by Stephen Fredkin of Salinas, filed a motion asking Judge Merhige to remove of all the trustees. The motion alleged that "the trustees have negligently failed to act prudently and expeditiously in setting up the claims resolution facility." The timing of the motion was remarkable. On September 23 the trust had been in existence for only sixty days; the trustees had custody of funds for six days. The motion had been signed by Fredkin on September 15, 1988. Ralph Mabey's report of September 9, 1988, was not filed in the public record until September 22, 1988. Yet Fredkin relied, as a ground to remove the trustees, on "acts of misfeasance and improprieties which have been disclosed by Mr. Mabey's investigation and report to this Court."

Fredkin's motion was warmly received by Judge Merhige. On September 27, 1988, just after Judge Bryan filed his decision disqualifying the Cadwalader firm, Merhige scheduled an evidentiary hearing on the motion to commence on October 31, 1988. A few days later, Merhige entered a pretrial order relative to this hearing. Fredkin had not asked for any discovery, and no one had asked to intervene. But Merhige authorized "depositions, interrogatories and requests for admission," and announced that motions for intervention must be filed within twenty days.

On September 29, 1988, the trustees, still trying to make peace with Merhige and now advised by new counsel, filed a unanimous statement in the court of appeals that undercut the basis for the claimants' committee's emergency motion. "The trustees reject any suggestion that the District Court or anyone else is interfering in the operation of the trust and, specifically, reject any implication that the Trustees' decisions are not made fully consonant with their individual and collective fiduciary responsibility." On October 6, 1988, the court (Judges Russell, Widener, and Chapman) denied the committee's emergency motion while "expressing no opinion on the merits of the appeal."

Meanwhile, in response to Judge Merhige's pretrial order, Fredkin filed interrogatories, requests for the production of documents, and notices of depositions to the trustees. Merhige later ordered that all the discovery requests be met. On October 11, 1988, Guerry Thornton, an attorney from Atlanta, moved to intervene on behalf of his 1,101 Dalkon Shield clients in support of the motion to remove the trustees. Merhige granted Thornton's motion the day it was received. Then, on October 26, 1988, Joe Friedberg filed notice of his intention to participate in the removal hearing. In a reversal of what had seemed a venerable policy in the Chapter 11 case—a policy that had, for example, prevented the participation of any attorney representing women injured by the Dalkon Shield at the estimation hearing—Merhige ruled that all three lawyers could examine each witness at the hearing on the removal motion.

The hearing consumed all of October 31 and November 1, 1988. The trustees jointly opposed the motion through their new counsel, Elihu Inselbuch of the Washington, D.C., law firm of Caplan & Drysdale. In a joint affidavit filed in opposition to the removal motion, the trustees took the position that the problems among them had now been resolved. The affidavit described the numerous organizational issues that had commanded the trustees' attention and stated that the option 1 offer would be promulgated within thirty days. With regard to the all-important issue of court supervision, the trustees stated:

It is the intention of the Trustees to continue to keep the Court informed contemporaneously of all significant developments and decisions involving the Trust. That will allow the Trustees the benefit of the Court's views, where appropriate, and should assist the Court in performing its supervisory role. The movants are therefore entirely wrong in charging that the Trustees are opposed to having their activities supervised by this Court for the protection of the Dalkon Shield claimants.

Just before the hearing on the removal motion, the *Wall Street Journal* reported that the "rifts among the trustees" were "fading" and that a "number of people familiar with the case said it is unlikely the Judge would grant the motion [to remove trustees] now that the trustees are working together more amicably."[13]

The reasons why the Judge went ahead and removed Blum, Locks, and Samani despite the clear signs of accommodation that had been forthcoming can be gleaned from the testimony at the removal hearing. For one thing, it was clear that Merhige and these trustees had a fundamental disagreement about the role of option 1 in the compensation of women injured by the Dalkon Shield.

Merhige was determined "to assure the accuracy of the court's estimate,"[14] meaning that he wanted to assure that the trust would not run out of money. To this end, the judge intended to structure option 1 so as to dispose of as many claims as possible at a relatively low cost and thereby reduce the number of claims that would make more substantial demands on the assets of the trust. In developing his option 1 proposal in early September, Merhige had deducted from the ranks of the 195,000 eligible claimants those making only future claims, those who mentioned other IUDs or insertion dates outside the period in which the Dalkon Shield was sold, and those represented by attorneys, who, it was assumed, would advise their clients not to accept an offer of a few hundred dollars. This left a target group of approximately 100,000 claimants. Allowing for the possibility of nearly 100,000 acceptances of option 1, the maximum amount that could be offered, within the $100 million start-up payment, was $1,000. Merhige consulted an "expert" of some sort and was advised that "you would get just as many at 750 as you would at 1,000."[15]

The letter Merhige drafted to accompany the $750 option 1 offer was designed to encourage acceptances. It said, in part:

Several appeals have been filed. The immediate effect is to prevent the Trustees from proceeding under options of the Plan other than Option 1 . . . The appeals will take several months and could conceivably take more than a year though the court will be asked to expedite them.

. . . [N]o other payments are contemplated until all appeals are finalized and only then if the Court's Order of Confirmation is upheld.

If you so elect, by properly completing the enclosed form, to be paid under Option 1, you will be mailed a check for $750.00 within 30 days after your election form is received by the Trust. The plan provides that even if an appeal results in reversal of the Order of Confirmation, you will be allowed to keep your $750.

The draft letter went on to describe the more demanding requirements for information and records under options 2 and 3, but did not mention that settlements under option 2, and particularly under option 3, would be far higher than the option 1 offer.[16]

At the removal hearing, Judge Merhige repeatedly emphasized his concern over the trustees' delay in getting out the option 1 offer and stressed that the money would no longer be available if the plan of reorganization were reversed on appeal.

MERHIGE: Well, are you satisfied, Mr. Sheppard, that each of the trustees is conscious of the fact that if we don't spend this money for Option 1, and if the confirmation order is reversed, Robins gets the money? Has that been conveyed to them by you?

SHEPPARD: I took it for granted, Your Honor. I think it has been discussed . . .

MERHIGE: Hasn't the court [in] correspondence referred to it as gambling money on the part of Robins and we better spend it?

SHEPPARD: Yes.

In his testimony, Gene Locks forcefully rejected this approach and emphasized instead that a short delay in issuing the option 1 offer would be worthwhile to assure that unrepresented women with serious compensable injuries did not accept a token settlement.

MERHIGE: It was contemplated that within . . . thirty days after confirmation, Option 1 would be on the way . . . Plus, we have got a hundred million risk. These people might not get a dime . . . If the confirmation order gets reversed, we are back at step one . . . But then these claimants are gone, Mr. Locks. They are gone . . . These women have waited over ten years.

LOCKS: There is no way that Option 1 is not going to get out and be processed before consummation . . . It will be done. But if it takes another week, or if it takes another two weeks, its going to be done right. And, Your Honor, somebody coined a phrase that I heard yesterday for the first time, and I find it objectionable, and I want to state it on the record. It is objectionable. This ain't gaming money, this ain't gambling money, this ain't play money, this is a hundred million dollars to be paid to valid claimants who used and were injured by the Dalkon Shield. And they are surrendering by the acceptance of that money a valuable legal right. And my fiduciary responsibility is to those claimants and nobody else.

Later, Locks explained what exactly was taking the additional time:

A great many plaintiff lawyers and claimants believe and expect that the mailing with Option 1 must contain Option 2 amounts. I don't agree with that, but I certainly think a fully informed judgment requires as much detail of Option 2 as we can give them. And hopefully there will be language that will satisfy what I consider the necessary informed consent to take Option 1.

Other testimony at the removal hearing confirmed the efforts among the trustees to assure that claimants, without legal advice, were not mistakenly "lured" into accepting option 1.[17] To Merhige's chagrin, the trustees were taking steps with the potential to minimize, rather than maximize, the number of claimants who accepted option 1.

Another factor that appeared to motivate Merhige to remove the trustees was their continued reservations about his authority. Although all the trustees had committed themselves to abide by Merhige's interpretation of his supervisory authority unless that interpretation was reversed, Merhige pried from Locks during his testimony the admission that he would prefer for that authority to be narrowed by the appellate court. Merhige read to Locks the portion of his confirmation memorandum to which Drabkin had objected, and asked:

MERHIGE: Now, that is the part you all would like to see out, isn't it?

LOCKS: Judge . . .

MERHIGE: I want you to know the court would not be unhappy about that, but I think the plan is going to fail if it is not there.

LOCKS: Well, I am not . . .

MERHIGE: I hope I am wrong.

LOCKS: I am not disagreeing.

MERHIGE: But I don't like the bouncing around, because I am satisfied that all of you, perhaps all of you, would like to have that out. And if so, say so. Because you have a perfect right to your opinion.

LOCKS: I would like to have it out, if you are asking me personally.

MERHIGE: You say you would?

LOCKS: I would like to go back to the trust document and deal with the trust document.

The Judge could reasonably conclude that Samani and Blum agreed.

Lastly, there was the matter of Ann Samani's conduct on July 25, 1988, when she disagreed with Merhige's interpretation of his powers. Several witnesses, including Samani, tried to convince Merhige that she had not intended to be rude, but Merhige would hear none of it.

SALTZBURG: I don't believe she intended to be rude. I believe she intended to be direct and forthright.

MERHIGE: She was rude. Let there be no question about it. And had we been in a courtroom, she would have been held in contempt of court. Have no question about it . . .

＊　　　＊　　　＊

LOCKS: I would have asked the question a little differently, or projected the response a little differently. But in no way in my view was she in contempt . . . And all due respect to Your Honor, I have only known Miss Samani since May. And I don't think she knows how to be rude . . .

MERHIGE: Do you recall Miss Samani saying that Mr. Drabkin said the court had no right to do what it was doing? Do you recall that?

LOCKS: No, I don't.

MERHIGE: Okay . . . Do you recall my saying, if that is your attitude, Miss Samani, perhaps you ought to consider resigning? Do you recall that?

LOCKS: I remember you saying that . . .

MERHIGE: Do you recall her saying that she had no intention of following it, and she was going to be a trustee whether I liked it or not? Do you recall that?

LOCKS: Not exactly those words, no . . .

MERHIGE: Let's take a five-minute recess. I know when it is appropriate to pour water on myself, on my face . . .

*   *   *

SAMANI: I . . . said in response to your saying, do you have any problems with that, that I did have a problem. I heard you say that you felt I was rude. I apologize for that because I . . .

MERHIGE: Well, you were excited, don't let that . . .

SAMANI: I was very excited, but I did not intend to be rude. I thought I was keeping my voice low. I am sure my face was red. It is probably red now. But I did not intend to be rude to the court. What I felt I had to say was how I saw the court's role, because I felt it was very different from what you had just said . . . I did say that I would not resign, but I don't think I said . . . I am going to serve as a trustee whether you like it or not . . .

MERHIGE: That is my recollection.

Judge Merhige removed Locks, Samani, and Blum as trustees on November 28, 1988. In a written opinion, he found that Samani and Locks were in "open defiance" of the court's authority and that Blum had "supported Samani and Locks in their pronounced disagreement with the law as enunciated by the Court."[18] Nevertheless, Merhige said that he was not removing the trustees because of their defiance but because of their "derelictions."[19] The "derelictions" listed by Merhige were the trustees' employment of Drabkin; the trustees' support for the claimants' committee's appeal (support that Merhige's found "nothing less than shocking"); and the trustees' failure to issue option 1 when and in the manner Merhige had wanted.[20]

In his opinion, Merhige did not mention that in his meeting with the trustees on July 25, 1988, just before they acted, he had said that he saw no problem with their retention of Drabkin. To the contrary, Merhige claimed that he had told the trustees "that the retention of Cadwalader, though perhaps not impermissible, would be detrimental to the trust," and he found that Locks had voted to retain Drabkin to defy the court. Locks had denied this in his testimony. "Any suggestion by Mr. Locks that his vote to retain the firm was not influenced by a desire to challenge the authority of the court is rejected as untrue," Merhige said.[21]

The most remarkable aspect of Merhige's opinion was his reliance, as proof that the employment of Drabkin was a dereliction of duty, on the decision of the first claimants' committee, "composed of thirty eight members including the most knowledgeable plaintiff's counsel with experience in Dalkon Shield litigation," to discharge Drabkin as its counsel in February 1986.[22] These kind words must have come as quite a surprise to those lawyers, whom Merhige had angrily ejected from the Chapter 11 case in response to their vote to discharge Drabkin.[23] Merhige had never before suggested that there was any justification for the committee's vote to discharge Drabkin. To the contrary, the day he dissolved the committee, Merhige appointed Drabkin legal representative of the Dalkon Shield claimants until a new committee could be appointed. Six weeks later, Merhige wholeheartedly approved the decision of the new committee to retain Drabkin—with no hint that it had committed a "dereliction" in doing so. The reason the members of the first claimants' committee had voted to discharge Drabkin was their perception, which time proved to be mistaken, that he was not willing to stand up to Merhige. It is no small irony that their vote, itself an effort to curb Merhige's dominance, should be dragged out years later to justify the expulsion of trustees who had sought their independence from the judge.

The day Judge Merhige's decision was issued, Nancy Worth Davis, the chairperson of the claimants' committee, condemned the removal of the trustees as "a cynical and ruthless breach of faith with Dalkon Shield victims, for whom the plan was created."[24]

As a result of the decision, there were only two remaining trustees, Steven Saltzburg and Kenneth Feinberg. On December 5, 1988, Judge Merhige appointed Georgene Vairo, an associate professor at Fordham University Law School in New York, as a third trustee. Vairo, at the time in her late thirties, had grown up on Staten Island in New York. She graduated from Sweet Briar College in Virginia and then earned a master of education degree at the University of Virginia. She graduated from the law school at Fordham in 1979 and was appointed to the faculty in 1982. Vairo was a college student in Virginia in 1972 and had followed the controversy occasioned by Merhige's decision requiring the consolidation of the Richmond-area school systems. As a result of his actions in that case, Merhige is Vairo's "only hero."[25]

Vairo met Merhige when they were both participants in a bar association program. Through this connection, she was appointed as a trustee of the Other Claimants Trust, established by Robins's plan of reorganization. In an interview with Ralph Mabey during his investigation, Vairo expressed disapproval of the delay in hiring Sheppard and of the decision to retain Drabkin. She criticized the trustees of the claimants' trust for their inaction and for being "suspicious of the Judge." She said she did "not think that the Judge is a problem."[26]

Barbara Blum and Ann Samani retained Peter B. Edelman, a professor at Georgetown Law School in Washington, D.C., to represent them in appealing Merhige's removal order. On December 12, 1988, Professor Edelman filed a motion in the court of appeals on behalf of Blum and Samani for a stay of the order during the appeal. On December 23, 1988, the motion was granted; the court of appeals (Russell, Widener, and Chapman, again) suspended the order removing Blum and Samani as trustees during the appeal. The case was set for an expedited argument on January 12, 1989.

Locks took no action until December 23, when he filed a notice of appeal. On December 28, 1988, Blum, Samani, and Locks filed a joint motion asking the court of appeals "to clarify" its December 23, 1988, order by stating that it applied to Locks, as well as Blum and Samani, and that it operated to block the appointment of Georgene Vairo. In opposition to the motion to clarify, the trust (Feinberg, Saltzburg, and Vairo) argued that a stay in favor of Locks did not follow from the stay in favor of Blum and Samani because there were two vacancies on the five-person trust when the Blum and Samani motion was granted. With Blum and Samani restored, there were no vacancies. They also argued that Vairo should not be displaced by Locks because the trust would then be controlled by three trustees operating under the cloud of Merhige's removal order.

The court of appeals took no action on the motion to clarify and heard arguments in the appeal on January 12, 1989. Peter Edelman argued for Locks, as well as Blum and Samani. Merhige was uneasy with Stephen Fredkin of Salinas defending his decision on appeal and arranged for Joseph Friedberg to argue in support of the removal order.[27] On March 30, 1989, the court of appeals denied Locks's motion for a stay, thus continuing the odd conglomeration of trustees—Feinberg, Saltzburg, Vairo, Blum, and Samani—until the appeal was decided.

On June 16, 1989, the same day the decisions affirming the confirmation of the plan of reorganization and the approval of the *Breland* settlement were released, the court of appeals issued decisions by Judge Chapman denying the claimants' committee's appeal relative to Merhige's supervisory authority and the appeals by the removed trustees.

In the claimants' committee's appeal, Chapman ruled that, because of the large number of claims and the large amount of money involved, Judge Merhige was correct in concluding that continued supervision of the trust was required "so long as its supervision does not interfere with the day-to-day operation of the Trust."[28] Chapman found that the specific acts of which the claimants' committee complained "do not amount to monitoring the day-to-day operations of the Trust or result in usurpation of or interference with the powers and duties of the Trustees." Relying on the statement submitted to the court of appeals by the trustees on September 28, 1988, just after the motion for their removal had been filed, Chapman said, "These acts did not interfere with the Trustees in the performance of their duties, but according to the Trustees, assisted them in getting things started."[29]

In the appeal by the removed trustees,[30] Judge Chapman condemned the conduct of Blum, Samani, and Locks:

The appellants attempt to present this case as a clash of personalities between the appellants and the district court and that this conflict is at the heart of the problems that have beset the Trust from its inception. We find this unpersuasive. The appellants have spent so much time, money and energy trying to assert their independence from the district court, that they have neglected their primary duty of administering the trust so as to promptly pay the Dalkon Shield claimants . . . The delays occasioned by the three trustees have increased administrative costs, have delayed the full funding of the Trust, which when fully funded will produce approximately $600,000 per day in interest income, and have endangered the very life of the Plan by delays that could extend consummation past July 24, 1989 and allow American Home Products to revoke its offer of merger.[31]

In fact except for defending against the effort to remove them, there is no indication that the trustees spent time or money asserting their independence from the court. Certainly, they did nothing that would delay full funding of the trust or consummation of the plan. On the other hand, after granting a motion for expedited treatment, it had taken Judge Chapman and his colleagues more than six months after argument to decide the appeal from the plan of reorganization. This delay really had postponed full funding of the trust and really had cost the trust tens of millions of dollars of lost interest.

Judge Chapman took a parting shot at the removed trustees and at Murray Drabkin:

It is obvious from the record that a real bone of contention among the trustees is the appointment of an attorney . . . to represent the Trust . . . Mr. Lock, Ms. Blum and Ms. Samani have refused to acknowledge that Mr. Drabkin . . . may have a conflict of interest because [he] has been and still is counsel to the Dalkon Shield Claimants Committee. The remaining trustees and the disqualification order of Chief Judge Albert Bryan, Jr. have found such a conflict, but this has not diminished the loyalty of the three trustees to Mr. Drabkin. This is a throw-back to the former bankruptcy scenario when the lawyer for the largest number of creditors elected the Trustee, and the Trustee then employed the lawyer to represent him. Such activity is no longer acceptable.[32]

Here again, the evidence was all to the contrary. At the hearing on the motion to remove the trustees, Locks had testified: "Cadwalader will never be hired again if I have anything to say about it. It is done." Samani had testified: "[Retention of the Cadwalader firm] is a totally dead issue. I think it is very clear after Judge Bryan's ruling, it is a totally dead issue." Blum was not asked about the matter.

21   Running the Trust

In July 1989, following the decision of the court of appeals upholding the removal of Gene Locks, Barbara Blum, and Ann Samani as trustees, Judge Merhige appointed John Dowd and Marietta Robinson to fill the two positions that were vacant. Dowd is a Washington, D.C., attorney who had frequently appeared before Judge Merhige. Like Georgene Vairo, the first replacement trustee, Dowd had been a trustee of the Other Claimants Trust. In that capacity, Dowd was present at the July 25, 1988, meeting at which Merhige and Ann Samani had their disagreement. In testimony at the hearing on the motion to remove the trustees, he was critical of Samani's resistance to Merhige's supervision of the trust. Dowd explained that the trustees should have welcomed the judge's involvement because his "sole object is justice." Marietta Robinson is an attorney from Detroit who represents plaintiffs in personal injury litigation. She was recommended by Stephen Saltzburg.

With all five trustees now appointed by Judge Merhige, the concept of the trust as an independent decision-making body quickly faded away. Management of the trust was lodged squarely in the hands of Merhige's nominee for executive director, former bankruptcy court clerk Michael Sheppard. In the months that followed, there was substantial additional turnover among the trustees, including the resignations of Saltzburg and Kenneth Feinberg, the last of the original trustees, and the appointment of two trustees from Richmond.[1]

Shortly after his appointment of Dowd and Robinson, Merhige made known that he wanted the trust to change lawyers. When Merhige removed three trustees in November 1988, the remaining two, Saltzburg and Feinberg, had replaced Elihu Inselbuch, who had been suggested by Gene Locks, with Edward Modell of the firm of Dickstein, Shapiro & Morin of Washington, D.C. Modell seemed like an agreeable choice. With Vairo and Dowd, he was the third trustee of the Other Claimants Trust. He was also a former law clerk to Judge Merhige.

But in July 1989, Merhige decided that he did not want any outside law firm to serve as general counsel of the trust, because of the expense involved and because, to paraphrase the judge, he did not want a law firm to run the trust. Merhige decided that outside counsel should be employed only for specific projects, as needed, and that an attorney should be employed to work full time for the trust. The Dickstein firm was promptly discharged.

For outside counsel, Merhige selected two of his former clerks, Michael Smith and Orran Lee Brown, who practice law in Richmond with the firm of Christian, Barton, Epps, Brent & Chappell. The judge is the godfather of Smith's child. For in-house counsel, Merhige chose Linda Thomason, who left her employment with Mays & Valentine, general counsel to the A. H. Robins Company, to accept the position. While with Mays & Valentine, Thomason had been active in the Robins bankruptcy. Her principal assignment had been to oppose motions by injured women for permission to file claims after the bar date and to oppose requests for reinstatement of claims that had been disallowed for failure to return the court questionnaire on time.

For example, fifteen women from Costa Rica alleging injuries from the Dalkon Shield were represented by Martina Langley, an attorney in Austin, Texas. Langley suffered a brain hemorrhage on April 26, 1986, four days before the bar date. On April 28, 1986, the completed claim forms from her Costa Rican clients arrived in her office. Langley submitted the claims when she was released from the hospital in June 1986 and then filed a motion asking that the court treat them as timely. For Robins, Thomason opposed the motion:

Presumably, the responsibility for directing the shipment of these persons' notices to Texas at this extremely late date lies with Langley. Langley could easily have arranged for the April 26 courier delivery to have been delivered to the Clerk's office . . . Notwithstanding the unfortunate events that befell Langley, she must shoulder responsibility for the consequences of her decision.[2]

Thomason also represented Robins in opposition to Kathryn Glascow's motion to treat her late claim as timely. Glascow, it will be remembered, learned after the bar date that the IUD she had used was a Dalkon Shield and that it had caused her to be infertile. She also had not been aware of the bar date. In opposition to Glascow's motion, Thomason argued: "There has been a lot of talk about justice and fairness and equity, but in this situation we have the law. We have got bankruptcy rules and case law . . . You open the bar date for Miss Glascow and really there is no more bar date."[3]

In connection with the disqualification of Murray Drabkin, who had supported the interests of the claimants during the Chapter 11 case, great stress had been placed on the need for "counsel who in fact are unconnected with the past deliberations and conflicts . . . [on] a fresh start . . . [with] counsel who are beginning anew in this matter."[4] Some of the trustees questioned whether Thomason, who had opposed the interests of injured women in the Chapter 11 case, should now be employed as chief counsel for the claimants' trust. Merhige saw no problem. He knew Thomason, he liked her, she was from Richmond, and he wanted her to have the job. Later, Ralph Mabey, the former examiner, who in his report recommending Drabkin's disqualification had cited his own advice to the original trustees to employ counsel with no prior connection to the case, was himself employed as special counsel to the trust.

The option 1 offer in the amount of $725 was issued on December 5, 1988, just a few days after Merhige's decision removing the three trustees. The offer met with an enormous response. In the first two months, it was accepted by some 65,000 of the 195,000 eligible claimants. The offer remained open, and as time passed with no indication of when the plan would be consummated or when the trust would be able to process claims at options 2 or 3, more and more claimants accepted option 1. When the plan of reorganization was finally consummated on December 15, 1989, a total of some 84,000 claims had been resolved through option 1, at a cost of approximately $55 million. This meant that 43 percent of the claims had been resolved for less than 3 percent of the funds that would be paid into the trust.

On the date the plan was consummated, the trust received $2.155 billion ($2.255 billion less the $100 million start-up payment) from American Home Products, and $75 million from Aetna in accordance with the settlement in *Breland*. Unfortunately, despite the lengthy appeal process, which provided sixteen months from confirmation to consummation, the trust was unprepared at that time to send out the materials offering option 2 and option 3 to the remaining 111,000 claimants.[5] It took three additional months, until mid-March 1990, before the package was ready for mailing.

There was also a significant delay before the trust was prepared to make payments for medical fertility procedures. The trustees were authorized under the terms of the plan of reorganization to use the start-up funds "to prepare for distributions to be made from the trust,"[6] and they were instructed to "establish a program for providing immediate payments to qualified claimants who could benefit from reconstructive surgery or in vitro fertilization."[7] Applications for participation in this program could have been sent to interested claimants, returned, evaluated, and approved by the trust during the sixteen-month interval between confirmation and consummation so that "immediate payments to qualified claimants" could indeed have been made when the plan was consummated. In fact, the application forms were not mailed out until late December 1989, after consummation, and there was a delay of several additional months before approval of expenditures for fertility procedures began in the late spring of 1990.[8]

In connection with the appeal from the plan of reorganization, Alan Morrison and his colleagues were reviled for delaying payments to injured women. The inability of the trust to complete the option 2 and option 3 materials, or to distribute and process applications for payments for medical fertility procedures, while the appeal was pending indicates either that the appeal did not delay payments to injured women, because more than sixteen months were required to make these preparations, or that the trust was not doing what it was mandated to do during the interim period. In contrast to his outrage in the fall of 1988 over the "dereliction" of the original trustees in failing to issue the option 1 offer within a few weeks of confirmation, Merhige had nothing but praise for the performance of the reconstituted trustees.

The forms with which to select an option and file a claim were mailed by the trust to all eligible claimants on March 15, 1990. A deadline of July 1, 1991, was set for the return of the forms. By January 14, 1991, the trust had received claims as follows:

Option 1	99,452
Option 2	8,216
Option 3	19,367

The option 1 number included more than 15,000 claims that were filed after the forms were mailed in March 1990. Almost 70,000 claimants had not yet responded. Some 10,000 of these had moved and could not be located by the trust.[9]

During the appeal the trust had undertaken various analyses of the best way to proceed with options 2 and 3. Michael Ciresi and Martha Wivell, an attorney in Ciresi's firm who had worked on the recent Copper 7 IUD litigation, were retained because of their knowledge of the evaluation of IUD injury claims. Economists and statisticians were employed to make mathematical projections. These included Thomas Florence, who had testified for Robins at the estimation hearing, Timothy Wyant, who had

Table 21.1. Amounts Offered by Dalkon Shield
Claimants Trust for Settlements in Option 2

Sterilizing surgery	$5,500
Nonsurgical infertility	3,900
Ectopic pregnancy	3,300
Pelvic inflammatory disease	1,250
Uncontrolled bleeding	850
Perforation or embedment (surgical removal)	1,500
Birth defect, congenital defect, or birth injury	1,150
Infant death	3,200
Septic abortion	2,500
Premature delivery	2,300
Spontaneous abortion	1,000
Induced abortion	850

assisted the claimants' committee in its preparation for the estimation hearing, and Charles Goetz, the economist at the University of Virginia who had previously been retained by the trust as a consultant with respect to option 1. Thirty attorneys who represent Dalkon Shield claimants were asked to assist by providing their evaluations of a sample group of cases.

The plan of reorganization requires that under option 2 a fixed dollar amount be offered for each injury category. In order to qualify for payment under option 2, a claimant must submit medical records that establish the use of the Dalkon Shield and an injury listed as compensable in the plan, but the trust will not examine issues of causation, that is, whether the injury was caused by the Dalkon Shield or by some other factor. For this reason, the trustees selected values for the option 2 offers that they considered appropriate only for claimants who have a significant problem relative to causation. The values shown in table 21.1 were adopted for option 2.

Using data from the McGovern sample, the trust's experts estimated the number of claims in each injury category that would be resolved under option 2 and the total cost of those resolutions. Projections were then made from the McGovern data and other available information of the number of claims that would be filed under option 3 and of the distribution of these claims among the various injury categories. Factors were identified that would affect the proper evaluation of a claim within an injury category, and the distribution of those factors was estimated. The trust has not publicly identified these factors, but the indications are that they relate to such matters as the strength of the proof of Dalkon

Shield use, whether there is more than one compensable injury, the likelihood of alternative causes of the injury or injuries, the length of incapacity, "special damages" (medical and hospital bills and lost wages), and, if infertility is claimed, the age and marital status of the claimant and whether she has children. All the factors considered by the trust are personal to the claimant and do not include such matters as geographical location (including foreign residence), representation by counsel, or the identity of the counsel.

On the basis of these projections, historical values, and the amount of money expected to be available for option 3 claims after claims under options 1 and 2 have been paid, a "rules-based" system was developed for arriving at option 3 offers. A base amount was established for each injury category. Predetermined amounts would then be added or subtracted depending on the relevant factors. Although the trust employs many claims evaluators, in theory the same value should be attached to a claim regardless of who evaluates it. The values were derived so that, if the claimants elect options 1, 2, and 3 in the proportions projected; if, within option 3, each claimant accepts the amount offered by the trust; and considering the expenses to operate the trust, nearly all the trust funds will be expended. The prevailing opinion among plaintiffs' counsel is that in many cases the trust's early option 3 offers are below, sometimes significantly below, the settlement levels in the period before the bankruptcy.

The plan of reorganization provides that a claimant who rejects the offer of the trust "may make a counteroffer, and the parties may resolve the matter at that or some other amount." The plan also provides that, if a resolution is not reached, the trust must "invite the claimant to a voluntary settlement conference," which must be followed by an exchange of offers.[10] Despite these provisions, the trust refuses even to discuss its offer until it has been rejected and a settlement conference held. And, according to policies announced by the trust, unless at the settlement conference the claimant can demonstrate that an error has been made in the application of the rules system, or supplies information the absence of which lowered the evaluation of the claim, the trust will not change its offer. The claimant's only alternative to accepting the offer is to go to arbitration or trial. Even after suit is initiated, there will be no further settlement discussions, before or during trial. The case will have to go to judgment. The rationale for this no-negotiation policy is that the initial offer was the "correct" offer, at least in terms of the available resources, and that there would be no incentive for anyone to accept that offer if the trust were willing to raise it to avoid litigation. And, because the initial offers have been calculated to use up almost all the trust funds, if they were regularly increased, the trust could run out of money.

The right of every claimant to seek an independent determination of the value of her claim, either through arbitration or through a local jury trial, has the potential for upsetting this system. It is possible that an arbitrator or a jury will liquidate the claim at a far higher level than the amount offered by the trust, and it is certain that the process will increase the expenses of the trust on account of the attorney fees and costs of defending the litigation. To reduce these risks, the trust, under Judge Merhige's auspices, has adopted policies intended to discourage litigation. The most dramatic of these is that the trust will not pay jury verdicts or arbitration awards in excess of its settlement offer. If a claimant rejects the trust's offer of settlement, goes to trial or arbitration, and succeeds in obtaining a higher award, the trust will only pay the amount of its offer and will "hold back" the balance. All or part of the excess amount will be paid, if ever, only after all the claimants have been given the opportunity to accept an offer from the trust, or until such earlier date that it is unmistakable that the trust will have sufficient funds to pay the additional amounts awarded in court or through arbitration. (If the award in court or arbitration is less than the trust's offer, the lesser amount will be paid.)

With the choice between an immediate payment in an amount the trust has concluded is appropriate, and a trial that will involve all the normal disadvantages of delay, expense, and risk, plus the added disadvantage that any recovery beyond the amount offered by the trust will not be paid for five or more years, and may never be paid, the trust hopes that very few women will choose to go to trial. The holdback policy also serves to reinforce the no-negotiation policy because it deprives the claimant of her only effective weapon in negotiations—a credible threat of taking the case to trial and obtaining a higher recovery.

The trust's objective system for the evaluation of claims, together with its holdback policy, is designed to compensate women on a uniform basis and to minimize trust fund expenditures on litigation. The concept is similar to a workers' compensation system, where each injury has an amount attached to it, the proof requirements for recovery are limited, and litigation is forbidden. The problem with this approach in the Robins bankruptcy is that the holdback policy violates the terms of the plan of reorganization and federal law.

The plan of reorganization, in recognition of the possibility that the liquidated value of all the claims may exceed the resources of the trust, includes the following provision:

3. *Payments.* The Trustees shall pay claims in a manner designed to ensure that all claims are paid in the same proportions. While it is intended that each claimant receive a substantial portion of his or her award immediately upon the determination of his or her claim, the Trustees may withhold some portion of the amounts awarded under option 3 for claims and pay the balance withheld at such times and in such amounts as necessary to ensure the equality in distribution among the claimants and the continued availability of funds to pay all valid non-subordinated claims. The Trustees may also determine that compensatory damages awarded under option 1 or option 2 shall be paid in full immediately upon liquidation.[11]

The mandate to "pay claims in a manner designed to ensure that all claims are paid in the same proportions" could not be clearer. It incorporates (except with respect to those claimants who accept small settlements under option 1 or option 2) the bankruptcy law principle of pro rata distribution within a class of creditors. The balance of the quoted provision instructs the trustees, if they are unsure that enough funds are available to pay the full liquidated value of all claims resolved at option 3, to pay claims as they are liquidated in a proportion that the trust is clearly able to afford and to make a second payment when the correct proportion (or the ability to make full payment) can be determined.

The trust's holdback policy disregards this mandate. Claimants who agree to liquidate their claims at the value proposed by the trust will be immediately paid in full; claimants who attain a higher award in arbitration or trial will be paid a fraction of the value at which their claims are liquidated. Hypothetically, a jury may award a woman many times the amount of the trust's offer, because it finds in her favor on an issue of causation that the trust resolved against her. The woman will nonethelss be paid the amount of the trust's offer, until such time, if ever, the trust determines that it has the resources to pay litigated claims. This is not merely economy; it is an arrogation of the power to override judicial determinations of the worth of individual claims.

This result is in sharp contrast to the representations relating to trial by jury on which the approval of the plan of reorganization and the *Breland* settlement were based. In the "Special Note to Women Who Used the Dalkon Shield" in the front of the disclosure statement, the following appears:

If you have a claim that has not yet been determined, the amount of your claim will be determined under the procedures set up by the Trustees of the Claimants

Trust. After following these procedures, if you are not satisfied with the settlement amount that the Trust offers to pay you, you can have the amount of the claim decided by an appropriate Court, as in a normal lawsuit . . .

THERE ARE NO MAXIMUM SETTLEMENT AMOUNTS OR MAXIMUM AMOUNTS THAT MAY BE AWARDED BY A JURY . . . YOU STILL HAVE THE RIGHT TO FILE A LAWSUIT . . . IF YOU ARE NOT SATISFIED WITH THE SETTLEMENT OFFERED BY THE TRUST.

And:

THE COURT MUST FIND . . . BEFORE THE PLAN GOES INTO EFFECT THAT THE PLAN PROVIDES ENOUGH MONEY TO SATISFY ALL DALKON SHIELD CLAIMS AND EXPENSES OF THE TRUST IN FULL.

The right of each eligible claimant "to elect to have her claim settled in a trial with all the procedural rights normally attaching to a jury trial" was also the basis on which the court of appeals rejected the constitutional challenge to the mandatory class in the *Breland* settlement.[12]

If Robins's plan of reorganization had provided for a holdback applicable only to claims that were liquidated in court, it would have violated the provision of Chapter 11 that mandates that every plan of reorganization "provide the same treatment of each claim or interest of a particular class."[13] In a bankruptcy context, "same treatment" does not mean paying every creditor an amount unilaterally determined by trustees to be appropriate; it means paying every creditor the same proportion of the liquidated value of her claim. A personal injury claim can be liquidated by agreement, but Congress has guaranteed personal injury claimants in a mass tort bankruptcy the right to liquidate their claims through a jury trial.[14] In their zeal "to assure the accuracy of the court's estimate," Judge Merhige and his trustees have so burdened the jury trial right as to all but eliminate it. The right remains meaningful only when the offer of the trust is so far below the expectations of the claimant and her attorney that, even with the holdback, there is potentially a substantial advantage to a jury verdict.[15]

Georgene Vairo, the chairperson of the trust, has described the holdback policy as "critical to the success of the plan."[16] What she meant is that the holdback policy guarantees that the trust funds will be adequate to support the settlement offers that will be generated by the system that the trust has adopted, and in that sense it guarantees that the trust will not run out of funds before all the claims are paid. The same result could also have been achieved by complying with the direction in the plan of reorganization to pay a clearly affordable percentage of each claim, however liquidated, until all claims had been paid, and then distribute the balance on a pro rata basis. The difference is that the latter approach would not have discouraged claimants from rejecting the trust's offer of settlement and seeking a liquidation of their claims in court and would have been more difficult to reconcile with the official position that the trust's funds are adequate to pay all claims in full.

Judge Merhige and the trust have adopted other policies calculated to discourage litigation. Under the plan of reorganization, a settlement conference must precede litigation. (Although the substantive purpose of the conference—to attempt to agree on a settlement—has been eliminated by the trust's no-negotiation policy, the procedural requirement remains.) In July and August 1990, several women represented by David Sabih, an attorney from Pacific Groves, California, rejected settlement offers issued by the trust under option 3. In a motion filed in October 1990, Sabih complained of the trust's failure to schedule settlement conferences in these cases despite his repeated requests. Judge Merhige declined to intervene. At the end of November 1990, the trust announced that the first settlement conferences would be held in March 1991 and at six-month intervals thereafter.[17] But by mid-January 1991, no settlement conference had been scheduled in any of Sabih's cases.

The plan of reorganization provides that:

[i]f a settlement is not sooner reached, not later than 60 days after the [settlement] conference, both parties must submit to the other a written settlement proposal which shall remain in effect until 90 days after the conference. If neither accepts the other's offer during this period, the claimant may proceed to arbitration or trial.[18]

Notwithstanding this explicit authorization, Judge Merhige and the trust have adopted rules that prohibit suit until the trust "certif[ies] the claimant's eligibility to choose either binding arbitration or trial," *and* until Merhige issues "an order allowing the claimant to proceed."[19] These requirements provide additional mechanisms by which the right to file suit can be delayed.

Another aspect of the effort to convince women to accept whatever offer they receive from the trust involves maintaining secrecy concerning the amounts paid in the resolution of Dalkon Shield injury claims before the bankruptcy. Jay H. Glasser, Ph.D., an associate professor at the School of Public Health at the University of Texas, was retained by the claimants' committee to assist it in connection with the McGovern process and claims estimation, and he had access at that time to the

McGovern data bases. In the fall of 1988, after the plan of reorganization was confirmed, Glasser offered his services to Dalkon Shield claimants in the selection of the appropriate option and in the submission of their claims to the trust, at charges below the fees generally charged by attorneys.

In June 1989, Robins moved to hold Glasser in contempt of court for violating confidentiality orders relating to the McGovern data. At a hearing the following month, in which Robins was represented by Linda Thomason, who had not yet left Mays & Valentine to become counsel for the trust, Merhige ruled that Glasser had violated the protective orders. Merhige found that "[i]n representing Dalkon Shield claimants and advising them as to the value of their claims, Glasser has necessarily utilized information gleaned from the closed files, even if he has not directly disclosed the data underlying his recommendations." Merhige's explanation of why the information on historic values should be secret is revealing:

[T]he closed files contain information concerning the exact dollar amounts of the judgments and settlements received by individual claimants prior to the filing of Robins' petition. It is exactly this data which was of crucial importance in reaching a valid estimation of Robins' total Dalkon Shield liability. The Court perceived that possession of this information, however, would also be very useful to anyone representing Dalkon Shield claimants in negotiations with or litigation against the trust.[20]

Information on prior settlements is not admissible in litigation. The trust refuses to engage in negotiations. The only use that could be made of information relating to historic values is in deciding whether the trust's offer is adequate and should be accepted—whether it is payment "in full," as advertised, or whether it is inadequate and should be rejected in favor of litigation.

The trust prepared and mailed to the claimants a series of newsletters. In soothing tones, suitable to a promotional brochure, these portray the trust as the beneficent guardian of the interests of the claimants.

This is the first issue of a newsletter designed to help provide you with the information and support you will need as you seek fair compensation from the Dalkon Shield Claimants Trust . . .

We hope that most claimants will be able to resolve their claims without the need to consult an attorney.

"We are satisfied that the Trustees are dedicated to expeditiously grant all deserving claimants their full and fair entitlement to their share of the funds available" [quoting Judge Merhige] . . .

"If there is one thing I would like to communicate to the claimants, it is we are on your side" [quoting Claims Manager Ann Peters] . . .

Above all, [Trustee Feinberg] wants claimants to know that "we are on your side" . . .

"We want to make sure that the Trust . . . puts the maximum amount of money in claimants' pockets in the minimum amount of time and with a minimum of expense . . . Both represented and unrepresented claimants will get the same fair offer from the Trust . . . All materials will be written in nonlegal language so that claimants without attorneys can understand the procedure" [quoting Trustee Georgene Vairo].

The trust's newsletters devote space to admiring profiles of the trustees.

VAIRO WORKS FOR CLAIMANTS

The door of the elevator opens and a slim, athletic woman hurries to the security desk, signs her name and quickly puts on her badge. Escorted by a staff member, she walks briskly through the door to the meeting room.

She will be at the Trust all day, conferring with staff members, conducting business on the phone, or chairing meetings. Throughout the day as she debates policy or guides meetings to a decision, she displays the same energy and intensity as when she entered.

She is Georgene Vairo, Chair of the Dalkon Shield Claimants Trust . . .

ROBINSON RELATES TO CLAIMANTS' FEELINGS

When you meet Marti (Marietta) Robinson, your first impression is that this is someone who enjoys herself. She likes to remain active, both on the job and in her free time. She is always ready to tell you a funny story and laugh about it with you.

But when the discussion turns to the Dalkon Shield Claimants Trust and the decisions she must make as one of the trustees, she quickly becomes serious . . .

If Marti could talk face to face with claimants, she says that she would like to tell them that "we are not A. H. Robins. I know how frustrating this process has been for claimants. I hope that the claimants can look beyond their justifiable anger and realize how hard we are working for them. I want claimants to understand that we are not the enemy, but we are doing our very best to protect the interests of all of them."

The unmistakable purpose of this public relations campaign is to induce women to rely on the trust and to accept its decision as to the value of their claims. Yet, in a number of respects, it is questionable whether the trust has lived up to its promise of the swift and fair resolution of claims. The trust's newsletters and the application materials sent to claimants in a variety of ways subtly encourage women to choose the lower options. They do not state that the low option 2 values are intended only for women who would have substantial problems connecting their injuries to the Dalkon Shield or that women without these problems should not accept option 2. To the contrary, they emphasize delays that will be encountered under option 3 as a reason to accept the lower options. One of the "factors" listed by the trust "in deciding which option to choose" is "[h]ow soon you desire payment." "Payment under option 1 will be made in 30 days; payment under option 2 will take more time. Payment under option 3 will require considerably more time than option 2."[21] A form letter sent by the trust to claimants who rejected an offer under option 2 stated: "Please be aware that you may still accept the Trust's option 2 offer or you may proceed to option 3 . . . Since option 3 requires a full review, it may take up to five years to settle your claim."[22]

The trust's materials have also exaggerated the obstacles to recovery under option 3 by suggesting that a claimant's medical records must show "that there is nothing else in her medical history [other than the Dalkon Shield] that could have caused [the injury]."[23] The applicable standard of liability for personal injuries is not absolute proof that the defective product was the sole cause of the injury but proof that the defective product was more likely than not to have been a contributing cause of the injury.[24]

In a section entitled "Choosing Your Best Option," one trust newsletter actually suggested that a woman who became pregnant with a Dalkon Shield in place and gave birth to an injured baby should consider accepting $725 under option 1. "But Jane does not want to submit her claim under option 3 because the full review may take a long time. Jane knows that if she files under option 3, the Trust will look closely at any other conditions that may have caused her abnormal pregnancy or injured baby."[25]

In addition, the trust encourages acceptance of the lower options by giving no hint of the amounts of money that may be available under option 3. In the context of option 1 at $725 and option 2, for most women, at less than $2,000, the newsletters refer vaguely to the possibility of "more money" at option 3. Consistent with this policy, if a woman chooses option 2 and submits medical records that show her to be entitled to greater compensation at option 3, her friends at the trust will not tell her as much; she will be paid the option 2 amount.[26] The necessary result is that a significant number of serious cases have been settled for nominal payments.

Consistent with Judge Merhige's position throughout the case, the trust has encouraged women to proceed without counsel by emphasizing that the involvement of counsel will not cause the trust to increase its offer of settlement. Some 150,000 of the 195,000 eligible claimants were unrepresented by counsel. Virtually all of the claimants who accepted option 1 and the great majority of those who accepted option 2 were unrepresented.[27]

It is true that, for some women, the cost of counsel would have been unjustified.[28] These include women for whom option 1 or option 2 was the correct choice and women who filed a fully documented claim under option 3 and whose best course was to accept the trust's offer of settlement. Many claimants, however, were disadvantaged by the absence of legal help, including women who could have qualified for compensation under option 3 but mistakenly filed under a lower option; women who filed under option 3 but failed to obtain and submit the necessary medical records or other documentation, such as affidavits from doctors that would correct gaps or explain ambiguities in the medical records; and women who would have been well advised not to accept the trust's option 3 settlement offer but to seek its modification, either by establishing through the settlement conference procedure that an error was made in the evaluation process or by seeking an independent determination through arbitration or trial.

The trust does not disclose its policies for the evaluation of claims filed under option 3. However, judging from offers it has made in response to option 3 claims, it appears that the trust discounts or disregards sworn statements submitted by claimants to overcome gaps in their medical records. For example, the plan of reorganization provides that under option 3 a woman whose medical records do not specify that her IUD was a Dalkon Shield may submit "an affidavit . . . stating that she used the Dalkon Shield and explaining the basis of this knowledge." This would imply, particularly in light of Judge Merhige's comments on the subject at the estimation hearing, that the requirement of proof of Dalkon Shield use can be fully met with a convincing affidavit. Yet it appears to be the policy of the trust to heavily discount the value of all claims in which medical records do not establish Dalkon Shield use, regardless of the credibility of the affidavit and the strength of the corroborating evidence.

Similarly, according to some reports, the trust has refused to pay more than nominal values in cases involving ectopic pregnancy or infertility where there is no medical documentation of pelvic infection associated with Dalkon Shield use. Presumably, the reason for the trust's decision on these claims is that the medical records do not prove that an infection related to use of the Dalkon Shield, rather than an unrelated infection, was the cause of the damage to the reproductive system that resulted in the ectopic pregnancy or infertility. In many cases, however, old medical records reflecting outpatient treatment of pelvic infections are unavailable. In others, women did not receive medical treatment because they did not identify a pelvic infection at the time it occurred ("silent PID") or attributed its symptoms to the pain or discomfort commonly associated with IUD use. The trust has not allowed (as a jury might) the missing link to be supplied by a sworn statement from the claimant describing symptoms of a treated or untreated pelvic infection during Dalkon Shield use or denying such symptoms at any other time.

The trust rapidly processes claims submitted under options 1 and 2, but it has been roundly criticized for its slow pace in processing option 3 claims. According to unofficial sources, by the end of 1990, the trust had issued settlement offers in approximately 1,100 claims filed under option 3. Some 18,000 option 3 cases were backed up for consideration, and many more were arriving every day. In a letter to counsel published in December 1990, in which she demanded "a modicum of patience," trust chairperson Georgene Vairo explained, "We are continuing to refine and streamline our claims process . . . The number of option 3 offers has steadily increased every month since the process began and will dramatically increase in a short time." Vairo refused, however, to reveal the specific number of option 3 claims processed by the trust because "[a]nnouncing our progress to date would mislead claimants into thinking that they will have to wait decades for payment which would be totally false, and would only cause claimants to panic."[29]

Under the most optimistic estimates the process of evaluating option 3 claims is scheduled to take at least through 1994. All claims must be submitted by July 1, 1991, so the bottleneck is at the trust. In 1990 the trust's investment income far exceeded its costs for resolving claims and operating expenses.[30] The problem is not money. Unquestionably, the process could be expedited by dramatically increasing the number of people involved in claims evaluation in the Richmond facility, or, if sufficient qualified employees were not available in Richmond, by contracting out some of the work or by establishing regional offices outside Richmond. The decision to organize the trust in a manner that will take five or more years from the consummation of the plan of reorganization to make offers on claims filed under option 3 suggests a greater interest in perpetuating the institution for those who benefit from its existence than in the expeditious resolution of the Dalkon Shield claims.[31]

Finally, there is the question of the trust's treatment of late claims. The plan of reorganization allows women to file late claims during the life of the trust, at a minimum for the purpose of sharing in any residual distribution after all timely claims are paid, but also with the right to request reclassification as a timely claimant under the "excusable neglect" provisions of the plan.[32] Inexplicably, in the spring of 1990, the trust announced that it would not accept any late claims filed after December 15, 1989, the date on which the plan was consummated. Following an angry letter from Stanley Joynes to the trustees, in which he threatened to sue them personally on behalf of future claimants, Judge Merhige ordered the trustees to continue to accept late claims.[33]

In the spring of 1990, the trust wrote to each of the some 35,000 women who had filed late claims advising them of their right to request reclassification of their claims. In August and December 1990, the trust submitted to the court its recommendations with respect to 10,220 requests that had been received. The trust recommended that 177 claimants be reclassified as timely because they had met the criteria in the plan relating to future claims that require reclassification (medical records showing the first manifestation of an injury related to the Dalkon Shield after the bar date, and lack of knowledge of the bar date or of the use of a Dalkon Shield–brand IUD). The trust recommended reclassification of 20 other claims, in which the claimant had established that the failure to file a timely claim was the fault of an attorney. The trust recommended that the other 10,023 requests for reclassification be denied.

Judge Merhige adopted the recommendations of the trust. He afforded those denied reclassification the opportunity to object and to seek review of the trust's decision but only if they presented themselves for hearing in Richmond.[34] More than 3,500 claimants filed objections, and the first set of hearings was held over the course of three days commencing October 19, 1990. Predictably, most of the objectors did not make the trip to Richmond and for that reason their objections were dismissed. During the hearings, it became clear that, apart from the 20 claims involving attorney error, the trust had automatically denied reclassification to every claimant who did not satisfy the criteria in the plan for mandatory reclassification. The trust had not exercised the intended discretion in the application of the excusable neglect standard. Accordingly, reclassification was denied to 21 women who proved a first manifestation of injury after the bar date but did not make the necessary attestation relative to lack of knowledge. In 151 other cases, the trust denied reclassification to women who had suffered or became aware of a major injury, such as ectopic pregnancy or infertility, after the bar date, for the reason that their medical records revealed minor symptoms, such as pain or bleeding, before the bar date. And reclassification was denied to thousands of women with pre–bar date injuries who swore that they had not been aware of the bar date. By April 1991, Judge Merhige had not ruled on the objections.[35]

22   Conclusion

Bankruptcy is the appropriate recourse when a business is unable, or can foresee that it will be unable, to pay the cost of mass tort liability. Novel and difficult questions are presented when the liabilities of a financially distressed business arise primarily out of personal injury claims, but no other mechanism is available and, with due regard for the exceptional context, these questions must be addressed and resolved within the bankruptcy system.

If, however, a company has the financial resources to withstand the cost of mass tort liability—if, for example, the Dalkon Shield had been manufactured by a company many times wealthier than Robins—a petition for reorganization would be an abuse of the bankruptcy process and an improper infringement of the rights of the personal injury claimants under nonbankruptcy law. This is true despite the burden and expense of defending and paying a large number of product liability claims all across the country, and despite the advantages to the defendant of establishing a mandatory claims resolution facility (particularly one with limited funding) for the liquidation and payment of all claims. Chapter 11 is not designed to ease the debt burden of financially secure businesses.

If reorganization procedures were available where there is no risk of financial distress, Chapter 11 would, in effect, constitute a general mandatory class action procedure for tort cases. Such an application of Chapter 11 would be unrelated to the purposes of the bankruptcy system and would conflict with the rule governing class actions in federal court. The aberration of *Breland v. Aetna* notwithstanding, the federal class action rule does not permit mandatory class actions in personal injury cases, except perhaps where the resources of the defendant are insufficient to pay all the claims (a circumstance that would qualify the defendant for bankruptcy). A persuasive case for a change in this rule has not been made. But if good grounds existed and the decision was made to allow a mandatory class action in federal court whenever there are numerous personal injury claims arising out of the same conduct, the place to make that change would be in the federal class action rule, not in federal bankruptcy law.

Early in the Robins bankruptcy, motions to dismiss were filed contending that Robins was able to meet its Dalkon Shield liability without reorganization and that it had entered Chapter 11 as a tactical maneuver after its other efforts to consolidate Dalkon Shield claims before Judge Merhige had proved unavailing. One of the motions to dismiss set forth information drawn from Robins's financial reports that the company's net operating profits exceeded its Dalkon Shield costs in every reporting period and that operating profits in the half year preceding the bankruptcy filing were at a record high.[1]

The motions to dismiss raised the important question of the legitimacy of Robins's need for reorganization and should have been heard and decided. Instead, Judge Merhige decided to duck this question, and to do this he imposed on the proponents of the motions the impossible, unnecessary, and inconsistent requirement of giving individual notice to each of the almost two hundred thousand women who by that time had responded to the bar date advertisements.[2]

This disposition was unfortunate because it fostered the widespread impression among plaintiffs' counsel that Judge Merhige had encouraged and was committed to protecting an illegitimate resort to Chapter 11. It was also unnecessary to the maintenance of the Chapter 11 case. The financial data on which the motion relied did not address the crucial question of Robins's ability to meet its future liabilities related to the Dalkon Shield. As the court held in denying a motion to dismiss in the *Johns-Manville* case, a business that can foresee insolvency is not required to wait until it is actually unable to pay its bills before petitioning for reorganization under Chapter 11.[3] Merhige would have had little difficulty addressing the issue and, on the basis of the perilous litigation situation facing Robins in the fall of the 1985 and beyond, concluding that the bankruptcy was proper.

The A. H. Robins Company entered Chapter 11 with the intention of creating a limited fund from which all Dalkon Shield claims would be paid and placing the value of the company in excess of the fund beyond the reach of the injured women. Initially, Robins assumed that it would continue as an independent company and that the excess value would take the form of the shareholders' continued ownership of the existing corporation. Later, when it appeared that Robins could not afford to finance an adequate fund and remain independent, the concept evolved; the excess value would take the form of stock issued to Robins's shareholders by an acquiring corporation. The basic idea, however, of a fixed fund for Dalkon Shield claims and the balance of the company's value vested in its shareholders never changed. Judge Merhige consistently supported this approach, and, by extending Robins's exclusivity period for the entire length of the proceeding, he precluded consideration of a plan that would first pay the debt and allow any excess value to vest in the shareholders only after that process was complete.

Any limited fund based on an estimate of the value of tens of thousands of unliquidated personal injury claims necessarily exposes the personal injury victims to the risk of underpayment. (If the fund constitutes a floor on the debtor's liability as well as a ceiling, as is the case in Robins's final plan of reorganization, there is also the possibility of overpayment. It is doubtful, however, that this is a gamble that personal injury claimants would want, if offered the choice of no more or less than full payment.) A limited fund is not necessary to preserve the economic value of the business, which is preserved when it is sold, or to avoid thousands of individual determinations of liability, which must occur in any event. Its principal purpose is to avoid delay in vesting the shareholders with what is assumed to be the value of the company in excess of its debt.[4] But a delay in ascertaining the interest of the shareholders is the consequence of the nature of the corporation's debt.[5] The shareholders have no interest unless the debts can be paid. That extended proceedings are required before the debts can be liquidated does not provide any reason for putting the creditors' right to absolute priority at risk.

The Bankruptcy Code does allow a class of creditors to waive its right under the absolute priority rule by voting to accept a plan of reorganization. But there are several reasons to doubt whether the lopsided vote in favor of Robins's plan constituted a proper measure of the will of the women whose claims had forced Robins into bankruptcy.

First, there are questions about the identity of the voters and the weight of their votes. By virtue of the bar date advertising and Judge Merhige's refusal to weight the votes in accordance with the value of the claims, women who would not have asserted claims against Robins outside of bankruptcy, and who in many cases had minor injuries or no injuries, controlled some 94 percent of the total voting strength within the class; the women who had filed or who could be expected to file claims against Robins outside of bankruptcy, most of whom had substantial injuries and large sums of money at stake, controlled 6 percent of the votes.[6] Judge Merhige found that it would be difficult or burdensome to weight the votes of the claimants in accordance with the value of their claims. A vote to accept a plan of reorganization by a class of impaired creditors constitutes an agreement to accept less than the law guarantees. If it is too difficult or too burdensome to conduct a vote that accords claimants a voice in that decision in proportion to the size of their claims, as required by the Bankruptcy Code, the appropriate conclusion is that there can be no effective waiver of the right to absolute priority, not that it can be waived under some lesser standard.

Second, the disclosure statement failed by a wide margin to provide the information necessary for the "informed suffrage which is at the heart of Chapter 11."[7] The Dalkon Shield claimants were told that the proposed trust fund exceeded Judge Merhige's estimate of the value of their claims, but they were denied any information that would provide a basis on which to make their own judgments on the adequacy of the trust fund to pay their claims.[8] In the absence of explanatory information, the statement of the total amount of the fund had no meaning whatsoever.

Third, Judge Merhige prevented the dissemination of any information or opinion in opposition to Robins's plan of reorganization. He accomplished this by refusing to make the names and addresses of the claimants available to independent voices on reasonable terms and by refusing to allow opponents of the plan to include a dissenting statement with the statements in support of the plan that were distributed to the claimants.[9] As a result, the claimants heard nothing other than endorsements of the plan.

If Robins's plan of reorganization had not been treated as accepted by the class of Dalkon Shield claimants, it is doubtful that the plan could properly have been crammed down based on Judge Merhige's estimate of the full value of the personal injury claims. In a cramdown, the court would have had to find that the plan would pay to each Dalkon Shield claimant "property of a value . . . equal to the allowed amount of [her] claim."[10]

One obstacle to a cramdown, apart from Judge Merhige's reluctance to explain his estimate, was the deficiencies in the factual record developed at the estimation hearing, particularly the failure to develop any evidence concerning the proportion of women who would participate in a claims resolution process notwithstanding their failure to participate in the McGovern process.[11] No court has ever addressed the proposition that the mandate to estimate unliquidated claims, contained in section 502(c) of the Bankruptcy Code, can be read to permit a value projected from an estimate of a sample of unliquidated claims to be used as the allowed amount of the universe of such claims for purposes of a cramdown. If it can, it would be essential that the evaluation of the claims in the sample be soundly based.

Another obstacle to a cramdown is the statutory guarantee of the right to a jury determination of the amount of a personal injury claim against a debtor in bankruptcy.[12] If there were a single unliquidated personal injury claim, a court could find that the holder is assured of full payment only if a plan provided sufficient funds to satisfy the highest verdict a jury would be permitted to return on that claim, that is, the amount above which a court would reduce a jury verdict as excessive. If the claim were estimated by the court at any lower level, then the value of the claim could be determined by the court and not by the jury in contravention of the jury trial right.

It follows that, if there can be a cramdown based on a group estimate of personal injury claims, the court would have to find at a minimum that the proposed plan provides sufficient funds to cover the cost of the settlements that could be expected in a context in which claimants have an untrammeled jury trial right, plus the cost of the potential judgments in the cases in which claimants could be expected to reject offers of settlement and go to trial. The manner in which the trust is operating under Judge Merhige's auspices, and particularly its holdback policy, makes plain that full payment of jury verdicts was not encompassed in the estimate, or even in the larger amount available under the plan of reorganization.[13]

The provisions eliminating the right of women injured by the Dalkon Shield to seek punitive damages constituted another obstacle to a cramdown of Robins's plan of reorganization. Demands for punitive damages are explicitly recognized in the Bankruptcy Code as a valid (although subordinated) component of a claim against the debtor; if this component is eliminated, the claim is not paid in full.[14] Judge Merhige issued a postconfirmation opinion in which he purported to disallow all claims for punitive damages on grounds other than the acceptance of the plan, but his reasons do not withstand scrutiny.[15] Merhige premised his analysis on the doubtful proposition that a bankruptcy court has the "equitable power" in a Chapter 11 case to disallow claims that would be enforceable outside of bankruptcy "if the Court determines that such [claims] would frustrate the successful reorganization of the Company."[16] He went on to assert that recognition of claims for punitive damages would destroy Robins's ability to reorganize both because punitive damage claims cannot be estimated and limited, and because the availability of punitive damages would threaten the rights of some claimants to recover compensatory damages.[17]

The first point assumes that Robins could not reorganize unless its liability for Dalkon Shield injuries was estimated and limited. A limitation on its liability is certainly what Robins wanted, but it was not necessary to a successful reorganization. Moreover, there is no reason why punitive damages could not have been estimated by reference to the prebankruptcy experience just as compensatory damages were. This could have been done, for example, by replicating the ratio of punitive damage awards to payments of compensatory damages before the bankruptcy ($20 million to $500 million, or 4 percent). Assuming the validity of Merhige's $2.475 billion estimate of compensatory damages, this would lead to an estimate of punitive damages of $95 million.

If the plan of reorganization provided that the fund for compensatory damages could not be used to satisfy punitive damage judgments, the existence of an additional fund for punitive damages could not threaten the right of any claimant to recover compensatory damages. To the contrary, in accordance with the policy of the Bankruptcy Code to subordinate punitive damage claims to compensatory damage claims, the fund for punitive damages could be retained until all claims had been liquidated and used to supplement the fund for compensatory damages, if necessary.[18] Far from jeopardizing full payment of compensatory damages, such an arrangement would increase the likelihood of full payment of compensatory damage claims.

If the punitive damages fund was not needed to pay compensatory damages, it could then be used to pay punitive damages awarded in jury trials, in full or pro rata, as appropriate. Alternatively, litigation over punitive damages could be precluded, as it was under the plan, and the amount estimated for punitive damages added to the general funds of the trust, to be distributed, with any other funds left in the trust, pro rata to all claimants. The point is that mechanisms were available to recognize claims for punitive damages consistent with a reorganization and with the superior right of all claimants to compensatory damages. There is certainly no provision in the code or any aspect of bankruptcy law or policy that suggests that claims that are valid and enforceable outside of bankruptcy should be extinguished simply to preserve value for the shareholders. If punitive damage liability were extinguished by a petition for reorganization, even when sufficient assets were available to pay these claims, there would be a strong incentive for the misuse of Chapter 11.[19]

The limitations on the recoveries of women injured by the Dalkon Shield that were occasioned by Robins's plan of reorganization were not the inevitable result of a Chapter 11 case arising out of mass tort liability. If the imperative of limiting Robins's liability and of paying the shareholders before liquidating and paying the Dalkon Shield claims had been put aside, a plan of reorganization could have been adopted that would have achieved a far closer approximation of the nonbankruptcy rights of all concerned. Such a plan would include the following provisions:

1. A bar date would only apply to women who had already filed suit against the company and who therefore could be personally notified. There would be no advertisements for claims.

2. Additional claims could be filed before or after confirmation of the plan of reorganization. The timeliness of these claims would be determined by the applicable nonbankruptcy statute of limitations.

3. On the basis of medical evidence concerning the latest date on which a Dalkon Shield injury could become manifest—evidence relating to the years of fertility of the youngest women who had worn the device—the plan of reorganization would establish a date, sometime in the mid-1990s, after which no further claims would be received or considered.

4. The businesses of the A. H. Robins Company would be sold in whatever form would produce the highest return.

5. The Dalkon Shield claimants would have the first call on the proceeds of the sale; the shareholders would have a remainder interest in those proceeds.

6. Dalkon Shield claimants would be required to submit their claims for possible settlement to a claimants' trust. The trustees would make offers to settle claims that were valid and timely based on comparable historic settlement values adjusted to present dollars. Claimants who did not accept an offer of settlement would be entitled to liquidate their claims in a jury trial against the trust. The normal rules governing such suits, including the right to seek punitive damages, would be unchanged, except that the applicable statute of limitations would be extended for the delay occasioned by the Chapter 11 case.

7. The trust would make projections relating to the sufficiency of the resources of the estate to pay all settlements and compensatory damage judgments in full. If there was any doubt whether full payments could be made, partial payments on a pro rata basis would be made without discrimination between settlements and judgments. Punitive damages would not be paid at this stage.

8. When the final cutoff date was reached and all claims had been liqui-

dated, the trust would pay any unpaid portion of settlements or compensatory damage judgments to the extent that there were sufficient resources in the estate to do so. If funds remained, punitive damages would be paid to the extent resources permitted.

9. Any remaining balance would be distributed to Robins shareholders. Alternatively, an interim distribution to shareholders could be made at the point it became clear that a portion of the proceeds from the sale of the corporation would not be needed to pay debt.

This plan would do exactly what a bankruptcy proceeding is intended to do: it would identify the women who had or would have made claims against Robins apart from the bankruptcy and would enable their claims to be paid to the extent available resources allowed. By not soliciting claims, it would not inflate the numbers of women seeking redress. This would reduce the delay in the disposition of the claims that were filed and would increase the likelihood that all claims would be paid in full. It could even result in the shareholders' realizing a greater return despite the delay in their distribution. The economic value of Robins's successful businesses would be preserved; only the owners would change.

Robins claimed in connection with its liquidation analysis that a sale of the company's assets would realize less than $2.3 billion (including cash and cash equivalents on hand). If that were true, this hypothetical plan of reorganization would produce less money to pay Dalkon Shield claims than the amount paid under Robins's actual plan of reorganization. Even in that event, the available funds would be directed to the injured women who actually had pressed claims against Robins, or could be expected to do so in the future, rather than diffused among a far larger group dominated by women whose claims were a product of the Chapter 11 case. But more to the point, no credible proof was presented at the confirmation hearing to support the assertion that a sale of Robins's assets would have attracted $1 billion less than the amount paid by American Home Products, and considering the intensity of the competition for the acquisition at prices in excess of $3 billion, it is unlikely that this is true.[20]

The focus of much of the opposition to Robins's plan of reorganization was the accompanying injunction prohibiting Dalkon Shield litigation against other potential defendants. The emphasis on this issue was a byproduct of the assignment of a large portion of Robins's value to its shareholders. If this money—ultimately amounting to more than $900 million—had been kept available to pay Dalkon Shield claims, there would have been far greater confidence that the trust could, in fact, pay all claims in full and correspondingly less concern for alternative or supplementary sources of recovery.

In addition, a substantial portion of the value diverted to the shareholders under Robins's plan of reorganization—nearly $385 million—was paid to the foremost potential individual defendants, E. Claiborne Robins, Sr. and Jr. If the right of Dalkon Shield claimants to sue third parties had not been extinguished, such suits would have provided a mechanism through which at least this portion of the shareholders' stake could have been reclaimed, as well as a means for holding the Robinses and other individuals responsible for their conduct.[21]

The prohibition of litigation against other potential defendants violated the spirit, if not the letter, of section 524(e) of the Bankruptcy Code, which provides that a "discharge of a debt of the debtor does not affect the liability of any other entity on . . . such debt." Indeed, the very purpose of the prevailing doctrine of "joint and several liability," by which all persons who participate in the wrongful conduct are independently liable to the injured party for the full amount of her damages, is to increase the likelihood that the victim will receive full recovery notwithstanding an inability to recover from one of the wrongdoers. Unless a plan of reorganization *guarantees* full payment of all claims, the abrogation of the liability of other wrongdoers because one is in bankruptcy denies this protection just when it is needed the most.

In December 1985, long before American Home Products was on the scene, Robins made clear that it would not agree to any plan of reorganization that did not include an injunction prohibiting litigation against individuals associated with the company. A prohibition to this effect was included in Robins's stand-alone plan filed in April 1987, its Rorer plan filed in August 1987, and its Sanofi plan filed in January 1988. Nevertheless, the prohibition against co-defendant litigation was defended and upheld on the ground that American Home Products insisted on it. American Home Products was said to be determined to avoid the distractions and the bad publicity generated by Dalkon Shield litigation.[22]

Its statement that it would not acquire Robins unless litigation against third parties was enjoined furthered American Home Products' goal of minimizing future Dalkon Shield litigation. It does not follow, however, that, if the court had declined to issue such an injunction, the acquisition would not have occurred. American Home Products' acquisition of Robins was described as the "steal of the century" by one drug industry analyst.[23] It was acclaimed throughout the financial community as a bonanza, providing a huge source of profits, a valuable distribution system, and tax benefits that will substantially reduce American Home Products' overall tax rate for years into the future.[24] Referring to Robitussin and Chapstick, an American Home Products executive said that "[f]ranchises that powerful come along only once every few decades."[25] The *Washington Post* explained that American Home Products had been able to purchase Robins at what it called "an extraordinary discount" because of its willingness to become involved "before all of [Robins's] legal difficulties were resolved."[26]

It is most unlikely that American Home Products would have given up this valuable acquisition merely because litigation against third parties could not be avoided. E. Claiborne Robins, Sr. and Jr., were terminated by American Home Products the day the acquisition was consummated. The other likely targets of litigation—McGuire, Woods & Battle, Hugh Davis, other former Robins officials—have no connection with American Home Products or its A. H. Robins subsidiary. Discovery against Robins had been concluded in the multidistrict proceeding before the bankruptcy; its product was available to all plaintiffs without seeking information from the successor corporation or its employees. And under the confirmed plan of reorganization, Dalkon Shield–related litigation against the trust is contemplated; under the settlement in *Breland*, the almost 3,000 class B members who opted out are permitted to bring suit against Aetna. There is no discernible difference with respect either to discovery demands or to adverse publicity between the litigation that is allowed and the litigation against third parties that is enjoined.

The remote possibility that American Home Products would have abandoned the deal if an injunction prohibiting third-party litigation had been refused by the court does not justify the issuance of the injunction. The courts cannot allow legal principles to be shaped by ultimatums from the litigants. With the Robins precedent, bankruptcy courts can expect many more instances in which plans of reorganization are conditioned by the debtor on an injunction immunizing its insiders from personal liability to the creditors.

If American Home Products had dropped out, Robins would have been sold to another buyer. It is possible, notwithstanding the positive evaluations of the American Home Products acquisition, that a substitute sale would have produced a lower price, as the proponents of the injunction contended. Even in that event, with proceeds from the American Home Products transaction more than $900 million in excess of the payment to creditors, there was an ample margin to assure that the funds available to pay Dalkon Shield claims would not be reduced.

Judge Merhige and the court of appeals adopted the best answer to a difficult question in deciding that claims for postpetition injuries attributable to past use of the Dalkon Shield were prepetition claims subject to disposition in bankruptcy. This interpretation is supported by the language of the Bankruptcy Code, and the apparent congressional intention to encompass in a bankruptcy proceeding all potential claims based on prepetition activity.[27] The treatment of future claims as prepetition claims avoids leaving future claimants without a remedy in liquidation cases, because provision for inchoate claims against the estate can be made when the assets are distributed. In reorganization cases, it avoids granting future claimants a better remedy than that accorded tort victims whose injuries preceded the bankruptcy. This interpretation also furthers the reorganization of the debtor corporation, whether through refinancing or a restructure of the equity interests, by permitting the separation of liability based on prepetition conduct from the going concern.

A distinct question relates to the provisions necessary to account for the unusual nature of future claims. During the first two years of the Chapter 11 case, Judge Merhige appeared to have adopted Robins's position that future claims were lost if not filed by the bar date. The idea that adequate notice of an obligation to file a claim by a fixed date can be afforded to persons without manifest injuries by advertisements in newspapers and on television is, as two courts have said, "absurd."[28] The right to seek damages for a wrongful injury is constitutionally protected by concepts of due process and cannot be extinguished on the basis of such a transparent fiction. Some provision must be made to pay future claims without reference to a bar date.

The direct way to handle the matter, assuming that a bar date is adopted for existing claims, is to specify that it is inapplicable to claims based on injuries that are manifest later than a reasonable time before the bar date and to make economic provision for these additional claims in constructing a plan of reorganization. Another route to the same end is to appoint a legal representative of future claimants and to treat a group claim filed by the representative before the bar date as satisfying the filing requirement for all future claimants. Stanley Joynes argued for both of these procedures in the Robins bankruptcy.

Conceptually, the least satisfying method of providing for the compensation of future claimants, but a method nonetheless, is for the court to reclassify late claims as timely claims on the ground of "excusable neglect" when the injury was manifest too late to expect compliance with the bar date. With important limitations, this is the approach adopted in the Robins bankruptcy. The plan of reorganization requires that claims from women whose injuries were first manifest after the bar date be treated as timely, but only if the claimant swears that she did not have knowledge of the bar date or that her IUD was a Dalkon Shield.[29]

This formulation has excluded many women with late-occurring injuries who cannot reasonably be held to compliance with the bar date, including uninjured women who did have knowledge of the bar date and of their use of the Dalkon Shield; women who first manifested an injury so soon before the bar date that it is unconscionable to insist on a timely filing; and women who experienced minor symptoms about which they did not choose to file a complaint before the bar date and then became aware of infertility or other major injury after the bar date.[30]

Apart from assuring that future claimants are eligible for compensation, funds must be provided for the payment of these claims. If a Chapter 11 case is to be resolved through the creation of a limited fund to pay personal injury claims, the size of the fund must be determined with reference to the amount necessary to pay future claims. This would require a finding by the court, based on competent epidemiologic evidence, of the expected number and the nature of future injuries, and of the cost of resolving them. In the Robins bankruptcy, no estimate was made of the value of unfiled future claims. As a result, future claims that are accepted as timely under the excusable neglect provision will be paid from the fund estimated and negotiated as adequate to pay pre–bar date claims. The cost will be borne by the other claimants rather than by the debtor.

A major shortcoming of the Robins bankruptcy was the failure prior to confirmation to provide funds for medical procedures designed to overcome infertility caused by the Dalkon Shield. Many women needlessly lost the opportunity to conceive because of the delay. The proponents of the emergency program approved by Judge Merhige demonstrated that preconfirmation payments for fertility procedures could be expected to reduce Robins's overall liability and were therefore justified as administrative expenses. The decision of the United States Court of Appeals for the Fourth Circuit overturning the program, of a piece with the performance of that court throughout the Chapter 11 case, failed even to mention this basis to sustain it.[31]

Even apart from the likelihood of reducing the liabilities of the estate, the pendency of a Chapter 11 case should not make impossible the disbursement of funds to treat or ameliorate personal injuries when it is highly probable that the beneficiaries will receive at least the amount of the payments in compensation for their injuries at the conclusion of the case. In 1988 Congress amended the Bankruptcy Code to authorize the payment of medical and disability benefits to retired employees during the course of a Chapter 11 case.[32] A similar amendment should be enacted to directly authorize the payment of urgent medical expenses of personal injury claimants against a Chapter 11 estate.

An irony of the court of appeals' perverse approach to preconfirmation disbursements for medical expenses is that the lawyers and other professionals officially retained in the case did not suffer under a similar handicap. In bankruptcy cases, the fees of attorneys and other professionals are paid from the assets of the estate and have priority over the claims of the creditors. The Bankruptcy Code specifically authorizes the bankruptcy judge to allow payments of fees to professionals during the course of the proceeding.[33] The payment of $27 million in interim fees to law firms during the course of the Robins bankruptcy provided an unseemly contrast with the inability of the system to find $15 million to pay for medical fertility procedures.

It was evident even before the Chapter 11 case was commenced that Judge Merhige concurred in Robins's basic goal of consolidating all Dalkon Shield injury claims under his control and of confining these claims to a limited fund fixed at a level that would salvage the shareholders' investment in the company. An unfortunate and ultimately discrediting characteristic of Merhige's management of the bankruptcy was that in the process of achieving this goal the judge's pattern was to preclude the effective presentation of opposing positions.

In part, Merhige did this by preventing those with a different agenda from participating in the proceeding. Most significant was the exclusion of Robins's natural adversary—the lawyers representing the injured women. This was accomplished initially by the dissolution of the first claimants' committee, and later by the exclusion of these lawyers from the prosecution of their clients' claims against Aetna, and even from participation in the hearing for the estimation of Robins's liability for Dalkon Shield injuries. Merhige initially believed that Murray Drabkin woud be "cooperative," as the judge likes to put it, but time proved him wrong, and after protecting Drabkin from discharge by his client, Merhige banished him as well as the trustees whose nominations he had sponsored. Merhige also stifled dissident voices by threats of contempt or other sanctions.[34]

In addition, Judge Merhige eviscerated unwelcome positions by preventing their proponents from acquiring the evidence necessary to support them, as in the cases of the challenge to the selection of the second claimants' committee and the opposition to the settlement of *Breland v. Aetna*. In other instances, Merhige simply refused to consider troublesome contentions (most significantly by preventing the submission of a plan of reorganization which would pay the Dalkon Shield claims before it paid the shareholders), ignored them (as in the case of the best interests requirement for plan confirmation), or, with respect to the validity of his estimate of the value of the Dalkon Shield claims, avoided scrutiny by failing to offer an explanation. Closely related was the judge's refusal to allow any opposition to Robins's plan of reorganization to be communicated to the Dalkon Shield claimants.

Conversely, Judge Merhige bestowed major roles (and compensated handsomely with funds provided by Robins, Aetna, or the claimants' trust) upon those who were prepared to carry out his wishes. The positions accorded Joseph Friedberg, Ralph Mabey, Michael Sheppard, and Georgene Vairo are cases in point.

The consequence of Merhige shuffling players in and out depending on the positions they would advocate and of his tight control over the issues that could be raised, together with extensive off-the-record activity by the judge, was that the case lacked the credibility of an adversarial proceeding. Many of the most important hearings in the case were little better than charades, as every knowledgeable observer understood that Merhige had orchestrated the presentation and that his decision was a foregone conclusion.

In the final analysis, what is most important to women injured by the Dalkon Shield about Judge Merhige's administration of the Robins bankruptcy and of the claimants' trust is the result: whether they will be compensated, how long it will take, and how much they will be paid.

As a consequence of publication of notice of the bar date, many more Dalkon Shield claimants will receive compensation than would have been the case if claims had not been solicited. To the extent that these women have suffered an injury attributable to the Dalkon Shield, this is a positive result of the procedure that was used, even though it is not within the focus of the bankruptcy system.

A negative result of the bar date procedure is that some women, particularly foreign women, who would have asserted claims against

Robins within the time periods established by nonbankruptcy law are not eligible claimants in the bankruptcy. There is no way to know how many of the more than 35,000 late claimants are in this category.

Some avenues of redress for these women were established after Robins reached an agreement with American Home Products in January 1988, because American Home Products was unwilling to accept the public relations implications of the exclusion of thousands of women with meritorious claims. Initially, American Home Products suggested abrogating the bar date entirely or extending it to the date of consummation, but Judge Merhige would not allow this. As an alternative, American Home Products reached the agreement with Aetna for outlier policies in the amount of $100 million, possibly augmented by any unused portions of the $250 million Aetna excess policy, directed to women who were not eligible claimants in the bankruptcy. A provision was also added to the plan of reorganization that entitles late claimants to be paid from any trust funds remaining after timely claims are paid. It has now been determined that the outlier insurance will not be adequate to pay late claims at the levels at which eligible claims are evaluated by the trust.[35] Whether spillover funds from the excess policy or trust funds will be available for this purpose is uncertain.

Although the Chapter 11 case undoubtedly seemed endless to women waiting for relief, judged by the standards of major reorganization cases, the case was handled relatively expeditiously in Judge Merhige's court. Merhige kept constant pressure on the attorneys and on the participants in the McGovern process to keep things moving, he refused to allow diversions from the central purpose of the proceeding, and he decided issues quickly, at least when it fit his strategy to do so.

The length of the delay in paying claims following consummation of the plan of reorganization varies widely. Women who filed claims before the bar date and who were willing to settle under options 1 or 2 have been paid quickly. The plan of reorganization requires the trust to accord priority to claims under option 3 filed by women who had sued Robins before the bankruptcy and by women who participated in the McGovern process. It is expected that the trust will make offers to these women by the end of 1991, two years after consummation. For women who reject the trust's offer, trial or arbitration will take much longer, and, if they are successful in obtaining an award above the offer of the trust, full payment, if it ever comes, will take longer still.

The trust has organized itself in such a manner that it will take at least through 1994 to evaluate and make offers on the balance of the option 3 claims. Here again, a refusal to accept the trust's offer could result in a much longer delay.

The funds available to pay Dalkon Shield claims are far greater than anyone expected when the bankruptcy began. The escalation from the $600 million or less paid over time initially contemplated by Robins to the $2,335 million cash plus $350 million in insurance finally provided is attributable to a series of factors: the staggering response to the bar date notice; Judge Merhige's refusal to allow Robins to file a plan in September 1986 calling for payments of $700,000 over several years; American Home Products' initial negotiations with Murray Drabkin in February 1987, which, despite American Home Products' quick withdrawal, had the effect of creating a floor of $1.75 billion on any trust fund; Drabkin's decision to oppose both the Robins stand-alone plan and the Rorer plan, despite their use of the $1.75 billion figure, and to propose a far larger fund in connection with the estimation hearing; Aetna's decision to submit an estimate of $2.5 billion, which effectively created a new floor and precluded a significantly lower estimate; Drabkin's insistence that the amount of Merhige's estimate, or nearly all of it, be paid in cash upon consummation of the plan of reorganization, not "over a reasonable period of time," as Merhige intended; and American Home Products' decision to use Aetna insurance not as a component of its bid but as protection against any shortfall in funds and as a mechanism to provide for ineligible claimants.

The structure of Robins's final plan of reorganization, by which the entire amount of the trust fund was paid at the outset and the universe of eligible claimants is relatively fixed, avoids the major problems of inadequate cash flow and uncertain claim volume that contributed to the difficulties experienced by the trust established in the Johns-Manville bankruptcy. Whether the funds paid to the Dalkon Shield claimants' trust will be large enough to pay all eligible claims at nonbankruptcy values is not only unknown; it will probably never be known. Most of the claims would not and, as a practical matter, could not have been asserted outside of bankruptcy, and for these there is no nonbankruptcy value. With respect to the more serious claims that will be processed under option 3, the trust will unilaterally determine "full value" in a manner that guarantees that the available funds will be sufficient, whether or not the offers in particular cases actually match what would have been paid if there had been no bankruptcy. The trust fund could prove inadequate, in the practical sense of not having enough money to pay the liquidated values of all of the claims, only if a significant number of claimants reject the trust's settlement offers and go to court. This would cause the trust to spend substantial amounts in the defense of these cases and could result in judgments far larger than the settlement offers. The disincentives to litigation created by the trust, particularly the holdback policy, make this most unlikely. The right of women with serious injuries to be paid in accordance with a jury determination of the value of their claims—a right guaranteed by the language of the plan of reorganization and by federal law—has been undermined in favor of a system designed to allocate a fixed fund among a far larger number of claims without the intrusion of independent evaluations.

Notes

Chapter 1

1. This introductory chapter draws on information contained in three excellent books that were written before the Robins bankruptcy concerning the development and marketing of the Dalkon Shield and the prebankruptcy litigation: Morton Mintz, *At Any Cost* (Pantheon 1985), Susan Perry and Jim Dawson, *Nightmare* (Macmillan 1985), Sheldon Engelmayer and Robert Wagman, *Lord's Justice* (Anchor Press Doubleday 1985).

2. *American Journal of Obstetrics and Gynecology*, February 1, 1970, p. 455.

3. Senate Select Committee on Small Business, Subcommittee on Monopoly, Competitive Problems in the Drug Industry, 91st Cong., 2d sess., pt. 15, pp. 5924–26 (January 14, 1970).

4. Id. at 5941.

5. The Food, Drug and Cosmetic Act was amended in 1976, largely as a result of the experience with the Dalkon Shield, to require FDA approval of intrauterine devices and other medical devices before they can be sold. Medical Device Amendments of 1976, 90 Stat. 540, 21 U.S.C. 360(d).

6. C. Donald Christian, "Maternal Deaths Associated with an Intrauterine Device," *American Journal of Obstetrics and Gynecology*, June 15, 1974, p. 19.

7. Howard J. Tatum, "The Dalkon Shield Controversy: Structural and Bacteriological Studies of IUD Tails," *Journal of the American Medical Association*, February 1975.

8. Roger L. Tuttle, "The Dalkon Shield Disaster Ten Years Later—A Historical Perspective," 54 *Okla. Bar Journal* 2501 (1983).

9. See 28 U.S.C. § 1407.

10. Janet Bamford, "The Dalkon Shield Starts Losing in Court," *American Lawyer*, July 1980, p. 31.

11. It has been suggested that the immediate stimulus for the letter was the preparation by CBS's "60 Minutes" of a segment highly critical of A. H. Robins and the Dalkon Shield. Perry and Dawson, *Nightmare, supra* n. 1 at 184. The report was aired on April 19, 1981.

12. The phrase "toughing it out" is Morton Mintz's categorization of Robins's defense strategy. *At Any Cost, supra* n. 1 at 173.

13. The name of the firm is now Robins, Kaplan, Miller & Ciresi.

14. *Reserve Mining Co. v. Lord*, 529 F. 2d 181, 185 (8th Cir. 1976).

15. The matter was assigned docket no. 83P-0139. The FDA did not act until

October 1986, when Dr. Frank Young, commissioner of food and drugs, denied the petition on the ground that the removal campaign undertaken by Robins in the fall of 1984 made the relief requested unnecessary.

16. *Gardiner v. A. H. Robins Co.,* 747 F. 2d 1180 (8th Cir. 1984).

17. Tuttle, *supra* n. 8.

Chapter 2

1. Shortly thereafter, some one hundred additional cases brought against Robins in Minnesota by non-Minnesota plaintiffs were transferred to Richmond by consent. The attorneys in those cases, John Cochrane and Ronald Meshbesher, allied themselves with Friedberg in processing those cases and in the class action litigation against Robins and Aetna that followed.

2. Emily Couric, "Judge Robert R. Merhige, Jr.," 8 *National Law Journal* 1, 21 (August 4, 1986).

3. See Ronald J. Bacigal and Margaret I. Bacigal, "A Case Study of the Federal Judiciary's Role in Court-ordered Busing: The Professional and Personal Experiences of U.S. District Judge Robert R. Merhige, Jr.," 3 *Journal of Law and Politics* 693 (1987). Ronald Bacigal, a professor at the University of Richmond Law School, is writing an "authorized biography" of Judge Merhige and has published several articles about various aspects of Judge Merhige's work. See nn. 24, 36. Professor Bacigal recently published an overview of the Dalkon Shield litigation with emphasis on Judge Merhige's role. *The Limits of Litigation* (Carolina Academic Press 1990).

4. 347 U.S. 483 (1954), 349 U.S. 294 (1955).

5. *Green v. School Board of New Kent County,* 391 U.S. 430, 437–38 (1968).

6. *Alexander v. Holmes County Board of Education,* 396 U.S. 19, 20 (1969).

7. On December 13, 1969, the Supreme Court granted a petition for a writ of certiorari to review the decision of the court of appeals and ordered the defendant school boards to prepare to implement unitary systems at the beginning of the spring semester. *Carter v. West Feliciana School Board,* 396 U.S. 226 (December 13, 1969). On January 14, 1970, the Supreme Court reversed the decision of the Fifth Circuit and ordered that the unitary systems be immediately implemented. *Carter v. West Feliciana School Board,* 396 U.S. 290 (1970).

8. *Bradley v. School Board of the City of Richmond,* 317 F. Supp. 555 (E.D. Va. 1970). See also 315 F. Supp. 326 (E.D. Va. 1970).

9. *Bradley v. Richmond City School Board,* 324 F. Supp. 456, 457 (E.D. Va. 1971). See also *Richmond Times-Dispatch,* January 9, 1971, p. A1, January 16, 1971, p. A1. Merhige was referring to *Swann v. Charlotte-Mecklenburg Board of Education,* decided in April 1971, in which the Court upheld mandatory bussing ordered by Judge James McMillan in North Carolina. 402 U.S. 1.

10. *Richmond Times-Dispatch,* January 5, 1971, p. B1.

11. Judge Merhige's letter is reprinted in *Bradley v. School Board of City of Richmond*, 324 F. Supp. 439, 451 (E.D. Va. 1971).

12. *Bradley v. School Board of the City of Richmond*, 325 F. Supp. 828 (E.D. Va. 1971); *Richmond Times-Dispatch*, May 11, 1971, p. A1.

13. *Bradley v. School Board of the City of Richmond*, 324 F. Supp. 439, 448 (E.D. Va. 1971).

14. *Bradley v. School Board of the City of Richmond*, 338 F. Supp. 67 (E.D. Va. 1972).

15. *Richmond Times-Dispatch*, January 11, 1972, p. A14.

16. Id. at A5.

17. *New York Times*, January 11, 1972, p. 1, col. 8.

18. *New York Times*, January 13, 1972, p. 41, col. 1.

19. *Richmond Times-Dispatch*, January 20, 1972, A2.

20. *Bradley v. School Board of the City of Richmond*, 462 F. 2d 1058 (4th Cir. 1972).

21. Id. at 1066.

22. *Bradley v. School Board of the City of Richmond*, 412 U.S. 92 (1973).

23. *Milliken v. Bradley*, 418 U.S. 717 (1974).

24. *Dabney v. Cunningham*, 317 F. Supp. 57 (E.D. Va. 1970); *Landman v. Royster*, 333 F. Supp. 621 (E.D. Va. 1971). The Supreme Court did not approve Eighth Amendment limitations on conditions in state prisons until *Estelle v. Gamble*, 429 U.S. 97 (1976), and *Hutto v. Finney*, 437 U.S. 178 (1978). See generally, Ronald J. Bacigal, "Annals of the Prisoners' Rights Movement: The Contributions of Judge Merhige," 24 *Criminal Law Bulletin* 521 (1988).

25. *Landman v. Royster*, 333 F. Supp. 621 (E.D. Va. 1971); *New York Times*, November 1, 1971, p. 1, col. 3.

26. *Landman v. Royster*, 354 F. Supp. 1292, 1304 (E.D. Va. 1973); *New York Times*, February 2, 1973, p. 7, col. 1.

27. *New York Times*, October 6, 1976, pp. 1, 17, col. 1.

28. *Fortune*, September 11, 1978, p. 18.

29. *Washington Post*, February 2, 1977, p. B1.

30. *Richmond Times-Dispatch*, February 2, 1977, A1, col. 2.

31. Virginia Environmental Endowment, *1985 Annual Report*, p. 6.

32. University of Richmond, "Connections," vol. 6, no. 3 (Summer 1986).

33. On Merhige's background, see *Who's Who in America*, p. 1917 (44th ed. 1986–87); B. D. Johnson, ed., I *Almanac of the Federal Judiciary*, pp. 28–30 (Lawletters, Inc., 1989); Ray McAllister, "Trying Times, Trying Cases," *ABA Journal*, January 1, 1988, pp. 48–52; Stephen Labaton, "A Case to Cap Controversial Career," *New York Times*, July 3, 1988, § 4, p. 4, col. 3; *Richmond Times-Dispatch*, January 8, 1967, p. B1, July 18, 1967, p. B1.

34. See *Richmond Times-Dispatch*, January 8, 1967, p. B1, January 12, 1967, p. B3, June 7, 1967, p. A1, July 18, 1967, p. A1.

35. *Richmond Times-Dispatch*, August 31, 1967, p. B1.

36. See Couric, *supra* n. 2; Larry Lempert, "Judge Shows Knack for 'Just

Getting Parties Talking,'" *Legal Times of Washington*, August 10, 1981, p. 6; Merhige, *The Role of the Judge in the Settlement Process*, 75 F.R.D. 203, 212 (1977); McAllister, *supra* n. 33; Christopher T. Lutz, "Interview with Robert R. Merhige, Jr., 12 *Litigation* 10 (1988); Ronald J. Bacigal, "An Empirical Case Study on Informal Dispute Resolution," 4 *Ohio State Journal of Dispute Resolution* 1 (1988).

37. Lutz, *supra* n. 36 at 14.

38. Bacigal, *supra* n. 36 at 23.

39. An account of this litigation is set forth in Bacigal, *supra* n. 36.

40. *In re Westinghouse Elec. Corp., Uranium Contracts Litig.*, 405 F. Supp. 316, 319 (1975).

41. Merhige, *supra* n. 36 at 213.

42. *Richmond Times-Dispatch*, June 4, 1978, p. F1, col. 1. See *Washington Post*, June 3, 1978, p. D8, col. 3.

43. E. Allan Farnsworth and William F. Young, *Cases and Materials on Contracts* 981, n. 6 (3d ed. 1980); Bacigal, *supra* n. 36 at 23; *Washington Post*, October 28, 1978, p. D8, col. 5. Merhige did not issue a written decision. Three years later, he did write a decision on similar facts and issues on an unresolved claim in one of the cases in the original group. See *In re Westinghouse Elec. Corp., Uranium Contracts Litig.*, 517 F. Supp. 440 (E.D. Va. 1981).

44. Bacigal, *supra* n. 36 at 27.

45. Id. at 23.

46. Id. at 26.

47. Id. at 23–25.

48. *Wall Street Journal*, October 3, 1979, p. 21, col. 1.

49. *New York Times*, August 2, 1979, p. D2.

50. 125 *Congressional Record* 30751–53 (November 2, 1979).

51. Jack Anderson, "Judge Has Ties to Defendant Bagley," *Washington Post*, November 5, 1979, p. B13, col. 4. See Jack Anderson, "Judge Incenses Bagley Prosecutors," *Washington Post*, November 6, 1979, p. B15, col. 4. See also *Washington Post*, November 2, 1979, p. A4, col. 1.

52. 125 *Congressional Record* 30751–53 (November 2, 1979); id. at 31061–63 (November 6, 1979).

53. James B. Stewart, *The Partners* 168 (Simon & Schuster 1983).

54. *Report of the Special Committee of the Bar Association of the City of Richmond, Re: Judge's Conduct of Trial in United States v. Smith W. Bagley, et al.*, pp. 4–5 (December 12, 1979).

55. *In re A. H. Robins Co.*, Transcript, March 14, 1986, p. 39.

56. Transcript, July 7, 1988, p. 3.

57. McAllister, *supra* n. 33 at 48, 51.

58. *New York Times*, July 3, 1988, § 4, p. 4.

59. The claim that successive awards of punitive damages violate due process of law has generally been rejected. E.g., *Leonen v. Johns-Manville Corp.*, 717 F. Supp. 272 (D.N.J. 1989) (Fisher, J.); *Jackson v. Johns-Manville Sales*

Corp., 781 F. 2d 394 (5th Cir. 1986) (en banc); *Cathey v. Johns-Manville Sales Corp.*, 776 F. 2d 1565 (6th Cir. 1985); *Celotex Corp. v. Pickett*, 459 So. 2d 375 (Fla. App. 1984); *State ex. rel. Young v. Crookham*, 290 Ore. 61, 618 P. 2d 1268 (1980). These courts reasoned that the prior awards of punitive damages can be taken into account by the jury in the present case in deciding whether another award of punitive damages is appropriate, or by the court in determining whether an award of punitive damages is excessive. See also *Restatement, Torts (Second)*, § 908, comment e (1979).

In March 1989, Judge Lee Sarokin, a federal district judge in New Jersey, held that due process of law prohibits the imposition of repeated awards of punitive damages, and ruled that he would dismiss a claim for punitive damages if the defendant could show that it had already paid a punitive damage award based on the same conduct. *Juzwin v. Amtorg Trading Corp.*, 705 F. Supp. 1053. A few months later, Judge Sarokin vacated his own decision. He adhered to the view that successive punitive damages awards raise due process issues but concluded that the problem could not be properly addressed by automatically denying punitive damages if there had been any such award in the past. 718 F. Supp. 1233 (D.N.J. September 5, 1989).

This issue has not been addressed by the Supreme Court of the United States. The Court did recently hold that the Eighth Amendment's prohibition of cruel and unusual punishment does not apply to punitive damages awarded in suits between private parties. *Browning-Ferris Inds. v. Kelco Disposal, Inc.*, 109 S. Ct. 2909 (1989). And, in March 1991, the Court rejected the contention that an award of punitive damages violated due process because of the absence of standards to guide the jury. *Pacific Mutual Life Ins. Co. v. Haslip*, 59 U.S.L. Week 4157.

60. See cases cited in chap. 18, n. 1.

61. Rule 23(b)(1)(B).

62. Notes of Advisory Committee on Rule 23(b)(1)(B) (1966).

63. Judge Jack B. Weinstein certified a mandatory class action limited to claims for punitive damages on the basis of a limited fund theory in the *Agent Orange* litigation in New York. *In re "Agent Orange" Product Liability Litigation*, 100 F.R.D. 718, 724–28 (E.D. N.Y. 1983), mandamus denied sub nom., 725 F. 2d 858 (2d Cir.), cert. denied, 465 U.S. 1067 (1984). Judge Weinstein did not find that there was a likelihood that punitive damage awards would exceed the resources of the defendants. Instead, he found that the courts were likely to limit the award of punitive damages out of fairness to the defendants so that, as far as the plaintiffs were concerned, there was a limited fund. The court of appeals in that case did not review this decision.

In late 1990, Judge Weinstein, relying on the limited fund theory, conditionally certified mandatory class actions on all claims in asbestos-related personal injury litigation against the trust established in the Johns-Manville chapter 11 case (discussed in chap. 3, nn. 29–33, and accompanying text) and against Eagle-Picher Industries, Inc. See 59 U.S.L. Week 2381 (November 30,

1990) (Manville trust) and *Wall Street Journal*, December 11, 1990, p. B4, col. 6 (Eagle-Picher). The certification in the Eagle-Picher case was immediately appealed, but the class proceeding was effectively mooted when the company petitioned for reorganization in bankruptcy several weeks later. *Wall Street Journal*, January 8, 1991, p. A3, col. 3.

Other courts have recognized the possibility that the limited fund theory could justify a mandatory class action in a personal injury case, but Judge Weinstein's decisions are the only reported instances, not reversed on appeal, in which this was done. In the following cases, courts of appeals reversed lower-court decisions certifying a mandatory class on the ground that the existence of a limited fund had not been established. *In re Temple*, 851 F. 2d 1269 (11th Cir. 1988); *In re Benendectin Products Liability Litigation*, 749 F. 2d 300, 305–7 (6th Cir. 1984); *In re School Asbestos Litigation*, 789 F. 2d 996, 1002–6 (3d Cir. 1986); *In re: Northern District of California "Dalkon Shield" IUD Products Liability Litigation*, 521 F. Supp. 1188, 526 F. Supp. 887 (N.D. Calif. 1981), rev'd, 693 F. 2d 847 (9th Cir. 1982), cert. denied, 103 S. Ct. 817 (1983).

64. *In re: Northern District of California "Dalkon Shield" IUD Products Liability Litigation*, 521 F. Supp. 1188, 526 F. Supp. 887 (N.D. Calif. 1981), rev'd, 693 F. 2d 847 (9th Cir. 1982), cert. denied, 103 S. Ct. 817 (1983).

65. 28 U.S.C. § 1407(a).

66. See 28 U.S.C. § 1404; rule 11(b) of the Rules of the Judicial Panel on Multidistrict Litigation.

67. The decision of the United States Court of Appeals for the Tenth Circuit is not reported. On June 10, 1985, the Supreme Court denied the company's petition for review of the Tenth Circuit decision. 472 U.S. 1008 (1985).

68. *In re A. H. Robins Co., "Dalkon Shield" Products Liability Litigation*, 107 F.R.D. 2 (1985).

69. Affidavit of Joseph S. Friedberg, March 6, 1986, docket no. 740, paras. 19 and 20 (hereafter "Friedberg affidavit").

70. Friedberg affidavit, para. 21.

71. Affidavit of Robert Manchester, February 12, 1986, attached to docket no. 695, para. 5. The affidavit was filed in support of a motion to disqualify Judge Merhige, which is discussed in chap. 5, nn. 9–12, and accompanying text.

72. Friedberg affidavit, para. 28; transcript, March 13, 1986, p. 37.

73. Friedberg affidavit, paras. 29, 39–40.

74. *In re Dalkon Shield Punitive Damages Litigation*, 613 F. Supp. 1112 (E.D. Va. 1985).

75. Id. at 1119.

76. *Richmond Times-Dispatch*, July 25, 1985, p. A1.

77. *Wall Street Journal*, July 25, 1985, p. 3, col. 2.

78. Transcript, March 14, 1986, p. 13.

79. Id. at 14.

80. See nn. 61–63, *supra*, and accompanying text.

81. Transcript, March 14, 1986, p. 17.

82. Transcript, March 14, 1986, pp. 17–18, 21; transcript, August 9, 1985, p. 3.

83. "Re: Dalkon Shield Cases Pending in the District of Massachusetts," p. 2 (D. Mass. August 7, 1985). In this order, Judge Skinner requested counsel in the Dalkon Shield cases pending in his court to "show cause" why the cases should not be transferred to Richmond.

84. By August 21, 1985, 9,500 cases had been resolved at a cost to Aetna and Robins of $530 million. A. H. Robins Co., *Annual Report*, 1986, p. 18; A. H. Robins Co., "Sixth Amended and Restated Disclosure Statement," p. 16 (March 28, 1988); Affidavit of Arvid Johnson, para. 10 (October 31, 1987), attached to docket no. PT 51.

85. *Wall Street Journal,* August 22, 1985, p. 3, col. 1.

86. *Richmond Times-Dispatch,* August 22, 1985, p. A1, col. 5.

87. Transcript, August 22, 1985, pp. 14–17.

Chapter 3

1. In the case of individual debtors, certain assets are exempted from the process. See 11 U.S.C. § 522.

2. 11 U.S.C. §§ 506, 507, 726.

3. 11 U.S.C. § 727.

4. 11 U.S.C. § 362.

5. Rules 2002(a)(8) and 3003(c), *Rules of Bankruptcy Procedure.*

6. 11 U.S.C. §§ 549, 365.

7. 11 U.S.C. § 547(b), (c).

8. See Thomas H. Jackson, *The Logic and Limits of Bankruptcy Law*, pp. 21–27 (Harvard 1986).

9. *Butner v. United States,* 440 U.S. 48, 54–55 (1979).

10. See chap. 2, n. 59.

11. Act of March 3, 1933, chap. 204, § 77, 47 Stat. 1467, 1474–82; Act of June 7, 1934, chap. 424, § 77B, 48 Stat. 912–22; Chandler Act, Pub. L. no. 75-696, 52 Stat. 840, 883 (1938). See *Case v. Los Angeles Lumber Co.,* 308 U.S. 106 (1939); Peter F. Coogan, "Confirmation of a Plan under the Bankruptcy Code," 32 *Case W. Res. L. Rev.* 301, 309–26 (1982).

12. By contrast, efforts at the reorganization of small, privately owned firms are usually unsuccessful. Typically, the shareholders are the managers, no one else wants the stock, and it is unclear whether the business would be economically viable even if some disposition could be made of the existing debt. The effort to reorganize in these circumstances often merely postpones an inevitable business failure.

13. 11 U.S.C. §§ 1101, 1107, 1108, 1123(a)(5)(D). A Chapter 7 Trustee, with the approval of the court, may "operate the business of the debtor for a limited period" if a sale of the going concern would maximize the value of the estate, and can even employ existing management to assist in doing so, but the

presumption under Chapter 7 is a rapid liquidation. See 11 U.S.C. §§ 704(1), 721.

14. The economic validity of the assumption that a publicly held business can be worth more than the price for which it can be sold is questionable. See Jackson, *supra* n. 8 at 218–24; Douglas G. Baird, "The Uneasy Case for Corporate Reorganizations," 15 *Journal of Legal Studies* 127, 138 ff. (1986).

15. 11 U.S.C. § 1129(a)(8).

16. 11 U.S.C. § 1121.

17. Report of the Committee on the Judiciary, House of Representatives, to accompany H.R. 8200, H.R. Rep. no. 95-595, 95th Cong., 1st Sess., pp. 231–32 (1977); *U.S. Code Cong. & Admin. News*, 1978, p. 6191. See *In re Timbers of Inwood Forest Associates, Ltd.*, 808 F. 2d 363, 372 (5th Cir. 1987), aff'd, 108 S. Ct. 626 (1988); *In re Public Service Co. of New Hampshire*, 88 B.R. 521, 533–37 (Bankr. D.N.H. 1988).

18. *In re Texaco Inc.*, 84 B.R. 893, 894 (Bankr. S.D. N.Y. 1988).

19. 11 U.S.C. § 1129(b).

20. 11 U.S.C. §§ 503, 507(a)(1).

21. Declaration of G. E. R. Stiles, p. 14 (August 21, 1985).

22. A. H. Robins Company, Incorporated, SEC Form 10Q for Quarter Ended June 30, 1988, p. 2 (August 11, 1988).

23. In order to eliminate "the strategic uses of current Chapter 11 practice," Professors Baird and Jackson have suggested prohibiting publicly held corporations from reorganizing under Chapter 11. They propose instead that the corporation be sold, without its liabilities, through a public offering or to a third party, and that the proceeds be distributed in accordance with the entitlements and priorities set forth in the Bankruptcy Code. Douglas G. Baird and Thomas H. Jackson, "Corporate Reorganizations and the Treatment of Diverse Ownership Interests," 51 *U. Chi. L. Rev.* 97, 125, n. 86 (1984). See also Jackson, *supra* n. 8 at 209–24; Baird, *supra* n. 14 at 127; Mark J. Roe, "Bankruptcy and Debt: A New Model for Corporate Reorganization," 83 *Colum. L. Rev.* 527 (1983).

24. 11 U.S.C. §§ 1125, 1126. The creditors may be divided into two or more classes for purposes of voting on a plan of reorganization on the basis of the similarity of their interests. 11 U.S.C. § 1122.

25. 11 U.S.C. § 1129(a)(7)(A)(ii).

26. 11 U.S.C. § 1141(d).

27. 11 U.S.C. § 1112(b)(2), (5).

28. Among the discussions of these issues in legal journals are Mark J. Roe, "Bankruptcy and Mass Tort," 84 *Colum. L. Rev.* 846 (1984); Note, "The Manville Bankruptcy: Treating Mass Tort Claims in Chapter 11 Proceedings," 96 *Harv. L. Rev.* 1121 (1983); Gregory A. Bibler, "The Status of Unaccrued Tort Claims in Chapter 11 Proceedings," 61 *Am. Bankr. L. J.* 145 (1987); Harvey J. Kesner, "Future Asbestos Related Litigants," 62 *Am. Bankr. L. J.* 69, 159 (1988).

29. See *In re Johns-Manville Corporation*, 68 Bankr. 618 (Bankr. S.D. N.Y.

1986), aff'd, 837 F. 2d 89 (2d Cir.), cert. denied, 109 S. Ct. 176 (1988). Others are *UNR Industries*, 725 F. 2d 1111 (7th Cir. 1984); *In re Amatex, Inc.*, 755 F. 2d 1034 (3d Cir. 1985); and *Eagle-Picher Industries, Inc., Wall Street Journal*, January 8, 1991, p. A3, col. 3.

30. *In re Johns-Manville Corp.*, 68 Bankr. 618, 622 (Bankr. S.D. N.Y. 1986) (Lifland, J.).

31. This situation was blamed on several factors: many more claims were filed with the trust than had been anticipated, and the trust was settling claims at a faster rate and for a higher average value than had been anticipated. In a large number of cases, settlement was not achieved and the trust was named as a defendant in litigation. This required the trust to spend substantial amounts for attorney fees. See *New York Times*, June 2, 1990, p. 1, col. 1; June 11, 1990, p. D2, col. 1; July 8, 1990, § 3, p. 1.

32. *Washington Post*, July 10, 1990, p. D1, col. 6. Judge Weinstein handled the mass tort litigation involving Agent Orange, the chemical defoliant used by the United States Army in Vietnam. See Peter H. Schuck, *Agent Orange on Trial* (Harvard 1986).

33. *Wall St. Journal*, November 20, 1990, p. A4, col. 3; *New York Times*, November 20, 1990, p. D1, col. 3. In addition to these funds, the proposal would allow the trust to raise other cash in the near term by dividing and selling a $1.8 billion bond originally issued by Manville to secure its obligation to pay $75 million to the trust for twenty-four years. The proposal also calls for basic changes in the administration of the trust, including the preclusion of individual litigation against the trust in favor of a class action settlement, priority payments to claimants with the most serious diseases (instead of the payment of claims in the order in which they were filed), and the partial payment of claims until the ability of the trust to make larger payments is determined. To facilitate this arrangement, on November 30, 1990, Judge Weinstein conditionally certified a mandatory class action against the trust on a limited fund theory, and enjoined all independent litigation against the trust. See *In re Joint Eastern and Southern Districts Asbestos Litigation*, 59 U.S.L. Week 2381; chap. 2, nn. 61–63, and accompanying text.

Chapter 4

1. 28 U.S.C. § 1334(a).
2. 28 U.S.C. § 157(a).
3. Transcript, March 14, 1986, pp. 23–24.
4. 28 U.S.C. § 157(b)(2)(B).
5. This distinction was recognized by the United States Court of Appeals for the Fourth Circuit in connection with the Robins bankruptcy:

The statute denies authority to the bankruptcy court to "estimate" contingent claims only if the purpose is to make a "distribution" of the assets of the debtor; the statute does not in express terms deny to the bankruptcy court the authority, or relieve it of the duty, to "estimate" the contingent "personal injury" claims for purposes of determining the feasibility of a reorganization . . . *Roberts v. Johns-Manville Corp.*, 45 B.R. 823, 825–26 (S.D. N.Y. 1984); *In re UNR Industries, Inc.*, 45 B.R. 322, 326–27 (N.D. Ill. 1984.) Both of these cases hold that estimations of the debtors' potential personal injury tort liabilities as an incident of the development of a plan of reorganization are core proceedings within the bankruptcy court's jurisdiction.

A. H. Robins Co. v. Piccinin, 788 F. 2d 994, 1012 (4th Cir.), cert. denied, 479 U.S. 876 (1986).

6. See 28 U.S.C. 157(b).

7. *New York Times*, July 3, 1988, § 4, p. 4.

8. Transcript, July 18, 1985, p. 12.

9. *A. H. Robins Co. v. Campbell*, Adv. Proc. 85-1006A, transcript of oral findings from the bench, October 9, 1985, p. 3.

10. *A. H. Robins v. Piccinin, supra* n. 5.

11. See chap. 15 text at nn. 12–15; chap. 19 text at nn. 8, 18, 34.

12. Public Law 98-353, Title I, § 102(a), 28 U.S.C. § 1411(a) (July 10, 1984). The statute provided that it does not apply to cases "pending on [its] date of enactment [July 10, 1984] . . . or to proceedings arising in or related to those cases." Public Law 98-353, § 122(b). Although the Johns-Manville bankruptcy was filed in 1982, the plan of reorganization confirmed by the bankruptcy court in 1986 provided each personal injury claimant the right to trial by jury in a local court if the claim is not settled with the trust.

13. 28 U.S.C. § 157(b)(5).

14. There is no explicit statutory authority for the transfer of cases to the court in which the bankruptcy is pending, but Robins persuasively argued that the authority to decide that jury trials will occur in the district where the bankruptcy was filed implies the authority to transfer the cases there from other federal courts. There is specific authority for a debtor to remove cases "related to" the bankruptcy, which includes suits pending against it, from a state court to the federal court for the district in which the state court is located. 28 U.S.C. § 1452. Because a federal court in Virginia has no power to transfer suits pending in state courts outside Virginia, Robins's intention, if a transfer order took effect, was to remove all Dalkon Shield cases pending in state courts to the local federal court, from which they would be transferred to Richmond. As Merhige's transfer order was reversed on appeal, Robins never effected the removal of cases from state to federal courts.

15. See chap. 5 text at n. 26; chap. 6 text at n. 20; chap. 8 text at n. 9; chap. 9. text at n. 5; chap. 16 text at n. 14.

16. *A. H. Robins Co. v. Piccinin, supra* n. 5, 788 F. 2d at 1014–16 (4th Cir. 1986).

17. A criminal grand jury investigation of Robins's officials and of the McGuire, Woods & Battle law firm was begun by the United States Department of Justice in 1986. The grand jury was disbanded in January 1990 without issuing indictments. See chap. 15, n. 12 and accompanying text.

18. Declaration of G. E. R. Stiles, August 21, 1985, p. 14.

19. *In re Johns-Manville Corp.*, 36 B.R. 727 (Bankr. S.D. N.Y. 1984).

20. See chap. 7 text at nn. 1–5.

21. Transcript, February 14, 1986, pp. 102–3. Judge Merhige's reference to $5 million was hyperbolic, as that figure represented the amount Robins was authorized to spend to give notice of the bankruptcy to Dalkon Shield users worldwide, not the cost of a mailing to two hundred thousand women. It made little actual difference, however, as either amount was prohibitive.

22. Memorandum in Support of Diana Beard's Motion to Dismiss, p. 2 (March 14, 1986).

Chapter 5

1. Transcript, September 21, 1985, p. 99.

2. 11 U.S.C. § 1102(b).

3. Supplemental memorandum of A. H. Robins Co., *Breland v. A. H. Robins Co.*, Adv. Proceeding 85-1001-R, p. 4 (November 4, 1985).

4. Order, November 12, 1985, p. 6.

5. Affidavit of Bradley Post dated March 22, 1986, p. 13, attached to Motion for Reconsideration of Order Denying Motion to Disqualify (March 24, 1986).

6. This issue is addressed in chap. 7 text at n. 4.

7. Affidavit of Mary Beth Ramey, dated March 13, 1986, pp. 3–4, attached to Motion to Reconsider Dissolution (March 14, 1986).

8. The Cadwalader firm was ultimately paid over $6 million in fees and expenses for its representation of the claimants' committee. See Stipulation and Order, May 22, 1990.

9. Motion of Diana R. Beard to Disqualify and supporting memorandum, March 4, 1986.

10. Memorandum (denying motion to disqualify), p. 39 (March 14, 1986).

11. Canon 3(A)(4) of the Code of Judicial Conduct (1973). See also Wayne E. Thode, *Reporter's Notes to Code of Judicial Conduct*, pp. 52–54 (ABA/ABF 1973).

12. Memorandum, *supra* n. 10 at 55, 58. The denial of the disqualification motion was affirmed by the court of appeals in February 1987. *In re Beard*, 811 F. 2d 818, 828–29, 830 (4th Cir. 1987). Writing for the court, Judge H. Emory Widener, Jr., found that Merhige's meeting with the Messrs. Robins did not violate the Code of Judicial Conduct because Friedberg had consented to it. He did not address the code's proscription of ex parte contacts concerning "impending proceedings." Id. at 828–29. Judge Widener did say that Merhige's pejorative remarks about Douglas Bragg were "ill-advised." Id. at 830.

13. *In re Beard*, nos. 86-3844, 86-3851, United States Court of Appeals for the Fourth Circuit, Order, December 19, 1987.

14. In a document filed in September 1988, Ralph Mabey, the court-appointed examiner, stated that the parties had agreed to ex parte contacts with Merhige "in order to receive appropriate direction and to effect compromise."

Examiner's Report, September 9, 1988, p. 11. There is no record of any such agreement. Certainly, the attorneys representing individual women were not parties to it.

15. Drabkin's time record reproduced in *Van Arsdale v. Clemo,* no. 86-3173, U.S.C.A. 4th Cir, Joint Appendix on Appeal, p. 517.

16. Transcript, September 4, 1986, pp. 185–86.

17. Id. at 235–36.

18. Id. at 192, 226–27.

19. Id. at 228–30.

20. Id. at 205–11.

21. Id. at 214.

22. Id. at 272.

23. Id. at 289.

24. A description by Szaller of the process for resolving Dalkon Shield claims under the confirmed plan of reorganization appears in 1 *Ohio Trial* 9 (Winter 1990).

25. H. R. Rep. no. 95-595, 95th Cong., 1st Sess. 236 (1977).

26. Order, July 21, 1986.

27. Transcript, August 28, 1986, pp. 17–18.

28. Memorandum, September 16, 1986.

29. *Van Arsdale v. Clemo,* 825 F. 2d 794 (4th Cir. 1987). Without reference to any of the facts indicating that counsel seeking employment dominated the process of selecting the members of the committee, Judge Robert Chapman, in his opinion for the court of appeals, ruled that the United States trustee is not prohibited "from receiving information and suggestions in his selection of a competent creditors' committee." Id. at 798. Compare chap. 20, n. 32, and accompanying text.

Chapter 6

1. Diane Goldner, "A. H. Robins," *American Lawyer,* October 1986, p. 32; Statement of Facts Submitted by United States, June 4, 1986, p. 1.

2. *Richmond Times-Dispatch,* March 7, 1986, p. c5, col. 3.

3. See Russell A. Eisenberg and Frances F. Gecker, "The Doctrine of Necessity and Its Parameters," 73 *Marquette Law Review* 1 (1989).

4. Consent Order Condition Rights of Debtor in Possession, para. 5 (August 23, 1985). See 11 U.S.C. § 549.

5. 11 U.S.C. § 1104(a).

6. Memorandum of the United States in Support of Motion for Finding of Contempt and Appointment of a Trustee, p. 19 (March 12, 1986).

7. *Wall Street Journal,* April 3, 1986, p. 6, col. 1.

8. Murphy, Weir and Butler's Motion to Withdraw (April 3, 1986).

9. *Washington Post,* April 9, 1986, p. G1, col. 3.

10. Dalkon Shield Claimants Committee's Memorandum in Support of the United States' Motion for Appointment of a Trustee, pp. 2–3 (June 4, 1986).

11. These payments were all outside the ordinary course of business. If Robins was insolvent when they were made, and the Bankruptcy Code presumes it was, these payments could be recovered ("avoided") in the Chapter 11 proceeding. 11 U.S.C. § 547(b), (c)(2), (f).

12. The Bankruptcy Code includes a procedure by which a debtor, with the advance approval of the court, can "assume" contracts for the delivery of goods or services that are necessary to the continued functioning of the business—so-called executory contracts. If the court approves the assumption of a contract, the debtor is authorized to pay the amounts past due on the contract to induce the supplier to resume performance. 11 U.S.C. § 365. After payments had been made and without mentioning the payments, Robins sought and obtained court approval for the assumption of contracts that accounted for approximately half of its disbursements for prepetition debt.

13. Statement of Facts Submitted by the United States, p. 38 (June 4, 1986).

14. Goldner, *supra* n. 1 at 32, 122.

15. *Wall Street Journal,* June 6, 1986, p. 4, col. 1.

16. *Washington Post,* June 6, 1986, p. B10, col. 2.

17. *Washington Post,* June 15, 1986, p. A10, col. 2.

18. Findings of Fact and Conclusions of Law as Stated from the Bench, p. 3 (June 14, 1986). The court of appeals affirmed Judge Merhige's decision not to appoint a trustee in September 1987. *Committee of Dalkon Shield Claimants v. A. H. Robins Co.,* 828 F. 2d 239 (4th Cir. 1987).

19. Findings of Fact and Conclusions of Law as Stated from the Bench, p. 7 (June 14, 1986).

20. Goldner, *supra* n. 1 at 32, 122.

21. In cases in which a trustee is not appointed, the Bankruptcy Code authorizes the court to order the appointment of an examiner "to conduct such investigation of the debtor as is appropriate." 11 U.S.C. § 1104(b). As indicated in the text, in the Robins bankruptcy the duties assigned to the examiner by Judge Merhige went well beyond investigations. Technically, in accordance with section 1104(c) of the Bankruptcy Code, the appointment of Mr. Mabey was made by United States Trustee William White with the "approval" of Judge Merhige.

22. *Washington Post,* August 6, 1986, p. G1, col. b.

23. *Washington Post,* October 13, 1987, p. E1, col. 6.

24. Order, October 14, 1987.

Chapter 7

1. The bar date also applied to claims for injuries that had not yet occurred—"future claims." This aspect of the bar date procedure is discussed in chap. 8.

2. *Mullane v. Central Hanover Bank & Trust Co.,* 339 U.S. 306, 314–15 (1950).

3. Bar Date Order, November 21, 1985, Exhibit C.

4. See chap. 3 text at nn. 29–33.

5. Bankruptcy Clerk's Memorandum, April 9, 1988.

6. Id.

7. Declaration of John C. Taylor, April 1, 1986, pp. 2–3, and Exhibits B & C; A. H. Robins Disclosure Statement, March 28, 1988, p. 16.

8. Declaration of Carl D. O'Hallahan, September 21, 1985, p. 7.

9. Schedule of foreign use distribution of the Dalkon Shield, p. 27, Joint Appendix, *Vancouver Women's Health Collective v. A. H. Robins Company,* no. 86-1159 (4th Cir.).

10. Memorandum, June 16, 1986.

11. As an additional ground for the denial of the motions, Merhige ruled that foreigners outside the United States are not entitled to due process of law, relying on a case addressing the procedural rights of aliens seeking admission to the United States. *Landon v. Plasencia,* 459 U.S. 1, 32 (1982). Whether or not that legal proposition can properly be applied in this context, the question of procedural fairness remains. When a foreign woman sues A. H. Robins, or its successor, for Dalkon Shield injuries in a court in her own country, that court will respect Merhige's judgment discharging the claim only if it is satisfied that the notice afforded to the plaintiff was adequate according to its own conceptions of public policy. See Eugene F. Scoles and Peter Hay, *Conflict of Law,* pp. 978–80 (West Publishing Co. 1982).

12. *Vancouver Women's Health Collective Society v. A. H. Robins Co.,* 820 F. 2d 1359, 1364 (4th Cir. 1987).

13. A. H. Robins' Motion for Order Approving Form of Notice of Bar Date and Approving Method of Notification, p. 8 (September 21, 1985); Response of A. H. Robins to Motion of Elana Mallari for order granting leave to file late claim, p. 6, n. 2 (September 8, 1987).

14. Declaration of Carl D. O'Hallahan, September 21, 1985, p. 8.

15. Affidavit of H. Arvid Johnson, Robins's senior vice-president and general counsel, October 31, 1987, p. 3.

16. Robins' Motion for an Order Authorizing Payment of Claims for Reimbursement of Medical Expenses Related to the IUD Removal Program, p. 5 (May 23, 1986).

17. Declaration of Carl D. O'Hallahan, September 21, 1985, p. 8.

18. Dalkon Shield Claimants Trust, Management Report, September 20, 1989.

19. Sixth Amended Disclosure Statement, p. LIQ-7 (liquidation analysis) (March 28, 1988).

20. Rule 9006(b)(1), Rules of Bankruptcy Procedure.

21. Order, September 18, 1987. See chap. 21 text at n. 2.

22. See Dalkon Shield Claimants Trust, Management Report, April 9, 1988.

23. Order, December 4, 1987; Order, February 17, 1988.

24. *In re A. H. Robins Co.,* 862 F. 2d 1092 (4th Cir. 1988).

25. *Maressa v. A. H. Robins Co.,* 839 F. 2d 220, 221 (4th Cir.), cert. denied, 109 S. Ct. 76 (1988).

26. See chap. 4 text at nn. 17–20.

27. Rule 3001.

Chapter 8

1. See Motion for Order Authorizing Reimbursement of Medical Expenses Related to the IUD Removal Program, pp. 6–8, 9–11 (May 23, 1986).

2. See transcript, November 9, 1987, pp. 2029–30 (Dr. Emanuel Friedman).

3. See 11 U.S.C. § 1141(d).

4. In 1983 the bankruptcy courts in the *UNR* and the *Amatex* reorganization cases ruled that persons who have not yet experienced any asbestos-related injury do not have "claims," because they do not have a "right to payment," and that their rights cannot be discharged in the reorganization. For this reason, these courts refused to appoint a legal representative of the interests of future claimants. *In re UNR Industries, Inc.*, 29 B.R. 741 (N.D. Ill. 1983); *In re Amatex Corp.*, 30 B.R. 309, aff'd, 37 B.R. 613 (E.D. Pa. 1983). Both of these decisions were appealed.

In January 1984, in the *UNR* case, the United States Court of Appeals for the Seventh Circuit in Chicago held that the lower-court order was not appealable. But a widely respected member of that court, Judge Richard Posner, took the occasion to question the lower-court's conclusion that future claimants did not have "claims," and to state that the issue was open as far as the appellate court was concerned. 725 F. 2d 1111, 1118–20 (7th Cir. 1984). In response, the bankruptcy court appointed a legal representative to act as a friend of the court on matters affecting future claimants. *In re UNR Industries, Inc.*, 46 B.R. 671 (Bankr. N.D. Ill. 1985). See also *In re UNR Industries, Inc.*, 71 B.R. 467 (Bankr. N.D. Ill. 1987); *In re Forty-Eight Insulations*, 58 B.R. 476 (Bankr. N.D. Ill. 1986).

In January 1985, in the *Amatex* case, the United States Court of Appeals for the Third Circuit in Philadelphia ruled that a legal representative of future claimants should be appointed, whether or not future claimants have "claims," because they are "parties in interest" (see 11 U.S.C. § 1109(b)) whose rights could be affected by the reorganization. 755 F. 2d 1034, 1041–44. A few weeks later, the Third Circuit, in a case arising under the pre-1978 Bankruptcy Act, which defined "claims" less broadly, ruled that a person without a present injury does not have a claim that can be discharged in a reorganization. *Schweitzer v. Consolidated Rail Corp.*, 758 F. 2d 936, cert. denied, 474 U.S. 474 (1985).

In the *Johns-Manville* case in New York, the bankruptcy judge appointed a legal representative of future claimants without deciding whether they had "claims" subject to discharge. 36 B.R. 743 (Bankr. S.D. N.Y. 1984), aff'd, 52 B.R. 940 (S.D. N.Y. 1985).

5. 11 U.S.C. § 1129(a)(11).

6. In the event of a liquidation, a reserve could be created to account for anticipated future claims. In some states, the creation of a reserve for anticipated

but unknown claims is mandatory in cases of corporate dissolution. See, e.g., California Corporations Code §§ 2005, 2008 (Deering 1987).

7. *Schweitzer v. Consolidated Rail Corporation,* 758 F. 2d 936, 943 (3d Cir.), cert. denied, 474 U.S. 864 (1985); *Gladding Corp. v. Forbes,* 20 B.R. 566, 568 (Bankr. D. Mass. 1982). See also *In re Amatex Corp.,* 37 B.R. 613, 614 (E.D. Pa. 1983); *Payton v. Abbott Laboratories,* 83 F.R.D. 382 (D. Mass. 1979).

8. Francine Rabinowitz, Estimation of Dalkon Shield Claims, p. 18 (November 2, 1987) (Aetna Exhibit 1, Estimation Hearing, November 8, 1987).

9. Order Denying Employment of Special Bankruptcy Counsel for the Legal Representative of Future Tort Claimants, May 12, 1986.

10. Memorandum of June 13, 1986, p. 1, n. 2.

11. In *Reading Co. v. Brown,* 391 U.S. 471 (1968), the Supreme Court held that a claim arising out of an automobile collision that occurred during a reorganization case constituted an "administrative expense," just like the other expenses of remaining in business during the reorganization, and was entitled to be paid as a priority claim at the conclusion of the proceeding. In that case, the conduct giving rise to the liability occurred during and not before the Chapter 11 case.

12. Order and memorandum, August 25, 1986.

13. In so ruling, Judge Merhige disagreed with a decision of the United States Court of Appeals for the Third Circuit, which had held that a claim exists for federal bankruptcy law purposes only when there is a right to sue under state law. *Matter of M. Frenville Co.,* 744 F. 2d 332 (3d Cir. 1984), cert. denied, 105 S. Ct. 911 (1985). Several lower courts outside the Third Circuit (Pennsylvania, New Jersey, and Delaware) had previously refused to follow the *Frenville* decision. *In re Edge,* 60 B.R. 690 (Bankr. M.D. Tenn. 1986); *Johns-Manville Corp.,* 57 B.R. 680 (Bankr. S.D. N.Y. 1986); *In re Yanks,* 49 B.R. 56 (Bankr. S.D. Fla. 1985); *In re Baldwin-United Corp.,* 48 B.R. 901 (Bankr. S.D. Ohio 1985). All these decisions related to claims other than future tort claims based on prepetition conduct of the debtor.

14. 1978 *U.S. Code Cong. & Admin. News* 5983 at 6266 (House Report) and 5785 at 5807–8 (Senate Report).

15. On appeal, Judge Merhige's ruling was affirmed. *Grady v. A. H. Robins Co.,* 839 F. 2d 198 (4th Cir.), cert. dismissed, 109 S. Ct. 201 (1988). Joynes filed a petition asking the Supreme Court to review the decision. He withdrew the petition, before it was acted on, when he agreed to the terms of a plan of reorganization. See chap. 15 text at n. 18.

Chapter 9

1. Only two decisions dismissing claims that Aetna was liable to women injured by the Dalkon Shield are reported. In *Bast v. A. H. Robins Co.,* 616 F. Supp. 333 (E.D. Wisc. 1985), the court based its decision on the insufficiency of the language of the complaint, without suggesting that an adequate claim

against Aetna could not be pleaded. In *Campbell v. A. H. Robins Co.*, 615 F. Supp. 496 (W.D. Wisc. 1985), the court did say, without explanation, that under Wisconsin law "an insurer owes no duty of care to injured third parties." Id. at 500. The responsibility of an insurer to warn consumers of defects in products it insures is analyzed, with particular reference to Aetna and the Dalkon Shield, by Morton Mintz in "The Dangers Insurance Companies Hide," *Washington Monthly,* January–February 1991, pp. 38–45.

2. It later developed that Skadden, Arps, Slate, Meagher & Flom, who had substituted for Murphy, Weir & Butler as special bankruptcy counsel for Robins, also represented Aetna. On October 29, 1986, following this disclosure, Judge Merhige disqualified Skadden, Arps from its representation of Robins. (Merhige did not disqualify Mays & Valentine, finding that the Richmond firm's situation "differs from Skadden, Arps' in that they fully disclosed all conflicts with Aetna at the inception of the case.") A week later, Skadden, Arps informed the court that it had terminated its representation of Aetna for the duration of the Robins Chapter 11 proceeding, and on November 10, 1986, the firm was reinstated as counsel for Robins.

3. See chap. 2 text at nn. 60–63; chap. 18 text at nn. 1–10.

4. See, e.g., Joint Brief for Appellees, *In re: A. H. Robins Co.* (Oberg), no. 88-1755 (U.S.C.A. 4th Cir.), p. 10; transcript, June 28, 1988, p. 36.

5. Order, May 21, 1986.

6. Transcript, October 30, 1985, p. 117.

7. Joynes's reference is to the inclusion of A. H. Robins Company, as well as its individual officers and directors, as defendants in the original April 9, 1986, filing in Minnesota. This was apparently done in error, and the next day Friedberg amended the complaint to delete these defendants.

8. Legal Representative's Memorandum regarding Plaintiff's Request for Attorneys Fees, p. 4 (January 28, 1987).

9. Order, June 15, 1987; Memorandum, June 15, 1987, p. 5.

10. The cases rejecting mandatory class actions in tort cases are cited in chap. 18, n. 1. See also chap. 2, n. 63. The legal issues and authorities relating to the maintenance of a mandatory class action against Aetna are addressed in chap. 18 text at nn. 1–10; chap. 19 text at nn. 9–12, 22–27, 37–39.

11. *Phillips Petroleum Co. v. Shutts,* 472 U.S. 797 (1985).

12. Transcript, September 21, 1985, p. 101.

13. See chap. 1 at n. 12 ff.

14. *In re A. H. Robins Co.,* 828 F. 2d 1023 (4th Cir. 1987), cert. denied, 108 S. Ct. 1246 (1988).

15. Id. at 1026.

16. Id.

Chapter 10

1. 11 U.S.C. § 507(a)(1).

2. Affidavit of Timothy Wyant, Ph.D., June 4, 1987, p. 3.

3. Examiner's Memorandum of Law in Opposition to Stay Pending Appeal, p. 12 (June 8, 1987). The figure is derived by multiplying $32,000, the presumed reduction in settlement cost, times 300, 30 percent of 1,000.

4. *In re Chateaugay,* 64 B.R. 990, 993–94, 998, 999 (S.D. N.Y. 1986) (retiree benefits), 80 B.R. 279 (S.D. N.Y. 1987) (worker's compensation). See also *In re Jewish Memorial Hospital,* 13 B.R. 417, 420 (Bankr. S.D. N.Y. 1981) (approving the preference for hospital operating expenses over other administrative expenses); *In re Eastern Air Lines, Inc.,* 98 B.R. 174 (Bankr. S.D. N.Y. 1989) (prepetition wages).

5. Brief in Support of Motion for Order Granting a Stay Pending Appeal, *Official Committee of Equity Security Holders v. Mabey,* pp. 16–21 (June 17, 1987).

6. Examiner's Memorandum of Law in Opposition to a Stay Pending Appeal, *Official Committee of Equity Security Holders v. Mabey,* p. 28, (June 24, 1987).

7. *Official Committee of Equity Security Holders v. Mabey,* 832 F. 2d 299 (4th Cir. 1987), cert. denied, 108 S. Ct. 1228 (1988).

8. 832 F. 2d at 302.

9. Id.

10. Id. at 301.

11. See n. 4. See also Russell A. Eisenberg and Frances F. Gecker, "The Doctrine of Necessity and Its Parameters," 73 *Marquette Law Review* 1 (1989).

12. *New York Times,* July 3, 1988, p. F4, col. 3.

Chapter 11

1. 11 U.S.C. § 1121.

2. See chap. 3 text at nn. 16–18.

3. See, e.g., *In re Public Service of New Hampshire,* 88 B.R. 521 (Bankr. D.N.H. 1988), and *In re Texaco Inc.,* 76 B.R. 322 (Bankr. S.D. N.Y. 1987).

4. Interest at 8.5 percent, compounded quarterly, on $2.335 billion (the total cash payments into the claimants' trust on consummation of the plan of reorganization), for the fifty-two months between August 1985, when the bankruptcy was filed, and December 1989, when the payment was made to the trust, is $1.027 billion.

5. Legal Representative of Dalkon Shield Claimants' Opposition to Motion to Extend Exclusive Period, p. 3 (March 26, 1986).

6. *Wall Street Journal,* July 1, 1986, p. 33, col. 1; *Richmond Times-Dispatch,* July 1, 1986, p. B1.

7. Resource Planning Corporation, Estimate of Cost and Timing of Pending and Future Dalkon Shield Actions in the United States, pp. 20–21 (March 26,

1985). The actual numbers in the estimate are 3,834 pending cases and 8,295 future cases, for a total of 12,129.

Based on Florence's estimate of $705 million, Robins had taken a $615 million charge on its books for the year 1984. The $90 million difference was attributable to available insurance.

8. In July 1990, after the Dalkon Shield claimants' trust had begun processing and paying claims, a motion was filed asking Judge Merhige to place a limit on fees paid to claimants' attorneys. See chap. 21, n. 28.

9. Section 502(c) of the Bankruptcy Code provides a procedure for the estimation of unliquidated and contingent claims against a debtor. The estimation of claims in the Robins bankruptcy is the subject of chaps. 12 and 13.

10. *Richmond Times-Dispatch*, September 30, 1986, p. A-1.

11. Transcript, February 14, 1986, p. 74. *See also* transcript, October 30, 1986 (in chambers), p. 25.

12. *Washington Post*, February 13, 1987, p. F1.

13. *Richmond Times-Dispatch*, February 15, 1987, p. A-1. See *Washington Post*, February 15, 1987, p. H6.

14. *Washington Post*, February 15, 1987, p. H6.

15. *Washington Post*, February 6, 1987, p. F2, col. 3.

16. *Richmond Times-Dispatch*, February 18, 1987, p. B2.

17. *Richmond Times-Dispatch*, April 19, 1987, p. B1.

18. Section 1121 of the Bankruptcy Code, which establishes the 120-day exclusivity period for the debtor to file a plan of reorganization, provides for an additional 60-day exclusivity period in which to obtain acceptances of a plan filed within the original 120 days. The first four times Judge Merhige extended the exclusivity period for filing a plan of reorganization, he provided for an additional exclusivity period for securing acceptances, but he had not done so when he extended the exclusivity period indefinitely on February 4, 1987.

19. The language is from the opinion of the court of appeals in *A. H. Robins Co. v. Piccinin*, 788 F. 2d 994, 1013 (4th Cir.), cert. denied, 479 U.S. 876 (1986).

20. *Wall Street Journal*, April 17, 1987, p. 3.

21. *Washington Post*, April 17, 1987, p. G1; *Wall Street Journal*, April 20, 1987, p. 2.

22. *Richmond Times-Dispatch*, May 12, 1987, p. A1.

23. *Washington Post*, May 7, 1987, p. E1.

24. *Richmond Times-Dispatch*, May 17, 1987, p. C1.

25. At a hearing on July 10, 1987, Judge Merhige rejected claims of privilege asserted by the Federal Reserve Board and the Federal Deposit Insurance Corporation, as well as the claims of these agencies that disclosure of their examination reports, even under an order prohibiting public disclosure, followed by a disapproval of the plan of reorganization could, by its negative implication, cause a run on the banks. Merhige said the suggestion was "asinine." *Richmond Times-Dispatch*, July 11, 1987, p. 1. By an order dated July 27, 1987, Merhige ordered the federal agencies to submit the examination reports for his "in camera" inspection. A few days later, Manufacturers Hanover withdrew from

its commitment to participate in the consortium of banks providing the letters of credit. *Wall Street Journal,* August 4, 1987, p. 44, col. 4. By that time, Robins had abandoned its stand-alone plan and agreed to be acquired by Rorer.

26. *Wall Street Journal,* May 4, 1987, p. 7, col. 2.

27. *Wall Street Journal,* July 6, 1987, p. 3, col. 2.

28. *Wall Street Journal,* May 5, 1987, p. 20, col. 2.

29. *Wall Street Journal,* July 6, 1987, p. 3, col. 2; *Wall Street Journal,* January 21, 1988, p.1, col. 6.

30. *Wall Street Journal,* July 6, 1987, p. 3, col. 2.

31. This change was made to assure that the claimants' trust would qualify under the Tax Reform Act of 1986 as a "designated settlement fund," a status that would allow the payments to the trust to be treated as deductible expenses in the tax year in which they were made, regardless of the sequence of payments from the trust to the claimants. 26 U.S.C. § 468B. See chap. 17, n. 13.

32. This present value calculation, using a 10 percent discount rate, is included in the Rorer plan, Exhibit 9, Financial Disclosure, p. 26.

Chapter 12

1. 11 U.S.C. § 1129(a)(8), (b)(1). See chap. 3 text at nn. 15–24.

2. S. Rep. no. 95-989, 1978 *U.S. Code Cong. & Admin. News* 5787, 5851 (1978); H. Rep. 95-595, 1978 *U.S. Code Cong. & Admin. News* 5963, 6310 (1978).

3. See, e.g., *Bittner v. Borne Chemical Co.,* 691 F. 2d 134 (3d Cir. 1982); *Nova Real Estate Invest. Trust,* 23 B.R. 62 (Bankr. E.D. Va. 1982); *Baldwin-United Corp.,* 55 B.R. 885 (Bankr. S.D. Ohio 1985); *In re Lane,* 68 B.R. 609 (Bankr. D. Ha. 1986). See generally Note, "Procedures for Estimating Contingent or Unliquidated Claims in Bankruptcy," 35 *Stanford L. Rev. 153* (1982).

4. The court in *Baldwin-United Corp.,* 55 B.R. 885 (Bankr. S.D. Ohio 1985), so held. Section 502(j) of the Bankruptcy Code provides for the reconsideration of the allowance of a claim, and this section has been cited by some courts as authority for the revision of an estimate to conform with the amount at which a claim was subsequently liquidated. *Baldwin-United Corp., supra; Nova Real Estate Invest. Trust, supra* n. 3; *In re Lane, supra* n. 3. An upward revision of an estimate, of course, is only possible before there has been a distribution of the assets of the estate other than the amount of the estimate. See section 502(j), third sentence.

5. 28 U.S.C. § 1411; see also 28 U.S.C. §§ 157(b)(2)(B), 157(b)(5), Pub. L. 98-353, Title I, 98 Stat. 335 (1984). The jury trial statute is quoted in chap. 4 text at n. 12.

6. *Katchen v. Landry,* 382 U.S. 323, 336–38 (1966), citing *Barton v. Barbour,* 104 U.S. 126, 133–34 (October Term 1881).

7. See chap. 22 text at nn. 12–13.

8. *A. H. Robins Co. v. Piccinin,* 788 F. 2d 994, 1012–14 (4th Cir.), cert.

denied, 479 U.S. 876 (1986); *In re UNR Inds., Inc.*, 45 B.R. 322 (N.D. Ill. 1984). In *Roberts v. Johns-Manville Corp.*, 45 B.R. 823, 825–26 (S.D. N.Y. 1985), the court spoke of the necessity to estimate unliquidated claims but did not specify whether this would be done individually or on a group basis.

9. 788 F. 2d 994 (4th Cir. 1986). See chap. 4 text at nn. 14–16.

10. 788 F. 2d at 1012–13.

11. Transcript, February 14, 1986, p. 74.

12. Debtor's Motion for an Order Requiring Group Estimation, etc., p. 4 (June 5, 1987).

13. Objection of the Equity Committee to Dalkon Shield Claimants Committee's Motion for Order Terminating Debtor's Exclusive Period to File a Plan, at p. 5 (July 22, 1987); Memorandum of Debtor Opposing Motion of Dalkon Shield Claimants Committee for Order Terminating Debtor's Exclusive Right to File Plan, at pp. 11, 13 (July 27, 1987).

14. Merhige stated:

It is the Court's intention, after said hearing, to make findings [as to the total value of allowable claims] for such further use as may be proper in assisting the Court in fulfilling its obligation to determine that which is required under . . . 11 U.S.C. s1129(b)(1) should the need for such consideration arise as a consequence of a failure of the proposed plan to garner a sufficient number of affirmative votes as required by law.

Order, July 27, 1987, p. 2. Section 1129(b)(1) is the provision allowing the court to cram down a plan of reorganization, over the dissent of a class of creditors, based on a finding that the class will be paid in full.

15. Professor McGovern has described this process in McGovern, "Resolving Mature Mass Tort Litigation," 69 *Boston U. L. Rev.* 659, 675–88 (1989).

16. Id. at 963.

17. Order, August 12, 1986.

18. In October 1987, the clerk of court reported that approximately 150,000 of the 195,000 eligible claimants were not represented by counsel. See affidavit of Rosemary Menard-Sanford, filed October 26, 1987.

19. McGovern, *supra* n. 15 at 687.

20. The results of the telephone survey are described in greater detail in chap. 13, nn. 3 and 4.

Chapter 13

1. See chap. 2 text at n. 87; chap. 5 text at n. 9.

2. 28 U.S.C. § 141. Judge Merhige was more obliging a decade earlier when, in the litigation between Westinghouse Electric Corporation and thirteen utility companies discussed in chap. 2 text at nn. 39–43, he traveled to London to rule on discovery objections. Merhige displays on his office wall a letter proclaiming

him the only United States judge to have held court in the American Embassy in London. In fond recollection of the event, Merhige told his authorized biographer that he would have traveled "to the ends of the earth" to promote settlement of that litigation. See Ronald J. Bacigal, "An Empirical Case Study of Informal Dispute Resolution," 4 *Ohio St. Journal of Dispute Resolution* 1, 13 (1988). The women injured by the Dalkon Shield who wanted to observe the estimation hearing could have been accommodated within a few hundred yards of the courthouse in Richmond.

3. Among the 455 nonresponding claimants contacted in Professor McGovern's telephone survey, 63 said they had not received the materials. Of the 392 who said they did receive the questionnaire, 92 said they had returned it; many of these had a copy of their response or a mailing receipt. These 92 were sent a duplicate form and 61 returned it, but their responses were not entered in the pending case database.

4. It is notoriously difficult, especially for nonlawyers, to secure old medical records. Substantial costs may be involved. More than 75 percent of the claimants contacted in the telephone survey of nonresponders who had received but not returned the questionnaire gave reasons for their nonresponse relating to the shortness of time or to the difficulty or expense of securing medical records.

5. The breakdown of Florence's additional items is as follows:

	No.	Amt.	Total (millions)
Future claims	99	$91,800	$9.1
Consortium claims	2,849	3,000	8.5
Minimal payments to excluded claimants	145,239	2,200 or 300	106.7
Administrative costs of trust			100.0
	Subtotal		$224.3

6. *Poffenberger v. Risser*, 290 Md. 631, 636, 431 A. 2d 677, 680 (1981). See Note, 41 *Md. L. Rev.* 451 (1982).

7. Annot. Code of Maryland, Courts and Judicial Proceedings § 5-203 (1988.)

8. Francine Rabinowitz, "Estimation of Dalkon Shield Claims," pp. 3–4 (November 2, 1987) (Aetna Exhibit 1, Estimation Hearing, November 8, 1987).

9. Dr. Rabinowitz testified that she tested the validity of these special evaluations by asking the same adjustors to evaluate the records in eighty-three resolved cases (without knowledge that they were resolved), and she found that their conclusions were very close to the amounts actually paid. Rabinowitz transcript, November 8, 1987, pp. 36–37, 39. These data were not introduced into evidence.

10. Rabinowitz transcript, pp. 79–82 (November 8, 1987).

11. The following is a summary of Dr. Rabinowitz's grid of the averages of the values found by the Aetna adjusters rounded to thousands of dollars.

Injury Category	No Complic. Factors	Minor Complic. Factors	Subst'l Complic. Factors	Maximum Complic. Factors
Death	—	—	—	$525,000
Birth Defect/Infant Death	$7,000	33,000	29,000	4,000
Infection/Infertility/ Surgery	33,000	64,000	15,000	63,000
Infection/Infertility	18,000	92,000	34,000	6,000
Infection/Surgery	70,000	9,000	3,000	8,000
Ectopic/Infected Abortion	29,000	19,000	10,000	4,000
Perforation	17,000	11,000	4,000	5,000
Pregnancy/Abortion	98,000	6,000	1,000	2,000
Infection/Pain/Other	7,000	7,000	2,000	19,000
Weighted Averages	56,000	24,000	6,000	27,000

Overall average per claim: $27,031

12. When all the cases in the sample were grouped by complication category without regard to injury, the average compensation paid to cases with no complicating factors was the highest; but that paid for cases with the maximum complications was not the lowest. See the next to last line in the chart in n. 11, *supra*.

13. Pifer adjusted the average values to reflect 1987 values. Florence had made no adjustment in the amounts that had been paid in the resolved cases in the ten years before the bankruptcy. Rabinowitz's adjusters valued the cases in present dollars.

14. The values computed through this process, rounded to the nearest thousand dollars, were:

1. Sterility—strong support $115,000
2. Same—some support   97,000
3. Same—no information   69,000
4. Nonsterility group A—strong support   43,000
5. Same—some support   32,000
6. Same—no information   21,000
7. Nonsterility group B—strong and some support   22,000
8. Same—no information   18,000
9. All—no support   8,000
10. Birth defect   459,000
11. Maternal death   346,000
12. Infant death   76,000

Because of the small number of cases in the last three categories in the McGovern resolved case database, Pifer drew the values for these injuries from Robins's file of all closed cases.

15. Pifer actually testified that he attributed values to the claims on the basis

of averages for those who did respond to McGovern, without even breaking down their claims by injury group, transcript, November 9, 1987, p. 2295. But that testimony is inconsistent with Pifer's exhibits 3 and 4, which show non-McGovern responders on average receiving less than the average for responders. Accordingly, the discussion in text assumes that Pifer misspoke and that he assigned values to the claims of nonresponders using responder averages by injury category.

16. The judge did not say this in so many words at the estimation hearing, but he did so later on more than one occasion. See transcript, October 24, 1988, p. 12 (Pifer's "credibility was negligible"); transcript of telephone conference, August 25, 1988, p. 9.

17. Transcript, November 11, 1987, pp. 2377, 2379

18. See chap. 7 text at nn. 22–24.

19. Interview with Robert R. Merhige, Jr., November 21, 1989.

Chapter 14

1. *New York Times,* December 12, 1987, p. 43, col. 3.

2. All present values in this chapter are computed at a 10 percent discount rate, compounded annually. This is the rate used for present value computations in the financial disclosure section (p. 26) of the Disclosure Statement filed in support of the Rorer plan (August 21, 1987).

3. See *New York Times,* December 21, 1987, p. D8, col. 6; *Richmond Times-Dispatch,* December 19, 1987, p. A19, col. 5, January 10, 1988, p. C1, col. 1.

4. *Richmond Times-Dispatch,* January 17, 1988, p. F3, col. 1.

5. Id.

6. Affidavit of Joseph S. Friedberg, July 7, 1988, para. 15, filed in *Breland v. Aetna Casualty & Surety* Co.

7. Interview with Louis L. Hoynes, Jr., January 23, 1990.

8. *Richmond Times-Dispatch,* December 25, 1987, p. C-1.

9. *New York Times,* January 13, 1968, p. D4, col. 5.

10. *Richmond Times-Dispatch,* January 5, 1988, p. 11, col. 6.

11. *Wall Street Journal,* January 4, 1988, p. 3, col. 3.

12. *Richmond Times-Dispatch,* January 5, 1988, p. A-11, col. 6.

13. *Washington Post,* January 7, 1988, p. F1, col. 3.

14. *Wall Street Journal,* January 4, 1988, p. 3, col. 2.

15. Under the terms of American Home Products' agreement with the equity committee, which was incorporated into the merger agreement that was ultimately entered into between Robins and American Home Products, the value of the American Home Products stock to be issued to Robins's shareholders was defined in terms of its then present value. When the merger was consummated twenty-three months later, there had been a substantial escalation in the market price of American Home Products stock, and the value of the stock issued to Robins's shareholders was worth $916 million, or $38 a share.

16. *Washington Post,* January 13, 1988, p. F-2, col. 6.

17. *Washington Post,* January 19, 1988, p. E-4, col. 1; *New York Times,* January 19, 1988, p. D2, col. 6.

18. Interview with Louis L. Hoynes, Jr., January 23, 1990.

19. Interview with Louis L. Hoynes, Jr., January 23, 1990.

20. The present value of the funds made available to both the claimants' trust and the Other Claimants Trust under the Rorer offer accepted by Robins in July 1987 was $1.55 billion. See chap. 11 at n. 32. This compares to $2.3 billion under the American Home Products proposal accepted in January 1988, plus rights against Aetna for more.

21. See chap. 17, n. 13 .

Chapter 15

1. Affidavit of Murray Drabkin, September 21, 1988, pp. 11–12, filed in *Official Dalkon Shield Claimants Committee v. A. H. Robins Co.,* no. 88-1753, U.S.C.A. 4th Cir. (hereafter cited as "Drabkin affidavit").

2. Examiner's Report, September 9, 1988, Appendix, p. 13.

3. See chap. 16 text at n. 11 ff.

4. Drabkin affidavit, p. 10.

5. Examiner's Report, September 9, 1988, p. 14; Drabkin affidavit, p. 12.

6. Drabkin affidavit, p. 13.

7. Transcript, October 30, 1986, p. 71.

8. Memorandum in Support of Class Plaintiffs' Motion for Final Approval of Settlement, *Breland v. Aetna Casualty & Surety Co.,* pp. 62–63 (June 28, 1988).

9. Id. at 69.

10. Stipulation and Settlement Agreement, February 1, 1988, para. 6 (a). A mandatory class action for punitive damages could be certified on a "quasi–limited fund" theory of the sort adopted by Judge Weinstein in the *Agent Orange* litigation. See chap. 2, n. 63. Although Aetna's funds were not limited in the sense that compensatory and punitive damage judgments against it in Dalkon Shield litigation would exceed its net worth, the funds available to pay punitive damages might be limited by the courts so that recovery of punitive damages by the first women to prevail would impair the ability of others to recover punitive damages. There is no analogous theory to support a mandatory class action on the compensatory damages claims, because the courts would not limit those claims until they had been paid.

11. Sixth Amended and Restated Plan of Reorganization, Section 6.06 (March 28, 1988); Agreement and Plan of Merger, March 21, 1988, Section 7.1(g).

12. *In re Grand Jury Proceedings, Company X v. United States,* no. 88-1243, cert. denied, 109 S. Ct. 3214 (1989). The order is printed in the appendix to the Brief of the United States in Opposition to Certiorari at 11a. The cases cited in the district court's order reveal that "Company X" is A. H. Robins. In

January 1990, just after the consummation of the plan of reorganization in the Chapter 11 case, the Department of Justice announced that indictments would not be returned against officers or employees of Robins or against McGuire, Woods & Battle. As is customary in such situations, there was no explanation for this decision. *Wall Street Journal,* January 12, 1990, p. B2, col. 3.

13. See chap. 19, n. 8.

14. See chap. 17 text at nn. 19–20; chap. 22 text at nn. 14–19.

15. As had the Rorer plan, the American Home Products plan established a separate "other claimants' trust" to provide a second layer of protection to potential co-defendants whom Robins had agreed to indemnify (reimburse) for liability related to the Dalkon Shield. If, despite the injunction, liability should be imposed against or costs incurred by these persons, this trust would provide reimbursement. Of the money American Home Products had agreed to pay to satisfy Dalkon Shield claims, $45 million was diverted to the "other claimants' trust." It was also agreed that $5 million of the money to be paid by Messrs. Robins would be paid into this trust, for a total funding of $50 million. To the extent that these trust funds were not necessary to indemnify co-defendants, they would be paid over to the claimants' trust beginning in the sixth year. The other $5 million from Messrs. Robins would be paid directly into the claimants' trust, on top of the other payments.

16. If the *Breland* settlement was not approved, Aetna would still provide $50 million of outlier insurance and $50 million of excess insurance with a spillover feature under terms of its agreement with Robins. See n. 11 and accompanying text.

17. See chap. 19 text at nn. 20–21; chap. 21, n. 35.

18. This additional language was added on March 21, 1988, the day of the hearing on the adequacy of the disclosure statement that would be distributed with the plan of reorganization. Joynes objected to the plan until this change was made.

19. The implementation of these provisions is discussed in chap. 21 text at nn. 32–35.

20. *Richmond Times-Dispatch,* February 11, 1988, p. B3, col. 4.

Chapter 16

1. Classes whose rights are altered by a plan of reorganization are said to be "impaired." 11 U.S.C. § 1124. Classes that are not impaired are not afforded the opportunity to vote and are assumed to have accepted the plan. 11 U.S.C. § 1126(f). Even assuming that the Robins plan of reorganization would allow for the eventual full payment of all Dalkon Shield claims, the provision of the plan prohibiting injured women from filing suit for the liquidation of their claims until their claims had been submitted to and processed by the claimants' trust and the provision precluding the recovery of punitive damages required that the class be treated as impaired.

2. Examiner's Report, September 9, 1988, Appendix, p. 42.

3. Id.

4. *Washington Post,* March 17, 1988, p. C11. col 2; *Richmond Times-Dispatch,* March 17, 1988, p. A1, col. 3; *New York Times,* March 17, 1988, p. D5, col. 4.

5. 11 U.S.C. § 1129(b).

6. The resolution of these questions is discussed in chap. 22 text at nn. 10–19.

7. Resource Planning Corporation, Estimate of Cost and Timing of Pending and Future Dalkon Shield Actions in the United States, pp.20–21 (March 26, 1985). This report found that, as of December 31, 1984, there were 3,834 Dalkon Shield claims pending against Robins and it estimated that another 8,295 would be filed in the future, for a total of 12,129. This is slightly more than 6 percent of the number of eligible claims in the Chapter 11 case.

8. By mid-January, 1991, 99,452 claimants, more than half of all the eligible claimants, had accepted $725 or less in an option 1 settlement. See chap. 21 text at n. 9.

9. In *Johns Manville,* 96 percent of the asbestos claimants voted in favor of the plan. On appeal, the court of appeals declined to rule on the legality of the equal vote procedure, finding that the plan would have been accepted if weighted voting had been used. "The alleged irregularities were at most harmless error." *Kane v. Johns Manville Corp.,* 843 F. 2d 636, 647 (2d Cir. 1988). There was no bar date advertising in *Johns Manville,* and there were no "post card" claims. The court attributed its conclusion in part to the expectation that, if weighted voting had been used, "all the votes would still have been weighted roughly the same since significant variations would not likely occur in the damages sustained by similar groups of people from similar kinds of injuries." Id. at 648.

10. Despite Merhige's instruction, the disclosure statement continued to refer to his estimate as a "decision." Disclosure Statement, p. 21. More significantly, the "Special Notice to Women Who Used the Dalkon Shield," which was written in plain English and placed at the front of the 250-page book containing the disclosure statement, the plan of reorganization, and related documents, stated that:

THE COURT MUST FIND, . . . BEFORE THE PLAN GOES INTO EFFECT, THAT THE PLAN PROVIDES ENOUGH MONEY TO SATIS-FY ALL VALID DALKON SHIELD CLAIMS AND EXPENSES OF THE TRUST IN FULL

Id., p. 4. (All capital letters in original.) Merhige made this recital in his confirmation order on the basis that the plan satisfied his estimate. See chap. 17, n. 4.

11. Memorandum in Support of Motion by Claimants Rosemary Menard-Sanford, et al., for Access to List of Dalkon Shield Claimants, p. 2 (May 8, 1987).

12. See 6 Collier, Bankruptcy, para. 7.12 (14th ed. 1978).

13. The code provides that "[a]n acceptance or rejection of a plan may not be solicited" before the distribution of the disclosure statement. 11 U.S.C. § 1125(b). In *Century Glove, Inc. v. First American Bank*, 860 F. 2d 94 (1988), the United States Court of Appeals for the Third Circuit held that this provision applies only to communications asking for a vote on a plan of reorganization that is available for approval. Id. at 102. The court said that a broader reading of section 1125(b) "can seriously inhibit free creditor negotiations" and stressed the importance of creditors "hav[ing] comparisons with which to judge the proposals of the debtor's plan." Id. at 101, 102.

14. Memorandum in Support of Dalkon Shield Claimants Committee's Motion for Authority to Send Letter, p. 7 (September 17, 1987).

15. The $2.255 billion referred to in Judge Merhige's letter is the $2.3 billion American Home Products agreed to provide, less the $45 million that was diverted to the Other Claimants Trust, subject to later transfer to the claimants' trust to the extent that it was not needed to indemnify co-defendants. See chap. 15, n. 15.

Chapter 17

1. The February 1986 issue of the *ATLA Advocate* (vol. 12, no. 1), a publication of the American Trial Lawyers Association, had reported that between $615 million and $750 million would be available through the Chapter 11 case for Dalkon Shield injury claims.

In June 1988, Thomas Morris of the Richmond Times-Dispatch polled the lawyers who were members of the first Dalkon Shield claimants' committee, and he reported that the seventeen who had responded told him of 6,101 votes in favor of the plan and 1,121 votes against. *Richmond Times-Dispatch,* June 26, 1988, p. A1.

2. In fact, while 64 cents per claimant's name and address was beyond the means of the International Dalkon Shield Victims' Education Association (IDEA), some enterprising law firms purchased portions of the list of claimants at this rate—ten or twenty thousand at a clip—and conducted mass mailings offering their services on a contingent fee basis.

3. See chap. 19 text at n. 6.

4. Although the acceptance of the plan meant that the Bankruptcy Code did not require a finding of full payment, the plan of reorganization included, at American Home Products' insistence, the condition that the confirmation order contain a finding that the funds provided under the plan were adequate to pay all Dalkon Shield claims in full. 7.02(a)(iii). Because the finding was not required by the Bankruptcy Code, the condition was deemed satisfied by a conclusory recitation without any statement of reasons or supporting facts. Confirmation Order, para. 11 (July 25, 1988). See also Confirmation Memorandum, p. 11 (July 25, 1988).

5. The question is whether the dissenting individual will receive less under the proposed reorganization than in a liquidation, not whether that is true of the class of which the dissenter is a member. See S. Rep. no. 989, 95th Cong., 2d Sess., 1978 *U.S. Code Cong. & Admin. News* 5787; Peter F. Coogan, "Confirmation of a Plan under the Bankruptcy Code," 32 *Case W. Res. L. Rev.* 301, 344 (1982).

6. 11 U.S.C. § 726(a)(5).

7. See *In re San Joaquin Estates, Inc.,* 64 B.R. 534, 536 (Bankr. 9th Cir. 1986); *In re Adcom, Inc.,* 74 B.R. 673 (Bankr. D. Mass. 1987); *In re Shaffer Furniture Co.,* 68 B.R. 827, 830 (Bankr. E.D. Pa. 1987).

The Bankruptcy Code also provides that claims for punitive damages will be paid in a liquidation before anything is paid to the shareholders. 11 U.S.C. § 726(a)(4). Robins's plan of reorganization prohibited the recovery of punitive damages. Analytically, the only difference is that the entitlement of all creditors to interest in a Chapter 7 liquidation was certain; the entitlement of any dissenting creditor to recover punitive damages is speculative (although her right to seek punitive damages was not). The disallowance of claims for punitive damages in Robins's plan of reorganization is discussed in chap. 22 text at nn. 14–19.

8. Under the plan, American Home Products and Robins would pay $2.255 billion to the Dalkon Shield claimants' trust, and $45 million to the Other Claimants Trust, and the full amounts due to trade creditors and to banks in repayment of unsecured loans, approximately $27 million and $29 million, respectively.

9. See chap. 14, n. 20. The liquidation value for Robins set forth in the liquidation analysis attached to the Rorer plan of reorganization was $2.667 billion without a disputed "risk adjustment," and $2.365 billion with the risk adjustment. A. H. Robins' Second Amended Plan Disclosure Statement, Exhibit 8, p. 3 (August 21, 1967).

10. See 11 U.S.C. § 363(f); *In re White Motor Credit Corp.,* 75 B.R. 944, 951 (Bankr. N.D. Ohio 1987).

11. Report of Examiner Regarding Objections to Debtor's Second Amended Disclosure Statement, December 1, 1987, p. 58. Mabey reiterated this point in more muted terms, with respect to the liquidation analysis supporting the plan of reorganization based on the American Home Products acquisition, by inserting in its note 3 that "[t]he examiner disputes Robins' position" that a prospective purchaser would discount the value of the company in a Chapter 7 liquidation.

12. Objections of the Dalkon Shield claimants' committee to the Second Amended Disclosure Statement filed by A. H. Robins Co., p. 31 (October 20, 1987).

13. Under section 382(b) of the Internal Revenue Code of 1954, which governed the carryover of Robins's operating losses following the acquisition, see Public Law 99-514, Section 621(e)(1), (f)(5), 100 Stat. 2266, 2268, American

Home Products was able to utilize as a deduction against income the entire payment of $2.255 billion to the claimants' trust. See Disclosure Statement, March 28, 1988, p. 52.

Moreover, the payment to the claimants' trust could be treated as a "qualified payment" into a "designated settlement fund," within the meaning of a provision of the Internal Revenue Code that was added in 1986. As a result, the entire $2.255 billion payment became a deductible expense in the year (1989) in which it was made, regardless of the sequence of the trust's payments to the injured women. See Pub. L. 99-514, Title XVIII, § 1807(a)(7)(A), 100 Stat. 2814 (Oct. 22, 1986), as amended, Pub. L. 100-647, Title I, § 1018(f)(1), (2), (4), (5)(A), 102 Stat. 3582 (November 10, 1988), 26 U.S.C. § 468B. See also Disclosure Statement, p. 52.

Because, however, the payment to the trust extinguished a liability of A. H. Robins, the deduction was only applicable to Robins's income; it could not be used as a deduction against other income of American Home Products. Treas. Reg. 1.1502-21 (C)(1) (Consolidated Returns—Separate Return Limitation Year). The amount of the trust payment, $2.255 billion, is greater by a factor of ten or more than Robins's recent annual taxable income, but the amount of the deduction that was not used in 1989 could be carried back for ten years and forward for fifteen years. 26 U.S.C. s172(a), (b)(1)(B),(I). This means that American Home Products was entitled to use part of the deduction to obtain a refund from the Internal Revenue Service of all the income tax that the A. H. Robins Company paid back to 1979. The amount not carried back can be deducted against future income of the Robins subsidiary until the year 2004. Assuming the Robins subsidiary will generate enough income to use it, the entire $2.255 billion will be deducted from taxable income over a period of years. The absolute value in federal tax savings is approximately $767 million (computed at 34 percent, the corporate tax rate). The present value is much less.

If Robins's businesses were purchased as assets, the purchaser would not realize any tax benefit related to the payment of Dalkon Shield claims. That deduction would remain with A. H. Robins Co., Inc. The purchaser would, however, realize a different substantial tax benefit that is not available in a corporate merger. The tax basis of the assets that are subject to depreciation or amortization would be "stepped up," from the $412 million on Robins's books to a far higher level related to the purchase price, that is, the actual price less the portion of the price that must be allocated to asset categories, such as goodwill, that cannot be amortized or depreciated. See Treas. Reg. 1.167(a)-3. The increase in the tax basis of the assets would become deductions against income over the life of the depreciation and amortization periods. If the amount of the step-up in assets subject to depreciation or amortization was $2 billion, for example, the absolute value of the resulting tax savings would be $680 million over a period of years. Again, the present value would be much less.

The actual calculation of the relative tax advantages of the two forms of transaction would require data that are not available. It is likely, however, that the additional depreciation or amortization deductions resulting from a step-up of assets in a purchase would be less than the $2.255 billion deduction that is available to American Home Products as a result of the merger. Further, depreciation and amortization deductions would all be applicable to future years, while the deduction resulting from American Home Products' payment to the trust can be carried back to obtain a refund of taxes paid in past years. For these reasons, the tax advantages of the American Home Products acquisition presumably are greater than the alternative advantages of a purchase of assets, but only by a relatively modest amount that does not begin to approach the $930 million reduction in price incorporated in Robins's liquidation analysis.

14. Plan of Reorganization, 8.05.

15. Affidavit of Murray Drabkin, September 21, 1988, p. 17, filed in *Official Dalkon Shield Claimants Committee v. A. H. Robins Co.*, no. 88-1753, U.S.C.A. 4th Cir.

16. *In re A. H. Robins Co.*, 88 B.R. 742 (E.D. Va.).

17. Id. at 751.

18. Id. at 751–52.

19. Confirmation Order, July 25, 1988, para. 31.

20. Although the disallowance of punitive damages was settled by the confirmation of the plan of reorganization, two weeks after the confirmation order had been entered Merhige issued another opinion in which he volunteered his view that Robins's punitive damages liability could and should have been eliminated in the Chapter 11 case, apart from the acceptance of a plan that eliminated punitive damages by the Dalkon Shield claimants. *In re A. H. Robins Co.*, 89 B.R. 555 (E.D. Va. 1988). Merhige's opinion is discussed in chap. 22 text at nn. 14–19.

Chapter 18

1. *McDonnell Douglas Corp. v. United States District Court*, 523 F. 2d 1083, 1086 (9th Cir. 1975), cert. denied, 425 U.S. 911 (1976); *In re Federal Skywalk Cases*, 680 F. 2d 1175 (8th Cir.), cert. denied, 459 U.S. 988 (1982); *In re Bendectin Products Liability Litigation*, 749 F. 2d 300, 305 (6th Cir. 1984); *In re Temple*, 851 F. 2d 1269, 1272 (11th Cir. 1988).

2. Class Plaintiffs' Brief in Support of Motion to Certify, *Breland v. Aetna Casualty and Surety Co.*, February 11, 1988, pp. 2, 5.

3. See chap. 15, n. 10, and accompanying text; Plan of Reorganization, 6.06(a); Merger Agreement, Sec. 7.1(g).

4. Rule 23(c)(2), Federal Rules of Civil Procedure. In two major mass tort cases, the courts had allowed optional class actions for compensatory damages under subpart (b)(3) of rule 23. *School Asbestos Litigation*, 789 F. 2d 996, 1008–11 (3d Cir. 1986); *In re "Agent Orange" Product Liability Litigation*, 100 F.R.D. 718, 721–24 (E.D. N.Y. 1983), mandamus denied sub nom., 725 F. 2d 858 (2d Cir.), cert. denied, 465 U.S. 1067 (1984).

5. See chap. 2, text at nn. 61–63.

6. David W. Louisell and Geoffrey C. Hazard, *Pleading and Procedure: State and Federal*, p. 719 (Foundation Press 1962), quoted in the Supplementary Note of Advisory Committee on Rule 23(b)(1)(A).

7. *McDonnell Douglas Corp. v. U.S. District Court*, 523 F. 2d 1083, 1086 (9th Cir. 1975), cert. denied, 425 U.S. 911 (1976).

8. Id. See also *In re Bendectin Products Liability Litigation*, 749 F. 2d 300, 305 (6th Cir. 1984); *In re Dennis Greenman Securities Litigation*, 829 F. 2d 1539, 1544–46 (11th Cir. 1987); *In re "Agent Orange" Product Liability Litigation, supra* n. 4, 100 F.R.D. at 724–25.

9. Stipulation and Settlement Agreement, February 1, 1968, pp. 2, 7, 18, and Exhibit E.

10. *Breland v. Aetna Casualty & Surety Co.*, Civil Action 86-0315-R (E.D. Va.), memorandum, April 12, 1988, p. 18.

11. A total of 2,960 members of class B filed timely requests to opt out. *In re A. H. Robins Co.*, 88 B.R. 755, 761 (E.D. Va. 1988). Some 37,000 members of class B who did not opt out filed notices of intent to participate in the proceeds of the outlier policies by the extended deadline of September 30, 1989. See. chap. 21, n. 35.

12. See *In re A. H. Robins Co. (Oberg)*, 828 F. 2d 1023 (4th Cir. 1987), cert. denied, 108 S. Ct. 1246 (1988). See chap. 9 text at nn. 14–16.

13. *Saylor v. Lindsley*, 456 F. 2d 896, 904 (2d Cir. 1972); *Girsh v. Jepson*, 521 F. 2d 153, 157–58 (3d Cir. 1975); *In re General Motors Corp., Engine Interchange Litigation*, 594 F. 2d 1106, 1123–26 (7th Cir.), cert. denied, 444 U.S. 870 (1979).

14. See chap. 2 text at n. 71; chap. 5 text at n. 9.

15. Affidavit of Joseph S. Friedberg, March 6, 1966, docket no. 740, para. 31.

16. Later, Merhige returned to the theme that McDowell had been late in seeking discovery when McDowell objected to the admission of a complex affidavit from Francine Rabinowitz estimating the value of the claims of members of class B, on the ground that the affidavit had not been provided to him in advance as required by the rules Merhige established for the hearing.

MERHIGE: I am sorry, Mr. McDowell . . . you have to do the best you can. If you can't examine, you can't examine. But I think everybody has had their opportunity. The case has been sitting here for some time. You were just late coming in seeking discovery. And I gave you as much as I thought fairly could be done, and I think you agreed with me.

MCDOWELL: Could I respond briefly, very briefly for the record, because I don't think I should leave the court without saying on the record that I don't agree we were tardy. I filed a motion to conduct discovery shortly after Your Honor, the Honorable Court, issued its April order making this a mandatory class.

MERHIGE: You didn't bring it on for hearing. You let it sit. I am not sure we were conscious it was here.

MCDOWELL: Your Honor, I can tell you I will say this as an officer of the court, that I brought this case on for hearing by calling the clerk's office of this court in the beginning of

May of 1988 within a very short period of time after the parties here objected, and the earliest date I was given was May 26 . . . After I got the response [to the court-ordered discovery] I filed certain motions. The second motion to conduct discovery and the motion to compel.

Transcript, July 7, 1988, pp. 209–11.
17. See chap. 9, n. 1.
18. *In re A. H. Robins Co.*, 88 B.R. 755 (E.D. Va. July 26, 1988).
19. Id. at 759.
20. Id. at 759–63.
21. Id. at 762–63.
22. Stipulation and Settlement Agreement, *Breland v. Aetna Casualty and Surety Co.* (February 1, 1988), paras. 5(e), 16.
23. Letter to Joseph McDowell, III, from Joseph S. Friedberg, June 20, 1988, para. 7.
24. Transcript, July 7, 1988, p. 242. Judge Merhige suggested that, after the settlement was final, there would be "no rule that you all can't talk about it and work it out on your own, is there?" Harkins responded, "Well, that may be, Your Honor. But, we haven't reached that point." Id. at 242–43.
25. Transcript, November 8, 1987 (Rabinowitz transcript), pp. 8–9 (the estimation hearing); transcript, May 26, 1988, p. 4 (the hearing on Joseph McDowell's motion for discovery concerning the settlement).
26. Friedberg said he had worked "4,200 hours"; Cochrane, "in excess of 2,500 hours"; Janus, "600 hours"; Douglas Thompson, "in excess of 800 hours."
27. The *Breland* action was filed in April 1986. Friedberg's affidavit states that his time was spent "from the Spring of 1985." Meshbesher included time expended from October 7, 1984. Herbert Newberg said his time dated from July 2, 1985.

Chapter 19

1. See nn. 4 and 5, *infra*.
2. An increase in the total amount paid to any individual could not be assumed because late claims had the first call on any funds remaining in the trust after timely claims had been paid. Only after all late claims had been paid would any remainder be distributed to those who had received payments.
3. As it turned out, when the trust was fully funded in December 1989, sixteen months after the appeal was initiated, it was not yet prepared to mail the claim application forms. See chap. 21 text at nn. 5–8.
4. *A. H. Robins Co. v. Piccinin*, 788 F. 2d 994 (4th Cir. 1986), cert. denied, 479 U.S. 876 (1986) (injunction against co-defendant litigation); *In re Beard*, 811 F. 2d 818 (4th Cir. 1987) (two appeals: motion to disqualify Merhige and motion to transcribe all proceedings); *Vancouver Women's Health Society v. A. H. Robins Co.*, 820 F. 2d 1359 (4th Cir. 1987) (motion to extend bar date for

foreign claimants); *Van Arsdale v. Clemo*, 825 F. 2d 794 (4th Cir. 1987) (challenge to selection of second claimants' committee); *Committee of Dalkon Shield Claimants v. A. H. Robins Co.*, 828 F. 2d 239 (4th Cir. 1987) (motion for an appointment of a trustee); *In re: A. H. Robins Co. ("Oberg")*, 828 F. 2d 1023 (4th Cir. 1987), cert. denied, 108 S. Ct. 1246 (1988) (prohibition of suits against Aetna); *Beard v. A. H. Robins Co.*, 828 F. 2d 1029 (4th Cir. 1987) (challenge to discharge of liability based on fraud); *Grady v. A. H. Robins Co.*, 839 F. 2d 198 (4th Cir. 1988), cert. dismissed, 109 S. Ct. 76 (1988) (whether victims of postpetition injuries are prepetition creditors); *In re A. H. Robins Co.*, 862 F. 2d 1092 (4th Cir. 1988) (denial of reinstatement of women who failed to return court questionnaire).

In the *Piccinin* decision, the panel also affirmed Judge Merhige's right to transfer all Dalkon Shield litigation to Richmond for trial but ruled that before the transfer was final the plaintiffs must be afforded notice and an opportunity to be heard. Robins ultimately abandoned its request for transfer of all cases to Richmond, and the final plan of reorganization provides that cases that are not settled before the trust can be tried where the plaintiffs' reside.

5. *Maressa v. A. H. Robins Co.*, 839 F. 2d 220 (4th Cir.), cert. denied, 109 S. Ct. 76 (1988) (late claim from women with a prepetition case pending in court); *Official Committee of Equity Security Holders v. Mabey*, 832 F. 2d 299 (4th Cir. 1987), cert. denied, 108 S. Ct. 1228 (1988) (emergency fund for fertility procedures). In another case the court of appeals reversed Judge Merhige's refusal to allow Aetna to pay attorneys it had retained for prebankruptcy services in defending Dalkon Shield litigation. *In re A. H. Robins Co. (Washburn & Kemp, P.C.)*, 846 F. 2d 267 (4th Cir. 1988).

6. *Kane v. Johns-Manville Corp.*, 843 F. 2d 636, 647–48 (2d Cir. 1988).

7. Brief of Appellants, *Rosemary Menard-Sanford, et al. v. A. H. Robins Co.*, October 28, 1988, pp. 18–22.

8. *Union Carbide Corp. v. Newboles*, 686 F. 2d 593 (7th Cir. 1982); *Underhill v. Royal*, 769 F. 2d 1426, 1432 (9th Cir. 1985); *United States v. Huckabee Auto Co.*, 783 F. 2d 1546 (11th Cir. 1986).

The plan of reorganization in the *Texaco* bankruptcy (which arose out of the litigation between Pennzoil and Texaco relating to their competition for the acquisition of Getty Oil) released officers of Texaco from claims against them that might be asserted by Texaco shareholders on behalf of the corporation (derivative claims). In approving this provision, Bankruptcy Judge Schwartzberg emphasized that the claims being released belonged to Texaco and stated that the release would not be allowed if the officers were liable to creditors of Texaco. "If these non-parties were possibly liable to creditors other than Texaco, such releases . . . would not be effective against the other creditors because such a result would be contrary to the principle expressed in 11 U.S.C. § 524(e), which . . . states in relevant part that a ' . . . discharge of a debt of the debtor does not affect the liability of any other entity on . . . such debt.'" 84 B.R. 893, 900 (Bankr. S.D. N.Y. 1988). This is the argument Morrison was making.

9. 472 U.S. 797, 812 (1985).

10. The court had said:

Due process requires at a minimum that an absent plaintiff be provided with an opportunity to remove himself from the class by executing and returning an "opt out" or "request for exclusion" form to the court. *Phillips Petroleum Co. v. Shutts*, 472 U.S. 797, 812 (1985).

In re A. H. Robins Co. ("Oberg"), 828 F. 2d 1023, 1027 (4th Cir. 1987), cert. denied, 108 S. Ct. 1246 (1988).

11. *McDonnell Douglas Corp. v. United States District Court*, 523 F. 2d 1983, 1086 (9th Cir. 1975); *In re Federal Skywalk Cases*, 680 F. 2d 1175 (8th Cir.), cert. denied, 459 U.S. 988 (1982); *In re Bendectin Products Liability Litigation*, 749 F. 2d 300, 305 (6th Cir. 1984); *School Asbestos Litigation*, 789 F. 2d 996, 1002 (3d Cir. 1986); *In re Temple*, 851 F. 2d 1269, 1272 (11th Cir. 1988). See chap. 2, nn. 60–63, and accompanying text.

12. See chap. 18 text at n. 6 ff.

13. *In re A. H. Robins Co.*, 880 F. 2d 694 (4th Cir. 1989), cert. denied, 110 S. Ct. 376 (1989).

14. Id. at 697.

15. Id. at 699, n. 4.

16. See chap. 13 text at nn. 9–12.

17. 880 F. 2d at 700. Actually, Dr. Rabinowitz's final figure was $2.5 billion, so Merhige's estimate of $2.475 billion was somewhat below it.

18. Id. at 701.

19. Id. at 700–701.

20. Individual Brief of Donna Oberg, p. 2.

21. See chap. 21, n. 35.

22. *In re A. H. Robins Co.*, 880 F. 2d 709 (4th Cir.), cert. denied, 110 S. Ct. 377 (1989).

23. Rule 23(b)(1)(A) of the Federal Rules of Civil Procedure.

24. See chap. 18 text at n. 6 ff.

25. 880 F. 2d at 741–42.

26. *School Asbestos Litigation*, 789 F. 2d 996, 1007 (3d Cir. 1986); *In re "Agent Orange" Product Liability Litigation*, 100 F.R.D. 718, 724 (E.D. N.Y. 1983), mandamus denied sub nom., 725 F. 2d 858, 861 (2d Cir.), cert. denied, 465 U.S. 1067 (1984).

27. 880 F. 2d at 745.

28. Id. at 749.

29. See chap. 15, n. 11, and accompanying text.

30. 880 F. 2d at 750–51.

31. Id. at 751.

32. Id. at 752.

33. Within this group, Joe McDowell had strongly argued against filing a petition in *Menard-Sanford* and in favor of filing only in *Breland*. McDowell

reasoned that this would avoid all risks and costs and at the same time enhance the prospects of review in *Breland* because, with the plan of reorganization already implemented, it would be unmistakable to the Supreme Court that review could be granted in *Breland* without delaying or jeopardizing the plan of reorganization, a point that otherwise seemed easily obscured. When McDowell's suggestion was rejected, he signed both petitions for the sake of unity.

34. See n. 8, *supra*.

35. *United States v. Huckabee Auto Co.*, 783 F. 2d 1546, 1548 (5th Cir. 1986).

36. That these eighteen lawyers or law firms represent more than 18,000 claimants underscored that the persons with the greatest stake in the matter were the lawyers. If each of those 18,000 claims was resolved for $20,000, certainly a modest sum and one well within the capacity of the trust, and assuming the normal one-third contingent fee, the eighteen lawyers or firms would each earn an average of $6.6 million.

37. The decisions are cited in n. 11, *supra*.

38. 472 U.S. 497 (1985).

39. *Menard-Sanford v. A. H. Robins Co.*, 110 S. Ct. 376 (1989); *Anderson v. Aetna Casualty & Surety Co.*, 110 S. Ct. 377 (1989).

40. *National Law Journal*, January 29, 1990, p. 31.

Chapter 20

1. See chap. 15 text at n. 6.

2. Examiner's Report, September 9, 1988, Appendix, p. 45.

3. Id., p. 71.

4. Id., pp. 58–59.

5. Id., p. 58.

6. Id., p. 58.

7. Id., pp. 58–59.

8. Transcript, November 1, 1988, p. 467.

9. Examiner's Report, September 16, 1988, Appendix, p. 87. See also id., p. 106.

10. Affidavit of Ralph R. Mabey, October 1, 1988, pp. 8–9, filed in *Dalkon Shield Claimants Committee v. A. H. Robins Co.*, no. 88-1753, United States Court of Appeals for the Fourth Circuit.

11. Memorandum Opinion, September 27, 1988, pp. 9–10.

12. Motion of Dalkon Shield Claimants Committee for Emergency Relief, September 20, 1988, pp. 15–16.

13. *Wall Street Journal*, October 26, 1988, p. B8.

14. Memorandum in Support of Confirmation Order, 88 B.R. 742, 752. (E.D. Va. July 25, 1988).

15. Transcript, October 31, 1988, p. 75. See also id., p. 314.

16. The closest the draft letter comes to acknowledging the possibility of higher payments is the following:

Reasons you may *not* wish to choose Option 1:

• You may feel that $750 is less than what you could reasonably expect under a more prolonged settlement process.

17. Transcript, October 31, 1988, pp. 119–20, 185–89; November 1, 1988, p. 317.

18. Memorandum, November 28, 1988, pp. 5, 17.

19. Id. at 5.

20. Id. at 14–15. Merhige also concluded that Ann Samani's "membership of the Claimants Committee, which continued even after their appeal was noted, represented a breach of her obligation to the trust . . . [which] alone is sufficient grounds for her removal." Id. at 16. This conclusion is difficult to reconcile with the circumstances of Samani's appointment. She was selected as a trustee *because* of her membership on the claimants' committee, pursuant to the agreement on that subject that had been reached by parties and accepted by Judge Merhige. In the disclosure statement, Ms. Samani is described as "Dalkon Shield claimant and member of Dalkon Shield Claimants Committee; will withdraw claim in order to serve as a trustee." On September 30, 1988, when it was first suggested to her that she should not be a member of the claimants' committee while she was a trustee, Samani resigned from the committee.

21. Id. at 8–9. Locks's testimony on this point is quoted, *supra*, text at n. 8.

22. Memorandum Opinion, November 28, 1988, p. 9.

23. See chap. 5 text at n. 8 ff.

24. *Wall Street Journal*, November 29, 1988, p. B8.

25. Interview with Georgene Vairo, July 24, 1990.

26. Examiner's Report, September 16, 1988, Appendix, pp. 94–96.

27. On July 13, 1989, after his decision had been affirmed, Judge Merhige approved the disbursement of $34,828 of trust funds to Stephen Fredkin for his efforts in seeking the removal of the trustees. Joe Friedberg did not seek fees separately from his application in the *Breland* case the following December. See chap. 18 text at nn. 22–27.

28. *Official Dalkon Shield Claimants Committee v. Mabey,* 880 F. 2d 769, 776 (4th Cir. 1989).

29. Id. at 777.

30. *Blum v. Unnamed Claimants,* 880 F. 2d 779 (4th Cir. 1989).

31. 880 F. 2d at 785–86, 787.

32. Id. at 787–88. Judge Chapman had reference to the statements in the legislative history of the Bankruptcy Code of 1978 evidencing an intention to assure that prospective counsel do not have a role in the selection of a creditor's committee. This is the material on which James Szaller relied, and that Judge Chapman ignored, in the challenge to the selection of the second claimants' committee. See chap. 5, nn. 25, 29.

Chapter 21

1. Saltzburg and Feinberg resigned in November 1989 and May 1990, respectively. Dowd resigned in February 1990. No one gave an explanation for his resignation beyond citing other professional commitments. To fill these vacancies, Judge Merhige appointed Ellen W. Bishop and Henry C. Spalding, Jr., both business people in Richmond, and Robert Bland Smith, a Washington lawyer who had worked in staff positions in the United States Senate. Following Saltzburg's departure, Georgene Vairo became the chairperson and leading figure among the trustees.

2. Response of A. H. Robins Co. to Motion of Yadira Sevilla Aragon, et al., for Reclassification of Late Proofs of Claims, September 14, 1987, pp. 3–4. On September 18, 1987, Merhige granted the motion of the Costa Rican women.

3. Transcript, July 27, 1987, pp. 15–19. Judge Merhige took the motion under advisement and later granted it. The Glascow motion is discussed in chap. 8 text following n. 15.

4. The quote is from the remarks of Louis Hoynes at the August 25, 1988, hearing before Judge Merhige on the equity committee's Motion to disqualify the Cadwalader firm. Transcript, pp. 38–40.

5. According to information released by the trust in January 1990, the 111,000 claims broke down as follows:

Users/nonusers	100,000/11,000
Represented by counsel/ not represented by counsel	46,000/65,000
Domestic/foreign	98,000/13,000

6. A. H. Robins Co., Sixth Amended Plan of Reorganization, March 28, 1988, Section 6.07.

7. A. H. Robins Co., Sixth Amended Plan of Reorganization, March 28, 1988, Exhibit C-Claims Resolution Facility, K (hereafter "Claims Resolution Facility").

8. By January 14, 1991, 504 applications had been filed for participation in the medical fertility procedure program. Ninety-five of these had been granted, 68 had been denied, and the balance were still pending. The trust had actually paid out $395,000 for the benefit of 54 women. Telephone interview with Michael Sheppard, executive director, Dalkon Shield Claimants Trust, January 14, 1991.

9. Sheppard Interview, *supra* n. 8. There is also an option 4, which is directed to claimants who are not yet aware of injuries or who are concerned that their injuries may worsen. Option 4 must be selected by the July 1, 1991, deadline for selecting an option, but women who accept option 4 within that period will be afforded a total of three years to submit their claims. By January 14, 1990, 148 claims had been submitted in option 4. In addition, 1,238 eligible claimants had withdrawn their claims.

10. Claims Resolution Facility, E(4).

11. Claims Resolution Facility, G(3). To complement this provision, Judge Merhige's confirmation order enjoins claimants who receive a jury verdict from using the legal process to collect the full amount of the judgment from the trust. Confirmation Order, July 26, 1988, para. 34.

12. *In re A. H. Robins Co.*, 880 F. 2d 709, 745 (4th Cir.), cert. denied, 110 S. Ct. 377 (1989). See chap. 19 text at n. 27.

13. 11 U.S.C. § 1123(a)(4). Section 1129(a)(1) provides that the "court shall confirm a plan only if. . .[t]he plan complies with all applicable provisions of this title."

14. 28 U.S.C. § 1411, Pub. L. no. 98-353, § 122 (July 10, 1984). See chap. 12 text at nn. 5–7.

15. The situation is ameliorated in one respect. If the calculations of the trust are correct, the Aetna excess insurance will be available at the conclusion of the claims resolution process to pay the unpaid portion of any jury verdicts and arbitration awards up to $250 million. This corrective will be more theoretical than real in many cases, because of the success of the efforts of the trust to discourage jury trials.

16. Interview with Georgene Vairo, July 24, 1990.

17. Dalkon Shield Claimants Trust, Claims Resolution Report, November 1990, p. 2.

18. Claims Resolution Facility, E(4).

19. Dalkon Shield Claimants Trust, Claims Resolution Report, November 1990, p. 2. The plan of reorganization does not grant Merhige the power to delay the filing of suit after completion of the trust procedures. It does grant "the power to stay the commencement of any trial upon a showing by the Trust of undue prejudice due to the multiplicity of ongoing trials." Claims Resolution Facility, E(5)(b). This provides another potential obstacle to trial and judgment.

20. Memorandum Opinion, July 19, 1989, p. 5. Glasser's appeal from Merhige's ruling was pending when this was written. *Glasser v. A. H. Robins Co.,* no. 89-1061, U.S.C.A. 4th Cir. The trust is defending the appeal.

21. The quoted language appears, under the heading "What is your best option," in the explanatory ("Read This First") materials accompanying the application forms mailed to the claimants in March 1990.

22. In a letter to the author dated August 6, 1990, Georgene Vairo, chairperson of the trust, advised that the form letter had been revised because "[w]e do not want anyone to choose one option over another out of timing considerations."

23. Dalkon Shield Claimants Trust, Claims Resolution Report, no. 5, February 1990, p. 4.

24. The application forms submitted to the claimants by the trust in March 1990 reiterated that option 3 claimants must submit proof that "the Dalkon Shield was the sole cause of the injury for which you are requesting compensation." In response to criticism from attorneys for claimants, the trust later stated

the lawyers had "pulled an isolated statement . . . out of context" and announced that the policy of the trust was not to deny payment under option 3 when the medical records indicated a cause of the injury in addition to the Dalkon Shield. If an alternative cause is suggested, "the settlement offer will be lower than if only the Dalkon Shield were responsible for the injury." Dalkon Shield Claimants Trust, Attorney Update, June 1990, p. 5.

25. Dalkon Shield Claimants Trust, Claims Resolution Report, February 1990, p. 5.

26. Dalkon Shield Claimants Trust, Claims Resolution Report, no. 5, February 1990, p. 7.

27. See n. 5.

28. In July 1990, an organization called the Coloradans for Professional Responsibility filed a motion asking Judge Merhige to limit the fees that can be charged by lawyers for Dalkon Shield claimants to 25 percent of the recovery. Judge Merhige did not act on the motion, but in a letter to counsel published in December 1990, Merhige stated that "there is nothing contingent about whether claimants with active valid Dalkon Shield claims will recover from the Trust," and that contingent fees of 33 percent or more "appear excessive." He left open the question of whether he would intervene in the matter. Dalkon Shield Claimants Trust, "Attorney Update," December 1990, p. 3. The proposed revision of the *Johns-Manville* plan of reorganization under consideration by Judge Weinstein (see chap. 3, n. 33, and accompanying text) provides for a 25 percent limit on fees of counsel for claimants. *New York Times*, November 20, 1990, p. D1, col 3.

29. Dalkon Shield Claimants Trust, "Attorney Update," December 1990, pp. 1–2.

30. In 1990 the trust spent $59 million in the resolution of claims and realized investment income of $180 million. After taxes and expenses, the trust's operating profit was $75 million. Dalkon Shield Claimants Trust, financial statement for the year ended December 31, 1990.

31. From the outset, Judge Merhige emphasized his determination to locate the trust in Richmond so that it would aid the local economy. See chap. 15 text at n. 1; chap. 16 text at n. 2. Consistent with this intention, at the end of 1990, the trust provided employment to more than 250 people, with annual earnings in excess of $5 million. Total trust expenses for 1990, mainly disbursed in Richmond, were over $15 million. See Dalkon Shield Claimants Trust, financial statement as of December 31, 1990. The executive director of the trust, former bankruptcy court clerk Michael Sheppard, was originally employed by the trust in 1988 under a five-year contract at $150,000 per year, more than double his previous salary. The trust now has employment contracts with Sheppard and others covering the years 1991–96. The trust's financial statement reports these, together with lease commitments, at a value of $6.3 million. The trustees, for whom the positions are extracurricular, are each paid $35,000 per year, plus $1,000 for every meeting they attend.

32. See chap. 15 text at nn. 18 and 19.

33. Order, March 30, 1990.

34. Order, August 6, 1990.

35. The *Breland* settlement agreement established a date by which members of class B—women who were not eligible claimants in the Chapter 11 case—were required to communicate their intention to make a claim under the two $50 million Aetna "outlier" policies. The date was later extended to September 30, 1989, and by that date approximately 37,000 such notices had been received. Presumably, many of these women are among the 35,000 late claimants. The claimants' trust has assumed the responsibility for administering the claims of class B members against the outlier insurance.

In September 1990 these women were mailed a packet offering them the choice of settling their claims in an option 1 type of procedure for $200, or completing a lengthy questionnaire similar to the option 3 questionnaire for eligible claimants. By mid-March 1991, almost 11,500 women had accepted the $200. Thomas Florence conducted a study of a sample of 300 of the returned questionnaires to determine the total value of the remaining class B claims under the same standards used to evaluate claims by the claimants' trust. On the basis of Florence's findings, the Breland trustee concluded that only 15 percent of the value of each claim could be paid from the first $50 million outlier policy. The intention is to make a second payment when the second $50 million outlier policy becomes available in 1995. *The Bulletin* (newsletter of the Breland Insurance Trust), April 1991. These class B members may receive additional payments up to the full value attached to their claims either from the spillover of any portions of the Aetna excess policy that is not used to pay eligible claims or, for class B members who also filed late claims in the bankruptcy case, from any unused portion of the regular trust funds.

Chapter 22

1. See chap. 4 text at nn. 17 and 18.

2. See chap. 4 text at nn. 20–22.

3. The decision in *Johns-Manville* denying the motion to dismiss is reported at 36 B.R. 727 (Bankr. S.D. N.Y. 1984).

4. A limited fund has other advantages for the equity interests. It makes possible a merger rather than a sale, which because of tax considerations may attract a higher price and allow a greater return to equity. See chap. 17, n. 13. A limited fund may also make possible a reorganization that does not involve a sale of the business and leaves the existing owners in place, but if the debtor's liabilities are a sufficiently small proportion of its assets to permit this, the appropriateness of a reorganization may be in question.

5. Under the law of some states, a corporation is not permitted to dissolve, or to make a distribution of its assets to its shareholders, without creating a reserve adequate to pay unliquidated and anticipated claims. See, e.g., California Corporations Code §§ 2005, 2008 (Deering 1987).

6. See chap. 16, nn. 7 and 8, and accompanying text.

7. *In re Lionel Corp.*, 722 F. 2d 1063, 1066 (2d Cir. 1983).

8. See chap. 16 text at n. 10.

9. See chap. 16 text at nn. 11–14.

10. 11 U.S.C. § 1129(b)(2)(B).

11. See chap. 13 text at nn. 3–4.

12. 28 U.S.C. § 1411. See chap. 12 text at nn. 5–7.

13. When a class of personal injury claimants properly votes to accept a plan limiting the funds that will be available to pay their claims, there is a potential conflict between the individual claimant's jury trial right and the scheme of the Bankruptcy Code, which authorizes departures from the absolute priority rule when a plan is accepted by an impaired class. Because an acceptance by a class of creditors is customarily allowed to modify an individual creditor's right to full payment of even a liquidated claim (where there is no doubt as to full value), it seems appropriate, subject to the best interests test, to treat acceptance of a plan of reorganization as a modification of the individual's right to be paid the full amount of a jury verdict, just as an insufficiency of assets modifies that right. In that situation, the jury verdict would constitute the allowed value of the claim against which a pro rata distribution (applicable to liquidated values determined by settlement as well as by litigation) would be made.

Under section 1129(a)(7)(A)(ii), which embodies the best interests test, a plan of reorganization cannot be confirmed if it would pay a dissenting creditor less than she would receive in a liquidation, regardless of the acceptance of the plan by the class of creditors. For the reasons stated in chap. 17, nn. 5–13, and accompanying text, insufficient evidence was submitted at the hearing on the confirmation of Robins's plan of reorganization to allow a determination of whether more money would have been available to pay Dalkon Shield claims if the company had been sold in the context of a liquidation rather than under the terms of Robins's plan of reorganization.

14. The failure of the plan of reorganization to pay interest to the Dalkon Shield claimants for the duration of the Chapter 11 case would not be an obstacle to a cramdown, because section 502(b) of the Bankruptcy Code excludes claims for unmatured interest from the allowed amount of a claim and the cramdown provision of the code is keyed to full payment of the "allowed amount." See section 1129(b)(2)(B)(i). By contrast, the failure of a plan of reorganization to pay interest is relevant to the best interest requirement of section 1129(a)(7)((A)(ii), because that provision requires payment to the dissenting creditor of not less than the amount the creditor would receive in a liquidation and section 726(a)(5) provides that in a liquidation creditors shall be paid interest for the duration of the bankruptcy, before there is any distribution to the equity interests.

15. *A. H. Robins Co.*, 89 B.R. 555 (E.D. Va. 1988).

16. 89 B.R. at 561. Merhige was unable to cite any authority that supported the proposition that a bankruptcy court has the power to disallow claims against the debtor that are valid and enforceable outside of bankruptcy in order

to foster a reorganization, and it is at odds with the fundamental principle that reorganizations are intended to enhance, and at a minimum cannot reduce, the rights of the creditors. Judge Merhige relied on three cases decided under the old Bankruptcy Act, *Vanston Bondholders Protective Committee v. Green*, 329 U.S. 156 (1946); *Heiser v. Woodruff*, 327 U.S. 726 (1945); *Pepper v. Litton*, 308 U.S. 295 (1939). In *Vanston*, the disallowed claims were invalid under state law. See 329 U.S. at 160; id. at 168 (Frankfurter, J., concurring.) In *Pepper v. Litton*, the disallowed claim was fraudulent. 308 U.S. at 311–12. In *Heiser v. Woodruff*, the Supreme Court held that the bankruptcy court *did not* have discretion to disallow a claim as fraudulent where the assertion of fraud had been litigated and rejected in state court. 327 U.S. at 739–40. See also *Kelleran v. Andrijevic*, 825 F. 2d 692 (2d Cir. 1987).

17. 89 B.R. at 562–63.

18. 11 U.S.C. §§ 726(a)(4); 510(c)(1).

19. In the *Johns-Manville* case, Judge Lifland concluded that punitive damages should be disallowed to preserve the money for future asbestos victims. The judge did not explain why the value—small as it was—reserved for the equity interests in the plan of reorganization should not be devoted to punitive damages. 68 B.R. 618, 627 (Bankr. S.D. N.Y. 1986), aff'd, 78 B.R. 407 (S.D. N.Y. 1987), aff'd sub nom., *Kane v. Johns-Manville Corp.*, 843 F. 2d 636 (2d Cir. 1988). As was the case in the *Robins* bankruptcy, Judge Lifland addressed the issue against the background of acceptance by the class of personal injury claimants of a plan of reorganization that disallowed claims for punitive damages.

Punitive damage claims were disallowed because they could only be paid at the expense of the other creditors in *In re GAC Corp.*, 681 F. 2d 1295, 1301 (11th Cir. 1982). Similarly, *In re American Federation of Television and Radio Artists*, 32 B.R. 672 (Bankr. S.D. N.Y. 1983), the court subordinated the penalty portion of a treble damage judgment to avoid prejudice to other creditors but allowed the claim to be paid to the extent the resources of the debtor allowed after nonpenalty claims had been paid. See also *Olympia Equipment Leasing Co. v. Western Union Telegraph Co.*, 786 F. 2d 794, 797 (7th Cir. 1986).

20. See chap. 17 text at n. 8 ff.

21. There are two reasons why the company's indemnity obligation would not render such suits superfluous. Under Virginia law indemnity obligations do not apply when liability is imposed for willful, as distinct from negligent, misconduct. Code of Virginia s13.1-704 (1989 Replacement Volume). Willful misconduct has been found to exist in connection with the Dalkon Shield. Moreover, if the total liability to women injured by the Dalkon Shield exceeded the total funds made available under the plan of reorganization to pay these claims and to pay claims for indemnification, the separate resources of other culpable defendants would be available to the claimants, regardless of their agreements with Robins.

22. See *In re A. H. Robins Co.*, 88 B.R. 742, 747, 751 (E.D. Va. 1988), aff'd,

880 F. 2d 695, 702 (4th Cir. 1989). Transcript, July 18, 1988, pp. 140 (Robert G. Blount).

23. *Washington Post,* December 15, 1989, p. F1, col. 1.

24. See *Washington Post,* December 15, 1989, p. F1, col. 1; *Forbes,* February 5, 1990, at p. 176; *Business Week,* June 11, 1990, pp. 80–81, February 1, 1988, pp. 27–28; *U.S. News & World Report,* February 1, 1988, p. 47. See also chap. 17, n. 13.

25. *U.S. News & World Report,* February 1, 1988, p. 47.

26. *Washington Post,* December 15, 1989, p. F1, col. 1.

27. See chap. 8 text at nn. 4, 14.

28. See chap. 8, n. 7.

29. See chap. 15 text at n. 18.

30. See chap. 21 text at nn. 33–35.

31. See chap. 10 text at nn. 7–11.

32. Retiree Benefits Bankruptcy Protection Act of 1988, 102 Stat. 610, Pub. Law 100-334 (June 16, 1988), codified at 11 U.S.C. § 1114.

33. See Bankruptcy Code, section 331.

34. The instances in which Judge Merhige threatened or imposed sanctions against attorneys representing women injured by the Dalkon Shield, on the ground that their actions were frivolous or taken for an improper purpose in violation of rule 11 of the Federal Rules of Civil Procedure, or were in violation of his injunction against co-defendant litigation, include the motion filed by Bradley Post, Douglas Bragg, and others to recuse the judge; the motion filed by James Szaller and others challenging the selection of the second claimants' committee; the suit against Aetna filed in Kansas by John Baker and twenty-two other attorneys after Joe Friedberg had filed the *Breland* action without protest; an effort by Sidney Matthew, a plaintiffs' attorney from Tallahassee, Florida, to collect from Aetna under a prebankruptcy settlement of a Dalkon Shield injury claim; a request to Judge Merhige by Robert Manchester for permission to investigate the extent of Robins's insurance coverage with Aetna and others; public statements by Guerry Thornton, a plaintiffs' attorney from Atlanta, Georgia, in opposition to one of Robins's early plans of reorganization (on the theory that Thornton's comments constituted impermissible solicitation of votes against the plan before a disclosure statement had been distributed); and the efforts of Cadwalader, Wickersham & Taft to call women injured by the Dalkon Shield as witnesses at the estimation hearing.

In addition, former United States senator Vance Hartke was fined $7,500 by Judge Merhige in July 1987 for filing on behalf of Prudential Bache Securities a "friend of the court" brief suggesting a plan of reorganization that would provide up to $2.5 billion to pay Dalkon Shield claims, at the cost of the dilution of the interests of Robins's existing shareholders, at a time when Robins proposed to pay $1.75 billion. Merhige found that the brief constituted a plan of reorganization in violation of Robins's exclusive right to file a plan.

35. See chap. 21, n. 35.

Table of Transcript Citations

(transcript citations for quotations or references not cited in endnotes)

Text Page	Quotation	Transcript Date, Page
Chapter 2		
43	"discuss some kind of procedure . . ."	7/18/85, 3
43	"Now I want to talk . . ."	7/18/85, 10–11
43	"we will confirm . . ."	7/18/85, 12
43	"initial view . . ."	7/18/85, 11
43	"I think my own idea . . ."	7/18/85, 3
43	"coercive practice."	7/18/85, 22
46	"Robins can respond . . ."	8/9/85, 2–3
46	"what the company . . ."	8/9/85, 11
46	"We view these lawyers . . ."	8/9/85, 23–24
46	"Regrettably, your committee . . ."	8/9/85, 23
47	"Had it taken, . . ."	8/22/85, 5–6
48	"You have been misinformed."	8/22/85, 14–17
Chapter 4		
62	"You are going to find . . ."	8/22/85, 19
62	"There are women who . . ."	9/21/85, 111–12
66	"under the whole theory . . ."	11/9/85, 65
66	"I think we'll get the cases . . ."	11/9/85, 74
Chapter 5		
71	"I will be delighted . . ."	9/21/85, 51
71	"I have dealt with . . ."	9/21/85, 101
71	"Mr. Cochrane, your group . . ."	9/30/85, 13–14, 21
72	"The first time . . ."	12/16/85, 116–17
77	Twice during the proceedings . . .	2/14/86, 7, 100
77	"delighted that we have . . ."	2/14/86, 6
78	"I predicted from the . . ."	3/4/86, 24–25, 34
78	"The record is replete . . ."	3/4/86, 13–14

Table of Citations to Statutes and Rules

(Page numbers refer to the text page on which the statute or rule is discussed or on which the reference to the endnote in which it is cited appears. To find the notes themselves, the reader should consult the running heads to the endnotes, pp. 343–386.)

391

Internal Revenue Code (United States Code, Title 26)

Judiciary and Judicial Procedure (United States Code, Title 28)

Rules of Bankruptcy Procedure

Federal Rules of Civil Procedure

Index

(Endnotes are cited to the text pages on which they are referenced. To find the notes themselves, the reader should consult the running heads to the endnotes, pp. 343–386)